TERTULLIAN'S
TREATISE AGAINST PRAXEAS

Q. Septimii Florentis TERTULLIANI ADVERSUS PRAXEAN LIBER

TERTULLIAN'S TREATISE AGAINST PRAXEAS

The Text edited, with an Introduction, Translation, and Commentary

by

ERNEST EVANS,

HONORARY D.D., GLASGOW

VICAR OF HELLIFIELD AND CANON OF BRADFORD

WIPF & STOCK · Eugene, Oregon

APOSTOLICAE REGIAEQVE SOCIETATI

COLLEGII ET VNIVERSITATIS

GLASGVENSIS

IVRE CONCESSO

QVICQVID HIC

HVMANARVM LITTERARVM COGNITIONIS

GRATO REDDEBAT ANIMO

ALVMNVS OBSERVANTISSIMVS

Wipf and Stock Publishers
199 W 8th Ave, Suite 3
Eugene, OR 97401

Tertullian's Treatise Against Praxeas
The Text Edited, with an Introduction, Translation, and Commentary
By Evans, Ernest

ISBN 13: 978-1-60899-745-9
Publication date 2/17/2011
Previously published by SPCK, 1948

CONTENTS

PREFACE

THIS book was not written for publication, but as a relaxation from the more exacting duties of my profession. If I had thought of the matter at all I should have suspected that I had written *ea quae nec indocti intellegere possent nec docti legere curarent*. Consequently it was a matter of some surprise when a learned friend, casually catching sight of the manuscript, suggested that it ought to be published. I have now come to hope that the introductory matter may be found to have the value of the judgement of one who during thirty years has made a careful study of the original contemporary authorities, and, being unable to procure many modern books, nor having the leisure to read them, has escaped the bondage of that modern scholasticism which accepts the brilliant but often unproven theories of famous scholars at the value of their authors' great names and proceeds to build upon them an edifice bearing little relation to that which the original documents portray. In editing the text I have kept as close to the manuscripts as possible. In a few places I have submitted my own conjectures, but only where the traditional text was notoriously faulty or unintelligible. In the notes I have drawn attention to the objectivity of Tertullian's habit of expression. His language is commonly supposed to be difficult; but it is so, I suggest, largely because he uses words in well authenticated though unusual ways, and retains in his mind the original sense of words which in ordinary Latin have had their primary meaning almost lost in metaphor.

The translation was an afterthought. My friend who first suggested publication strongly advised it. I venture to hope that it will (among other things) serve as a commentary on such matters of Latin grammar and syntax as are hardly worth the dignity of a formal note.

I was also advised to add a bibliography. That, however, I could not have done without an extended visit to the libraries of Oxford or London, for which I could afford neither the time nor the expense. But there is what appears to be an exhaustive list of books on Tertullian in Lupton's edition of *De Baptismo*, which only needs to be supplemented by reference to the index to the *Journal of Theological Studies.*

As a contribution to theological discussion Tertullian's treatise must be allowed to speak for itself. It has also a religious value, which should not be overlooked. From the fourth century down to the present, theological discussion has frequently been conducted in such a way as to suggest, without doubt unintentionally, a false religious outlook which regards our Lord Jesus Christ as no more than a kind of appendage to God—a secret and undetected legacy from Arianism. Tertullian and his contemporaries had a fundamentally different conviction and experience. To their mind all that has ever been known of God has from the beginning been mediated by the Word or Son of God, who afterwards was incarnate and is Jesus Christ our Saviour; and therefore every valid approach to God from the beginning has been, and must to the end continue to be, mediated by Him. It may be that our present half-heartedness and consequent ineffectiveness is, at least in part, due to our having overlooked this aspect of the divine economy.

If this work of mine is favourably received, I propose to continue it by producing, at not nearly so great length, editions of Tertullian's treatises *On the Soul*, *On the Body of Christ*, and *On the Resurrection of the Body*, for which I have already made large preparations. If circumstances should give me leisure, it would be my further ambition to supply the second volume of Tertullian's works, which was promised fifty years ago in the Vienna Corpus, but which has not yet appeared, nor, in the present state of continental scholarship, is likely to appear for many years to come.

My thanks are due to Professor S. L. Greenslade and to the late Dr. J. K. Mozley, for a number of valuable suggestions. How much this book owes of accuracy and self-consistency to Messrs. Constable's readers, it would be exceedingly difficult to say.

HELLIFIELD,
January 1948.

NOTE.—Citations from the Apologists are quoted by the page and letter of Otto's text. Irenaeus *Against the Heresies* is quoted by Harvey's numbering. The translations of Irenaeus *On the Apostolic Preaching* are borrowed, with this acknowledgement, from the *Patrologia Orientalis*, volume 12. Quotations from Tertullian are according to Oehler's text.

INTRODUCTION

I. TERTULLIAN'S LIFE AND WORKS

AFRICAN Christianity [1] first comes into public notice towards the end of the second century, though there are reasons for thinking that it was then no new thing. By the middle of the third century the Churches were already numerous and flourishing, and as early as our first knowledge of them (through Tertullian) they had developed liturgical and other usages with characteristics of their own. The Church of Carthage, whose bishop became the acknowledged leader and spokesman of the bishops of the three provinces, was pre-eminent in numbers and influence, in this reflecting the prestige of the senate of that city, who were *principes semper Africae*.[2] The African Christians appear for the most part to have belonged to the Latin-speaking section of the population, though possibly already, as certainly two centuries later, a number of them were of Punic race and speech. But the native Berbers of the country districts seem to have remained almost untouched by Christianity—which is suggested as one of the reasons why the impact of Islam, following on the Donatist and Vandal disorders, so speedily obliterated almost all trace of Churches which had once been of such account in Christendom.[3]

It was in Africa, not in Italy, that the first Christian Latin literature was produced, and that at a time when (except for legal text books and a few trivial copies of verses) Latin was hardly being written. But that is not to say that it was not spoken: it was still a living tongue, which in the late fourth century was once more to produce an aftermath of non-theological, even self-consciously pagan, literature: and if Tertullian was the first to

[1] The designation Africa is applied in its ancient sense, denoting the provinces now called Tunisia, Tripolitania, Algeria, and Morocco, but excluding Egypt and Libya which in language and in general interest were more closely related to the Levant than to the West.

[2] Tertullian, *De pallio*, 1.

[3] On this subject see Holme, *The Extinction of the Christian Churches in North Africa* (Hulsean Prize Essay 1895), ch. ix. But there is some slight epigraphic evidence which may possibly suggest that Donatism was in one of its aspects a revolt of the native Christians against the Latin and Punic elements: see W. H. Frend, in the *Journal of Roman Studies*, vol. xxx.

use in writing the theological terminology which is still in use in the Latin-speaking Churches and their vernacular-speaking offspring, the ease with which the words flow from his pen suggests that he had often heard them and employed them in speech before he set pen to paper—in other words, he may have been the inheritor, not the inventor, of them.

Quintus Septimius Florens Tertullianus[1] was born probably at Carthage about A.D. 160, his father being a centurion in the proconsular service. He received the excellent literary and professional education which the municipalities then provided, becoming a ready writer in Greek as well as Latin. For some years he practised as an advocate and legal consultant. The juristic cast of his mind is shown in his writings, both by his employment of legal turns of phrase and in his presentation of his case: first and last, he is always a pleader. When he wishes, he can make a parade of erudite knowledge of the poets and historians whose works were the staple of the pre-professional education of that day—knowledge which at other times he will affect to despise. Shortly before 197 he became a Christian—through what precise influences he fails to indicate—and immediately began to write in defence of the faith. About 213 he joined the sect of the Montanists, separating himself from the Church, which he now proceeded to attack for its unspirituality, by which he meant its rejection of the Montanist revelations, and also what he regarded as the laxity of its moral code (e.g. its allowance of second marriages) and its disciplinary system. That he was a married man is certain: whether or not he was a presbyter, either of the Church of Carthage or of the Montanist sect, remains an open question: that at some period of his life he spent some time in Rome is probable, but not important. St Jerome, a century and a half later, says that he lived to extreme old age, *ad decrepitam aetatem*, which would place his death perhaps as late as 240. That he ever returned to the Church is not suggested; but it is significant that half a generation later Montanism seems almost to have disappeared from Africa (as it was bound to do, as soon as the too confident prophecies of Montanus were falsified by non-fulfilment), and that Cyprian, who had little patience with

[1] This account of Tertullian's life and works, especially in the dates assigned to the several treatises, is largely indebted to that in Bardenhewer's *Patrologie* (3rd German ed. 1910).

disturbers of Christian unity, admired and read his writings, apparently without a thought of their sectarian origin.[1]

Tertullian's works fall into three classes, apologetic, controversial, and disciplinary: in the last two groups there is also a cross division according as the works were written before or after his acceptance of Montanism. The treatise *Against Praxeas* belongs to the second group, and to the Montanist period. The following brief description of some of his other works is intended merely to assist the reader in estimating the significance of the quotations from them adduced in the commentary.

(1) Of the *apologetic treatises*, i.e. those addressed to non-Christians, the most comprehensive is the *Apologeticus* (A.D. 197), which presents in forensic form the standard and often-repeated Christian answers to the charges of ritual murder, immorality, and cannibalism, as well as to the graver accusations of atheism and political disloyalty. Bearing on our present subject is a notable declaration (§§ 17-21) of the Christian doctrine of God, of revelation, of the *Logos* and the Incarnation, from which it appears that the theological doctrine in its essential features which Tertullian produced in opposition to Praxeas was already in hand (without any controversial intention) sixteen or more years earlier, immediately after his conversion. The two books *Ad nationes* (also 197) were a preliminary draft of the *Apologeticus*. The "golden book" (the description is Bardenhewer's) *De testimonio animae naturaliter Christianae*, developing an incidental remark in the Apology, is a brilliant exposition of the thesis (already attempted by Justin, Theophilus, and Athenagoras) that the characteristic Christian and scriptural themes of the unity of God, of divine providence, of the immortality of the soul, and of judgement to come, are admitted to be true by the common consent of mankind, as is shown by the expressions used by the heathen themselves when they allow themselves to speak their natural thoughts. The open letter *To Scapula* (proconsul of Africa, 211) is a protest against the ineffective cruelty of persecution. The unfinished work *Adversus Iudaeos* is a report of a dis-

[1] But, according to Augustine (*Adv. haer.* 86), a sect of Tertullianists, few in number and gradually declining in importance, continued until his own day, when their last remaining basilica was, with their consent, transferred to the Catholic Church. They were schismatics rather than heretics, for their peculiar tenet of the corporeal nature of the soul was not considered important enough to be regarded as heretical.

cussion covering some of the same ground as Justin's *Dialogue with Trypho.*

(2) The *controversial works*, the most important for our purpose, are with one exception attacks on specific heresies, combined with the defence of the traditional Christian faith on the points involved. The exception is the discourse *De praescriptione haereticorum*, in purpose, as apparently in date, a general introduction to the works of this group, though with a particular reference to the gnostic speculators. In it Tertullian propounds the rule (which he insists on as axiomatic in his Montanist as in his pre-Montanist period) of *principalitas veritatis et posteritas mendacitatis*,[1] and makes a specious plea (to which there is an obvious rejoinder) that the heretics have no right to appeal to the Scriptures, since these are the property of the Church, from which they have seceded. The five books *Against Marcion* (of which the first in its present revised form was published in 207, the others at intervals during several years later) may be taken as representing Tertullian's considered opinions on the faith, and on the interpretation of the Scriptures in accordance with the faith, before the influence of Montanism seriously took effect, and serve to show how little difference the "new prophecy" made to the essentials of Christian belief. A treatise *Against Hermogenes*, apparently of early date, combats the suggestion (which often appears in various disguises) that the material out of which the world was made existed independently of the Creator, and was somewhat intractable under his manipulation. The work *Against the Valentinians* (in which first Tertullian represents himself as a Montanist) is largely based on data supplied by Irenaeus, and contains little of Tertullian's own: *Scorpiace* (i.e. antidote to serpent bites) is pure Tertullian on the same subject. The homily *On baptism* is only by accident controversial: it contains much information bearing on the customs observed in the African Churches in the administration of that sacrament, along with some of Tertullian's personal views—notably his objection (in which he stood almost alone) to the baptism of infants. The two treatises *De carne Christi* and *De resurrectione carnis* combat the docetic view, favoured by the gnostic sects, that the human body, being material, is in itself and of necessity an evil thing: from which it would follow, (*a*) that

[1] So *Adv. Prax.* § 2: *id esse verum quodcunque primum, id esse adulterum quodcunque posterius.*

the Body of Christ could not have been a real one and that there was no true Incarnation, and (*b*) that the human body can have no part in the resurrection—a supposition which is liable to have disastrous consequences upon moral conduct. The last work of this series is the present treatise *Against Praxeas*, which, though occasioned by the recrudescence in Africa of modalistic unitarianism, may be taken as representing the official doctrine of the African Churches on the holy Trinity and the Incarnation, as set forth by Tertullian *ut instructior per paracletum*: for the practical concordance of this late work with those written shortly after his conversion suggests that, while the argument and its presentation are Tertullian's, the doctrine and to a large extent the terminology are the common property of the Church.

(3) It is in the *disciplinary works* that Tertullian's peculiar views, as developed in accordance with Montanist principles, are most in evidence. To the catholic period belong the tract *On patience*, and the homilies *On prayer* (including an exposition of the Lord's Prayer) and *On penance* (*poenitentia*, the ecclesiastical disciplinary system) as well as the oration *On the public games* and two books *On the dress of women*. In the other treatises of this group, Tertullian inculcates, with much violent language, the intolerant ethical puritanism which was characteristic of African Montanism and which (in respect at least of the sin of apostasy, real or alleged) left indelible traces in African Christianity. Though marked by a fierce animosity against the official Church, both African and Roman, yet in the expression of the faith (except for some difference in the presentment of the doctrine of the Holy Spirit) they hardly differ from the works of the earlier period. Bearing on our present purpose is the statement of the *regula fidei* which introduces the argument of *De virginibus velandis* (perhaps 215): concerning the Father and the Son, Tertullian repeats in substance what he has frequently said elsewhere, but (his statement having omitted all reference to the Holy Spirit) the rest of the treatise is a plea that the Paraclete, as *vicarius domini*, is presently guiding the Church into that moral truth which an earlier Christian age was not able to bear.

Two books stand outside all these groups. *De pallio* (the philosopher's gown) is of no religious interest, being a half-serious, half-satiric, address to the populace of Carthage, not perhaps without a side-glance at the *Florida* of Appuleius. The treatise *De anima* is an essay in Christian psychology, in which it is to be observed that Tertullian is unable to conceive of real existence except as in some sense corporeal (cf. *Adv. Prax.* 7), that almost alone among Christian thinkers he adopts concerning the origin of the individual soul the doctrine known as traducianism, and that he is probably the first to raise and attempt to answer, from a Christian standpoint, the questions connected with sleep and death.

II. THE MONARCHIAN CONTROVERSY

The double series of discussions known as the monarchian controversy began in the last decade of the second century and continued intermittently for about eighty years. The monarchian theories attracted some attention in Alexandria, in Libya, and in Africa, though only in Rome and in Antioch is there reason to think that they seriously disturbed the general Christian public. But the monarchian theory strictly so called—that which is attacked by Tertullian in the present treatise, and was afterwards known as Sabellianism—remained sufficiently alive in the memory of the learned to be a bugbear to theologians both orthodox and heretical a century and more after the controversy was at an end.

It is sometimes suggested [1] that monarchianism was a reaction against gnosticism. There seems to be little or no evidence of this. The term *monarchy* was introduced into Christian theology by the apologists as a protest against polytheism.[2] It was after-

[1] E.g. by Dr Bethune-Baker, *History of Christian Doctrine*, p. 96.

[2] The term μοναρχία (in three forms, ἡ τοῦ θεοῦ μοναρχία, ἡ μοναρχία ἡ κατὰ τὸν θεόν, ἡ μοναρχία) was in use from the middle of the second century, usually in contrast with polytheism. Justin, *Dial.* 1 (Otto, p. 4 e), οὐχ οἱ φιλόσοφοι περὶ θεοῦ τὸν ἅπαντα ποιοῦνται λόγον . . . καὶ περὶ μοναρχίας αὐτοῖς καὶ προνοίας αἱ ζητήσεις γίγνονται ἑκάστοτε; *Cohort. ad gent.* 17 (p. 64 e), τὴν γὰρ μοναρχίαν ἄμαχον εἶναι συμβαίνει (a parallel between politics and theology, introduced by the Homeric quotation οὐκ ἀγαθὸν πολυκοιρανίη, εἷς κοίρανος ἔστω. Tatian, *Orat.* 14 (p. 64 b), τὴν πολυκοιρανίην μᾶλλον ἤπερ τὴν μοναρχίαν ἠσκήσατε (another reference to the Homeric quotation). Theophilus, *Ad Autol.* ii. 8 (p. 74 b), the gentile poets, inconsistent among themselves, πλὴν καὶ πληθὺν εἰσήγαγον ἢ καὶ μοναρχίαν εἶπον, *ibid.* p. 76 d, ἀκόλουθα τοῖς προφήταις . . . περί τε θεοῦ μοναρχίας καὶ κρίσεως καὶ τῶν λοιπῶν ὧν ἔφασαν: so also *ibid.* 35 (p. 16 c): *ibid.* 38 (p. 184 b), καὶ περὶ πλήθους οὖν θεῶν οἱ συγγραφεῖς εἰπόντες κατῆλθον εἰς μοναρχίαν: iii. 7 (p. 204 b), Πλάτων δέ, ὁ τοσαῦτα εἰπὼν περὶ μοναρχίας θεοῦ καὶ ψυχῆς ἀνθρώπου. But Theophilus in two places uses the term in opposition to dualism: ii. 4 (p. 54 c), εἰ δὲ θεὸς ἀγένητος καὶ ὕλη ἀγένητος, οὐκέτι ὁ θεὸς ποιητὴς τῶν ὅλων κατὰ τοὺς Πλατωνικούς, οὐδὲ μὴν

wards used as a catchword by the professors of that form of unitarian doctrine which denied the distinction of the Father, the Son, and the Holy Spirit.[1] The description "monarchian" is applied both to these and (possibly by contemporaries but more commonly by modern writers) to those other unitarians who denied both the true deity of our Lord Jesus Christ and the personality of the Holy Spirit. But it does not appear that monarchianism in either form was a reaction against any particular doctrine: the two theories (both of them unsatisfactory, and the second on occasion deliberately profane) arose in the attempt to answer questions which were bound to be asked as soon as Christians became conscious of the implications of their immemorial devotional practice.

Christianity inherited from Judaism the fundamental conviction that there is one God and that there can be no other, and that God alone can be legitimately worshipped, either in adoration or in prayer. The very idea of deity implies unity, and it is impossible to conceive of God consenting to share with any other the prerogatives of the incommunicable Name. But, since the beginning of Christianity, invariable and unquestioned

μοναρχία θεοῦ δείκνυται ὅσον τὸ κατ' αὐτούς: *ibid.* 27 (p. 136 b), Adam and Eve were not created separately, lest it might be thought that one god made the man and another the woman, οὐ μὴν ἀλλὰ καὶ ἵνα διὰ τοῦτο δειχθῇ τὸ μυστήριον τῆς μοναρχίας τῆς κατὰ τὸν θεόν, ἅμα ἐποίησεν ὁ θεὸς τὴν γυναῖκα αὐτοῦ. But here again it is philosophic dualism, not Marcionism, that is under consideration. Eusebius, *H.E.* iv. 18. 3, mentions a work of Justin, περὶ θεοῦ μοναρχίας (apparently not the same as that printed with Justin's works): he also, *H.E.* v. 20, mentions a letter of Irenaeus to Florinus, περὶ μοναρχίας ἢ περὶ τοῦ μὴ εἶναι τὸν θεὸν ποιητὴν κακῶν, perhaps a tract against Marcionism. [A strange use, if the text is correct, is Tertullian, *De cult. fem.* ii. 6, *hanc incorruptibilitatem habemus superinduere ad novam domum domini quam monarchia pollicetur*: but *monarchia* as a synonym for *deus* is unparalleled, and, despite the remarks of Rigaltius (quoted by Oehler, *ad loc.*), cannot be defended. Perhaps read *acacia* (a cosmetic), making *incorruptibilitatem* (not *domum*) the antecedent of *quam.*]

In Liddell and Scott, μοναρχία is quoted only in the political sense: ἀρχή however means (*a*) origin, first principle: (*b*) sovranty, dominion, empire, magistracy. Athenagoras, *Suppl.* 22, combines the two senses ἀρχικὸν ἡ φιλία κατὰ τὸν Ἐμπεδοκλέα, ἀρχόμενα τὰ συγκρίματα, τὸ δὲ ἀρχικὸν κύριον· ὥστε ἐὰν μίαν καὶ τὴν αὐτὴν τοῦ τε ἀρχομένου καὶ τοῦ ἄρχοντος δύναμιν θῶμεν, λήσομεν ἑαυτοὺς ἰσότιμον τὴν ὕλην . . . τῷ ἀγενήτῳ . . . ποιοῦντες θεῷ. The term, still in a political sense, was adopted from the apologists as a convenient catchword by the school of Noetus: Hippolytus, *Philos.* ix. 10, referring to Cleomenes, οὕτως γὰρ δοκεῖ μοναρχίαν συνιστᾶν, ἓν καὶ τὸ αὐτὸ φάσκων ὑπάρχειν, πατέρα καὶ υἱὸν καλούμενον, κτέ. The metaphysical sense first appears in [Athanasius] *C. Arian.* iv. 1 (quoted below).

[1] It is also suggested that monarchianism arose from a reaction, among the more simple sort, against speculations about the Logos. But the evidence hardly proves that: the monarchians were not *simplices et idiotae*; rather these latter were persons whom the monarchians found it easy to lead astray.

Christian practice had associated our Lord Jesus Christ with God as the one and only object of public and private worship. Whereas both Jews and Christians maintained that between God and even the highest of created existences there is a sharp and clear distinction as between the infinite and eternal Creator and the finite and temporal creature, Christian thought and liturgical practice from the apostles downwards had always regarded Christ and the Holy Spirit as being on the divine side of that distinction. The trinitarian blessing is of apostolic origin, and from the time of St Stephen Christians had addressed to the Lord Jesus such prayers as may be directed to none but God.[1] The strength of the Christian conviction behind this practice is shown by the fact that it was not until the end of the second century that it occurred to anyone that an articulated justification was necessary.

If justice is to be done to Christian devotional usage, and to the scriptural *data* to which there is always a final appeal, there are three facts which must have full regard paid to them. The divine unity is the first. That our Lord Jesus Christ is the Son of God and is in the highest sense worshipful is the second. The third is that the Son of God is in some sense (into which Christian intelligence may reverently enquire) not identically the same with God the Father. The monarchians, of both schools, thought that the combined acknowledgement of the second postulate and the third amounted to a denial of the first, introducing the idea of a duality of gods. Consequently, holding fast to the fact of the divine unity, the (self-styled) monarchians with whom Tertullian is in controversy wished to relinquish the third fact so as to establish the second, making God the Son identically one with God the Father with the purpose of maintaining his worshipfulness: while the humanitarian school (of whom Tertullian does not seem to have heard, unless he is referring to them in § 27) relinquished the second fact so as to establish the third, denying that Jesus is in any real sense God, with the purpose of safeguarding his personal subsistence.

The theologians whom the common consent of Christendom has come to regard as orthodox, found part of the solution of the

[1] Acts 7. 59: 9. 14. The verb ἐπικαλεῖσθαι implies this. For the principle involved see Novatian, *De trinitate*, 14: *si homo tantummodo Christus, quomodo adest ubique invocatus? . . . si homo tantummodo Christus, cur homo in orationibus mediator invocatur, cum invocatio hominis ad praestandam salutem inefficax iudicetur?*

problem to be involved in the word ***monarchy***. In itself this term is as unobjectionable as the term ***unity***. Tertullian, taking the word in its original political sense, and hardly distinguishing between the objective meaning "empire" and the subjective meaning "imperial authority", points out that the delegation of imperial authority to a second and a third person involves no division of the Empire, so long as it is a fact that the delegated authority derives from one and reverts again to the one. This is evidently no more than an ***argumentum ad hominem*** directed against those who harp on a word without considering its implications. The term is however susceptible of a metaphysical sense, as implying that in the divine Being the Father is the sole ἀρχή or origin of the Being of the Son and of the Holy Spirit. This sense is referred to occasionally by Greek fathers,[1] and Tertullian (though no longer professedly discussing the term) perhaps has it in mind in his three similes of the root, the fountain, and the sun (§ 8). In this way the doctrine of the divine unity in trinity is placed upon a metaphysical (the only finally satisfactory) basis: and the unity is further safeguarded by the doctrine of reciprocity, apparently first suggested by Novatian,[2] summarised in the phrase εἰς αὐτὸν οὗ καὶ ἔστιν ἀναφέρεται in the foregoing quotation from Athanasius, and developed by the Cappadocian fathers as the doctrine which a later age called περιχώρησις.[3]

The monarchianist leaders for the most part found their way to Rome, and obtained a precarious welcome there, during the episcopates of Victor (193-202), Zephyrinus (202-219), and Calixtus (219-223). Apart from such indications as are given by Tertullian and Novatian, our contemporary information about them and their doctrines comes from Hippolytus, who was

[1] The earliest of which I am aware is [Athanasius], *C. Arian.* iv. 1: τοῦ ἑνὸς γὰρ θεοῦ υἱὸς ὢν ὁ λόγος, εἰς αὐτὸν οὗ καὶ ἔστιν ἀναφέρεται, ὥστε δύο μὲν εἶναι πατέρα καὶ υἱόν, μονάδα δὲ θεότητος ἀδιαίρετον καὶ ἄσχιστον. λεχθείη δ' ἂν καὶ οὕτω μία ἀρχὴ θεότητος καὶ οὐ δύο ἀρχαί. ὅθεν κυρίως καὶ μοναρχία ἐστίν.

[2] Novatian, *De trin.* 31: *deus quidem ostenditur filius, cui divinitas tradita et porrecta conspicitur: et tamen nihilominus unus deus pater probatur, dum gradatim reciproco meatu illa maiestas atque divinitas ad patrem qui dederat eam rursum ab illo ipso filio missa revertitur et retorquetur: ut merito deus pater omnium deus sit, et principium ipsius quoque filii sui quem dominum genuit.* Athenagoras, *Suppl.* 10 (p. 10 d), has a similar expression of the Holy Spirit: ἀπορρέον καὶ ἐπαναφερόμενον ὡς ἀκτῖνα ἡλίου.

[3] Prestige: *God in Patristic Thought*, ch. xiv, "The earlier Latin Fathers were fruitful in anticipating the results of later Greek theology, throwing out suggestions of great fertility."

resident at Rome during most of this period; though as for other reasons he was no friend of the Popes concerned, we must regard it as possible that they were better theologians and men of more steadfast character than he gives them credit for. In our account of the history of the movement it will be convenient to consider first that school with which Tertullian was in conflict, the line of teachers beginning with Noetus and ending with Sabellius. These are in modern times described as *modalists* (a term devised by Dr Harnack), since their theory was that Father, Son, and Holy Spirit are three modes or aspects of one divine existence. Their description of themselves was apparently *monarchians*: the Greek fathers call them *Sabellians*, after the name of Sabellius, who expressed the theory in its most philosophic form: the Latins call them *patripassians*, on the ground that their identification of the Son with the Father implies that it was the Father, in the guise of Son, who suffered and died.

Tertullian says that the first teacher of this doctrine was one Praxeas who, during the episcopate of Victor, came from Asia to Rome, where he did two things, both of which annoyed Tertullian: he gave Victor such information about the Asiatic Montanists as caused him to give up his project of sending them his approval, and he began to teach (Tertullian does not say, with the Pope's approval) that there is one God the Father, who himself came down from heaven and was born of a virgin, and himself is Jesus Christ. Some time later a disciple of his found his way to Africa, where his heresy was detected by Tertullian, and he was forced by the African Church to sign a document of recantation. It seemed as though the mischief was stamped out, for the unnamed teacher gave no more trouble; but, like seed that has lain dormant for a while, it began again to germinate, and Tertullian (who by this time had left the Church and become a Montanist) now took up the controversy in writing.[1]

A suggestion is made,[2] with some plausibility, that Praxeas (which could be a rather unusual Greek word for "busy-body") is a nickname designed to cover some well-known person, possibly Calixtus, who afterwards became Pope. Hippolytus mentions no such name, but (after remarking that this heresy was the most dangerous that had hitherto divided the

[1] Tertullian, *Adv. Prax.* § 1.
[2] By P. de Labriolle, referred to by Bethune-Baker, *op. cit.* p. 432.

Church) gives the following account of its origin and its propagation in Rome:

There was a person named Noetus, of Smyrna by origin. He introduced a heresy derived from the doctrines of Heraclitus. He had for his servant and disciple one named Epigonus, who settled at Rome and disseminated the godless opinion. This man's pupil was Cleomenes, a man by conduct and character alien from the Church, who gave vogue to the teaching. At that time Zephyrinus, an ignorant and grasping person, supposed himself to be ruler of the ⟨Roman⟩ Church. He, in consideration of a bribe that was offered him, allowed those who asked for permission, to become disciples of Cleomenes: and he himself after a time was induced to take the same course, his counsellor and abettor in evil being Callistus, whose life and the heresy invented by him I shall expose a little later on. These men's school continued through a succession of masters, strengthening itself and increasing on account of the adherence of Zephyrinus and Callistus, although I by no means acquiesced, but often resisted them and proved them wrong and forced them against their will to admit the truth: and they, being for a time abashed and convinced by the truth, admitted it, but not long afterwards returned to wallow in the same mire.[1]

Hippolytus proceeds to illustrate his contention that these theorists, whether they knew it or not, were followers of Heraclitus (*c.* 520 B.C.) described as "the obscure". They had adopted his doctrine of the universal monad, which (he said) comprised in itself all contradictory qualities (which he, of course, regarded not as contradictory but as complementary), being both divisible and indivisible, created and uncreated, mortal and immortal, and so forth. He then gives the following summary of the opinions of the Noetic school:

Cleomenes says: "So, when as father he had not yet come into existence, he was rightly addressed as Father. But when it was his good pleasure to submit to generation, he was born and became his own Son, not another's." In this fashion he thinks he establishes the monarchy, by saying that there exists one and the same Being, called Father and Son, not one derived from the other, but himself from himself, nominally called Father and Son according to the changing of times: and that

[1] Hippolytus, *Philos.* ix. 7 sqq.

this One is he that appeared [sc. to the patriarchs], and submitted to birth from a virgin, and conversed as man among men: on account of his birth that had taken place he confessed himself to be the Son to those who saw him, while to those who could receive it he did not hide the fact that he was the Father. He adds that he who was nailed to the passion of the cross, and commended to himself his spirit, who died and did not die, and raised himself the third day, and was buried in the sepulchre and wounded with the spear and pierced with nails, is the God and Father of all: and by so saying, Cleomenes and his company bring Heraclitean obscurity upon many.[1]

These are evidently the opinions with which Tertullian is in conflict. Some further information about Noetus is given by Hippolytus in a separate discourse,[2] which from its conversational tone and its concluding doxology appears to be a homily rather than a treatise. Noetus, besides saying that Christ is identical with the Father and that it was the Father who was born and suffered and died, was expelled from the ministry for blasphemy against the Holy Spirit, as having claimed that he himself was Moses and his brother was Aaron. He was twice examined by the presbyters, at first professing not to understand,[3] but afterwards making the excuse, "But what harm do I do in glorifying Christ?" On his expulsion from the Church he founded a school of his own. The texts by which the Noetians supported their opinion were these: Is. 45. 14, "Surely God is in thee, and there is none else, there is no God": Baruch 3. 35, "This is our God, and there shall none other be accounted of in comparison of him": Rom. 9. 5, "Christ . . . who is God over all, blessed for evermore": John 10. 30, "I and the Father are one": John 14. 9, "He that hath seen me hath seen the Father". Once more Tertullian agrees: all these texts except that from Baruch find a place in his discussion.

So far as this, the modalist doctrine amounts to no more than an identification of the Son with the Father, speciously supported by appeal to a few scriptural texts. Its metaphysical basis was supplied by Sabellius, who appeared in Rome about A.D. 220 and, having been at first favourably received, was afterwards

[1] Hippolytus, *Philos.* ix. 10.
[2] Hippolytus, *C. Noet.*, §§ 1, 2.
[3] Ὁ δὲ ἠρνεῖτο, λέγων τὰς ἀρχὰς μὴ φρονεῖν. The version of Turrianus, printed by Routh (*S.E.O.S.* vol. 1), hardly does justice to this sentence.

excommunicated by Calixtus: Hippolytus claims that Calixtus took this action through fear of his censure,[1] which may in a sense be true. Precise indications as to what Sabellius' doctrines were are first given by fourth-century authorities,[2] from whom it appears that he made use of philosophical language of Stoic origin: nor is it impossible that he was acquainted with the work of Tertullian, whose terminology he uses to expound the opposite opinion. His theory indeed seems to be a reply to Tertullian's refutation of Noetus. In the divine being, he said, there is one substance (or person) but three operations. The Deity is a monad, a singular individual unity, which possesses internal powers of expansion, appearing in the act of creation as the Father, in redemption as the Son, and in grace and inspiration as the Holy Spirit, the Three being not three realities but three aspects of one reality. Sabellius apparently did not make it clear whether he meant that the one reality is the Father, who by process of expansion becomes the Word and the Holy Spirit, or whether the One is something more recondite which expands into Father and Word and Holy Spirit: in either case he seems to have held that the process of expansion is balanced by a process of contraction by which the Three cease to be three, being withdrawn again into the One.[3]

This is no doubt a great advance upon the naïveté of Noetus and his school: it amounts to a new theory, which needed a separate discussion—which it apparently did not receive until the fourth century. But the Sabellians made further difficulties, and were not in agreement among themselves, as to the precise incidence of the titles Word and Son. Some of them said that the Son is Christ's human nature, not the Word at all: others said that the Word and the humanity together constitute the Son: while others would have it that the Word himself became Son at the Incarnation.[4] St Athanasius (or whoever is the author of the fourth so-called Oration against the Arians) points out

[1] Hippolytus, *Philos.* ix. 12.
[2] Notably [Athanasius], *C. Arian.* iv. 13 sqq.
[3] Besides the term *substance*, Sabellius (if Epiphanius reports correctly, *Haer.* 62. 1) adapted to his own purposes Tertullian's illustration of the sun and its ray. This would make the Son (the light) and the Holy Spirit (the heat) emissions from, not representations of, the Father. Sabellius shortsightedly makes those emissions (πρόσωπα) temporary, though as a fact of nature the light and the heat are as permanent as the sun.
[4] [Athanasius], *op. cit.* 15.

that since the Father is father of the Word, and since father and son are correlative terms, evidently the Word is the Son: the Son is not an aspect of the Word, nor the Word an aspect of the Son, but these are two titles of one divine Person who is always the Word of God and always the only-begotten Son of the Father: the Gospel itself makes this identification: difficulties only arise when speculation is allowed to override the scriptural evidence. But it is conceivable, once more, that these speculations were affected by Tertullian's discussion of the Incarnation.[1] The early monarchians, Tertullian says, wished to distinguish between a human Jesus-Son and a divine Christ-Word-Father. This distinction he shows to be impossible: though, since he admits the existence of two *substantiae*, each with its *proprietas*, the temptation remained to make a division between them and to give to each a proper name.

It is sometimes alleged [2] that the Sabellian speculations had a reflex restrictive action upon orthodox terminology, in that the word πρόσωπον, which ought to have been the equivalent of the Latin *persona*, had through the associations of the Attic theatre suggested that the three divine Persons were no more than temporary roles like those assumed by an actor in a drama, and that consequently the orthodox tended to avoid this term as misleading. In fact there does not seem to be any evidence that the term was used by the monarchians in this sense—or even at all except for the precarious example quoted by Epiphanius—and the theatrical usage upon which such an interpretation would have depended had been obsolete for several centuries: moreover the orthodox continued to use the term as indicating a living self-conscious active ὑπόστασις.[3] In any case the Latin word *persona*, which by its legal associations means one who has an existence and a status and rights of his own as well as relations and obligations in respect of others, was not unsuitable for safeguarding the Christian conviction of the immutability of the three divine Persons: and in particular, if the salvation of mankind by the incarnate Word is a permanent thing, then the Incarnation once accomplished must be a permanent fact, and the Word

[1] *Adv. Prax.* § 27.
[2] E.g. by Bethune-Baker, *Christian Doctrine*, pp. 105, 234.
[3] This sentence was written before the editor had read Dr G. L. Prestige's *God in Patristic Thought*: he can only be gratified at finding himself in agreement in this and in other matters with so weighty and well-documented a book.

who was incarnate cannot be regarded as a temporary and transitory aspect of deity. It is on the doctrine of the Atonement that Sabellianism, like other heresies, finds itself wrecked: that, whether explicitly or not, is the fathers' final criterion.

The opposing school of humanitarian monarchians [1] is of interest here only in so far as the Church writers who controvert them—Novatian and the fathers of Antioch—make use of material furnished by Tertullian in this treatise. The descriptions "adoptionist" or "dynamic monarchians", now frequently applied to them, are not very appropriate, except perhaps the latter in a specific sense of the term δύναμις: they, like the corresponding term "modalist", are due to Dr Harnack. Our information as to the origin of the sect comes once more from Hippolytus.[2] Early in the episcopate of Victor a certain Theodotus, a Byzantine, came to Rome. This man, unlike the Marcionites and gnostics, admitted that God is the creator of all things, but, like the Ebionites and gnostics, said that Jesus was a mere man (though born of a virgin) and that at his baptism the heavenly Christ, who is the same as the Holy Spirit, came down upon him in the form of a dove. He did not say that Jesus became God at the descent of the Spirit, though some of his school thought that he did so after his resurrection. This piece of amateur theology was improved on by another Theodotus, a banker, who said that the Christ who came down upon Jesus was a kind of celestial copy of a "great power" Melchizedek, but for the rest agreed with his namesake.

Here we have that faulty exegesis (to which Tertullian draws attention) which fails to see that the title Christ signifies an office rather than a person, and that the office of Christ is the office of a man. Once the false distinction has been made, or copied from the gnostics, between the heavenly Christ and the human Jesus, the identification of Christ and the Holy Spirit naturally results, as a reaction from the virtual polytheism of the gnostics. That something important happened at our Lord's

[1] Origen, *Comm. in Ioa.*, ii. 2, associates the two schools, as φιλοθέους εἶναι εὐχομένους, but εὐλαβουμένους δύο ἀναγορεῦσαι θεούς, the one party as ἀρνουμένους ἰδιότητα υἱοῦ ἑτέραν παρὰ τὴν τοῦ πατρός, the other as ἀρνουμένους τὴν θεότητα τοῦ υἱοῦ τιθέντας δὲ αὐτοῦ τὴν ἰδιότητα καὶ τὴν οὐσίαν κατὰ περιγραφὴν τυγχάνουσαν ἑτέραν τοῦ πατρός. The latter are the Theodotians, but there is no evidence that they either called themselves monarchians or were so called by their contemporaries: see Tixeront, *Histoire des Dogmes*, vol. i. p. 310.

[2] Hippolytus, *Philos.* vii. 35, 36.

baptism is clear from the conspicuous place it occupies in the Gospel narrative: the Church writers, when they do not avoid the question, seem to think it was the occasion of his apprehension of the implications and powers of his ministry: if that is too little, it is certainly too much to say that it represents the seizure (one might almost say the obsession) of a human person by a hitherto alien celestial "power"—for it must be remembered that "power", to the persons who use this language, always means a semi-divine personage of some sort. The second Theodotus, having read in the Epistle to the Hebrews that Melchizedek, King of Salem, was made like unto the Son of God, twisted this into the fancy that the supposed celestial Christ was made like unto Melchizedek, and invented a heavenly Melchizedek who should be the prototype of the heavenly Christ. The wonder is that such exegesis obtained a hearing: apparently no one thought it worth answering.

Further information about this school comes to us from an unnamed contemporary writer quoted by Eusebius,[1] who says that the founders of the school, and Artemon (or Artemas) their successor, claimed that their doctrine was that of the primitive Church, having been maintained at Rome from the apostles until the death of Victor, after which Zephyrinus falsified the faith. There are those to whom such a claim as this, reported at second hand and without its supporting facts (if there ever were any), will always carry more weight than the main body of the available evidence: and it is not surprising that from the seventeenth century to the present the statement has repeatedly been made that until the end of the second century the Roman Church (if no other) held humanitarian or adoptionist views of Christ, and that attempts have been made, by digging beneath the surface of the evidence, to ferret out the appearance of proof. But, as Bishop Bull showed, and as has frequently been repeated, our unnamed author is by the extant evidence abundantly justified in his remark that this claim to antiquity is discountenanced both by the Scriptures and the writings of the apologists, "in all of which Christ is glorified as God", as well as by the works of theologians such as Irenaeus and Melito, who proclaim that Christ is God and Man, and by psalms and hymns composed by the brethren in praise of "the Word of God, the Christ". Also, our author adds,

[1] Eusebius, *H.E.* v. 28. For theories as to this writer's identity see Lightfoot, *Clement of Rome*, vol. ii. pp. 377 sqq.

the statement about Victor is palpably false, for it is well known that it was he who excommunicated the author of this "god-denying apostasy", who first presumed to say that Christ was a "mere man".

Concerning Artemon (or Artemas) very little is known, though as the school was for a time called by his name it is to be supposed that in his day he was of some importance. Conceivably he was the propagator of that more thoroughgoing humanitarianism or naturalism against which Novatian directed a long section of his treatise. The two Theodoti had taught that the Christ is a celestial "power" who took possession of the man Jesus: those whom Novatian has in view regarded Christ as a "mere man" and as nothing more than that,[1] though apparently they still retained the practice of addressing prayers to Christ and had not ceased to regard him as mediator and saviour.[2] They did, however, overlook many texts, and indeed the whole tenor of Scripture, which throughout presents Christ as God and Man. Novatian does not, like Eusebius' unnamed author, say that they had corrupted or mutilated the Scriptures under the pretence of correcting them.

The most notorious disciple of this school was Paul of Samosata, bishop of Antioch, *c.* 260-270. Eusebius, from whom most of our information is derived,[3] was only one generation removed from him in date, but seems to have been more interested in his supposed or real offences against ecclesiastical propriety than in his theological opinions: he does however mention that Paul held low and earthbound views of Christ, contrary to the teaching of the Church, that he said that Christ was a man like other men, and that he would not admit that the Son of God came down from heaven, but frankly affirmed that he was "from beneath"—this last being a reference to John 8. 23 and a deliberate reversal of our Lord's words there recorded. It is consistent with this that in the articles of his condemnation by the synod of Antioch he is reported to have forbidden the use of hymns

[1] Novatian, *De trin.* §§ 11 sqq.: *hominem tantum et solum defendentibus . . . hominem illum nudum et solitarium probare cupientibus.*

[2] See the sentences quoted above, p. 9: Novatian's remonstrance would have been pointless if they had been able to reply, "But we do not pray to him".

[3] Eusebius, *H.E.* vii. 27-30. Eusebius had access to a shorthand report of the final Antiochene synod: his information therefore must be regarded as authentic.

in praise of Christ, on the ground that they were of recent composition.[1]

During the years 265-270 a series of synods was held at Antioch to discuss Paul's beliefs and conduct.[2] One of the early synods, dealing gently with Paul, sent him a letter in which they stated the Church's faith in one God, and in Christ the Son of God, both God and Man, a letter which (as we shall indicate below) shows evident acquaintance with the work of Hippolytus and through him (if not directly) is beholden to Tertullian. At the final meeting, in 270, it was ascertained after some verbal fencing that Paul's views were that Christ is not the very Word and Wisdom of God, but that the Word and Wisdom of God dwelt in Christ in the same manner as in the prophets but to a greater degree. This is not the view of either Theodotus, nor is it the doctrine of the New Testament or of the Church at large: it may be the doctrine of Artemas, and it is certainly the doctrine which now prevails under the guise of undenominational religion.

The deposition of Paul brings to an end the direct line of Tertullian's influence, and there we may leave the history and turn to the literature in which that influence makes itself felt. The humanitarian tradition apparently came to an end with Paul: but adoptionism and modalism strangely reach a reconciliation in the opinions professed in the middle of the fourth century by Photinus, the disciple of the suspected Sabellian Marcellus of Ancyra.

III. TERTULLIAN'S TREATISE AND ITS INFLUENCE

The treatise *Against Praxeas*, written perhaps in A.D. 213,[3] is directed against the modalist teaching in its unmetaphysical Noetic form. That Tertullian in this answer managed to cover

[1] In this he was mistaken, as the evidence shows. The accompanying statement that he substituted hymns in praise of himself need not be untrue: the synod of Antioch (which made the statement) was composed of grave men, and we have known preachers who, while belittling Christ, are prone to magnify themselves.

[2] The relevant documents, drawn from Eusebius, Athanasius, Basil, and Hilary, are collected by Routh, *R.S.* vol. iii. pp. 287-367.

[3] This, the date usually given, seems to have been suggested by the reference in § 3 to the assumption by certain emperors of their sons as colleagues. Caracalla was the colleague of Septimius Severus from 198 to 211: Severus, Caracalla, and Geta were colleagues from 209 to 211, and Caracalla and Geta from 211 to 212. So Liebenam, *Fasti Consulares Imperii Romani*, p. 110.

all the necessary ground becomes evident from the fact that his successors not only use his materials (some of which he inherited from the apologists) but also follow the general lines of his arrangement and presentation of them. That his answer in its general conception was not extemporised, but represents his own considered opinion and a respectably supported Church tradition, will appear from his earlier works and those of second-century authors.

Hippolytus, though aware of the existence of Sabellius, is also dealing with the Noetic form of the heresy. His discourse follows Tertullian's general lines—brief historical narrative, correction of faulty exegesis, scriptural proof of the existence of the Word or Son, statement of the doctrine of the Incarnation: and, although there is at least one important difference of presentation, he borrows much of Tertullian's material and all his most significant terminology.

Novatian must have been personally acquainted with Hippolytus, and it is perhaps the case that he allowed himself to become the leader of that anti-papal opposition, perhaps one may say that conservative group, of which Hippolytus had been the spokesman.[1] In the latter part of the second section of his book *On the Trinity* he briefly adverts upon the Sabellians: the greater part of his treatment of the second paragraph of the Creed is concerned (after a repudiation of the Marcionite and Gnostic Christ) to disprove a humanitarian doctrine which is neither Ebionite nor Theodotian, but may perhaps be that of Artemas. He too uses Tertullian's Old Testament texts (originally collected by Justin Martyr), gives special attention to the testimony of St John's Gospel and to the contrast between God who cannot be seen and God who has been seen, and controverts an unsatisfactory interpretation of the words of the Annunciation. The arguments used by Tertullian and Hippolytus against those who denied that the Son is a second Person beside the Father, prove equally apposite against those who, while admitting Christ's personal existence, deny that he is more than man.

[1] If Hippolytus correctly represents the facts (*Philos.* ix. 12) the conventicle founded by Callistus will (through the attraction of its relaxed penitential system) have drawn into itself the great body of the Roman Christians, so that his διδασκαλεῖον came to be taken for the catholic body. But that is a subject on which Cyprian would have had something to say, for the facts (if they had been facts) could not have been forgotten in so short a time.

The correspondence between Dionysius of Rome and Dionysius of Alexandria (*c.* 260) was occasioned by the dissemination of Sabellian doctrine in Libyan Pentapolis, a district over which the bishops of Alexandria had extended their patriarchal oversight. The bishop of Alexandria, taking steps to counteract the Sabellian influence, wrote a number of letters, one of which was severely criticised (apparently as unduly subordinationist in tone), and formal complaint was made to Dionysius of Rome. A Roman synod discussed the matter and demanded explanations, while the Pope issued a document which impartially condemned both tritheists and adoptionists and patripassians,[1] and wrote also a private letter of remonstrance to the bishop of Alexandria, who in due course returned a long and careful reply.[2] Of the fragmentary remains of this correspondence one can say that the Roman bishop says little that is not by this time common form: while the Alexandrian, though (having been trained in the school of Origen) he has an independent mind which makes him no mere copyist of other men's matter, has (whether or not he was conscious of their origin) made further use of Tertullian's materials, rescuing them from the interpretation which Sabellius seems to have put upon them.

The letter of the synod of Antioch to Paul of Samosata (*c.* 265),[3] for all that it was composed by pupils of Origen, again has so much in common with Tertullian that his influence, either directly or through Hippolytus, has to be acknowledged. But beyond this point, monarchianism in both its forms being dead, or at least discredited, it seems that the recognisable influence of its first adversary also comes to an end. The revived Sabellianism (suspected or real) of Marcellus of Ancyra was attacked by Eusebius of Caesarea from the same scriptural armoury, though the arrangement and treatment of the materials suggest that they were collected afresh by Eusebius himself, and that he owes more to Origen than to any other. The rationalism of Photinus owes nothing to the Ebionites or Theodotus or Paul of Samosata: it

[1] Preserved by St Athanasius, *De decret. Syn. Nic.*: Routh, *R.S.* vol. iii. pp. 373 sqq. Routh thinks this document is not part of the correspondence with the bishop of Alexandria. Feltoe, *The Letters of Dionysius of Alexandria*, p. 176.

[2] Fragments preserved chiefly by St Athanasius, *De sententia Dionysii*: Routh, *R.S.* vol. iii. pp. 390 sqq.: Feltoe, p. 182.

[3] Routh, *R.S.* vol. iii. pp. 287 sqq.

was the spontaneous outgrowth of an irreverent mind, and the weapon with which it was met was the new one of sorrowful amazement not untempered with invective. At the same period St Hilary of Poitiers found Sabellianism almost as pressing a danger as Arianism: he is evidently acquainted with the work of Tertullian (whom he rarely mentions) and on several occasions seems to be tacitly correcting phrases which are suggestive, but capable of leaving a false impression.

In the following pages we give a brief outline of the contents of each of the works referred to, drawing attention to those respects in which Tertullian's ideas and method of presentation appear to have been influential.

Tertullian against Praxeas

After an introductory chapter describing the circumstances under which Praxean teaching was imported to Rome and Africa, Tertullian lays his foundation by stating the traditional faith in the holy Trinity which it is his purpose to defend. The argument itself begins with an analogy intended to remove the fears of the more simple brethren: The Roman Empire is one, though it is ruled by the emperor and his sons whom he has co-opted as his colleagues, and no one supposes that the existence of three emperors imperils the monarchy, i.e. the unity of the Empire. In like manner the monarchy of God is not imperilled by the existence of the Son and the Holy Spirit consubstantial with him: the more so as it is clearly stated that the Son's kingship is committed to him by the Father, to whom he will also deliver it up again.

Secondly, addressing the more instructed, Tertullian adduces scriptural testimony to the existence of the Son, who is also the Word and the Wisdom of God, proceeding by generation from the Father, as a second Person beside the Father. We do not, he maintains, by the terms generation and prolation give countenance to the Valentinian theory of prolation: for the Son is not by generation separated from the Father, seeing that the holy Trinity are three "not by diversity but by distribution, not by division but by distinction". The monarchians suggest that the Father made himself his own Son: the scriptural evidence is to the effect that it was another beside himself whom the Father brought forth from himself, and the Scriptures consistently present two who are called God and Lord, but not two gods or two lords.

A third line of argument arises from the pronouncement that no man can see God's face and live, brought into comparison with those many places in which it is written that God was seen, by the patriarchs and others. This must mean that he who cannot be seen is the Father, while God who was seen is the Son: and in fact since the foundation of the world all the Father's acts have been mediated by the Son, for the Father's attributes and powers are the Son's also. The possession of a Son no more destroys the Father's unity than the sunlight destroys the unity of the sun in the sky.

Fourthly: the monarchians rest their whole case on three texts, "I am God, and beside me there is none else", and "I and my Father are one", and "He that hath seen me hath seen the Father". They insist on these texts, in their own short-sighted interpretation of them, in spite of the numberless places of Scripture which discountenance that interpretation. To confute them Tertullian extracts from St John's Gospel all the passages in which our Lord speaks of the Father as other than himself, adding also summary references to the same teaching in St Matthew and St Luke. He adds that the words of the Annunciation to Mary, which the monarchians wrest to their own purpose, support this distinction, and that the very name, or rather title, of "Christ" presumes the existence of One who anoints and Another who is anointed.

Lastly: not only are the monarchians wrong, even blasphemous, in suggesting that the Father became the Son and as the Son was passible, but the Son, moreover, himself is impassible in his divine nature, becoming passible in the flesh. The words from the cross, "Why hast thou forsaken me?", and "Into thy hands I commend my spirit", his raising up by the Father, his session at the right hand of the Father, as well as the mission of the Holy Spirit by the Son from the Father, are only possible if the Son is not identical with the Father. Therefore we affirm that so to believe in the divine unity as to deny the Son and the Holy Spirit, is to deny the Father also, and is Judaism and not Christianity.

Hippolytus against Noetus

This discourse [1] begins with a brief account of Noetus and of the nature of his heresy, after which Hippolytus recites the texts on which Noetus chiefly relied [2] and remarks that there are two facts we need to establish: the unity of God, and the economy—by which (like Tertullian) he means the holy Trinity.

Thereafter the discourse falls into three parts, of which the first consists of a detailed examination of the Noetian texts, intended to show that within their own context they will not bear the interpretation put upon them. Throughout this section the influence of Tertullian is evident, the method of approach and even the phraseology being identical.

Part two (§§ 8-14) presents proof from the Scriptures of the need to confess God the Father Almighty, and Christ Jesus the Son of God, who became Man, and to whom the Father hath subjected all things except himself and the Holy Spirit, and that these are verily three subsistences (*καὶ τούτους εἶναι ὄντως τρία*).[3] God is one because his power is one: in respect of his power there is one God, but in respect of the economy the demonstration is triple (or, reading *τριχῶς*, "proceeds on three lines").[4] Before the creation, God, though alone, was manifold, having in him Word, Wisdom, Power. When he so willed, he displayed the Word in creation: that is, the Word invisible he made visible. So he had Another beside him, as light kindled from light, as river from fountain, as radiance from the sun. To the fathers the Word spoke of himself as of one who was to come: which eventually came to pass, as St John says, when the Word was made flesh. Hence Jeremiah can say (by anticipation) that men see the Word, whereas the human word is merely heard.

[1] Routh (*S.E.O.S.* vol. i. p. 49) describes it as the concluding portion of a lost work against all the heresies. It is certainly the concluding part of a longer discourse which treated of several heresies, including that of Theodotus: but it is not part of the *Philosophumena*, which had not been discovered when Routh wrote. The conversational style, and the concluding doxology, suggest that it was a homily.

[2] See above, p. 12.

[3] It was perhaps this neuter *τρία* to which Callistus objected, saying *οὐκ ἄλλο εἶναι πατέρα, ἄλλο δὲ υἱόν, ἓν δὲ καὶ τὸ αὐτὸ ὑπάρχειν* (Hippolytus, *Philos.* ix. 12): he accused Hippolytus of ditheism.

[4] *Εἰ δε βούλεται μαθεῖν πῶς εἷς θεὸς ἀποδείκνυται, γινωσκέτω ὅτι μία δύναμις τούτου, καὶ ὅσον μὲν κατὰ τὴν δύναμιν εἷς ἐστι θεός, ὅσον δὲ κατὰ τὴν οἰκονομίαν τριχὴς ἡ ἐπίδειξις.*

St John's testimony is our proof that there is one God, but two Persons, "and by the economy the grace of the Holy Spirit is third"[1]: and these Three are one "by an economy of unison".[2] It was because our Lord knew that only so was it the Father's will to be glorified, that he gave his disciples the trinitarian formula: "it was the Father's will, the Son's act, the Spirit's manifestation".

Here again Tertullian's influence is beyond question, though Hippolytus is by no means a slavish copyist. The term πρόσωπον, evidently a translation of Tertullian's *persona*, fills a blank in Greek theological terminology, making for the future unnecessary such a circumlocution as Justin's ἄλλος καὶ ἄλλος. Tertullian, repudiating the suggestion that by maintaining the existence of three Persons he is rejecting the monarchy, begins by thinking of the monarchy as subjective but ends by objectifying it as *regnum*: Hippolytus avoids this equivocation by maintaining one δύναμις, thus placing the ground of unity (as Tertullian does when he gets down to the subject) in the inmost being of God. Hippolytus is rather less guarded than Tertullian in the suggestion that the Word was displayed for the purpose of creation, though the language of both is probably defensible in terms of later orthodoxy. He borrows the illustrations of the sun and the fountain (but not the root), and adds from elsewhere the kindred image of light kindled from light. The text from Jeremiah which anticipates the Word made visible in the Incarnation may have been suggested by Tertullian's *non alius quam sermo qui caro erat futurus* (§ 16); but the striking though unsatisfactory phrase οἰκονομία συμφωνίας, and the suggestive thought that the trinitarian formula was communicated by our Lord because it is only through the Son and in the Holy Spirit that the Father is willing to be worshipped, are due to Hippolytus himself.

The third part of the homily treats of the Incarnation. There are those[3] who deny the identity of the Son with the Word who (as the apostle says) was incarnate: but these are refuted by Apocalypse 19. 13 where "a garment dipped in blood" can only mean the flesh with which the Word clothed himself: and St Paul

[1] Εἰ δὲ οὖν ὁ λόγος πρὸς τὸν θεὸν θεὸς ὤν, τί οὖν φήσειεν ἄν τις δύο λέγεις θεούς; δύο μὲν οὐκ ἐρῶ θεοὺς ἀλλ' ἢ ἕνα, πρόσωπα δὲ δύο, οἰκονομίᾳ (so Routh, for οἰκονομίαν) δὲ τρίτην τὴν χάριν τοῦ ἁγίου πνεύματος.

[2] Οἰκονομίᾳ συμφωνίας συνάγεται εἰς ἕνα θεόν.

[3] I.e. a section of the monarchians: see above, p. 13.

explicitly says that God sent his own Son. That it was not the Father himself who was incarnate is evident from such a text as "I came forth from the Father" and from the Father's words "Out of the womb before the dawn have I begotten thee"—which Hippolytus, like Tertullian,[1] takes as referring to the Incarnation, not to the eternal generation. The incredulity of these people was foreseen, as is shown by the often repeated text, "Who hath believed our report?" But we must believe that the Word was incarnate for our salvation, and that, being incarnate, he is both heavenly and earthly, and that not in mere appearance, nor by change from one to the other, but God who has been made Man in very truth.

Here Hippolytus is much more independent. The themes indeed are those of Tertullian, but Hippolytus approaches the subject from a new direction. If the language of Tertullian insisting on the permanence of the *proprietas utriusque substantiae* in the Word incarnate suggests that of Leo the Great, Hippolytus maintaining the unity of Christ's Person in his sufferings as in his glories approaches more nearly to the standpoint of Cyril of Alexandria—in theology a much more satisfactory guide. The whole section abounds in suggestive phrases which Hippolytus apparently owes to no one but himself.[2]

Novatian on the Trinity

St Jerome says[3] that Novatian's *grande volumen* is a sort of epitome of a work of Tertullian. This has been called in question, since Tertullian is not known to have written a book expressly on the Trinity, nor is Novatian's work an epitome of any particular treatise of his. Probably what Jerome (or his informant) had in mind was that Novatian combines in one volume the results of Tertullian's dispersed discussions. And this is substantially true: for the first section of this work, on God the Father, the Creator, undoubtedly owes something to passages in Tertullian's *Apology*, while the second section, on God the Son, though largely occupied in combating an opposite heresy, shows evident acquaint-

[1] *Adv. Marc.* v. 9.

[2] The parallels between Tertullian and Hippolytus are set out in full by Semler (printed in Oehler's vol. iii. pp. 688 sqq.).

[3] Jerome, *De viris illustribus*, 70.

ance with the treatise *Against Praxeas.* Only in the third section, on the Holy Spirit, does Novatian strike a line of his own, and here he is expository, almost encomiastic, rather than controversial or theological.

As already indicated, Novatian's book, being not in the first instance a work of controversy but of instruction, an exposition of the leading sentences of the Rule of the Faith, falls naturally into three parts. In part *one*, having summarised the scriptural teaching of the work of God in the creation of the world and of man, and having briefly stated the fact of the fall, and of heaven and hell, Novatian goes on to say that God, who is above all, also contains all, being infinite and eternal, far transcending the powers of human thought and speech. Yet as creator he manifests himself in his works: he is good, always the same, without peer, without name, immortal and incorruptible. When the Scripture speaks of the wrath of God it indicates no defect in his nature, since his wrath affects not him but us: and likewise the other anthropomorphisms of holy Scripture are meant to help man's understanding, certainly not for a description of God. Even the statement "God is a spirit" (and here Novatian disagrees with Tertullian) is not an exhaustive definition of his essence, any more than "God is love", "God is light", "God is a consuming fire". The Scripture also shows that God's providential care extends both to the whole and to every smallest part of his creation.

The *second* and by far the longest section of the book is concerned with Christ Jesus the Son of God, who was promised of old in the law, the prophets, and the psalms. Neither the Marcionite Christ nor the Christ of the docetists and the gnostics is of any use to us Christians: Christ comes to us not as an unannounced stranger into an alien world, but as the saviour of his own creation: he is also fully human. But he is not merely human, being both God and Man. There are places in the Old Testament which promise a saviour who is God: God says, in Hosea, "I will save them by the Lord their God", and, Isaiah says, our Saviour is Emmanuel, "God with us". The apostles John and Paul bear the same testimony.

Now follows a long argument directed against those who will have it that Christ is nought but man. These are evidently not Ebionites, nor adherents of either Theodotus: we have suggested that this thoroughgoing humanism was the teaching of Artemas.

In this section the influence of Tertullian is very apparent: the themes and the scriptural quotations and many of the interpretations are borrowed from him, but with the difference that what he uses to prove that the Son is a second divine Person beside the Father, Novatian (whose adversaries admit Christ's personal existence) finds equally apposite to prove his deity (which Tertullian's adversaries did not deny).

First, the testimony of St John's Gospel is adduced in detail, and it is shown that both Moses and David anticipate John's teaching. Next, asserting the principle that "No man hath seen God at any time", Novatian (like Tertullian) remarks that as God did appear to the patriarchs and others it must have been God the Son whom they saw. In some of these places the visitant is described as both "God" and "Angel of the Lord": and as it is impossible to suppose that the Father could be the angel or messenger of any greater than himself, we must conclude that Christ the Son, the Father's messenger, is here declared to be God. In the wrestling at Penuel, Jacob's antagonist is called Man as well as God, the former by anticipation of the Incarnation. These two points Novatian seems to owe not to Tertullian but directly to Justin. If the heretics contend that an ordinary angel is here indicated, they do not improve their case: for it is declared that all things in heaven and earth are subject to Christ, and consequently he is superior to the angels and (on the heretics' contention) to the angel who is described as God and Lord. Further, Christ's own testimony concerning himself is that he is both God and Man. And again, if Christ were nought but man, he would be in the image of God (as are all men) but not in the form of God (as St Paul affirms): and moreover a mere man by being born is not "emptied" but increased, and it is impossible that to a mere man every knee should bow. The Sabellians and the docetists, though we do not approve of their errors, at least testify to the strength of the scriptural evidence for Christ's deity. If the heretics allege the words of the Annunciation as saying that the Son of Mary as such is the Son of God, they have misread their text: the word "also" must not be disregarded. And finally, if they object that God cannot die, we reply that in the Passion of Christ it was not the godhead but the manhood that died, even as in the death of every man it is the body that dies and not the soul.

Having thus dealt at length with the humanitarians, Novatian turns to deal briefly with the Sabellians. The references to the obedience of Christ are sufficient proof that the Son is not the Father, for no one is obedient to himself. An examination of the texts "I and my Father are one" and "He that hath seen me hath seen the Father" which concludes the second part of the book, follows Tertullian's general line, but with a few details of Novatian's own.

The *third*, a very brief, section of the work, expounds, on what seem to be Novatian's own lines, the doctrine of the Holy Spirit. If there are differences in the manner of the Holy Spirit's operations as between the Old Testament and the New, there are sufficient likenesses to prove that it is the same Spirit. His present working is by no means only in the so-called "spiritual gifts": for the Holy Spirit rested fully upon Christ, and operates fully from him, working in the Christian person both for the formation of character and for moral power, as well as in prophetic and intellectual enlightenment and in ascetic self-mastery. Novatian here greatly improves upon Tertullian, who regarded the Paraclete as acting almost exclusively in the revelations of the "new prophecy", and had little conception of the general Christian life as one lived in the grace of the Holy Spirit: indeed, to Novatian apparently belongs the credit of rescuing this Pauline teaching from the oblivion into which since apostolic days it had (except for Irenaeus) for the most part been allowed to fall.

The work ends with two chapters of recapitulation of the doctrine of God and of Christ, which contain the remarkable sentence (already quoted) which seems to anticipate the doctrine afterwards called περιχώρησις. This thought also seems to be Novatian's own, though Athenagoras has something like it in reference to the Holy Spirit: ἀπορρέον καὶ ἐπαναφερόμενον ὡς ἀκτῖνα ἡλίου.

THE CORRESPONDENCE OF THE TWO DIONYSII

The fragment of the letter of Dionysius of Rome preserved by Athanasius is directed against persons whom he accuses of the unlikely heresy of tritheism, and others who make the Son a created being. Its expressions seem to be such as had by now become common form. Christ is the Word and Wisdom and

Power of God, and as it is impossible to conceive that God can ever have been devoid of these, it is equally impossible that the Son should ever have been non-existent, and consequently he cannot be a creature. A misinterpretation of "The Lord created me" is corrected with the remark that ἔκτισε here means ἐπέστησε. "Out of the womb before the dawn" and "Before all the hills doth he beget me" are adduced as proof-texts, as are "I and the Father are one" and "I am in the Father and the Father in me". The "preaching of the monarchy" is insisted on as essential: Dionysius perhaps regarded Sabellianism as a lesser evil than subordinationism.

The *epistula quadripartita* of Dionysius of Alexandria (the fragments of which are again for the most part preserved by Athanasius) seems to have been largely occupied with the defence of a former epistle. In this use had been made of the image ἀπαύγασμα φωτὸς ἀιδίου, and the term ὁμοούσιος had been remarked on as non-scriptural (apparently it was already an accepted expression even in other than Origenistic circles, and Dionysius here regards it as equivalent in the divine sphere to ὁμογενής in the human or to ὁμοφυής in vegetable life). He uses the figures of plant springing from seed or root, and river from fountain, his purpose in these and in the figure of the light being to illustrate homogeneity but distinctness. There is a λόγος which is ἀπόρροια νοῦ, ἕτερος τοῦ ἐν καρδίᾳ λόγου, ὁ διὰ γλώσσης νοῦς προπηδῶν: the one λόγος remains where it was, after emitting the other, yet both are in each other, καὶ ἕν εἰσιν, ὄντες δύο: so the Father and the Son are ἕν, and within each other. This seems a new illustration, perhaps suggested by Tertullian, but certainly not one which he would have thought it safe to use. Again, father and son being relative terms, the mention of the Father implies (even without express mention) the acknowledgement of the Son. But Dionysius is greatly concerned to avoid Sabellianism: the Word who was in the beginning was not sent forth by the Word, but was "with God": we must acknowledge three ὑποστάσεις, or we deny the Trinity. On the text "My heart hath sent forth a good Word", he remarks that λόγος is so to speak the child of νοῦς, the angel and interpreter of νοῦς, but is not itself νοῦς. Once more we may suspect that Tertullian's arguments and illustrations have become by now common property: in any case, the pupil of

Origen was not likely to be entirely beholden to a western tradition.

The Synod of Antioch to Paul of Samosata

This letter, a statement of the faith delivered by the blessed Apostles and preserved in the holy catholic Church, declares: (1) that God is unbegotten, one only, without beginning, invisible, immutable, whom no man hath seen nor can see, of glory beyond description, yet known (to the measure to which he is known) through the revelation of his Son. (2) That the only begotten Son of God, the Wisdom and Word and Power of God, exists before the ages, not in foreknowledge, but God in actual subsistence,[1] as both Old and New Testaments testify, Ps. 45. 6, 7: Is. 35. 4, 5: 45. 14: Rom. 9. 5: Hos. 11. 9, 10. (3) That the Son, being ever with the Father, fulfilled the Father's counsel in the creation of the world, and it was he who appeared to the patriarchs Abraham and Jacob: this also is evident from the Scriptures, Ps. 148. 5: Gen. 1. 26: John 1. 3: Col. 1. 16: Prov. 8. 30: and Gen. 18. 1: 19. 24: Is. 9. 6: Gen. 22. 11, 15: 31. 11-13, in some of which places the Lord is called Angel, an appellation inapplicable to the Father but appropriate to the Son. (4) That the Son was the mediator at the giving of the Law, and was seen by Moses, though he testifies that God the Father cannot be seen. (5) That the Son, sent by the Father, was incarnate, and the body born of the virgin received the whole fullness of the Godhead bodily, being without detriment to its proper nature (*ἀτρέπτως*) united to the Godhead and deified, wherefore the prophets preached beforehand of Jesus Christ the same both God and Man: the signs and wonders were the work of God, but in that he became partaker of flesh and blood he, the same, was in all points tempted like as we are, apart from sin: Lam. 4. 20: 2 Cor. 3. 17: 1 Cor. 10. 4, 9: Heb. 11. 26: 1 Pet. 1. 10: 1 Cor. 1. 24.

The similarities, both in detail and in general construction, of this letter with the works of Tertullian and Hippolytus, seem too close to be accidental, and it appears likely that the work

[1] *Πρὸ αἰώνων ὄντα, οὐ προγνώσει ἀλλ' οὐσίᾳ καὶ ὑποστάσει θεὸν θεοῦ υἱόν.* The three verbal substantives are evidently here more verbal than substantival, and the sentence would lose nothing if rewritten *οὐ μὴν προεγνώσθη ἀλλ' ἦν τε καὶ ὑπέστη θεός.*

of one or other of the western writers had become known in the East. One might suggest that the connecting link was Firmilian, the correspondent of Cyprian: his name does not appear in the superscription of the letter, but he is known to have been in close touch with the composers of it.

IV. TERTULLIAN'S DEBT TO HIS PREDECESSORS

Tertullian, though by no means a slavish copyist of other men's matter, would have been the last to claim for himself any credit as an original thinker. His purpose, in his dogmatic treatises, is to make a competent and forceful forensic presentment of the case for the traditional Christian faith. His qualifications, besides his command of language and his skill as an advocate, were a comprehensive grasp of the Scriptures, the sound common sense which enabled him to disentangle their matter-of-fact meaning from the mists of speculation with which the gnostic schools had enveloped it, and appreciative and retentive reading of such works of the apologists as had come into his hands. Of these last he was most indebted to Justin, whose expositions he reproduces without the tentativeness and reserve which were natural to that gentler mind: he was also acquainted with the work of Tatian, and perhaps with that of Theophilus and Athenagoras: and if the present book does not afford much scope for borrowing from Irenaeus, the *Praescriptio haereticorum* and the treatise against the Valentinians show that he could on occasion make extensive use of that father. The following notes show his indebtedness in respect of the doctrine of the Logos (§ 5). Concerning his constant claim (for which he has some New Testament authority, and in which he is at one with all the fathers until the fourth century and with many after that) that the Lord who in the Old Testament appeared to the patriarchs and others is God the Son who afterwards was incarnate, reference should be made to the notes to §§ 12-16: and for the identification of the Logos with the divine Wisdom and for the interpretation of Pss. 45 and 110 to the notes on §§ 6, 7.

ΛΟΓΟΣ.

This term comes into Christian theology from John 1. 1, to which there is always a reference either explicitly or by implication, as *Adv. Prax.* 5, *sermonem . . . in primordio apud deum fuisse.* Christian writers do sometimes, when addressing a pagan audience, make some small apologetic capital out of the fact that it was in use among the philosophers: so Tertullian, *Apol.* 21, *apud vestros quoque sapientes* λόγον, *id est sermonem atque rationem, constat artificem videri universitatis. hunc enim Zeno determinat factitatorem, qui cuncta in dispositione formaverit: eundem et fatum vocari et deum et animum Iovis et necessitatem omnium rerum.* But they can hardly have been unaware that λόγος in the philosophers is neither speech nor reason, far less a divine person (though they designate it "god"—for god to them is depersonalised), but is little more than mathematical ratio: for the Stoics see the excerpts quoted from Diogenes Laertius by Ritter and Preller, § 493 (8th ed.), especially *δοκεῖ δ' αὐτοῖς ἀρχὰς εἶναι τῶν ὅλων δύο, τὸ ποιοῦν καὶ τὸ πάσχον· τὸ μὲν οὖν πάσχον εἶναι τὴν ἄποιον οὐσίαν, τὴν ὕλην, τὸ δὲ ποιοῦν τὸν ἐν αὐτῇ λόγον, τὸν θεόν . . . καὶ ὥσπερ ἐν τῇ γονῇ τὸ σπέρμα περιέχεται, οὕτω καὶ τοῦτον σπερματικὸν λόγον ὄντα τοῦ κόσμου τοιόνδε ὑπολίπεσθαι ἐν τῷ ὑγρῷ ἐνεργὸν αὐτῷ ποιοῦντα τὴν ὕλην πρὸς τὴν τῶν ἑξῆς γένεσιν.* "Ratio in matter" and "spermatic ratio of the world" are as far as can be from the real sentiments of the Christian apologists, and their references to Stoic theories can have amounted to no more than a plea that the Christian doctrine of the Logos, the creator of the world, who was incarnate and is Jesus Christ, must not be summarily dismissed as unreasonable. When Tertullian says, *Apol.* 23, *Christus . . . dei virtus et dei spiritus et sermo et sapientia et ratio*, he is saying things which (in their own peculiar sense of the word "god") the Stoics might have understood; but when he adds, *et dei filius*, he speaks of what to them is inconceivable.

The same can be said of the use of the term by Philo Judaeus (see Ritter and Preller, §§ 609, 610): it has little in common with Christian theology. *De cherubim*, 27, Philo claims a transcendental illumination: *ἔλεγε δέ μοι κατὰ τὸν ἕνα ὄντως ὄντα θεὸν δύο τὰς ἀνωτάτω εἶναι καὶ πρώτας δυνάμεις ἀγαθότητα καὶ ἐξουσίαν, καὶ ἀγαθότητι μὲν τὸ πᾶν γεγεννηκέναι, ἐξουσίᾳ δὲ τοῦ γεννηθέντος ἄρχειν, τρίτον δὲ συναγωγὸν ἀμφοῖν μέσον εἶναι λόγον· λόγῳ γὰρ καὶ ἄρχοντα καὶ ἀγαθὸν εἶναι τὸν θεόν.* Here (as R. and P. remark, § 609 note *b*) λόγος is either the ratio which reconciles God's goodness and his power, or else something superior to and transcending them both, but inferior to God: in either case it is a mathematical mean and has evidently no connexion with Christian usage. *Quis rer. div. haer.* 42, τῷ δὲ ἀρχαγγέλῳ καὶ πρεσβυτάτῳ λόγῳ δωρεὰν ἐξαίρετον ἔδωκεν ὁ τὰ ὅλα γεννήσας πατήρ, ἵνα μεθόριος στὰς τὸ γενόμενον διακρίνῃ τοῦ πεποιηκότος. ὁ δ' αὐτὸς ἱκέτης μέν ἐστι τοῦ θνητοῦ κηραίνοντος ἀεὶ πρὸς τὸ ἄφθαρτον, πρεσβευτὴς δὲ τοῦ ἡγεμόνος πρὸς τὸ ὑπήκοον . . . οὔτε ἀγέννητος ὡς ὁ θεὸς ὢν οὔτε γεννητὸς ὡς ὑμεῖς, ἀλλὰ μέσος τῶν ἄκρων, ἀμφοτέροις ὁμηρεύων. Here, and in the passages referred to by Ritter and Preller § 610 note *a*, the λόγος is substantified or even personified; but again it is a mathematical mean which Philo has in mind, and although some of the words have an almost Christian sound their sense is not that taken up by Christian theology.

So we are brought back to the opening words of the Fourth Gospel, where the word is so evidently due to recollection of the Old Testament texts "and God said", "by the word of the Lord were the heavens made", "he spake and it was done", that one can only wonder at the perverse ingenuity of those who look for Greek sources of the Johannine terminology.

JUSTIN MARTYR uses the term, but sits loosely to it: it is no fundamental element in his thought. That he was acquainted with the Gospel according to St John is evident from many reminiscences of its language (for which see Otto's Index); but he does not refer to the Prologue. He appears to some degree to accommodate his language to his auditors: in the *Dialogue* he paraphrases λόγος (which does not occur in the required sense in the Hebrew Scriptures) into δύναμίς τις λογική: in the *Apology* there is less need for anticipatory explanation, for the philosopher emperor was aware of the Stoic use of the term and would think he knew more or less what Justin meant. *Dial.* 61: μαρτύριον δὲ καὶ ἄλλο ὑμῖν . . . ἀπὸ τῶν γραφῶν δώσω ὅτι ἀρχὴν πρὸ πάντων τῶν κτισμάτων ὁ θεὸς γεγέννηκε δύναμίν τινα ἐξ ἑαυτοῦ λογικήν, ἥτις καὶ δόξα κυρίου ὑπὸ τοῦ πνεύματος τοῦ ἁγίου καλεῖται, ποτὲ δὲ υἱὸς, ποτὲ δὲ σοφία, ποτὲ δὲ ἄγγελος, ποτὲ δὲ θεὸς, ποτὲ δὲ κύριος καὶ λόγος· ποτὲ δὲ ἀρχιστράτηγον ἑαυτὸν λέγει ἐν ἀνθρώπου μορφῇ φανέντα (quaero an legendum φανεὶς) τῷ τοῦ Ναυῆ Ἰησοῦ· ἔχει γὰρ πάντα προσονομάζεσθαι ἔκ τε τοῦ ὑπηρετεῖν τῷ πατρικῷ βουλήματι καὶ ἐκ τοῦ ἀπὸ τοῦ πατρὸς θελήσει γεγενῆσθαι. ἀλλ' οὐ τοιοῦτον ὁποῖον καὶ ἐφ' ἡμῶν γινόμενον ὁρῶμεν; λόγον γάρ τινα προβάλλοντες λόγον γεννῶμεν, οὐ κατ' ἀποτομὴν ὡς ἐλαττωθῆναι τὸν ἐν ἡμῖν λόγον προβαλλόμενοι. Similarly fire kindles fire, without any diminishing of the parent fire. Justin proceeds to quote Prov. 8, texts from Gen. 1-3, and Josh. 5. 13: 6. 3. On Gen. 3. 22 he comments: ἀλλὰ τοῦτο τὸ τῷ ὄντι ἀπὸ τοῦ πατρὸς προβληθὲν γέννημα πρὸ πάντων τῶν ποιημάτων συνῆν τῷ πατρὶ, καὶ τούτῳ ὁ πατὴρ προσομιλεῖ, but comes back immediately to the identification with σοφία and ἀρχιστράτηγος κυρίου. Evidently Justin is thinking not in terms of philosophy, but of the exegesis of the Old Testament, especially the theophanies, and *Son* is nearer to his mind than *Word*. At *Dial*. 128 he seems almost afraid of the term: he refers to some who by anticipatory explanations (τινας προλέγειν ταῦτα βουλομένους) weaken the force of his illustrations: these λόγον καλοῦσιν ἐπειδὴ καὶ τὰς παρὰ τοῦ πατρὸς ὁμιλίας φέρει τοῖς ἀνθρώποις, and suggest that this δύναμις is ἄτμητος καὶ ἀχώριστος τοῦ πατρός, and that the Father ὅταν βούληται . . . δύναμιν αὐτοῦ προπηδᾶν ποιεῖ, καὶ ὅταν βούληται πάλιν ἀναστέλλει εἰς ἑαυτόν. With these anticipators of Sabellius Justin does not agree: ἡ δύναμις αὕτη . . . οὐχ ὡς τὸ τοῦ ἡλίου φῶς ὀνόματι μόνον ἀριθμεῖται, ἀλλὰ καὶ ἀριθμῷ ἕτερόν τί ἐστι: the illustration of fire lighted from fire, the offspring permanent and the parent undiminished, is better than that of the sun emitting and withdrawing its rays. He concludes (§ 129): νοεῖτε, ὦ ἀκροαταί, εἴ γε νοῦν προσέχετε· καὶ ὅτι γεγεννῆσθαι ὑπὸ τοῦ πατρὸς τοῦτο τὸ γέννημα πρὸ πάντων ἁπλῶς τῶν κτισμάτων ὁ λόγος (*sc*. our argument) ἐδήλου, καὶ τὸ γεννώμενον τοῦ γεννῶντος ἀριθμῷ ἕτερόν ἐστι, πᾶς ὁστισοῦν ὁμολογήσειε. Once more γέννημα is closer to Justin's mind than λόγος. In *Apol*. ii. 6 (to the Senate) the words ὁ λόγος could drop out without altering the sense: ὁ δὲ υἱὸς ἐκείνου, ὁ μόνος λεγόμενος κυρίως υἱὸς, ὁ λόγος, πρὸ τῶν ποιημάτων συνὼν καὶ γεννώμενος, ὅτε τὴν ἀρχὴν δι' αὐτοῦ πάντα ἔκτισε καὶ ἐκόσμησε, Χριστὸς μὲν . . . λεγεται, Ἰησοῦς δὲ καὶ ἀνθρώπου καὶ σωτῆρος ὄνομα καὶ σημασίαν ἔχει. At *Apol.* ii. 5 it is essential to the argument: οὐ γὰρ μόνον ἐν Ἕλλησι διὰ Σωκράτους ὑπὸ λόγου ἠλέχθη ταῦτα, ἀλλὰ καὶ ἐν βαρβάροις ὑπ' αὐτοῦ τοῦ λόγου μορφωθέντος καὶ ἀνθρώπου γενομένου καὶ Ἰησοῦ Χριστοῦ κληθέντος: so also *ibid.* 21: τὸν λόγον, ὅ ἐστι πρῶτον γέννημα τοῦ θεοῦ, ἄνευ ἐπιμιξίας . . . γεγεννῆσθαι, Ἰησοῦν Χριστὸν τὸν διδάσκαλον ἡμῶν. The last two passages suffice to show that though he neither quotes nor refers to John 1. 1-14, the sense of it was in his mind, and that he probably read ὃς . . . ἐγεννήθη.

Tatian reproduces some of Justin's phrases, e.g. λόγου δύναμις, δύναμις λογική, and his illustration of fire kindled from fire yet leaving the parent fire undiminished; but he differs from his master in that his thought is based on λόγος rather than on υἱός or γέννημα and that the λόγος concept is essential to his argument. *Orat. ad Graecos* 5: θεὸς ἦν ἐν ἀρχῇ, τὴν δὲ ἀρχὴν λόγου δύναμιν παρειλήφαμεν. ὁ γὰρ δεσπότης τῶν ὅλων, αὐτὸς ὑπάρχων τοῦ παντὸς ἡ ὑπόστασις, κατὰ μὲν τὴν μηδέπω γεγενημένην ποίησιν μόνος ἦν· καθὸ δὲ πᾶσα δύναμις ὁρατῶν τε καὶ ἀοράτων αὐτὸς ὑπόστασις ἦν, σὺν αὐτῷ τὰ πάντα· σὺν αὐτῷ διὰ λογικῆς δυνάμεως αὐτὸς καὶ ὁ λόγος ὃς ἦν ἐν αὐτῷ ὑπέστησε·[1] θελήματι δὲ τῆς ἁπλότητος αὐτοῦ προπηδᾷ λόγος· ὁ δὲ λόγος οὐ κατὰ κενοῦ χωρήσας, ἔργον πρωτότοκον τοῦ πατρὸς γίγνεται. τοῦτον ἴσμεν τοῦ κόσμου τὴν ἀρχήν. γέγονε δὲ κατὰ μερισμὸν, οὐ κατὰ ἀποκοπήν· τὸ γὰρ ἀποτμηθὲν τοῦ πρώτου κεχώρισται, τὸ δὲ μερισθὲν οἰκονομίας τὴν αἵρεσιν προσλαβὸν οὐκ ἐνδεᾶ τὸν ὅθεν εἴληπται πεποίηκεν. There follows an illustration of torch kindled from torch, and a carefully drawn comparison between the human word giving order and arrangement to the minds of the audience, and the divine Word first fabricating and then ordering the constituent elements of creation. It seems likely that Tertullian had Tatian's exposition in mind while writing the *Adv. Prax.* 5: he avoids some of the Assyrian's crudities of thought, but cannot altogether divest himself of the idea that the Λόγος reaches complete subsistence as the result of a time-process, and that the holy

[1] Otto wrongly translates *substitit*: Maranus, more correctly, *sustentabat*: but *fieri fecit* would be best: "caused all things to be".

Trinity is in some sense a development. *Orat.* 7 (146 B) and 20 (159 C), quoted in the notes on § 8, equate λόγος and πνεῦμα.

THEOPHILUS, possibly misled by the false application of ἐξηρεύξατο from Ps. 45. 1 (see the note on § 7), boldly introduces the contrasting terms ἐνδιάθετος, προφορικός: he substantifies ἀρχή and identifies it with λόγος: identifies λόγος with the voice of the Lord which Adam heard in the Garden: and makes the first explicit citation of John 1. 1-3. *Ad Autol.* ii. 10: ἔχων οὖν ὁ θεὸς τὸν ἑαυτοῦ λόγον ἐνδιάθετον ἐν τοῖς ἰδίοις σπλάγχνοις ἐγέννησεν αὐτὸν μετὰ τῆς ἰδίας σοφίας ἐξερευξάμενος πρὸ τῶν ὅλων . . . οὗτος λέγεται ἀρχή, ὅτι ἄρχει καὶ κυριεύει πάντων τῶν δι' αὐτοῦ δεδημιουργημένων. *Ibid.* 22: The Word ἀναλαμβάνων τὸ πρόσωπον τοῦ πατρὸς καὶ κυρίου τῶν ὅλων came into the Garden and talked with Adam: the Scripture says that Adam heard the voice: φωνὴ δὲ τί ἄλλο ἐστὶν ἀλλ' ἢ ὁ λόγος ὁ τοῦ θεοῦ, ὅς ἐστιν καὶ υἱὸς αὐτοῦ; There is nothing here akin to the poetic fables of sons of gods, ἀλλὰ ὡς ἀληθεία διηγεῖται τὸν λόγον τὸν ὄντα διὰ παντὸς ἐνδιάθετον ἐν καρδίᾳ θεοῦ. πρὸ γάρ τι γίνεσθαι τοῦτον εἶχεν σύμβουλον, ἑαυτοῦ νοῦν καὶ φρόνησιν ὄντα· ὁπότε δὲ ἠθέλησεν ὁ θεὸς ποιῆσαι ὅσα ἐβουλεύσατο, τοῦτον τὸν λόγον ἐγέννησεν προφορικόν, πρωτότοκον πάσης κτίσεως, οὐ κενωθεὶς αὐτὸς τοῦ λόγου, ἀλλὰ λόγον γεννήσας καὶ τῷ λόγῳ αὐτοῦ διὰ παντὸς ὁμιλῶν. Then, quoting John 1. 1, 3, with explanatory notes, he concludes: θεὸς οὖν ὢν ὁ λόγος καὶ ἐκ θεοῦ πεφυκώς, ὁπόταν βούληται ὁ πατὴρ τῶν ὅλων πέμπει αὐτὸν εἴς τινα τόπον, ὃς παραγινόμενος καὶ ἀκούεται καὶ ὁρᾶται, πεμπόμενος ὑπ' αὐτοῦ, καὶ ἐν τόπῳ εὑρίσκεται. [There is probably no need to regularise the grammar of this sentence by reading πέμπειν and omitting ὅς.]

ATHENAGORAS stands somewhat outside the Justin-Tatian-Theophilus sequence, and does not repeat their stock phrases. *Suppl.* 10: νοοῦμεν γὰρ καὶ υἱὸν τοῦ θεοῦ . . . ἔστιν ὁ υἱὸς τοῦ θεοῦ λόγος τοῦ πατρὸς ἐν ἰδέᾳ καὶ ἐνεργείᾳ· πρὸς αὐτοῦ γὰρ καὶ δι' αὐτοῦ πάντα ἐγένετο, ἑνὸς ὄντος τοῦ πατρὸς καὶ τοῦ υἱοῦ. ὄντος δὲ τοῦ υἱοῦ ἐν πατρὶ καὶ πατρὸς ἐν υἱῷ, ἑνότητι καὶ δυνάμει πνεύματος, νοῦς καὶ λόγος τοῦ πατρὸς ὁ υἱὸς τοῦ θεοῦ . . . ἐξ ἀρχῆς γὰρ ὁ θεός, νοῦς ἀΐδιος ὤν, εἶχεν αὐτὸς ἐν ἑαυτῷ τὸν λόγον, ἀιδίως λογικὸς ὤν. The nearest he gets to the contrast ἐνδιάθετος, προφορικός, is in the sentence (omitted in the previous quotation) οὐχ ὡς γενόμενον . . . ἀλλ' ὡς τῶν ὑλικῶν ξυμπάντων . . . ἰδέα καὶ ἐνέργεια εἶναι προελθών, which is capable of an interpretation to which later orthodoxy would not have objected. Compare also with Tatian's expression κατὰ μερισμόν, *Suppl.* 18, "as the empire is subject to the emperors, father and son", οὕτως ἑνὶ τῷ θεῷ καὶ τῷ παρ' αὐτοῦ λόγῳ υἱῷ νοουμένῳ ἀμερίστῳ πάντα ὑποτέτακται.

Irenaeus has the identification *filius, id est verbum,* too often to need quotation. Warned by gnostic error, he sees the danger of certain expressions and illustrations which had hitherto been in good repute. He does not like the comparison with the human voice, nor any idea of emission or prolation. *Haer.* ii. 42. 3: *vos autem generationem eius ex patre divinantes et verbi hominum per linguam factam prolationem transferentes in verbum dei, iuste detegimini a vobis ipsis quod neque humana nec divina noveritis* . . . (4) *non ergo magnum quid invenerunt qui emissiones excogitaverunt neque absconditum mysterium, si id quod ab omnibus intelligitur transtulerunt in unigenitum dei verbum.* He knew and used Justin's work, but he is an interpreter of Scripture rather than an original thinker, and therefore avoids the pitfalls in which others were caught.

Tertullian found the term already in use, with *sermo* as its conventional Latin equivalent (*Adv. Prax.* 5): from which it would appear either that the African Churches possessed theologians before him, or else that the title λόγος and the Johannine prologue were familiar to the unlearned. He can, when addressing pagans, lend himself to that bit of special pleading involved in the reference to the Stoic use of the term: but in the present treatise, an address to Christians (mistaken though they may be), he goes back to the Gospel text. Warned by Irenaeus, he safeguards the idea from the suspicion of affinity with gnosticism (§ 8); but he is chiefly concerned, as against the monarchians, to exclude any suggestion that the Logos is an impersonal attribute or function of God. The Logos is Jesus Christ the Son of God, and so cannot by any means be impersonal: that, though unexpressed, is at the back of his mind as a postulate, and the Gospel text must be expounded in accordance with it. In this respect he has left the apologists behind him: the apologetic value of the term is forgotten: it is to him, as to the evangelist, a positive contribution to Christian theology.

V. TERTULLIAN'S THEOLOGICAL TERMINOLOGY

Una substantia in tribus personis, an expression with which Tertullian is commonly credited, sufficiently represents his position, for though *tres personae* does not seem actually to occur, it is certainly there by implication, as the following discussion will show. Professor Bethune-Baker (*Early History of Christian Doctrine*, p. 138), writing in 1903, said: "Tertullian was perhaps less of a philosopher than a jurist, and we are helped to understand his theory . . . by the legal use of the terms he employs." He proceeds to explain that *substantia* in legal usage means property, and *persona* a being with legal rights. "Such a person's position or circumstances would be his status or condition—perhaps even his nature (*natura* or *proprietas*) when looked at from an inward point of view—and obviously a number of persons might occupy the same status, or be in the same condition, or have the same nature." Equally also, he implies rather than states, three persons could be joint possessors of one undivided property (*substantia*), and one of those persons could, without relinquishing that property, become also the possessor of another. The theory is due to Harnack, whose brilliant guesses it was the fashion in some quarters at that date to accept at the value of their author's great name: but apparently Bethune-Baker had his doubts, for in a footnote (after a reference to Harnack, *DG.* (Eng. Tr.) vol. iv. pp. 122-3) he remarks: "The conceptions and expressions of Tertullian were by no means entirely controlled by legal usage, and the philosophical sense of the terms must also be borne in mind." In fact, as the following examination will show, the philosophical (that is, the logical) sense is the only one worth considering. Tixeront was more reserved; he wrote (*Histoire des Dogmes*, vol. ii. p. 338 footnote): "M. Harnack a prétendu que Tertullien avait pris ces mots seulement dans leur sens juridique de personne morale et de fortune, biens possédés. Cette opinion n'est pas soutenable."

Substantia

is not quoted from Latin authors earlier than Quintilian. It is evidently a translation of ὑπόστασις, capable of being made to mean whatever the Greek word means: which gives wide possibilities.

(*a*) That it occurs in the sense of property is undeniable: *Apol.* 39, *ex substantia familiari fratres sumus, quae penes vos fere dirimit fraternitatem* (where *substantia* is apparently equivalent to *res* in the next sentence): *De cult. fem.* i. 9, *tantarum substantiarum usuram uno et muliebri corpusculo baiulare : De exhort. cast.* 10, *per continentiam enim negotiaberis magnum substantiam sanctitatis, parsimonia carnis spiritum acquires: Adv. Marc.* iv. 15 (quoting Is. 5. 14, *Inhonorabitur vir*), *utique ob substantiam honorabilis.*

(*b*) It occurs in several subsidiary senses of ὑπόστασις: *De cult. fem.* ii. 2, *debemus quidem ita sancte et tota fidei substantia incedere ut confisae et securae simus de conscientia nostra* (equivalent to ὑπόστασις in the sense of confidence or standing-ground, according to the figure of Ps. 69. 2, ἐνεπάγην εἰς ἰλὺν βυθοῦ καὶ οὐκ ἔστιν ὑπόστασις, and parallel with Heb. 11. 1, ἐλπιζομένων ὑπόστασις, "confidence concerning things hoped for"): *Adv. Prax.* 25, *post Philippum et totam substantiam quaestionis istius* ("subject-matter", cf. Liddell and Scott (8th ed.), s.v. B. II.): and compare *ibid.* 31, *quod opus evangelii, quae est substantia novi testamenti statuens legem et prophetas usque ad Ioannem . . .?* (where *substantia* may conceivably mean "whole content", though more probably the sense is "with what confidence does the New Testament terminate the law and the prophets with John, unless from thenceforth, etc.?"): and again *De orat.* 4, *petimus ergo substantiam et facultatem voluntatis suae subministret nobis* (the addition of *facultas* suggests the meaning "entire resources", though the idea of confidence is not absent): *ibid., dominus . . . cum substantia passionis infirmitatem carnis demonstrare iam in sua carne voluisset* ("toleration", "sufferance": L. and S., s.v. ὑφίστημι, refer to Demosthenes, p. 1421, where ὑφίστασθαι is apparently a synomym of ὑπομεῖναι and πεπονθέναι, so that Ursinus' conjecture *sub instantiam* is unnecessary).

(*c*) The philosophical (logical) sense. Since ὑφίστασθαι is by one of its uses a synomym of εἶναι, ὑπόστασις and οὐσία can also be synomyms, and when by convention they are distinguished, *substantia* remains untouched by the Greek development and continues to represent οὐσία. Further, since οὐσία is the abstract noun of εἶναι, it could have meant "being" in any sense in which the verb means "to be", i.e. either as copula or as existential verb. In practice it seems always to have represented the existential verb, as φύσις (*natura*) represents attributes attached by the copula, though without any necessary definition (expressed or implied) of what "being" is.

As representing the existential verb, οὐσία is the first of the categories. Unlike the Stoic ὑποκείμενον, it begs no questions, though the Aristotelian explanation, *Cat.* 4. 1 *b* 25, ἔστι δὲ οὐσία μὲν ὡς τύπῳ εἰπεῖν οἷον ἄνθρωπος ἵππος, perhaps unduly confines the meaning to visible objects. That Tertullian regarded *substantia* as in this sense equivalent to οὐσία appears from the following passages.

> *De anima*, 11: *sed ut animam spiritum dicam praesentis quaestionis ratio compellit, quia spirare alii substantiae adscribitur. . . . spiritum necesse est certa condicione dicamus, non status nomine sed actus, nec substantiae titulo sed operae, quia spirat, non quia proprie spiritus est. . . . illic de substantia quaestio est: spirare enim substantiae actus est. . . . solam eam* (*sc. animam*) *constat ante eventum spiritus utriusque* (*sc. dei et diaboli*)*: si solam, et simplicem et uniformem substantiae nomine, atque ita non aliunde spirantem quam ex substantiae suae sorte.*

That is, *anima* being in the category of οὐσία, *spiritus* (in the sense in which the soul is in Scripture called spirit) is in the category of ποιεῖν: but not as an accident, since spiration is by nature (apart from either inspiration or obsession) an activity of soul.

> *De anima*, 32: *nam etsi quidam homines bestiis adaequantur pro qualitatibus morum et ingeniorum et affectuum . . . non ideo milvi ex rapacibus fient, etc. . . . quasi eadem substantia animae ubique naturam suam in animalium proprietatibus repetat. aliud est autem substantia, aliud natura substantiae, siquidem substantia propria est rei cuiusque, natura vero potest esse communis. . . . substantia est lapis, ferrum: duritia lapidis et ferri natura substantiae est. duritia communicat, substantia discordat..*

> *mollitia lanae, mollitia plumae, pariant naturalia earum, substantiva non pariant. . . . naturae similitudo notatur cum substantiae dissimilitudo conspicitur. . . . sic et divina pronuntiatio* (Ps. 49. 20) *sapit, pecudibus adaequans hominem natura non substantia. ceterum nec deus hominem hoc modo notasset si pecudem de substantia nosset.*

That is to say, a thing is what it is, and cannot be another thing. The examples given are of *δεύτεραι οὐσίαι*, but the same would hold good of *οὐσίαι πρῶται*. This has a close bearing on our present subject. Tertullian nowhere says (as Harnack would seem to suggest) that God *substantiam obtinet*: rather God IS *substantia quaedam*, even *res quaedam* (e.g. *Adv. Prax.* 9, *pater enim tota substantia est*: and *Adv. Marc.* iii. 6, Christ IS the Son and spirit and substance of the Creator), and that substance cannot be other than it is. Moreover, in the examples quoted, *substantia discordat*; but with God *substantia communicat*, the Son and the Holy Spirit being *consortes substantiae patris* (not *participes*), one and the same substance, even (if you insist) one and the same thing. The divine substance is something necessarily one and necessarily indivisible and incommunicable, which each of the three Persons (not "has" but) is: we are discoursing in the category of *οὐσία* not of *ἔχειν*.[1]

Substantia, it appears, though it might have meant "existence", comes in practice to mean an existent thing: and since God is not a species or genus, it must mean a *πρώτη οὐσία,* a single individual Being. A consideration of some of the derivatives of *substantia* will illustrate this conclusion.

Substantialis: De res. carn. 45, *tam vetustatem hominis quam novitatem ad moralem non ad substantialem differentiam pertinere definimus* ("old man" and "new man" signify not a difference of identity but of character): *Adv. Val.* 7, referring to the Valentinians' god, *hunc substantialiter quidem αἰῶνα τέλειον appellant, personaliter vero Προαρχὴν et τὴν Ἀρχήν, etc.* (he is a singular individual thing, a *πρώτη οὐσία,* described as "perfect æon", and is also a person named Proarche, etc.: and, one may add, God is a *πρώτη οὐσία* described as *deus*, and his personal name

[1] Thinking in similar terms, Athenagoras, *Suppl.* 5, remarks that Euripides seems to have been aware that the so-called gods were non-existent, they were not οὐσίαι: οὔτε τὰς οὐσίας αἷς ἐπικατηγορεῖσθαι τὸ ὄνομα συμβέβηκεν ὑποκειμένας ἑώρα . . . οὔτε τὰ ὀνόματα καθ' ὑποκειμένων κατηγορεῖσθαι πραγμάτων.

is "the LORD": and similarly, *Adv. Prax.* 7, the Logos is *res et persona quaedam*): *Adv. Val.* 27, *patitur vero animalis et carneus Christus in delineationem superioris Christi qui ad Achamoth formandam substantivali non agnitionali forma cruci id est Horo fuerat innixus* (the tragedy of the "superior Christ" was represented as a fact, though outside the range of perception).

Substantivus: Adv. Hermog. 7, *nam et ipsum principium in quo deus fecit et caelum et terram aliquid volunt fuisse quasi substantivum et corpulentum: ibid.* 36, ⟨*motus*⟩ *substantiva res* ⟨*non est*⟩ *quia nec corporalis, sed accidens si forte substantiae et corpori: De res. carn.* 40, *ita vocabulum homo consertarum substantiarum duarum quodammodo fibula est, sub quo vocabulo non possent esse nisi cohaerentes. interiorem hominem . . . non substantiam ipsam sed substantiae saporem . . fidem quidem et dilectionem non substantiva animae ponens sed conceptiva.*

In every case we seem to be dealing with the Aristotelian categories: certain persons wish to take *in principio* not in the category of ποτέ but of οὐσία: motion is not οὐσία but ποιεῖν or πάσχειν: faith and charity are not οὐσία but are activities of the understanding: the inner man is not οὐσία but ποῖον. A few passages from *Adv. Prax.* will provide further illustration of these derivatives.

Adv. Prax. 7: *non vis enim eum* (sc. *sermonem*) *substantivum habere in re per substantiae proprietatem, ut res et persona quaedam videri possit . . . quid est enim, dices, sermo nisi vox et sonus oris, et sicut grammatici tradunt aer offensus intelligibilis auditu, ceterum vacuum nescio quid et inane et incorporale?*

The monarchians will have it that the Logos is a mere function of God, while Tertullian maintains that he is substantive, as being a substance which is himself and nothing but himself, an objective entity (*res*), and moreover a person (which is a kind of *res*), and in effect corporal (since he is spirit, which is *corpus sui generis*). It would follow, *per substantiae unitatem* (§ 2), that the substance which is the Logos himself is identical with the substance which is the Father and which also is the Holy Spirit: for *unitas* is not union but arithmetical unity.

Adv. Prax. 26. In the text Luke I. 35, since by the rules of grammar *spiritus dei*, though a *substantiva res*, is not *ipse deus* (i.e. the Spirit of the Lord which was to come upon Mary is not the Lord whose Spirit he is, viz. the Father), *multo magis*

> *virtus altissimi non erit ipse altissimus, quia nec substantiva res est quod est spiritus, sicut nec sapientia nec providentia: et haec enim substantiae non sunt sed accidentia uniuscuiusque substantiae.*

"God is a spirit", and therefore the Spirit of God is what God is, a *substantiva res*, though not personally identical with God, as the genitive dependence shows. But *virtus* and *sapientia* and *providentia* are not substantive, but are in the subordinate categories (*accidentia*): and consequently the text *Virtus altissimi obumbrabit te* gives no authority for saying that it was the Father who was the subject of the Incarnation. Here it is to be observed (in contrast with *De anima*, 11, quoted above) that spirit is not a function of the divine substance: it is the divine substance: the divine substance is that kind of substance which is spirit.

We return to the term *substantia*, with further examples of the same meaning.

> *Adv. Prax.* 5: *quia sermo ratione consistens priorem eam ut substantiam suam ostendat. tamen et sic nihil interest.*

Λόγος means both *ratio* and *sermo*: the latter is the more usual translation, though the former might be preferable, since as a matter of human experience speech is an activity proceeding from reason: i.e. *ratio* being in the category of οὐσία, *sermo* is in the category of ποιεῖν. Even so it makes no difference, since reason is only reason if it is articulate, and in God, whose reason is always articulate, *ratio* and *sermo* are not distinguishable except in thought. Consequently:

> *ibid.* 7: *ergo, inquis, das aliquam substantiam esse sermonem, spiritu et sophia et ratione* (so C. H. Turner, for MSS. *sophiae traditione*) *constructam? plane.*

Sermo, the divine Logos, cannot be a mere function, but must be *res et persona quaedam*, someone *substantivus in re per substantiae proprietatem.* It is impossible that that which has proceeded from the divine substance (*de tanta substantia*) should be devoid of substance, or that the maker of created substances (*tantas substantias*) should be unsubstantial. See the note on this passage, and compare:

> *ibid.* 6: *nam ut primum deus voluit ea quae cum sophiae* (qu. an legendum, *sophia et*) *ratione et sermone disposuerat intra*

> *se in substantias et species suas edere, ipsum primum protulit sermonem . . . ut coram quoque in suis speciebus atque substantiis cognoscerentur atque tenerentur:*

where, since *species* are evidently δεύτεραι οὐσίαι, *substantiae* must be πρῶται οὐσίαι.

On the other hand, at § 8 ⟨*Achamoth*⟩ *paene devoratur in reliquam substantiam, substantia* seems to mean matter in general: though in the same chapter:

> *nam et istae species* (sc. *frutex, fluvius, radius*) προβολαὶ *sunt earum substantiarum ex quibus prodeunt,*

substantiae (the root, the fountain, the sun) are once more singular things, while *species* are not δεύτεραι οὐσίαι but aspects of the several substances.

Having, as we think, established the point that *substantia* means a concrete individual thing, we pass on to Tertullian's discussion of the unity of the divine Trinity. The Three are one *per substantiae unitatem*, because they are one identical substance, one single Thing. The Son and the Holy Spirit are *consortes substantiae patris*, in contrast with the angels who (if the reconstructed text is correct) are *alieni a substantia patris* (§ 3). The Son (and by implication the Holy Spirit) is *de substantia patris* (§ 4), *de tanta substantia processit* (§ 7), whereas man is only *ex substantia eius animatus*, has become a living soul as a secondary result (*ex*, not *de*) of the action of the spirit of life which is the kind of substance God is (§ 5). The unity depends on this, that the Father is the whole substance, *pater tota substantia est*, while the Son is *derivatio totius et portio* (§ 9). It is tempting here, and in § 26 (*portio totius quae cessura erat in filii nomen*) to claim that *portio* does not mean part but inheritance, and that *totius* is a descriptive, not a partitive, genitive; but it seems from Novatian (see the note *ad loc.*) that in the third century *portio* was regularly used for *pars*, and in fact in the present passage Tertullian admits a certain minoration of the Son (not only in the Incarnation but) in his divine being. But there is no division or partition of the divine substance: the Son is *alius* (not *aliud*) *personae non substantiae nomine, ad distinctionem non ad divisionem* (§ 12): the divine substance is not divided into three nor shared among the Three, but is *una substantia in tribus cohaerentibus* (*ibid.*). The illustrations of the root, the fountain, and the sun, though they claim "prophetic" authority, are admittedly no more than illustrations: if they seem to divide the substance, it must be observed that at this point Tertullian has reached the end of his self-defence against the charge of tritheism, and is now concerned to maintain that the Three are really three. And moreover, though the smallest created substance is indefinitely divisible, it is common ground to both disputants that the divine substance is necessarily incomposite and indivisible: and therefore the illustration of the light and the radiance which, being of scriptural origin, is the least faulty of the three, must, for the purpose in hand, be understood in the sense required by the absolute indivisibility of the divine substance—*et solem et radium eius tam duas res et duas species unius et indivisae substantiae numerabo quam deum et sermonem eius* (§ 13).

The divine unity being thus safeguarded, there remains the question of the trinity. The mystery of the economy (*οἰκονομίας sacramentum*, § 2) must be acknowledged, though it remains a mystery. The scriptural data prove beyond question that the Father and the Son are *alius et alius*, that there are two and even three who are called God and Lord, though there are not three gods or three lords: on that set of facts, not on any explanation of them, Tertullian rests his case. But the question arises, three *what* are the Three? Justin had been content to say ἄλλος καὶ ἄλλος, and Tertullian on occasion uses the same expression; but now another term is necessary, which Tertullian supplies. The Word, he says, is *res et persona quaedam*: he is that *per substantiae proprietatem*, because that which he is is himself and not another: *quaecunque ergo substantia sermonis fuit, illam dico personam* (§ 7). It will appear in what follows that Tertullian, having first applied this designation to the Word, goes on afterwards to use it of the Father and the Holy Spirit: and this is correct Christian procedure, for (since he that hath seen the Son hath seen the Father) as it is a matter of apostolic experience that the Son is a person, it follows of necessity that the Father also is a person, and so is the Holy Spirit. But first we need to enquire what the term is intended to mean.

Persona

is found in the following senses:

(*a*) Mask: *De spect.* 23, *iam vero ipsum opus personarum quaero an deo placeat qui omnem similitudinem vetat fieri, quanto magis imaginis suae: De carne Christi,* 11, *nemo ostendere volens hominem cassidem aut personam ei inducit.* It must be observed that *persona* means the mask itself, not the person who wears it, or the role that person assumes.

(*b*) A quasi-dramatic sense: *Adv. Prax.* 11, *omnes psalmi qui Christi personam sustinent filium ad patrem, id est Christum ad deum, verba facientem repraesentant* (all the Messianic psalms, the psalms which sustain the role of Christ): *ibid.*, *animadverte etiam spiritum loquentem ex tertia persona de patre et filio* (as a third character.: but possibly a grammatical sense is here to be understood, "in the third person"): *ibid.*, *sic et cetera quae nunc a patre de filio vel ad filium, nunc a filio de patre vel ad patrem, nunc a spiritu pronuntiantur, unamquamque personam in sua proprietate constituunt*: i.e. the five groups of citations thus summarised, with other possible ones, indicate that Father and Son and Spirit are three distinct characters (possibly the dramatic sense is in mind, but it is no longer prominent, and we have reached the point where we are almost ready to speak of three Persons). The dramatic sense perhaps also underlies *ibid.* 7 (the first appearance of the term in this treatise), *in persona illius . . . filius ex sua persona* (the Son quoting the Father's words . . . the Son speaking as himself): and *ibid.* 21, *quo dicto utriusque personae constituit distinctionem, et filii in terris, quem Petrus agnoverat dei filium, et patris qui in caelis, qui Petro revelaverat, etc.* The same, or a kindred grammatical sense, is apparently in view *ibid.* 22, *qui non videant . . . "Sumus" non ex unius esse persona* (the plural verb is not used for the singular number, or by a character representing one individual): *Adv. Marc.* ii. 26, *Christum non agnoscitis in persona Moysi figuratum, patris deprecatorem et oblatorem animae suae pro populi salute* (the two roles are parallel, and so Moses is a type of Christ).

(*c*) Face: *Adv. Prax.* 14, quoting Lam. 4. 20 in the form *Spiritus personae eius Christus dominus*, he remarks that *Christus personae paternae spiritus est*, and proceeds to equate *persona* with *facies*, so that when the Son says to Moses "My face cannot be seen", "my face" means the Father: *mira res plane an facies filii pater accipi possit qui est caput eius* (see the note *ad loc.*).

(*d*) In the sense of "person", with no psychological or metaphysical or juristic reference, but simply as equivalent to *homo* or *vir: De paenit.* 11, *ad omnem occursum maioris cuiusque personae decrescentes* (personage): *De cor.* 1, *persona iam ex ordine decesserat* (the man in question): *De monog.* 7, *post vetera exempla originalium personarum aeque ad vetera transeamus instrumenta legalium scripturarum* (personal examples as contrasted with legal precepts): *Adv. Marc.* ii. 23, *si vero etiam circa personas levem* (sc. *deum*) *vultis intelligi* (men, such as Saul, as opposed to institutions such as the sabbath, images, sacrifices): *ibid.* iv. 14, *et utique si nondum venisset* (sc. *filius hominis*) *non potuisset nominis odium quod agitur hodie personam nominis antecessisse* (persecution of Christians could not have preceded the coming of Christ, the person to whom the name belongs): *Apol.* 36, *nullum bonum sub exceptione personarum administramus* (a reminiscence of Gal. 2. 6): *Adv. Prax.* 14, *non* (i.e. *nonne*) *enim et de aliqua maiore persona congruit dicere, Facies mea est ille homo, et, Faciem mihi praestat?* (some older or greater person): and in a slightly derivative sense *Adv. Marc.* ii. 24, *circa personam Saulis honorandam* (referring to his presence or outward appearance, and quoting *optimus qualis non erat in filiis Israelis*).

(*e*) We are left with the passages bearing a theological import, and our suggestion is that they are based on an analogy with things human, being saved from anthropomorphism not by any special meaning of the term *persona* but by consideration of the fact that the substance which the three Persons are is the divine Substance. Also it will appear that the term is first used of the Son (as *sermo*) and is afterwards applied to the Father and the Holy Spirit. There seems nowhere to be any sign of juristic usage.

> *Adv. Prax.* 7: *non vis enim eum substantivum habere in re per substantiae proprietatem, ut res et persona quaedam videri possit.*

The existence of substance constitutes a *res*, and a person is that particular kind of *res* which is conscious of itself, of its own existence and relationships.

> *ibid. ad fin.*: *quaecunque ergo substantia sermonis fuit, illam dico personam, et illi nomen filii vindico.*

The possession of a name indicates personality: cf. *Adv. Marc.* iv. 14 (quoted above), *personam nominis.* So also of common nouns, *De carne Christi* 13, *fides nominum salus est proprietatum.* Tertullian elsewhere remarks on the distinction between the proper and the attributive name: *Adv. Prax.* 28, *quorum nominum* (sc. *Iesus et Christus*) *alterum est proprium quod ab angelo impositum est, alterum accidens quod ab unctione convenit*: so that the possession of both a name and a title does not imply division of personality. But neither "father" nor "son" is a title, and consequently *dum filium agnosco secundum a patre defendo,* observing that there is a Son I maintain that he is another beside the Father.

> *ibid.* 12: *quia iam adhaerebat illi filius, secunda persona, sermo ipsius, et tertia, spiritus in sermone, ideo pluraliter pronuntiavit Faciamus et Nostram et Nobis.*
>
> *ibid.*: *habes duos, alium dicentem ut fiat, alium facientem. alium autem quomodo accipere debeas iam professus sum, personae non substantiae nomine, ad distinctionem non ad divisionem.*

The dramatic sense of two interlocutors is by the nature of the argument there, but very much in the background: we have reached the point when we may explicitly acknowledge three Persons. Moreover, if the dramatic sense is there, it is not in the form which the Sabellians are (apparently without warrant) said to have suggested, for the two Interlocutors are on the scene together, and there is no question of one actor sustaining three successive roles. The result of the scriptural evidence is again by negative inference indicated:

> *ibid.* 13: *si enim una persona et dei et domini in scripturis inveniretur, merito Christus non esset admissus ad nomen dei et domini . . . et futurum erat ut ipse pater descendisse videretur.*
>
> *ibid.* 18: *sine filio autem nominatur cum principaliter determinatur ut prima persona, quae ante filii nomen erat proponenda, quia pater ante cognoscitur et post patrem filius nominatur.*

The descriptions "second" and "third" person have already occurred, not necessarily meaning anything more than an enumeration of characters: now "first person" is introduced, not as enumerative but as indicating a metaphysical priority of the Father.

> *ibid.* 24: *et ideo suggillatur patrem videre desiderans quasi visibilem, et instruitur visibilem eum in filio fieri ex virtutibus non ex personae repraesentatione.*

> *ibid.*: *igitur et manifestam fecit duarum personarum coniunctionem, ne pater seorsum quasi visibilis in conspectu desideraretur et filius repraesentator patris haberetur.*

The former of these sentences might have recalled the equation *persona=facies* (§ 14): but the second makes it evident that in both cases *persona* means "his very self".

> *ibid.* 26: *nam nec semel sed ter, ad singula nomina in personas singulas, tinguimur.*

> *ibid.* 31: *sic deus voluit novare sacramentum ut nove unus crederetur per filium et spiritum, ut coram iam deus in suis propriis nominibus et personis cognosceretur.*

We return to the starting point: the possession of a name is a sign of personality: the scriptural revelation of three names indicates that God is three Persons.

And lastly, the Son is one single Person. The error of one group of the monarchians was to attempt to locate the distinction of Father and Son in that one Person: *ibid.* 27, *ut aeque in una persona utrumque distinguant, patrem et filium.* The truth is that in the Son of God *videmus duplicem statum, non confusum sed coniunctum, in una persona deum et hominem Iesum*: and it is in Jesus that we are able to observe what is the nature of personality, whether human or divine, since his is both.

Una substantia, tres personae: "one thing, three men" seems to have been the analogy from which Tertullian began, but the severest critic will not accuse him of having stopped there: *Adv. Marc.* ii. 16, *discerne substantias, et suos eis distribue sensus tam diversos quam substantiae exigent, licet vocabulis communicare videantur.* "One subject, three consciousnesses" will hardly serve as an equivalent, for consciousness is an abstract term, while *persona* is concrete. It would be advisable to retain "one Substance, three Persons", writing capital letters to indicate that the substance is the divine Thing, and that the Persons are not men.

D

There remains the question of the relation between the three Persons, and the passage which calls for elucidation is:

> *Adv. Prax.* 2: *quasi non sic quoque unus sit omnia dum ex uno omnia, per substantiae scilicet unitatem, et nihilo minus custodiatur* οἰκονομίας *sacramentum quae unitatem in trinitatem disponit, tres dirigens patrem et filium et spiritum, tres autem non statu sed gradu, nec substantia sed forma, nec potestate sed specie, unius autem substantiae et unius status et unius potestatis, quia unus deus ex quo et gradus isti et formae et species in nomine patris et filii et spiritus sancti deputantur.*

The terms are in part recapitulated *ibid.* 19:

> *rationem reddimus qua dei non duo dicantur nec domini sed qua pater et filius duo, et hoc non ex separatione substantiae sed ex dispositione, cum individuum et inseparatum filium a patre pronuntiamus, nec statu sed gradu alium, qui etsi deus dicatur quando nominatur singularis non ideo duos deos faciat sed unum, hoc ipso quod et deus ex unitate patris vocari habeat.*

The key-words are translated by Bethune-Baker (*op. cit.* p. 140) as follows: "Three, however, not in condition but in relation, and not in substance but in mode of existence, and not in power but in special characteristics." This is no more lucid than the Latin. In a footnote he quotes Bull, *Def. Fid. Nic.* ii. vii, to the effect that *gradus* means the relative order of the three Persons, while *forma* and *species* indicate different modes of subsistence, τρόποι ὑπάρξεως. A further footnote adopts a suggestion that *forma* and *species* are identical in meaning, being equivalents of the Greek ἰδέα. This still leaves Tertullian's meaning far from clear: for what is a τρόπος ὑπάρξεως, and which of the many senses of ἰδέα is indicated? A new examination of the terms seems necessary.

Status

is found to mean:

(*a*) Rank or position, or condition of life: *De idol.* 18, *Daniel qui per captivitatem statum verterat* (i.e. from freedom to slavery): *De pud.* 6, The flesh *statum vertit et in Christum tincta induit Christum.*

(*b*) Established usage or fact: *De cor.* 3, *habentes observationem inveteratam quae praeveniendo statum fecit: Adv. Marc.* iv. 12, *adversus statum scripti et voluntatem creatoris* (opposed to the fact of Scripture and to the Creator's will).

(*c*) A state or national polity: *Adv. Marc.* iv. 6, *alium* (sc. *Christum*) *qui a deo creatore* (i.e. Marcion's creator god) *in restitutionem Iudaici status sit destinatus quandoque venturus.*

(*d*) That which is permanent and unchangeable: *De pud.* 6, *coepimus . . . ab eo statu legis quem Christus non dissolvit sed implevit* (those permanent elements of the Law): *De fuga*, 4, *non sensus hominis praeiudicat statui rerum sed status sensui: status enim unusquisque certum quid est et dat sensui legem ita sentiendi statum sicuti est: si autem statu bonum quod a deo venit . . . sensui vero malum videtur, erit status in tuto sensus in vitio* (*status* is a matter of fact, not of opinion): *Adv. Marc.* ii. 16, *et haec ergo imago censenda est dei in homine, quod eosdem motus et sensus habeat humanus animus quos et deus, licet non tales quales deus: pro substantia enim et status eorum et exitus distant* (*status* is permanent because it depends on *substantia*: and it might not be quite beside the point that social status was to some extent dependent on *substantia*, property: but this instance approaches towards the meaning of the following).

(*e*) In the preceding instance possibly, and certainly in these that follow, *status* means *existentia*, ὕπαρξις: *De anima*, 3, *alii immortalem negant animam, alii plusquam immortalem affirmant, alii de substantia alii de forma alii de unaquaque dispositione disceptant, hi statum eius aliunde ducunt, hi exitum aliorsum abducunt: ibid.* 11 (quoted above), *non status nomine sed actus: Adv. Marc.* i. 22, *omnia enim in deo naturalia et ingenita esse debebunt, ut sint aeterna secundum statum ipsius, ne obvenientia et extranea reputentur ac per hoc temporalia et aeternitatis aliena* (*secundum statum ipsius*=κατὰ τὸ εἶναι αὐτοῦ).

That *stare* easily passes over to mean *esse* is shown by the fact that the Romance languages have all borrowed a supposed participle of *stare* to supply the deficient participle of *esse*. But *status* has a sense of objectiveness and permanency, as the following citations show:

> Novatian, *De trin.* 4: *Ego ait sum deus et non sum mutatus, statum suum tenens semper dum id quod natum non est converti non potest . . . merito in deo manet semper status suus, dum sine detrimento commutationis semper sui et similis et aequalis est.*

ibid.: *utroque* (sc. *esse immortalis et esse incorruptibilis*) *invicem sibi et in se conexione mutua perplexo et ad statum aeternitatis vicaria concatenatione producto* (so that *status* cannot mean rank, but is rather something permanent, not in externals only or in position, but in *esse*).

ibid. 26: *alii haeretici erumpentes statum in Christo religionis concutere machinantur* (stability).

Tertullian, *adv. Marc.* i. 28: *o deum usquequaque perversum . . . cuius non statum non condicionem non naturam non ullum ordinem video constare.*

We shall therefore suspect that the difference between *status* and *substantia* is that the former means "existence", while the latter means the existent thing: i.e., if *substantia* is indicated by the existential verb, *status* represents the copula in so far as it attaches attributes which are permanent (the *proprietates*), those which are *secundum condicionem*, and constitute the *natura* of the object: so, *Adv. Marc.* ii. 6, *oportebat igitur imaginem et similitudinem dei liberi arbitrii et suae potestatis esse, in quo hoc ipsum imago et similitudo dei deputaretur . . . in quam rem ea substantia homini accommodata est quae huius status esset, afflatus dei utique liberi et suae potestatis* (i.e. God possesses free will, and God's spirit breathed into man gives him the same as a permanent endowment): *ibid.* ii. 17, ⟨*bonitatem*⟩ *semotam a iudiciariis sensibus et in suo statu puram* (i.e. possessing only those characteristics which are proper to goodness, and not yet discharging those adventitious functions which it undertakes on account of man's disobedience).

Also, since (§ *d* above) *status* depends on *substantia*, the unity of the divine substance precludes the possibility of there being a plurality of degrees of the divine existence or any difference of *natura* or any greater or less sharing of the *proprietates* within the godhead: i.e. none of the Three is more or less existent or more or less possessed of the divine attributes than the others.

Gradus.

Two figurative uses may be ruled out of present consideration. (*a*) A metaphor from the original meaning "footstep": *De pud.* 10, *quid itaque in gradu totus es?* (Why is your attention all on your steps, why do you not extend yourself to a larger purpose?).

(*b*) A metaphor from the gladiatorial combats, indicating a position taken up and defended in argument: *De pud.* 7, *decedam nunc paulisper de gradu isto: Adv. Prax.* 8, *hic mecum gradum fige:* and frequently.

(*c*) A possible meaning is relative place or position, and something of the kind is apparently what is intended here and at § 4, *hoc mihi et in tertium gradum dictum sit, quia spiritum non aliunde puto quam a patre per filium.* Undoubtedly singularity of *substantia* and of *status* precludes difference of rank; but since the Father is *primarius fons deitatis* there is a sense, albeit not a temporal one, in which the Son is "after" the Father and the Holy Spirit after the Son, in that the Son and the Holy Spirit derive their being from the Father and are in practice mentioned after him: so § 8, *trinitas per consertos et connexos gradus a patre decurrens:* and *Adv. Marc.* i. 23, *sit nunc et a secundo gradu incipiens ratio bonitatis, in extraneum scilicet, nec secundus illi gradus ratione constabit alio modo destructus* (the goodness of God must be as rational in regard to man as it is in God himself).

Substantia

has already been sufficiently discussed. Evidently, in juxtaposition with *forma*, it does not mean property or possessions: the whole context demands a metaphysical sense, and we have suggested that that is to be found in the Aristotelian οὐσία, albeit the divine οὐσία, which on all Jewish and Christian principles is one and indivisible and incommunicable. Tertullian was unable to conceive of existence except as in some sense involving corporeity: *De paenit.* 3, *omne quod est corpus est sui generis: Adv. Prax.* 7, *quis enim negabit deum corpus esse, etsi deus spiritus est? spiritus enim corpus sui generis in sua effigie* (spirit is body, though of a special kind and with a character of its own). But it does not follow that "body" in the sense intended is necessarily material. Novatian seems to have been of the same mind: of God he says (*De trin.* 5), *est enim simplex et sine ulla corporea concretione, quicquid illud est totus, quod se solus scit esse, quandoquidem spiritus sit dictus.* Here he is not denying corporeity so much as *concretio*: he has already said (*paullo supra*) of passions such as anger and hatred, *habent igitur ista vim suam quam exerceant, sed ubi praecedit passibilis materia, non ubi praecedit impassibilis substantia.* There is therefore a substance which, though, being real, it may be described as *corpus sui generis*, is nevertheless not material. The metaphysical discussion is not apparently taken any further.

Forma

(*a*) in a number of passages means, by juristic or forensic usage, the statute or custom on which an advocate bases his plea: *Apol.* 2, *itaque nec in illo ex forma malorum iudicandorum agitis erga nos:* and metaphorically, *De idol.* 18, *tu vero nullius servus . . . ex forma dominica agere debebis: Adv. Marc.* ii. 10, (*deus*) *qui et angelum ex forma operum bonorum instituit bonum* (in consonance with the general principle that all his works are good): *De res. carn.* 5, *caro autem et sermone dei constitit, propter formam, ne quid sine sermone.*

(*b*) an architect's plan, or the map used by agrarian commissioners in the allocation of public lands: in many instances it is difficult to say whether this or the juristic sense is in Tertullian's mind.

(*c*) The obvious meaning is "shape": *De test. anim.* 3, *Minervam calcias furvis galeam formis* (you give her a leather helmet with terrifying shapes): *De anima*, 9, *recogita enim, cum deus flasset in faciem hominis flatum vitae et factus est homo in animam vivam, totum utique per faciem statim flatum illum, in interiora transmissum et per universa corporis spatia diffusum simulque divina aspiratione densatum, omni intus linea expressum esse quam densatus impleverat et velut in forma gelasse* (the soul "set" in the body like a jelly in a mould, and received shape from the body): *De res. carn.* 59, *nec alia erit forma nationum credentium nisi quae et non credentium, de carne, de anima.*

(*d*) More generally, form as an attribute of substance: *De anima*, 3, *alii de substantia alii de forma alii de unaquaque dispositione disceptant:* and consequently

(*e*) Form as that by which a substance becomes visible or otherwise cognisable by the senses: *Adv. Marc.* ii. 5, *liberum et sui arbitrii et suae potestatis invenio hominem a deo institutum, nullam magis imaginem et similitudinem dei in illo animadvertens quam eiusmodi status formam* (human *status* is one of free will, etc., and the form of that *status* is such outward manifestations as make it a fact which can be observed): *Adv. Prax.* 8, *sol et radius duae formae sunt sed cohaerentes.*

Scriptural precedent here gives no help. Phil. 2. 6, *ἐν μορφῇ θεοῦ ὑπάρχων*: in St Paul's sense there is one form of God, not three. Mark 16. 12, *ἐφανερώθη ἐν ἑτέρᾳ μορφῇ*, would give something less than Tertullian's meaning, which is that *forma* is unchangeably characteristic of each Person. Μόρφωσις, 2 Tim. 3. 5, indicates form divorced from substance, mere speciosity: at Rom. 2. 20 it seems to mean that knowledge and truth have been given visible shape in the Law.

The difficulty is to explain how one substance, singular and undivided and unshared, can display itself in three forms. What Tertullian succeeds in saying (and in a sense he seems to have meant it) is that the three divine Persons, being each what the others are, are distinguishable one from the other as three men otherwise alike are distinguishable *in aspect*. If this sounds dangerously anthropomorphic, the answer would be that in any case we are bound to think in terms which we understand: *substantia* is a thing, and *persona* is a man, and *forma* is an aspect, but in applying these analogies to God, *discerne substantias* and you will be discreet in other respects as well.

Potestas

(*a*) means δύναμις, strength or power, either as inherent in its possessor or as exercised by him: hence it may be substantified to indicate on the one hand the possessor of the power (as certain angels are called *potestates*) or on the other hand the effects of its exercise (e.g. miracles):

(*b*) *ἐξουσία*, authority, either as inherent in the person to whom it is committed, or by substantification that person himself (as magistrates are called *potestates*).

All these meanings are found in Novatian:

(*a*) *De trin.* 11, *maiestates in illo affirmant divinam potestatem: ibid.* 19, *qui aut hominem Christum aut angelum tantummodo dicit subtracta illi divini nominis potestate:* angels, *ibid.* 13, quoting Col. 1. 16: miracles, *ibid.* 11, *infirmitates carnis recolunt, potestates divinitatis excludunt.*

(*b*) *ibid.* 17, *ut merito nec veteris testamenti circa personam*

Christi vacillet auctoritas . . . nec novi testamenti intercepta sit potestas (*auctoritas* and *potestas* are not quite equivalent: the former implies priority, which the latter does not): *ibid.* 20, *divini enim nominis potestatem et super omnia et in omne tempus accepit* (a combination of both senses, the inherent δύναμις indicated by the divine name, and the committed ἐξουσία received from the Father): *ibid.* 31, *omnis creaturae subiectam sibi habens a patre proprio potestatem:* magistrates, *ibid.* 25, *hortans nos ad martyrium et ad contemptum omnis humanae potestatis.*

Especially noteworthy is (*ibid.* 27): *dicendo, Ego et pater, proprietatem personae suae, id est filii, a paterna auctoritate discernit atque distinguit, non tantummodo de sono nominis sed etiam de ordine dispositae potestatis* (the Father has *auctoritas* as *primarius fons deitatis*: that the Son is a Person distinct from the Father is indicated by his name of Son: and, being the Son, he has the δύναμις and the ἐξουσία *de ordine*, as second, *dispositam*, κατ' οἰκονομίαν).

According to Tertullian the three divine Persons possess and exercise one *potestas* (i.e. δύναμις, which includes ἐξουσία), neither dividing it among them nor dividing the sphere of its exercise, but (as Cyprian says of the episcopate) each holding it *in solidum.* He may have had in mind as an illustration Severus and his colleagues, under whom the imperial power remained a unity and the Empire a unity, though three held the *imperium* (not as later under the successors of Theodosius, where there was theoretical unity but actual partition). He refers to that fact *De pall.* 2, *praesentis imperii triplex virtus . . . deo tot Augustis in unum favente*: and Athenagoras had already so used a similar situation when Marcus and Commodus were colleagues, *Suppl.* 18, ὡς γὰρ ὑμῖν πατρὶ καὶ υἱῷ πάντα κεχείρωται ἄνωθεν τὴν βασιλείαν εἰληφόσι . . . οὕτως ἑνὶ τῷ θεῷ καὶ τῷ παρ' αὐτοῦ λόγῳ υἱῷ νοουμένῳ ἀμερίστῳ πάντα ὑποτέτακται. But it is to be observed that the illustration is no more than an illustration: the divine *potestas* is not (like the imperial *potestas*) a detachable accident of the persons who happen to possess it, but is a necessary characteristic of the divine substance: it is only on that consideration that Hippolytus (following Tertullian) is justified in making the divine δύναμις the centre of the divine unity: *c. Noet.* 8, εἰ δὲ βούλεται μαθεῖν πῶς εἷς θεὸς ἀποδείκνυται, γινωσκέτω ὅτι μία δύναμις τούτου, καὶ ὅσον μὲν κατὰ τὴν δύναμιν εἷς ἐστι θεός, ὅσον δὲ κατὰ τὴν οἰκονομίαν τριχῆς ἡ ἀπόδειξις.

Species.

Cicero (*Topica*, 7, referred to by Bethune-Baker, *loc. cit.*) proposes to treat *forma* and *species* as synonyms, equivalent to the Greek ἰδέα, with a preference for the former because the latter is defective in the plural (a nicety of grammar which would not trouble Tertullian). But Cicero is speaking of scientific division into *genera* and *species: formae igitur sunt hae in quas genus sine ullius praetermissione dividitur, ut siquis ius in legem morem aequitatem dividat.* This is certainly not what Tertullian means: God is not a genus divided into three species.

That *forma* and *species* are alike but not identical in meaning appears from *Adv. Prax.* 8, *nam et radix et frutex duae res sunt sed coniunctae, et fons et flumen duae species sunt sed indivisae, et sol et radius duae formae sunt sed cohaerentes.* A technical legal usage may indicate wherein they differ. In a number of places *species* means *causa*, *casus*, ὑπόθεσις, *argumentum* (so Oehler, index), i.e. a particular application of the appropriate *forma*: *Apol.* 1, *si ad hanc solam speciem auctoritas vestra de iustitiae diligentia in publico aut timet aut erubescit inquirere.* So then, as *potestas* is *substantia* in action, *species* will be *forma* brought into view: the divine *potestas*, being one and indivisible, is displayed by the Father primarily as creative, by the Son as redemptive, and by the Holy Spirit as informative, though all three Persons are one Creator and Redeemer and Sanctifier. So we translate "not in power but in its manifestation", and with this agrees *Adv. Prax.* 7, where *species et ornatus sermonis* are interpreted as the *sonus et vox* by which God said "Let there be light". Cf. also *Adv. Marc.* ii. 14, where it is said that Marcion seizes upon the equivocation which confuses *duas malorum species*, whereas we, *adhibita distinctione utriusque formae*, assign each to its own author: the two *species* of evils are real evil and remedial evil in their manifestations, while their two *formae* are real evil as inherent in the devil, and chastisement as having its ground in the rational goodness of God.

The two sentences therefore seem to mean:

"Though of course the One may be all these on this ground also, that they are all from the One, namely by unity of substance, and for all that there may be preserved the mystery of that economy which distributes the unity into a trinity, setting out the Father and the Son and the Spirit as three, three however not in quality but in sequence, not in substance but in aspect, not in power but in its manifestation, but of one substance and one quality and one power, seeing it is one God from whom in the name of Father and Son and Holy Spirit those sequences and aspects and manifestations are reckoned."

"We duly give reason why, though we may not say 'two gods' or 'two lords', yet the Father and the Son are two, and that not by partition of substance but by distribution, while we pronounce the Son indivisible and inseparable from the Father, another not in quality but in sequence, and although he is designated God when he is mentioned by himself, he does not on that account make two gods but one, by this very fact that he must be called God in consequence of his unity with the Father."

One difficulty remains. The sentence "*unus deus ex quo . . . deputantur*", if taken literally, sounds dangerously like the theory of one section of the Sabellians that there is an original monad anterior to the three Persons and from which the three Persons are produced by expansion. That this is not what Tertullian means the whole tenor of the treatise shows. The difficulty would be removed if we might suppose either (*a*) that only the Son and the Holy Spirit are referred to as *gradus et formae et species*, or (*b*) that "*ex quo*" is a slip for "*in quo*".

Tertullian on the Incarnation

I

In the early work, the *Apologeticus*, Tertullian had already, for a pagan audience, expressed the doctrine of the Incarnation in terms which in his later treatises were to need no correction, but only explanation and scriptural justification. Throughout his writings there is a consistency of statement which suggests that, in this matter at least, he had either worked out his theology down to its smallest detail surprisingly soon after his conversion, or else had learned it and the forms of its expression from his instructors in the faith. Except for the discarding of one inappropriate word, he had nothing to unlearn: and neither from Montanism nor from elsewhere does he seem, in the essentials of his doctrine, to have learned anything new during the twenty years of his literary activity.

The passages of the *Apology* which bear on the Person of Christ and on the Incarnation are these:

Apol. 17: *quod colimus deus unus est qui totam molem istam cum omni instrumento elementorum corporum spirituum verbo quo iussit, ratione qua disposuit, virtute qua potuit, de nihilo expressit in ornamentum maiestatis suae.*

The object of our worship is the one God: who by the *word* with which he commanded, the *reason* by which he ordained, the *power* by which he was able, formed out of nothing this whole world with all its appurtenance of elements, bodies, and spirits, for the adornment of his majesty.

Apol. 21: *sed prius substantiam edisseram ut et nativitatis qualitas intellegatur. iam ediximus deum universitatem hanc mundi verbo et ratione et virtute molitum. apud vestros quoque sapientes* λόγον, *id est sermonem atque rationem, constat artificem videri universitatis. . . . et nos autem sermoni atque rationi itemque virtuti per quae omnia molitum deum ediximus propriam substantiam spiritum inscribimus cui et sermo insit pronuntianti et ratio adsit disponenti et virtus praesit perficienti. hunc ex deo prolatum didicimus et prolatione generatum et idcirco filium dei et deum dictum ex unitate substantiae. nam et deus spiritus. et cum radius ex sole porrigitur portio ex summa: sed sol erit in radio quia solis radius est nec separatur substantia sed extenditur. ita de spiritu spiritus et de deo deus ut lumen de lumine accensum. manet integra et indefecta materiae matrix etsi plures inde traduces qualitatis mutueris: ita et quod de deo profectum est deus est et dei filius et unus ambo. ita et de spiritu spiritus et de deo deus modulo alternum numerum*[1] *gradu non statu fecit, et a matrice non recessit sed excessit. iste igitur dei radius, ut retro semper praedicabatur, delapsus in virginem quandam et in utero eius caro figuratus nascitur homo deo mixtus. caro spiritu instructa nutritur adolescit adfatur docet operatur et Christus est.*

But I shall first declare his substance so that you may also understand the quality of his nativity. We have already stated that God by word and reason and power made this world and all that is in it. Among your philosophers also there is agreement to regard *logos*, i.e. speech and reason, as the

[1] The meaning of these three words has been much discussed, and the accuracy of the text has been questioned. I take *modulus*, by an extension of its meaning the abacus or counting-board, to mean "numeration", and *alternus numerus* to mean "duality".

artificer of the universe. . . . And to that speech and reason and moreover power by which we have stated that God made all things, we also ascribe as proper substance spirit which has in it speech as it pronounces and with it reason as it ordains and as its assistant power as it brings to pass. This spirit, we have been taught, was brought forth from God and by that bringing forth was begotten, and therefore is called Son of God, and God, as a consequence of unity of substance. For God also is spirit. And when a ray stretches forth from the sun, there is a portion from the whole: but the sun will be in the ray, because the ray belongs to the sun, and because the substance is not separated but extended. There is spirit from spirit and God from God in the same way as there is light kindled from light. The original matter [*lit.* "the matrix of the matter"] remains intact and undiminished, although you borrow therefrom a number of offshoots of its quality: so also that which has come forth from God is God and Son of God, and both are one ⟨God⟩. So also spirit from spirit and God from God has made duality in counting, in sequence not in quality, and has not withdrawn from its original but has gone beyond it. So that ray of God, as was always prophesied beforehand, came down into a certain virgin, and was fashioned as flesh in her womb, and was born man commingled with God. Flesh accoutred by spirit receives nourishment, grows up, becomes articulate, teaches, works ⟨miracles⟩, and is Christ.

ibid.: *quem igitur hominem praesumpserant de humilitate, sequebatur uti magum aestimarent de potestate, cum ille verbo daemonia de hominibus excuteret, etc. . . . ostendens se esse verbum dei, id est* λόγον, *illud primordiale primogenitum virtute et ratione comitatum et spiritu fultum, eundem qui verbo omnia et faceret et fecisset.*

Him therefore whom they had supposed a man for his humility, they must needs regard as a magician for his power, seeing he with a word cast out devils from men . . . making it evident that he was the Word of God, that is, the Logos, that primordial first-begotten Word with power and reason for its escort and spirit for its basis, that same Logos who with a word both was making and had made all things.

ibid.: *et tamen suffixus multa mortis illius propria ostendit insignia: nam spiritum cum verbo sponte dimisit praevento carnificis officio.*

And yet, when crucified, he made evident many notable

peculiarities of that death: for of his own accord he let depart the spirit along with the Word, anticipating the function of the executioner.

It was the apologist's purpose to persuade his audience that Christians are not atheists. He might be supposed to have done so when he had declared in categorical terms their belief in one God, the creator of the universe. Christians are monotheists: that there is no god but one is a fundamental fact which admits of no compromise: for that faith they suffer persecution. If he could have left the matter there, he would have been saved a complicated explanation. But he could not leave it: Christ is too important to be left out, and it is Christianity, not mere monotheism, that he is defending. So he has to explain who Christ is and why he is worshipful, in such terms as not to compromise the essential fact of the divine unity. And the terms are ready to his hand: they are the common property of the Christian apologists and theologians, to be traced back through Irenaeus, Theophilus, Athenagoras, Justin, to the Gospel of John, and so well established in Christian thought as to have found their way even into gnostic travesties of the Gospel.

Like his predecessors, he begins at the beginning. There is no question of beginning with Jesus of Nazareth and working upwards to the divine Word: not in this way is it possible to account for the worshipfulness of Jesus while safeguarding the divine unity. His *substance* must be explained first, or the *quality of his nativity* will not be understood. The word, the reason, the power, by which God created the world, which indeed is the artificer of the world, is itself a substance, which we designate *spirit*—for God is spirit—who manifests himself in speech, reason, and power. That Greek philosophers used the term λόγος to describe the creative principle, may save our doctrine from appearing strange to the heathen, though that does not exhaust its content. For the Logos of whom we speak is spirit, which implies objective reality and moreover personality, and the word, reason, and power displayed at the creation are activities of his but are not he.

Who is he? He is one who was brought forth from God, and by that bringing forth was begotten, and so is called the Son of God; and because of unity of substance, because he is what God is, he is called God. He is called God, not as a mere appellative:

deum dictum, spoken of as God in those Scriptures of ours which treat facts as facts, and treat only facts as facts. Of unity of substance, not shared between two, but which both are, not by division or separation but by extension, you have a working example in the relation between the sun and its ray: of substance which transfers itself to another without thereby diminishing itself, you have an example in light kindled from light—an example, be it said, which is only applicable on the theory of the old physicists that fire is a natural element: of quality or attributes accurately copied without mutilation or exhaustion of the original, you have an example in the seal,[1] which remains what it was however many identical impressions are taken from it. The examples illustrate, but no more. The essential fact is that that which came forth from God is God and Son of God, and both are one God. But there is a duality, of relative order, not of being: the procession or extension, which is no withdrawal, *modulo alternum numerum fecit*—a difficult expression, partly repeated *Adv. Prax.* 9, and apparently meaning "brought about duality in counting". And this ray of the divine substance came down into a virgin and in her womb was formed as flesh and was born as man commingled with God: and this is no surprise to us who know the history of divine revelation, for it was preached beforehand in all the prophets that so it would be. Flesh fashioned by and actuated by spirit—and spirit is the divine substance—is suckled as a babe, grows into manhood, is articulate, teaches, works miracles, and is Christ. That is who Christ is: that is why he is worshipful as God, without compromise to the divine unity.

Homo deo mixtus, an expression repeated elsewhere (e.g. *De carne Christi*, 15), is afterwards rejected as unsatisfactory (*Adv. Prax.* 27). Also the phrase *caro spiritu instructa* (which does not seem to recur and may be considered to have been tacitly rejected), whether it means "flesh accoutred with spirit" or "flesh constructed by spirit", might have been thought to make the humanity of Christ the centre of his personality, except that the whole tenor of the passage is against this view, as also is the phrase which shortly follows, *ostendens se esse verbum dei, id est λόγον*. In this sentence the genders are carefully managed, the transition from *verbum dei illud primordiale primogenitum* to *eundem qui verbo omnia et faceret et fecisset* indicating once more that the recognition

[1] "Seal", not "womb", appears to be the meaning of *matrix*.

of the personality of the Word of God is essential to the understanding of who Christ is.

The divine substance is habitually described by Tertullian as spirit, in a specialised sense of that word which was apparently not so obvious a deduction from the pronouncement *deus spiritus est* as not to call for remark almost every time it was used. Novatian saw the danger of making too much of this idea—and indeed of making too much of any of those descriptions of the divine nature and attributes which can never be more than partial: and in the present instance it has led Tertullian into a false interpretation of Luke 23. 46, when he suggests that Christ's human nature so to speak gave his divine nature permission to depart at the moment of his death—a suggestion which is in substance repeated *Adv. Prax.* 30, *spiritu enim manente in carne caro omnino mori non potest*. The same principle, that God is spirit, caused him to adopt a theory of the method of the Incarnation which is probably not well founded on the scriptural text, though it was held by many others besides: this is the next matter to be considered.

II

The words of the annunciation to Mary, quoted by Tertullian in the form *Spiritus dei superveniet in te*, are taken to mean that God the Word came upon the blessed virgin and was the agent of his own incarnation. Since God is spirit (John 4. 24), Holy Spirit in the Scriptures can, he thinks, be a term of substance, denoting, in any particular scriptural text, all or any one of the three divine Persons, In this particular case a comparison with John 1. 14 is thought to require the identification of *spiritus dei* with the Word who was made flesh. The following passages present this interpretation directly: there are others where it is implied, and apparently nowhere does Tertullian suggest the possibility of any other.

Adv. Prax. 26: *dicens autem, Spiritus dei, etsi spiritus dei* [leg. *deus*], *tamen non directo deum nominans portionem totius intellegi voluit quae cessura erat in filii nomen. hic spiritus dei idem erit sermo. sicut enim Ioanne dicente, Sermo caro factus est, spiritum quoque intellegimus in mentione sermonis, ita et hic sermonem quoque agnoscimus in nomine spiritus. nam et spiritus substantia est sermonis et sermo operatio spiritus, et duo unum sunt.*

ceterum alium Ioannes profitebitur carnem factum, alium angelus carnem futurum, si non et spiritus sermo est et sermo spiritus.

He proceeds to defend this exegesis at some length, his purpose being to discountenance the monarchian suggestion that it was *ipse deus*, i.e. the Father, who was incarnate: and he refers to it again in his discussion of their alternative suggestion that the Father is Christ's divine nature, while the Son is his manhood:

> *ibid.* 27: *certe enim de spiritu sancto virgo concepit, et quod concepit id peperit. id ergo nasci habebat quod erat conceptum et pariundum, id est spiritus, cuius et vocabitur nomen Emmanuel, etc.*

This harmonisation of Luke and John is also prominent in the argument of *De carne Christi*, where the purpose is to maintain, against Marcionites and gnostics, the truth of the human substance of Christ. As before, his divine substance is described as spirit: the human substance, the flesh, is that of the old Adam, born of the virgin. Both the divine substance and the human remain each in its own true nature.

> *De carne Christi*, 5: *quae proprietas conditionum, divinae et humanae, aequa utique naturae cuiusque veritate dispuncta est, eadem fide et spiritus et carnis.*

> *ibid.* 14: *qua autem spiritus dei et virtus altissimi, num potest infra angelos haberi, deus scilicet et dei filius?*

> *ibid.* 17: *in vulvam ergo deus verbum suum detulit, bonum fratrem, ut memoriam mali fratris eraderet.*

> *ibid.* 18: *ergo iam dei filius ex patris dei semine, id est spiritu, ut esset hominis filius caro ei sola erat ex hominis carne sumenda sine viri semine . . . sic denique homo cum deo, dum caro hominis cum spiritu dei.*[1]

At John 1. 13 he reads *ex deo natus est*, with suggestions as to the dishonesty of those who read otherwise, and comments:

> *De carne Christi*, 19: *et ex deo natus est. merito, quia verbum dei, et cum verbo dei spiritus, et in spiritu dei virtus, et quicquid dei est Christus.*

Further, *De carne Christi*, 20, commenting on Gal. 4. 4 *factum ex muliere*, he points out the accuracy of the apostle's language.

[1] *Caro sola* here must be understood to include *anima*: he has already said, *ibid.* 14, *sic infra angelos deminutus dum homo fit, qua caro et anima et filius hominis.*

The verb *factum* sets the seal on *Verbum caro factum est*, and affirms the truth of the flesh born of the virgin. The preposition *ex*, which the heretics wish to supplant by *per*, signifies that the substance of Christ's flesh was of a truth derived from his mother, and excludes all docetic views. Moreover, the description of his mother as *mulier*, in view of St Luke's reference to the opening of the womb, indicates that the virginity which was conserved at the conception became womanhood at the nativity. So firmly does Tertullian insist on the verity of Christ's human substance that he will not admit even the secondary suspicion of docetism which was already in his day current in apocryphal legend.[1]

The identification of *spiritus dei* with the Word who was incarnate, was regarded by Tertullian as part of the received tradition. It can be referred to in controversy with the Jews:

> *Adv. Iud.* 13: *cum virgo Maria a verbo dei praegnans inveniretur:*

and it finds a place in the *regula veritatis*.

> *Adv. Prax.* 2: *hunc* (sc. *sermonem*) *missum a patre in virginem et ex ea natum.*

It is in fact found in a large number of writers, both before and after Tertullian, and probably until the fourth century was the accepted view, as will appear from the following citations:

HERMAS, *Simil.* v. 6:

> *τὸ πνεῦμα τὸ ἅγιον τὸ προόν, τὸ κτίσαν πᾶσαν τὴν κτίσιν, κατῴκισεν ὁ θεὸς εἰς σάρκα ἣν ἐβούλετο. αὕτη οὖν ἡ σάρξ, ἐν ᾗ κατῴκησε τὸ πνεῦμα τὸ ἅγιον, ἐδούλευσε τῷ πνεύματι καλῶς, ἐν σεμνότητι καὶ ἁγνείᾳ πορευθεῖσα, μηδὲν ὅλως μιαίνασα τὸ πνεῦμα.*

Hermas as a theologian need not be taken seriously, and the terms in which he introduces this theory show that it was not received from the Church tradition, but was his own invention, of which he is somewhat proud. It is vaguely adoptionist, but the adoption is not of the divine person described as "Holy Spirit", but only of the humanity which had faithfully served the Spirit. It is

[1] One does not rashly disagree with St Augustine, but it is difficult to avoid a suspicion that there is something constructively docetic or Apollinarian in the statement *post partum virgo mansit*, if it is meant (as Augustine does mean it) in the physiological sense indicated in the *Protevangelium of James*.

possible that he had Luke 1. 35 in mind, though the text is not quoted—indeed Hermas does not quote texts, and his verbal knowledge of the Scriptures is probably less than that of any other reputable author.

PSEUDO-CLEMENT, *Epist.* ii. 9:

> Χριστὸς ὁ κύριος ὁ σώσας ἡμᾶς, ὢν μὲν τὸ πρῶτον πνεῦμα, ἐγένετο σάρξ, καὶ οὕτως ἡμᾶς ἐκάλεσεν.

The reference to Luke 1. 35 is not explicit: but that the homilist was acquainted with John 1. 14 and 4. 24 is too evident to admit of denial, and the association of these texts with the words of the Annunciation is probable.

JUSTIN MARTYR evidently interprets Luke in the light of John, and it was probably from him that Tertullian copied this exegesis, as he copied so much else. Having quoted the angelic message—as his custom is, in a free paraphrase—he comments:

> *Apol.* i. 33 : τὸ πνεῦμα οὖν καὶ τὴν δύναμιν τὴν παρὰ τοῦ θεοῦ οὐδὲν ἄλλο νοῆσαι θέμις ἢ τὸν λόγον . . . καὶ τοῦτο ἐλθὸν ἐπὶ τὴν παρθένον καὶ ἐπισκιάσαν οὐ διὰ συνουσίας ἀλλὰ διὰ δυνάμεως ἐγκύμονα κατέστησε.

In his discussion of the eucharist he draws a parallel between the Incarnation, and the consecration of the sacrament, apparently meaning that as the Word of God was the agent of the Incarnation, so the word of Christ is the effective means of the consecration of the eucharist:

> *ibid.* 66 : . . . διὰ λόγου θεοῦ σαρκοποιηθεὶς Ἰησοῦς Χριστὸς ὁ σωτὴρ ἡμῶν καὶ σάρκα καὶ αἷμα ὑπὲρ σωτηρίας ἡμῶν ἔσχεν.

He refers again to the subject:

> *Dial.* 100 : παρθένος γὰρ οὖσα Εὔα καὶ ἄφθορος, τὸν λόγον τὸν ἀπὸ τοῦ ὄφεως συλλαβοῦσα, παρακοὴν καὶ θάνατον ἔτεκε· πίστιν δὲ καὶ χαρὰν λαβοῦσα Μαρία ἡ παρθένος, εὐαγγελιζομένου αὐτῇ Γαβριὴλ ἀγγέλου ὅτι Πνεῦμα κυρίου, κτέ . . . ἀπεκρίνατο Γένοιτό μοι κατὰ τὸ ῥῆμά σου· καὶ διὰ ταύτης γεγέννηται οὗτος.

This passage (which incidentally introduces the preposition διά=*per*, to which he objects) was known to Tertullian, who summarises it:

De carne Christi, 17: *in virginem adhuc Evam irrepserat verbum aedificatorium mortis: in virginem aeque introducendum erat dei verbum exstructorium vitae.*

IRENAEUS, *Haer.* v. 1. 3:

quemadmodum ab initio plasmationis nostrae in Adam ea quae fuit a deo adspiratio vitae unita plasmati animavit hominem et animal rationale ostendit, sic in fine verbum patris et spiritus dei adunitus antiquae substantiae plasmationis Adae viventem et perfectum effecit hominem capientem perfectum patrem.

Elsewhere (iii. 25. 1) Irenaeus quotes Luke 1. 35, without comment: here, though the texts are not quoted, the identity of Word and Spirit of God is apparently a generally admitted fact which may be referred to without explanation.

CLEMENT ALEX., *Strom.* v. 3. 16, apparently has this theory of the Incarnation in mind, though his purpose is speculative rather than exegetical. The term λόγος θεοῦ is, he says, the barbarian (i.e. Hebrew) equivalent of the Platonic ἰδέα ἀληθείας, which is ἐννόημα τοῦ θεοῦ.

προελθὼν δὲ ὁ λόγος δημιουργίας αἴτιος. ἔπειτα καὶ ἑαυτὸν γεννᾷ ὅταν ὁ λόγος σὰρξ γένηται ἵνα καὶ θεαθῇ.

And when the word cometh forth it is the cause of creation. Afterwards also it begets itself, when the Word is made flesh with a view to becoming visible as well.

HIPPOLYTUS, *Canon Euch.*:

. . . *qui est verbum tuum inseparabile*[*m*] *per quem omnia fecisti et beneplacitum tibi fuit: misisti de caelo in matricem virginis, quique in utero habitus incarnatus est et filius tibi ostensus est ex spiritu sancto et virgine natus.*

NOVATIAN, *De trin.* 24, has a long discussion of Luke 1. 35, which owes much to Tertullian, and in which this sentence occurs:

. . . *ut principalitas nominis istius "filius dei" in spiritu sit domini qui descendit et venit: ut sequella nominis in filio dei et hominis sit, etc.*

. . . so that the primary right to the title *Son of God* is with the spirit of the Lord, who descended and came: and consequently the secondary use of the title is in the Son of God and of man, etc.[1]

CYPRIAN, *De idol. van.* 6:

sermo et filius dei mittitur . . . hic est virtus dei, hic ratio, hic sapientia eius et gloria, hic in virginem illabitur: carnem spiritus sanctus induitur.

Sic cod. German. et iv. MSS. Pamelii: but Fell reads *carnem Spiritu sancto cooperante induitur*, which is more in keeping with Cyprian's argument, and may be right.

LACTANTIUS, *Div. inst.* iv. 12:

descendens itaque de caelo sanctus ille spiritus dei sanctam virginem cuius utero se insinuaret elegit. at illa divino spiritu hausto repleta concepit et sine ullo attactu viri virginalis uterus intumuit.

Lactantius had certainly read Tertullian, and not always understood him, and it is possible that here he is not giving the customary (even if incorrect) interpretation of the angelic message, but has made a thorough identification of the Word and the Holy Spirit. He has already said (*ibid.* 8) that while the angels are silent spirits, created for ministry and not for doctrine, the Son and Word of God, who also is spirit, came forth from God accompanied by voice and sound: between the angels and the Son there is a difference similar to that between the breath that proceeds from the nostrils and that which proceeds from the mouth. Spirit therefore, to Lactantius, is not the divine substance in the sense that in any text we need to ask which of the three divine Persons is meant by the term: it is no more than a divine activity, and when he refers to "that holy spirit of God" seeking out the holy virgin, he is not referring to Luke 1. 35, but only to his own previous argument, in which he is more anxious to claim the support of Hermes Trismegistus and to make debating points against the Jews, than to expound the gospel text.

[1] Fausset, *Camb. Patr. Text*, p. 89, not observing this identification of Word and "spirit of the Lord", can only make sense of the sentence by straining the grouping of the words.

MARCELLUS OF ANCYRA (*ap.* EUSEB. *C. Marc.* ii. 2 p. 35 D):

> *τί τοίνυν ἦν τὸ κατελθὸν τοῦτο πρὸ τοῦ ἐνανθρωπῆσαι; πάντως που, φησὶν, πνεῦμα· εἰ γάρ τι παρὰ τοῦτο ἐθέλοι λέγειν, οὐ συγχωρήσει αὐτῷ ὁ πρὸς τὴν παρθένον εἰρηκὼς ἄγγελος, Πνεῦμα ἅγιον ἐπελεύσεται ἐπί σε.*

Eusebius points out that this interpretation is constructively Sabellian—this being not the only occasion on which the bishop of Caesarea threw new light on an old-established theory, and procured its tacit rejection by theologians who would have thought him too dangerous a man for their overt agreement:

> EUSEB. *ibid.*: *εἰ δὲ πνεῦμα εἶναι φήσει, ἄκουε τοῦ σωτῆρος λέγοντος, Πνεῦμα ὁ θεός. σαφῶς ἐντεῦθεν τοῦ σωτῆρος περὶ τοῦ πατρὸς εἰρηκότος, Πνεῦμα ὁ θεός, ἐλέγχεται Μάρκελλος αὐτὸν τὸν πατέρα ἐνηνθρωπηκέναι εἰπών.*

[ATHANASIUS], *Orat. c. Arianos*, iv. 32:

> *σαφέστερον δὲ καὶ ἀναμφισβητητότερον παντὸς λογισμοῦ τὸ πρὸς αὐτὴν τὴν θεοτόκον πρὸς τοῦ ἀρχαγγέλου ῥηθὲν τὴν ἑνότητα τοῦ θείου λόγου καὶ ἀνθρώπου δείξειε. φησὶ γάρ, Πνεῦμα ἅγιον, κτέ.*
>
> *ibid.* 34: *ἐν γὰρ τῇ ταύτης νηδύι ὁ λόγος ἑαυτῷ τὸν οἶκον διεπλάσατο, ὃν τροπὸν ἐξ ἀρχῆς τὸν Ἀδὰμ ἐκ τῆς γῆς. μᾶλλον δὲ θειοτέρως . . . ἡ σοφία ᾠκοδόμησεν ἑαυτῇ οἶκον . . . καὶ ἀλλαχοῦ δὲ ναὸν προσαγορεύει, καθότι πρέπον θεῷ ἐν ναῷ κατοικεῖν.*

The writer is controverting a Sabellian theory similar to that discussed by Tertullian, *Adv. Prax.* 27. His acquaintance with Irenaeus and (perhaps indirectly) with Tertullian is sufficiently evident. This seems to be the last appearance of this piece of exegesis: the common-sense objection of Eusebius apparently discredited it. It has indeed recently been suggested that the two clauses of the Creed "conceived by the Holy Ghost, born of the virgin Mary" enshrine this theory of the Incarnation, the former signifying the godhead, the latter the manhood, of Christ: but neither these nor any similar words occur in any creed until the fourth century, the earliest being that presented at Rome by Marcellus of Ancyra (340). If Marcellus did understand the clauses in that sense (as is possible), evidently neither the Pope nor anyone else did, or this interpretation of Luke 1. 35 would not so soon have become obsolete.

Probably the intended meaning of Luke I. 35 is that the Holy Spirit, exercising the power of the Most High, is the operative agent of the miracle of the virginal conception. The manner of the Incarnation of the Word is not there under consideration, for the corollary "Wherefore also, etc." is not directly an affirmation of the deity of *τὸ γεννώμενον ἅγιον*, but a statement that he fulfils the prophetic promises concerning the Son of God. This is the interpretation given by Cyril of Alexandria, who attributes to the operation of the Holy Spirit the formation and sanctification of the *ναός* of the Word.

> CYRIL ALEX. *Comm. in Joa.* p. 366A: *τοῦ δὲ μακαρίου Γαβριὴλ τῇ τοῦ πνεύματος ἐνεργείᾳ τὴν τοῦ θείου σώματος ἀνατιθέντος ποίησιν.*
>
> *ibid.* p. 993B: *λογιζόμεθα δὲ οὖν ὅμως ἡγιάσθαι τε τὴν σάρκα διὰ τοῦ πνεύματος καθ' ὁμοιότητα τῆς ἄλλης κτίσεως τὸν ἴδιον ἐν αὐτῷ καταχρίοντος ναὸν τοῦ κατὰ φύσιν ἁγίου καὶ ἐκ πατρὸς ὄντος λόγου.* (Lk. I. 35 and Ps. 45. 7 *ὁ θεὸς ἔχρισέ σε.*)

Thus, according to Cyril, the Word is the agent of his own incarnation in the sense that he, by the operation of the Holy Spirit, formed and sanctified for himself his own Temple: but the precise method by which the Word entered into his temple is left a mystery.

Origen, who would offer an explanation of all mysteries, had postulated a previous union between the Word and the preexistent soul of Christ. In that case the union between the Word (with the soul) and the body conceived by Mary would be neither more nor less mysterious than the union of any soul with any body: and the previous union, between the Word and the soul, could be supposed to have been analogous. Neither the one union nor the other can be explained; but if, on Origen's creationist presupposition, the earlier union was a fact, the later and analogous fact would present no difficulty.

III

Tertullian's discussion of the Incarnation, like his discussion of the holy Trinity, is occasioned always (though never controlled) by the needs of controversy. His first complaint against the monarchians is that by identifying the Father and the Son, and by alleging that the expression *spiritus dei* in the words of the Annunciation signifies the Father, they make the Father both the subject and the agent of his own incarnation (*Adv. Prax.* 26). Convicted (rather than convinced) on this point, they now shift their ground and offer a new theory (*ibid.* 27 *ab init.*) that both Father and Son are to be seen in one Person because the Son is the flesh, the man, Jesus, while the Father is the spirit, God, Christ.

Waiving for the moment the elementary point that the designation *Christ* is an adjective, not a substantive, and that the fact of One being anointed requires the existence of Another who anoints, Tertullian refers again to the narrative of the Annunciation. "By holy spirit did the virgin conceive, and what she conceived, that she brought to birth", that is "holy spirit", namely, the Word. Flesh is not God, that of it should be said "It shall be called holy, the Son of God"; but the Word is in the flesh and is God. Christ therefore is not two, but one: he cannot be divided or distinguished into two persons or into a father-son relationship in one person. He is wholly the Son, not the Father.

It is possible to enquire how the Word was made flesh, whether by conversion into flesh or by being clothed with flesh. The answer must immediately be, by being clothed with flesh, *indutus carnem*. For the conversion of one thing into another involves either the destruction of what was, or else a mixture of both, which is neither the one nor the other—as electrum is a mixture of gold and silver, yet is neither. But the facts recorded in the Gospel narrative, and the balanced statement of St Paul, make it evident that there was no destruction of either divine substance or human, and no mixture of the two: both the divine and the human preserve unimpaired their several characteristics and their appropriate designations:

> *Adv. Prax.* 27: *invenimus illum directo et deum et hominem expositum . . . usquequaque filium dei et filium hominis . . . sine dubio secundum utramque substantiam in sua proprietate distantem, quia neque sermo aliud quam deus neque caro aliud quam homo.*

> *ibid.: videmus duplicem statum, non confusum sed coniunctum, in una persona deum et hominem Iesum . . . et adeo salva est utriusque proprietas substantiae ut et spiritus res suas egerit in illo . . . et caro passiones suas functa sit.*

> *ibid.: quia substantiae ambae in statu suo quaeque distincte agebant, ideo illis et operae et exitus sui occurrerunt.*

Tertullian here differs only verbally from himself some ten years earlier. In controversy with Marcionites (*De carne Christi*, 3) he admits, and even defends, the term *conversum*, though he means by it precisely what he means here when he rejects it. Marcion, he says, denies the reality of Christ's flesh, on the ground that "if he had been born and had of a truth clothed himself with manhood (*hominem vere induisset*) he would have ceased to be God, losing what he was while becoming what he was not": and he denies that God was of a truth changed into man (*in hominem vere conversum*). Tertullian replies that the case is different as between created things and God:

> *ubi erit diversitas divinitatis a ceteris rebus, nisi ut contrarium obtineat, id est ut deus et in omnia converti possit et qualis est perseverare?*
>
> Where will lie the difference between deity and the rest of things, unless the opposite be the case, namely, that God can be changed into all things while remaining like as he is?

It is recorded in Scripture that angels appeared in human flesh, and yet remained angels: God is mightier than they, and will you deprive him of this power, by suggesting that Christ was not capable, while truly clothing himself with manhood (*vere hominem indutus*), of continuing to be God? At our Lord's baptism, the Spirit who descended was truly spirit and truly a dove, and had not destroyed his proper substance through his assumption of an alien one. The flesh in which the Son appeared in the theophanies was truly flesh, and the Son was truly spirit: but there is this difference between the theophanies and the Incarnation, that in the theophanies the flesh was created expressly for the occasion, but at the Incarnation, because the flesh was assumed with the intention of dying for man's redemption, it must needs be born of the flesh of the old Adam which was to be redeemed.

The term *conversum* is thus used in a specialised sense to mean the assumption of something else without the destruction of what already was. Elsewhere in the same treatise, arguing against the Valentinian theory that the so-called human nature of Christ was not truly human but was derived either from celestial materials or from soul made visible as flesh, he uses similar terms: *agnoscunt hominem deo mixtum et negant hominem* (*De carne Christi*, 15). His own view is:

> *ibid.* 16: *sicut terra conversa est in hanc carnem sine viri semine, ita et dei verbum potuit sine coagulo in eiusdem carnis transire materiam.*
>
> As earth was changed into this flesh without man's seed, so also the Word of God was able without man's seed to pass into the material of this same flesh.

But evidently, whether he says "change" or "transition", he means nothing of the kind. The flesh of Christ is truly human flesh, of the substance of Adam, neither created for the occasion, nor derived from celestial materials nor from the Valentinian "soul-stuff": far less then can it be supposed to have been of divine origin, through any conversion of godhead into flesh, and Tertullian's subsequent rejection of dangerous terminology is a matter of words only.

Moreover, as Christ's human nature is truly human, it is also fully human, consisting of both body and soul. There are times when the term *caro* stands by itself, as alone under consideration: but it must be supposed then to include *anima*, since man is *carnis animaeque textura* (*De res. carn.* 34, cf. *De carni Christi*, 14, quoted above). And, on Tertullian's traducianist theory, the soul of Christ, like his body, is of the substance of Adam, being derived through the blessed virgin from that original soul which was the breath of God breathed into Adam's nostrils.

And finally, what Christ was on earth, that he now remains:

> *De res. carn.* 51: *adhuc Iesus ad dexteram patris, homo etsi deus, Adam novissimus etsi sermo primarius, caro et sanguis etsi nostris puriora, idem tamen substantia et forma qua ascendit, talis etiam descensurus. . . . hic sequester dei atque hominum appellatus ex utriusque partis deposito commisso sibi, carnis quoque depositum servat in semetipso, arrabonem summae totius. quemadmodum enim nobis arrabonem spiritus reliquit, ita et a nobis arrabonem carnis accepit, et vexit in caelum pignus totius summae illuc quandoque redigendae.*
>
> Still Jesus is at the right hand of the Father, Man albeit God, the last Adam albeit the Word which was in the beginning, flesh and blood albeit more pure than ours, yet the same in the substance and the aspect in which he ascended, and as such he will also come down again. . . . He is called the mediator of

God and men because of the deposit of each party entrusted to him; and moreover he conserves in himself the deposit of flesh, as an earnest of the whole sum. For as he has left with us the earnest of the Spirit, so he has received from us the earnest of the flesh, and has carried it to heaven as a token that the whole sum is some time to be brought thither.

IV

In these discussions of the Incarnation the terms *substantia, status, forma, proprietas*, are still the keywords. Jesus is one Person: the evident facts of the Gospel narrative as well as the requirements of the doctrine of redemption demand that that be acknowledged: he can only be *sequester dei et hominum* (*De res. carn.* 51: *Adv. Prax.* 27) if he is one, not if he is two. But he is now two substances. As before, it is not a question of having substance, of one person possessing two pieces of property, but of his being two substances. And as the divine substance was seen to be a *πρώτη οὐσία*, a single Thing which each of the three Persons completely and indivisibly is, human substance (of which Tertullian speaks in precisely similar terms) is assumed by the Word not partially but wholly. It is the substance of Adam, which is the substance of all humanity, that he takes from the holy virgin: for substance is not the same as *materia*. Each substance, the divine and the human, carries its own *status* and has those attributes which are its *proprietas*. The attributes and activities which constitute each *status* are perceptible (*videmus duplicem statum*), and present the two not confused but conjoined: the *substantiae* are not perceptible, but what we observe of the double *status* indicates that the *substantiae* also preserve each its *proprietas*. Tertullian offers no "solution" of the problem or mystery of the Incarnation, but merely a statement of it and of the scriptural *data* which have to be taken into account: and his statement is that our Lord Jesus Christ, the Word of God who has been made flesh, that is, has clothed himself with flesh, is one living conscious Person but two Things, possessing the attributes and displaying the activities of each several Thing, without confusion of the Things or division of him the Person. Only so can he be understood to be the mediator of God and men.

For this is no academic question. Tertullian is as conscious as any of the fathers that the reason for the Incarnation was man's regeneration. In the concluding paragraph of *Adv. Prax.* he seems to say that the purpose of the Incarnation was the revelation of the divine Trinity: this might have been cause enough, since it is only through the Son and in the Holy Spirit that the Father will consent to be worshipped. But the Incarnation, having a redemptive purpose, has a bearing on man's *status* and *forma* as well as on his knowledge, and of that fact Tertullian was not ignorant:

> *De carne Christi*, 17: *haec est nativitas nova, dum homo nascitur in deo. in quo homine deus natus est carne antiqui seminis suscepta sine semine antiquo, ut illam novo semine, id est spiritaliter, reformaret exclusis antiquitatis sordibus expiatam.*
>
> The new birth takes place when manhood is born in God. In this manhood God was born, taking to him flesh of the ancient seed without the agency of the ancient seed, so that by new seed (that is, spiritually) he might reshape it, having first by sacrifice expelled the ancient defilements.

VI. MONTANISM

The authors of most ancient heresies alleged that they had discovered (or inherited by a secret tradition) the authentic teaching of our Lord, which the apostolic Churches had either corrupted or failed to receive. Montanism frankly claimed to be a new revelation supplementing the original Gospel given to the Apostles, and by them to the Church. Montanus had been a priest of Cybele, whose disreputable bands of dervishes were a byword even among the heathen.[1] After he became a Christian he began (or continued) to have ecstatic visions, in consequence of which he declared himself the agent of the third and final revelation. The movement spread from Phrygia to the neighbouring provinces of Pontus, Cappadocia and Syria, in all of which it survived as late as the sixth century. It just failed to obtain a footing in Rome. Apparently about 180 the brethren in Gaul, hearing of the various opinions which were held concerning the prophecies of Montanus, Alcibiades and Theodotus, sent letters expressing their own judgement and expounding letters written in prison by their martyrs, to the brethren in Asia and Phrygia and to Eleutherus, bishop of Rome (177-192), τῆς τῶν

[1] So Appuleius, and his imitator [pseudo-]Lucian: the former at least had no objection to religion, even if only moderately respectable.

ἐκκλησιῶν εἰρήνης ἕνεκα πρεσβεύοντες.[1] Eleutherus, according to Tertullian,[2] refused to countenance the movement; but some twenty years later Victor, ignorant of his predecessor's policy, or preferring to disregard it, was inclined to approve of the prophets, until Praxeas arrived in Rome and, while giving him fresh information to their discredit, reminded him of his predecessor's ruling; whereupon he changed his mind. At the beginning of the third century there were many Montanists in proconsular Africa, of whom the most notable was Tertullian: possibly the martyrs Felicity and Perpetua belonged to the sect.[3] In the fourth century there were great numbers of them in Constantinople.

There is some evidence that the "spiritual gifts", which were so impressive (though so potentially troublesome) a characteristic of apostolic Christianity, had by no means disappeared by the end of the second century. Tertullian in his pre-Montanist days appears to say that the existence of prophets in the Church is a proof that it is the true Church, as opposed to Marcion's church which cannot produce prophets.[4] Certainly St Irenaeus knew of the existence of the whole galaxy of apostolic *charismata*: his words are:

> In his name his true disciples, receiving grace from him, accomplish for the benefit of other men as each one of them has received from him the gift. Some with finality and truth drive out devils, so that oftentimes those who have been cleansed from evil spirits even become believers, and are in the Church. Some also have foreknowledge of things to come, and visions, and prophetic narrations. Some by the imposition of hands

[1] Eusebius, *H.E.* v. 3. On this passage of Eusebius, Valesius has a curious note, in which (*a*) he conjectures that the advice given to the Asiatic brethren was to treat the prophets kindly by exhorting them to repentance, and if they should return to their senses admitting them to the Church; but if they should remain pertinacious in their error to cut them off from the Church: and (*b*) he affirms that the Gallic Churches in this matter studied to respect the prerogatives of the Roman bishop, so that by his authority the Asiatic dissension might be set at rest. This is almost the opposite of the truth: the language of Eusebius leaves it at least possible that the advice of the Gallic Churches was to allow the "prophecy", and he clearly states that these Churches were not asking for the Pope's ruling but giving him theirs, or rather that of their martyrs.

[2] Tertullian, *Adv. Prax.* 1.

[3] J. A. Robinson, *Texts and Studies*, vol. 1, no. 2, pp. 6. 51.

[4] Tertullian, *Adv. Marc.* v. 15. The above is probably his meaning: but there is just a chance that by the Church's prophets he means the Old Testament prophets, whom Marcion repudiated.

heal the sick and restore them whole. And, as I have said, it has been known for dead men to be raised, and to remain with us a number of years. Indeed it is not possible to tell the number of the *charismata* which the Church in all the world, by the gift of God, in the name of Jesus Christ who was crucified under Pontius Pilate, accomplishes every day for the benefit of the gentiles, neither deceiving any nor exacting a price: for as it has freely received from God, freely it also ministers.[1]

It is therefore hardly correct to represent Montanism as an attempt to restore spirituality to a lifeless Church, or to revive the Church's latent spiritual powers. There seems to have been something pathological about the movement from the beginning. The writers quoted by Eusebius,[2] who were acquainted with the immediate disciples of Montanus, and give the impression of being observant men, without apparent collusion concur in this. One of them, Miltiades the apologist, writes:

> The false prophet speaks in artificial ecstasy, which produces boldness and lack of restraint: he begins with a voluntary ignorance, and ends in an involuntary madness of the soul.

The writings of Montanus and his adherents consisted chiefly of collections of prophecies, which have disappeared except for a few quotations. The Church writers [3] say that, apparently about 170, Montanus, who was accompanied by two women named Prisca and Maximilla, claimed to be the organ of the revelation of the Paraclete. Apparently he made a distinction between the Holy Spirit who came at Pentecost, and the Paraclete promised

[1] Irenaeus, *Haer.* ii. 49. 3. His judgement on Montanism is given at iii. 11. 12, where Zahn, without MS. authority, has altered the text to make Irenaeus favour the Montanists. According to Harvey's text he appears to be criticising the sect (without naming them) for rejecting St John's Gospel because it records our Lord's promise to send the Paraclete, for denying that prophecy exists within the Church, and for separating themselves from the Church on that account. He suggests that in consistency with themselves they ought to reject St Paul, seeing that in the epistle to the Corinthians he speaks of the prophetic *charismata* and is aware of both men and women prophesing in the Church. Irenaeus, it appears, approves of prophecy, but not when it calls itself "new", or rejects one of the four Gospels, or goes into schism.

[2] Eusebius, *H.E.* v. 3 and 16-19.

[3] The references are collected by Bonwetsch, *Kleine Texte*, no. 129. The writers are (*a*) contemporaries of Montanus, or nearly so, viz. Irenaeus : Gaius, Apollinarius, Miltiades, Apollonius, Sarapion (these five quoted by Eusebius) : Hippolytus : Origen : Tertullian : (*b*) in the fourth century, Pseudo-Tertullian, Epiphanius, Philastrius, Didymus, Jerome. I have not been able to consult de Labriolle, *La Crise montaniste*.

by our Lord (John 14. 16)—a promise only now being fulfilled. This explains the statements that the Montanists accept the Old and New Testaments and (like the Church) believe in the Father, the Son, and the Holy Spirit, and the resurrection of the dead; but that they blaspheme when they say that the Apostles indeed had the Holy Spirit, but that the Paraclete said more and better and greater things in Montanus than Christ revealed in the Gospel. There is no need to believe that Montanus himself claimed to be the Paraclete: such a saying as "I am the Lord God Almighty come down into a man"[1] was probably to be understood as the voice of the Paraclete speaking in the prophet. The most notorious of his prophecies was that New Jerusalem would shortly come down from heaven and settle on a certain mountain-top near the obscure village of Pepusa in Phrygia: from that place Christ would reign on earth for a thousand years, and after that the end would come. In expectation of that millennium multitudes of people collected at Pepusa and at the neighbouring village of Tymium, and Montanism became the occasion of a good deal of unhealthy religious excitement.

This excitement was one of the grounds of complaint against Montanus and his prophetesses. Other criticisms were that through excess of asceticism they separated husbands and wives, and instituted additional fasts besides those prescribed by the Church.[2] Montanus organised a system of church dues, with collectors who had power to demand payment, as well as making additional demands under the guise of "freewill offerings". He paid his preachers a fixed salary, and (most shocking of all) some of his preachers were women.[3] The prophetesses wore fine clothes and jewels, and used cosmetics, and Montanist preachers had been known to play at dice, dye their hair, and lend money on usury. The heads of the Montanist ministry were the patriarchs,

[1] Quoted by Epiphanius, *Haer.*, 48. 11, from the Montanist collection of prophecies.

[2] This and the following are from Apollonius (ap. Euseb. *loc. cit.*), who wrote forty years after the beginning of the movement. The Church fast days were Wednesdays and Fridays: the Montanists extended the Friday fast until the evening of Saturday. At one time apparently the Roman Church adopted this innovation, traces of which survive four times a year at the Ember Days. This and the doctrine of Purgatory (see below) seem to be the only permanent effects of the prophetic movement.

[3] For this innovation the Montanists cited as precedent the four daughters of Philip the Evangelist. The Church writers replied that there is no evidence that they or Miriam or Deborah or Hannah or Huldah or the blessed Virgin Mary ever prophesied in public, though all of these were prophetesses.

whose seat was at Pepusa, under whom were officials known as "fellows" (*κοινωνοί*), so that the bishops were reduced to insignificance.[1] According to Hippolytus [2] one section of the Montanists (not apparently very numerous) adopted the heresy of Noetus: Didymus and Jerome accuse Montanists in general of Sabellianism, which may have been true in the fourth century, but certainly was not true in the second and third. It was also pointed out that after the death of Montanus and Prisca and Maximilla the sect ceased to give evidence of prophetic powers: though since Montanus had professed to be the last of the prophets, this is hardly a legitimate complaint.[3]

Such was Montanism in the eyes of its opponents. But there can be no doubt that Tertullian was too great a man to have become a member of a sect of mere freaks, and we must surmise that the New Prophecy as it reached Africa was in many respects a different thing from the movement in its original home. Tertullian would have had no toleration for women preachers. Moreover, he was in no sense unorthodox, and nowhere makes any claim that the new prophecy supersedes the apostolic faith: rather he says that it confirms and illuminates the old faith, while it imposes a new and more stringent moral code. Nor is he likely

[1] Jerome, *Epistle* 41.

[2] Hippolytus, *Philos.* viii. 19. Montanists in general *τὸν μὲν πατέρα τῶν ὅλων θεὸν καὶ πάντων κτίστην ὁμοίως τῇ ἐκκλησίᾳ ὁμολογοῦσι καὶ ὅσα τὸ εὐαγγέλιον περὶ τοῦ Χριστοῦ μαρτυρεῖ, καινίζουσι δὲ νηστείας καὶ ἑορτὰς καὶ ξηροφαγίας καὶ ῥαφανοφαγίας, φάσκοντες ὑπὸ τῶν γυναίων δεδιδάχθαι. τινὲς δὲ αὐτῶν τῇ τῶν Νοητιανῶν αἱρέσει συντιθέμενοι τὸν πατέρα αὐτὸν εἶναι τὸν υἱὸν λέγουσι, καὶ τοῦτον ὑπὸ γένεσιν καὶ πάθος καὶ θάνατον ἐληλυθέναι.* Pseudo-Tertullian, *Adv. omn. haer.* 7, names the former sect *Cata Proclum*, the latter *Cata Aeschinem.*

[3] For completeness the following information is recorded. Gaius, during the episcopate of Zephyrinus, composed a dialogue against Proclus, then leader of the sect, in which he rebuked their boldness and rashness in composing new scriptures. An unnamed author, writing thirty years after the death of Maximilla, says that after much consideration the Asiatic bishops expelled the prophets from the Church: he has stories (which he does not know whether to credit) that Montanus and afterwards Maximilla hanged themselves, and that Theodotus, practising levitation with the help of an evil spirit, fell to the earth and was killed. This author quotes Miltiades, who wrote fourteen years after the death of Maximilla, *περὶ τοῦ μὴ δεῖν προφήτην ἐν ἐκστάσει λαλεῖν* (in which occurs the sentence quoted above, p. 77). Apollonius said that Prisca and Maximilla had deserted their husbands: that a certain Themiso bought his release from prison and then boasted of his confessorship, and had the audacity to write a catholic epistle as though he were an apostle: that Alexander, a famous confessor of theirs, was a man of bad life and rapacious habits, but that the prophet during many years' companionship never found him out: and that a certain Zoticus tried to exorcise Maximilla's evil spirit but was prevented by her adherents. Serapion, Bishop of Antioch, tells this last story, but of Priscilla.

to have thought that the millennial reign of Christ would be established at an obscure barbarian village: he probably expected that the New Jerusalem would descend upon Mount Zion, as did many others of quite unimpeached orthodoxy.[1] His view is that so long as the Rule of the Faith is not infringed, other matters of discipline and order admit of corrective innovation, "since the grace of God operates and progresses unto the end". Is it reasonable, he asks, that while the devil is always active to invent devices of iniquity, God's works should have come to an end and progress ceased? It is for no other reason that the Lord has sent the Paraclete, "so that, since human infirmity could not receive all things at once, discipline might be by degrees directed and ordered and brought to perfection by the Lord's deputy the Holy Spirit. . . . For what is the administration of the Paraclete except this, that discipline is directed, the Scriptures are revealed, understanding is reformed, and progress is made? . . . In this way also righteousness was first rudimentary, fearing God by nature: then through the law and the prophets it moved forward to infancy: thereafter through the Gospel it bubbled up into youth: now through the Paraclete it is settling down to maturity." Before this new revelation Church custom must prove its validity, or else give way: *dominus noster Christus veritatem se, non consuetudinem, cognominavit.*[2]

Tertullian is quite unaware of the existence of a Noetian group among the Montanists. "The new prophecies", he says, "are set at nought, not because Montanus and Prisca and Maximilla preach another god, or because they 'resolve Jesus Christ' (1 John 4. 3), or because they subvert any rule of faith and hope, but because they specifically teach men to fast more often than they marry."[3] Again, "for no other reason are they compelled to deny the Paraclete, than because they regard him as the establisher of a new discipline, and one very grievous to themselves". Quoting John 16. 12, 13, "I have yet many things to say . . . he will guide you into all truth", he remarks, "He sufficiently indicates that the Paraclete will do things which may be

[1] Cf. *De res. carn.* 22, where he discusses the Lucan apocalypse (maintaining that on scriptural evidence there can be no resurrection until the Lord's coming), without any reference to the new prophecy, and pointing out that there are yet no signs of the approach of the end. He appears to have disregarded this aspect of Montanist teaching.

[2] *De virg. vel.* 1.

[3] *De ieiunio*, 1.

regarded as new . . . and sometimes burdensome". Is it then possible for every burdensome discipline to be ascribed to the Paraclete, whatever its source? Certainly not: for false prophets always begin by falsifying the faith, *quae prior est disciplina*, whereas the Paraclete always glorifies Christ.[1] In this vexed question of second marriages, "why should not the Paraclete have taken away the permission which Paul granted? Hardness of heart reigned even unto Christ: let infirmity of the flesh end its reign at the dispensation of the Paraclete."[2] Moreover, this discipline is not entirely new: there is a sense in which, even in ethical matters, the Paraclete is *potius restitutor quam institutor*.[3]

This is a sufficiently large claim. Before he became a Montanist Tertullian had declared that the existence of prophecy in the Church, or the Church's possession of the Scriptures of the prophets, proved it to be the true Church, in contrast with Marcion's church, which had no prophets. As a Montanist he seceded from the Church of Carthage, of which possibly he had been a presbyter. He now speaks with contempt of its members: they are *psychici*, the natural men, who cannot understand the things of the Spirit of God, while the Montanists are the spiritual men, who understand all things. But when we ask what was this new revelation of which he makes so much, we meet with some disappointment. Certainly it demanded the adoption (or, if you will, the restoration) of a stringent moral code, by which second marriages were to be forbidden and there was to be no remission of capital sins: for the Paraclete is supposed to have said, by one of the prophets, "The Church can forgive the sin, but I will not do it, lest they also commit other sins".[4] On doctrinal matters he claims to be *instructior per paracletum*: but of specific facts all that he mentions are the doctrine of purgatory (which he indicates was a Montanist innovation),[5] the elucidation of scriptural obscurities (he does not state which),[6] the three illustrations of

[1] *De monogamia*, 2.

[2] *Ibid.* 14: *regnavit duritia cordis usque ad Christum, regnaverit et infirmitas carnis usque ad paracletum.*

[3] *Ibid.* 3.

[4] *De pud.* 21: *ipsum paracletum in prophetis novis habeo dicentem, Potest ecclesia donare delictum, sed non faciam, ne et alia delinquant.*

[5] *De anima*, 55: *Perpetua fortissima martyr sub die passionis in revelatione paradisi solos illic commartyres suos vidit . . . habes etiam de paradiso a nobis libellum, quo constituimus omnem animam apud inferos sequestrari in diem domini : ibid.* 58 *omnes ergo animae penes inferos . . . supplicia iam illic et refrigeria.*

[6] *De res. carn.*, 63.

the unity of the holy Trinity[1] (two of which in any case are as old as the New Testament), and a revelation made to a woman visionary of the corporeal constitution of the soul.[2] A prophecy of Prisca, quoted from the Montanist book of prophecies,[3] seems to mean that the holiness of the minister is essential to the effect of his ministrations, *quod sanctus minister sanctimoniam noverit ministrare*: the words that follow,[4] in so far as they mean anything, apparently identify sanctimony with spiritualistic experiences. Two other prophecies, trivial enough in their expression, cited to discountenance flight from persecution,[5] stand in sharp contrast with the dignified scriptural conclusion of the treatise in which they occur: *non quaeritur qui latam viam sequi paratus sit, sed qui angustam. et ideo paracletus necessarius, deductor omnium veritatum, exhortator omnium tolerantiarum. quem qui receperunt neque fugere persecutionem neque redimere noverunt, habentes ipsum qui pro nobis erit, sicut locuturus in interrogatione, ita iuvaturus in passione.*

If that had been the temper of Montanism, it might have been entirely admirable. Unfortunately it must be averred that many, even most, of its so-called revelations were of negligible spiritual value, and that it is a great mistake to encourage the religious imaginations of persons of not eminently stable mind. It is true enough that the Church has need of men of spiritual insight and enlightenment: if such men remain loyal to the Church they can bring about a religious revival which may have lasting effects; but if they allow themselves to despise their fellow Christians, their pride may stultify their goodness. Tertullian at first was fortunate: a few years after his death, his vagaries had apparently been forgotten, and he became the revered master of Cyprian, the bishop of the Church of the "natural men": but the seed sown by him *subdola vivacitate latitavit* and after more than a century produced the poisonous harvest of Donatism.

VII. MANUSCRIPTS AND EDITIONS

[The information here given concerning manuscripts and early editions is summarised from the Preface to *Q. Septimii Florentis*

[1] *Adv. Prax.*, 8. [2] *De anima*, 9. [3] *De exhort. castitatis*, 10.

[4] *Purificantia enim concordat, ait, et visiones vident et ponentes faciem deorsum etiam voces audiunt manifestas, tam salutares quam et occultas.*

[5] *De fuga*, 9.

Tertulliani opera: pars iii: ed. Aemilius Kroymann: Vienna and Leipzig, 1906.]

The primary authorities for the text are:

M. Codex Montepessulanus: early eleventh century (Montpellier).

P. Codex Paterniacensis: late eleventh century (Peterlingen).

H. Codices Hirsaugienses, no longer extant, but used by Rhenanus in the preparation of his first edition: date unknown, but probably later than *M* and *P*.

These three MSS. are supposed by Kroymann to have been copies of a MS., not much earlier than the eleventh century, which he suggests came from Cluny: this would be the parent of all existing authorities.

R^1. The first edition of Rhenanus, based upon *P* and *H*, but with the editor's own corrections.

R^3. The third edition of Rhenanus, for which he also used the two following MSS.:

F. Codex Florentinus Magliabechianus, written in 1426, *in coenobio Pforzhiniensi*: a copy of a copy of *H*.

G. Codex Gorziensis, known only from the citations of Rhenanus and from

N. Codex Florentinus Magliabechianus, which is a copy of it, and from which it seems likely that *G* was a copy of *M*.

Consequently the only authorities of primary value are *M*, *P*, and R^1, which last must be used with caution.

The printed editions of note are these:

R^1, R^3. The first and third editions of Beatus Rhenanus, 1521, 1539. Rhenanus was an editor of excellent industry and skill in emendation, but does not always distinguish between MS. readings and his own conjectures, with the result that subsequent editors have emended his emendations instead of reverting to the MSS.

B. Editio Gangneiana, by Martinus Mesnartius, 1545, was based upon R^3, but records reading from other MSS., which are, however, not distinguished from the editor's own conjectures.

Gel. Sigismundus Gelenius, 1550, does not always acknowledge his own conjectures, which are frequently rash and unnecessary.

Pam. Jacobus Pamelius, 1562-1579, used (besides the earlier editions) an English MS. of untraceable origin and now lost, as well as two Vatican MSS., one of which appears to have been either *N* or a copy of it, and the other a copy of *F*. Pamelius was incompetent as a judge of the relative value of MSS. and did much harm to the text: among other iniquities he accommodated the scriptural quotations to the Latin vulgate. The standard chapter divisions are his.

Jun. Franciscus Junius, 1597, displays a wonderful sense of Tertullian's style, and great acumen and erudition. Unfortunately he made the edition of Pamelius his starting point.

Rig. Nicolaus Rigaltius, 1634, is sparing but felicitous in conjecture. He based his work on the older MSS., especially *M*, but also used as though they were ancient testimony the conjectures of Fulvius Ursinus written in the margin of a copy of Pamelius. These conjectures are of great value, and Ursinus is to be classed with Rhenanus and Junius as one of the great benefactors of the text of Tertullian.

The eighteenth and early nineteenth century editions are of no special value.

Oeh. Franciscus Oehler, 1853-4, made it his business to collect and record all previous variants, but examined afresh no MSS. except comparatively worthless ones from Leyden and Vienna. His own emendations, Kroymann remarks, are ridiculous and exasperating, and as an editor he was unequal to his task—an unduly harsh judgement.

Kroy. Aemilius Kroymann, 1906, takes *M* as his main authority, with *P* as subsidiary: where *P* fails he uses *F* to support or check *M*: R^1 he also cites as recording the Cluny tradition, but at a greater distance. He thinks there is still room for conjectural emendation, especially (1) in the restoration of missing words, and (2) in the correction backwards of deliberate scribal alterations. His own conjectures comprise (1) restorations of the correct order of words, or even of whole sentences which he supposes have got displaced, and (2) the insertion of marks of parenthesis and the assignment of some sentences to a presumed interlocutor.

Unfortunately, though he acknowledges faithfully in the footnotes his own conjectures, he has introduced them into his text without distinguishing marks, so that the reader has the distraction of not being able to read the text without continual reference to the foot of the page. Moreover his conjectures are numerous, and too often uncalled for: it is commonly expected that an editor will record his MS. text and print it intact except in places where it will not make sense; but Kroymann several times on a page alters a text which makes a tolerable sense already. On the other hand, a valuable feature of his work is that, besides some of his own suggestions, he records the judgements of his friend Augustus Engelbrecht, who (1) frequently expresses his dissent from Kroymann's alterations, and (2) in places offers suggestions for the interpretation of the traditional text or for its discreet emendation. Of these last it is sufficient to say that many of them had occurred to the present editor as obvious corrections of what he took to be accidental misprints in Oehler's edition: a number of them are so clearly right that the wonder is that during four centuries they had not been made already. Such places are indicated in the critical notes.

The text here printed follows the manuscript authorities as closely as possible: all emendations or additions, except such as have already become common form, are indicated in the text by italics or < >. Except for improved punctuation the editor has only presumed to print his own conjectures in ten places. The improved punctuation consists largely of the omission of unnecessary commas, of which books printed in Germany usually have far too many: but there are places where the removal of commas, or their transference, has made sense of what previously was meaningless or obscure.

TEXT AND TRANSLATION

TERTULLIANI
ADVERSUS PRAXEAN
LIBER

1. Varie diabolus aemulatus est veritatem. adfectavit illam aliquando defendendo concutere. unicum dominum vindicat, omnipotentem mundi conditorem, ut et de unico haeresim faciat. ipsum dicit patrem descendisse in virginem, ipsum ex ea natum, ipsum passum, denique ipsum esse Iesum Christum. excidit sibi coluber, quia Iesum Christum post baptisma Ioannis temptans ut filium dei adgressus est, certus filium deum habere vel ex ipsis scripturis de quibus tunc temptationem struebat: Si tu es filius dei, dic ut lapides isti panes fiant: item, Si tu es filius dei, deice te hinc; scriptum est enim quod mandavit angelis suis super te, utique pater, ut te manibus suis tollant necubi ad lapidem pedem tuum offendas. aut numquid mendacium evangeliis exprobra*b*it dicens, Viderit Matthaeus et Lucas; ceterum ego ad ipsum deum accessi, ipsum omnipotentem cominus temptavi: ideo et accessi, ideo et temptavi; ceterum si filius dei esset nunquam illum fortasse dignarer ? sed enim ipse potius a primordio mendax est, et si quem hominem de suo subornavit, ut Praxean. nam iste primus ex Asia hoc genus perversitatis intulit Roma*m*, *ho*mo et alias inquietus, insuper de iactatione martyrii inflatus ob solum et simplex et breve carceris taedium, quando etsi corpus suum tradidisset exurendum nihil profecisset, dilectionem dei non habens cuius charismata quoque expugnavit. nam idem tunc episcopum romanum, agnoscentem iam prophetias Montani, Priscae, Maximillae, et ex ea agnitione pacem ecclesiis Asiae et Phrygiae inferentem, falsa de ipsis prophetis et ecclesiis eorum adseverando et praecessorum eius auctoritates defendendo coegit et litteras pacis revocare iam emissas et a proposito recipiendorum charismatum concessare. ita duo negotia diaboli Praxeas Romae procuravit, prophetiam expulit et haeresim intulit, paracletum fugavit et patrem crucifixit. fruticaverant avenae

16 exprobrabit R^3 : exprobravit *PMF*.
19 fortasse *PMF* : temptasse *coniecit Urs.*
22 Romam, homo *Oeh.* : romanae humo *PM* : romanae humo homo *Eng.*
33 fruticaverant *M* : fructificaverant *P*.

Praxeanae hic quoque superseminatae, dormientibus multis in simplicitate doctrinae: traductae dehinc per quem deus voluit, etiam evulsae videbantur. denique caverat pristinum doctor de emendatione sua, et manet chirographum apud psychicos apud quos tunc gesta res est. exinde silentium. et nos quidem postea agnitio paracleti atque defensio disiunxit a psychicis. avenae vero illae ubique tunc semen excusserant: ita aliquamdiu per hypocrisin subdola vivacitate latitavit et nunc denuo erupit. sed et denuo eradicabitur, si voluerit dominus, in isto commeatu: si quo minus, die suo colligentur omnes adulterae fruges et cum ceteris scandalis igni inextinguibili cremabuntur.

2. Itaque post tempus pater natus et pater passus, ipse deus dominus omnipotens, Iesus Christus praedicatur. nos vero et semper, et nunc magis ut instructiores per paracletum, deductorem scilicet omnis veritatis, unicum quidem deum credimus, sub hac tamen dispensatione, quam *οἰκονομίαν* dicimus, ut unici dei sit et filius, sermo ipsius qui ex ipso processerit, per quem omnia facta sunt et sine quo factum est nihil: hunc missum a patre in virginem et ex ea natum hominem et deum, filium hominis et filium dei, et cognominatum Iesum Christum: hunc passum, hunc mortuum et sepultum secundum scripturas, et resuscitatum a patre et in caelo resumptum sedere ad dexteram patris venturum iudicare vivos et mortuos: qui exinde miserit, secundum promissionem suam, a patre spiritum sanctum paracletum, sanctificatorem fidei eorum qui credunt in patrem et filium et spiritum sanctum. hanc regulam ab initio evangelii decucurrisse, etiam ante priores quosque haereticos nedum ante Praxean hesternum, probabit tam ipsa posteritas omnium haereticorum quam ipsa novellitas Praxeae hesterni. quo peraeque adversus universas haereses iam hinc praeiudicatum sit id esse verum quodcunque primum, id esse adulterum quodcunque posterius. sed salva ista praescriptione ubique tamen propter instructionem et munitionem quorundam dandus est etiam retractatibus locus, vel ne videatur unaquaeque perversitas non examinata sed praeiudicata damnari, maxime haec quae se existimat meram veritatem possidere dum unicum deum non alias putat credendum quam si ipsum eundemque et patrem et filium et spiritum sanctum dicat: quasi non sic quoque unus sit omnia dum ex uno omnia, per

37 spiritum *PM*: spiritum sanctum *FR vulgo*.

substantiae scilicet unitatem, et nihilo minus custodiatur *οἰκονομίας* sacramentum quae unitatem in trinitatem disponit, tres dirigens patrem et filium et spiritum, tres autem non statu sed gradu, nec substantia sed forma, nec potestate sed specie, unius autem substantiae et unius status et unius potestatis, quia unus deus ex quo et gradus isti et formae et species in nomine patris et filii et spiritus sancti deputantur. quomodo numerum sine divisione patiuntur procedentes tractatus demonstrabunt.

3. Simplices enim quique, ne dixerim imprudentes et idiotae, quae maior semper credentium pars est, quoniam et ipsa regula fidei a pluribus diis saeculi ad unicum et verum deum transfert, non intellegentes unicum quidem sed cum sua oeconomia esse credendum, expavescunt ad oeconomiam. numerum et dispositionem trinitatis divisionem praesumunt unitatis, quando unitas ex semetipsa derivans trinitatem non destruatur ab illa sed administretur. itaque duos et tres iam iactitant a nobis praedicari, se vero unius dei cultores praesumunt, quasi non et unitas irrationaliter collecta haeresim faciat et trinitas rationaliter expensa veritatem constituat. Monarchiam, inquiunt, tenemus: et ita so*n*um ipsum vocaliter exprimunt etiam Latini, et tam opifice ut putes illos tam bene intellegere monarchiam quam enuntiant; sed monarchiam sonare student Latini, *οἰκονομίαν* intellegere nolunt etiam Graeci. at ego, si quid utriusque linguae praecerpsi, monarchiam nihil aliud significare scio quam singulare et unicum imperium: non tamen praescribere monarchiam ideo quia unius sit eum cuius sit aut filium non habere aut ipsum se sibi filium fecisse aut monarchiam suam non per quos velit administrare. atquin nullam dico dominationem ita unius sui esse, ita singularem, ita monarchiam, ut non etiam per alias proximas personas administretur quas ipsa prospexerit officiales sibi: si vero et filius fuerit ei cuius monarchia sit, non statim dividi eam et monarchiam esse desinere si particeps eius adsumatur et filius, sed proinde illius esse principaliter a quo communicatur in filium, et dum illius est proinde monarchiam esse quae a duobus tam uni*t*is continetur. igitur si et monarchia

3 spiritum *PM*: spiritum sanctum *F vulgo*.

20 sonum ipsum *R*[3]: solium ipsum *PMR*[1] (*quod forsan reponendum*): *paene scripserim* solum solium (*vel etiam* solisolium) ipsi.

20 et tam opifice *PFMR*[1] *quod dubites an latinum sit: alia alii tentaverunt: quaero an scribendum* etiam opifices.

35 unitis *ego, Eng.*: unicis *PMF*.

divina per tot legiones et exercitus angelorum administratur sicut scriptum est, Milies centies centena milia adsistebant ei et milies centena milia apparebant ei, nec ideo unius esse desiit, ut desinat monarchia esse quia per tanta milia virtutum procuratur, quale est ut deus divisionem et dispersionem pati videatur in filio et in spiritu sancto secundum et tertium sortitis locum, tam consortibus substantiae patris, quas non patitur in tot angelorum numero et quidem tam ⟨alienorum⟩ a substantia patris? membra et pignora et instrumenta et ipsam vim ac totum censum monarchiae eversionem deputas eius? non recte. malo te ad sensum rei quam ad sonum vocabuli exerceas. eversio enim monarchiae illa est tibi intellegenda cum alia dominatio suae condicionis et proprii status ac per hoc aemula superducitur, cum alius deus infertur adversus creatorem *cum Marcione*, cum plures secundum Valentinos et Prodicos: tunc in monarchiae eversionem cum in creatoris destructionem.

4. Ceterum qui filium non aliunde deduco, sed de substantia patris, nihil facientem sine patris voluntate, omnem a patre consecutum potestatem, quomodo possum de fide destruere monarchiam quam a patre filio traditam in filio servo? hoc mihi et in tertium gradum dictum sit, quia spiritum non aliunde puto quam a patre per filium. vide ergo ne tu potius monarchiam destruas, qui dispositionem et dispensationem eius evertis in tot nominibus constitutam in quot deus voluit. adeo autem manet in suo statu, licet trinitas inferatur, ut etiam restitui habeat patri a filio, siquidem apostolus scribit de ultimo fine, Cum tradiderit regnum deo et patri. oportet enim eum regnare usque dum ponat inimicos eius deus sub pedes ipsius, scilicet secundum psalmum, Sede ad dexteram meam donec ponam inimicos tuos scabellum pedum tuorum. cum autem subiecta erunt illi omnia absque eo qui ei subiecit omnia, tunc et ipse subicietur illi qui ei subiecit omnia, ut sit deus omnia in omnibus. videmus igitur non obesse monarchiae filium, etsi hodie apud filium est, quia et in suo statu est apud filium et cum suo statu restituetur patri a filio. ita eam nemo hoc nomine destruet ⟨si⟩ filium admittat cui et traditam eam a patre et a quo quandoque

8 alienorum *suppl. Gel. qui et post* patris *periodum statuit.*
14 cum Marcione *coniecit Oeh.*: tunc male *PMF*: tunc mage *Eng.*
36 si *suppl. R*[3].

restituendam patri constat. hoc uno capitulo epistulae apostolicae potuimus iam et patrem et filium ostendisse duos esse, praeterquam ex nominibus patris et filii, etiam ex eo quod qui tradidit regnum et cui tradidit, item qui subiecit ⟨et cui subiecit⟩, duo sint necesse est.

5. Sed quia duos unum volunt esse, ut idem pater et filius habeatur, oportet et totum de filio examinari, an sit et qui sit et quomodo sit, et ita res ipsa formam suam scripturis et interpretationibus earum patrocinantibus vindicabit. aiunt quid*am* et Genesim in Hebraico ita incipere, In principio deus fecit sibi filium. hoc ut firmum non sit alia me argumenta deducunt ab ipsa dei dispositione qua fuit ante mundi constitutionem ad usque filii generationem. ante omnia enim deus erat solus, ipse sibi et mundus et locus et omnia. solus autem quia nihil aliud extrinsecus praeter illum. ceterum ne tunc quidem solus: habebat enim secum quam habebat in semetipso rationem, suam scilicet. rationalis enim deus, et ratio in ipso prius, et ita ab ipso omnia: quae ratio sensus ipsius est. hanc Graeci λόγον dicunt, quo vocabulo etiam sermonem appellamus: ideoque iam in usu est nostrorum per simplicitatem interpretationis sermonem dicere in primordio apud deum fuisse, cum magis rationem competat antiquiorem haberi, quia [non] sermonalis a principio sed rationalis deus etiam ante principium, et quia ipse quoque sermo ratione consistens priorem eam ut substantiam suam ostendat. tamen et sic nihil interest. nam etsi deus nondum sermonem suum miserat, proinde eum cum ipsa et in ipsa ratione intra semetipsum habebat, tacite cogitando et disponendo secum quae per sermonem mox erat dicturus: cum ratione enim sua cogitans atque disponens, sermonem eam efficiebat quam sermone tractabat. idque quo facilius intellegas, ex te ipso *ante* recognosce ut ex imagine et similitudine dei, quo habeas et tu in temetipso rationem qui es animal rationale, a rationali scilicet artifice non tantum factus sed etiam ex substantia ipsius animatus. vide, cum tacitus tecum ipse congrederis ratione, hoc ipsum agi intra te, occurrente ea tibi cum sermone

4 et cui subiecit *suppl. R.*
9 quidam *edd. post Ciacconium*: quidem *libri.*
22 non *seclusi.*
31 ante recognosce *Urs.*: amore cognosce *MF*: a me recognosce *P*: amo, recognosce *K* (*quod vix Septimianum*).

ad omnem cogitatus tui motum, ad omnem sensus tui pulsum. quodcunque cogitaveris sermo est, quodcunque senseris ratio est: loquaris illud in animo necesse est, et dum loqueris conlocutorem pateris sermonem, in quo inest haec ipsa ratio qua cum eo cogitans loquaris per quem loquens cogitas. ita secundus quodammodo in te est sermo per quem loqueris cogitando et per quem cogitas loquendo: ipse sermo alius est. quanto ergo plenius hoc agitur in deo cuius tu quoque imago et similitudo censeris, quod habeat in se etiam tacendo rationem et in ratione sermonem? possum itaque non temere praestruxisse et tunc deum ante universitatis constitutionem solum non fuisse, habentem in semetipso proinde rationem et in ratione sermonem quem secundum a se faceret agitando intra se.

6. Haec vis et haec divini sensus dispositio apud scripturas etiam in sophiae nomine ostenditur. quid enim sapientius ratione dei sive sermone? itaque sophiam quoque exaudi, ut secundam personam conditam: primo, Dominus creavit me initium viarum in opera sua, priusquam terram faceret, priusquam montes collocarentur; ante omnes autem colles generavit me— in sensu suo scilicet condens et generans. dehinc adsistentem eam ipsa separatione cognosce: Cum pararet, inquit, caelum aderam illi simul; et quomodo fortia faciebat super ventos quae sursum nubila, et quomodo tutos ponebat fontes eius quae sub caelo, ego eram cum illo compingens, ego eram ad quam gaudebat; cottidie autem oblectabar in persona ipsius. nam ut primum deus voluit ea quae cum sophia *et* ratione et sermone disposuerat intra se in substantias et species suas edere, ipsum primum protulit sermonem habentem in se individuas suas rationem et sophiam, ut per ipsum fierent universa per quem erant cogitata atque disposita, immo et facta iam quantum in dei sensu: hoc enim eis deerat, ut coram quoque in suis speciebus atque substantiis cognoscerentur et tenerentur.

7. Tunc igitur etiam ipse sermo speciem et ornatum suum sumit, sonum et vocem, cum dicit deus, Fiat lux. haec est nativitas perfecta sermonis, dum ex deo procedit; conditus ab

17 primo, Dominus *ita punxi*.
22, 23 quomodo (*bis*) *PMF*: quom (*bis*) *R*.
24 quem *PMFR*[1]: quam *R*[3] *vulgo*.
26 sophia et *ego*: sophiae *vulgo*.

eo primum ad cogitatum in nomine sophiae—Dominus condidit me initium viarum; dehinc generatus ad effectum—Cum pararet caelum aderam illi; exinde eum pa*t*rem sibi faciens de quo procedendo filius factus est primogenitus, ut ante omnia genitus, et unigenitus, ut solus ex deo genitus, proprie de vulva cordis ipsius secundum quod et pater ipse testatur, Eructavit cor meum sermonem optimum; ad quem deinceps gaudens proinde gaudent*em* in persona illius, Filius meus es tu, ego hodie genui te, et, Ante luciferum genui te. sic et filius ex sua persona profitetur patrem in nomine sophiae, Dominus condidit me initium viarum in opera sua, ante omnes autem colles generavit me. nam si hic quidem sophia videtur dicere conditam se a domino in opera et vias eius, alibi autem per sermonem ostenditur omnia facta esse et sine illo nihil factum, sicut et rursum, Sermone eius caeli confirmati sunt et spiritu eius omnes vires eorum—utique eo spiritu qui sermoni inerat—apparet unam eandemque vim esse, nunc in nomine sophiae, nunc in appellatione sermonis, quae initium accepit viarum in dei opera, et quae caelum confirmavit, per qu*a*m omnia facta sunt et sine qu*a* nihil factum est. nec diutius de isto, quasi non ipse sit sermo et in sophiae et in rationis et in omnis divini animi et spiritus nomine, qui filius factus est dei, de quo prodeundo generatus est. ergo, inquis, das aliquam substantiam esse sermonem, spiritu et sophia *et* ratione constructam? plane. non vis enim eum substantivum habere in re per substantiae proprietatem, ut res et persona quaedam videri possit et ita capiat secundus a deo constitutus duos efficere, patrem et filium, deum et sermonem: quid est enim, dices, sermo nisi vox et sonus oris, et sicut grammatici tradunt aer offensus intellegibilis auditu, ceterum vacuum nescio quid et inane et incorporale? at ego nihil dico de deo inane et vacuum prodire potuisse, ut non de inani et vacuo prolatum, nec carere substantia quod de tanta substantia processit et tantas substantias fecit; fecit enim et ipse quae facta sunt per illum. quale est ut nihil sit ipse sine quo nihil factum est, ut inanis solida et vacuus plena et incorporalis corporalia sit operatus? nam etsi potest ali-

3 patrem *MF* (*restituit K*): parem *P vulgo*.
8 gaudentem *Pam.*: gaudenti *libri*.
19 quam . . . qua *vulgo*: quem . . . quo *libri* (*ut videtur*): *mallem* nunc in appellatione sermonis *post* confirmavit *transposuisse et* quem . . . quo *retinuisse*.
23 sophia et ratione *C. H. Turner*: sophiae traditione *libri et edd.*
24 non vis *MFR*: novimus *P*.

quando quid fieri diversum eius per quod fit, nihil tamen potest fieri per id quod vacuum et inane est. vacua et inanis res est sermo dei qui filius dictus est, qui ipse deus cognominatus est, Et sermo erat apud deum et deus erat sermo? scriptum est, Non sumes nomen dei in vanum. hic certe est qui in effigie dei constitutus non rapinam existimavit esse se aequalem deo. in qua effigie dei? utique in ali*qu*a, non tamen in nulla: quis enim negabit deum corpus esse, etsi deus spiritus est? spiritus enim corpus sui generis in sua effigie. sed et si invisibilia illa, quaecunque sunt, habent apud deum et suum corpus et suam formam per quae soli deo visibilia sunt, quanto magis quod ex ipsius substantia emissum est sine substantia non erit. quaecunque ergo substantia sermonis fuit, illam dico personam et illi nomen filii vindico, et dum filium agnosco secundum a patre defendo.

8. Hoc si qui putaverit me προβολὴν aliquam introducere, id est prolationem rei alterius ex altera, quod facit Valentinus alium atque alium aeonem de aeone producens, primo quidem dicam tibi, non ideo non ut*i*tur et veritas vocabulo isto et re ac ce*n*su eius quia et haeresis ut*a*tur: immo haeresis potius ex veritate accepit quod ad mendacium suum strueret. prolatus est sermo dei an non? hic mecum gradum fige. si prolatus est, cognosce προβολὴν veritatis, et viderit haeresis si quid de veritate imitata est. iam nunc quaeritur quis quomodo utatur aliqua re et vocabulo eius. Valentinus προβολὰς suas discernit et separat ab auctore, et ita longe ab eo ponit ut aeon patrem nesciat; denique desiderat nosse nec potest, immo et paene devoratur et dissolvitur in reliquam substantiam. apud nos autem solus filius patrem novit, et sinum patris ipse exposuit, et omnia apud patrem audivit et vidit, et quae mandatus est a patre ea et loquitur, nec suam sed patris perfecit voluntatem, quam de proximo immo de initio noverat. quis enim scit quae sint in deo nisi spiritus qui in ipso est? sermo autem spiritu structus est, et ut ita dixerim sermonis corpus est spiritus. sermo ergo et in patre semper, sicut dicit, Ego in patre: et apud deum semper, sicut scriptum est, Et sermo erat apud deum: et nunquam separatus a patre aut alius a patre,

7 aliqua *K* (*ego*): alia *PMF*.
19 utitur . . . utatur *ego*: utitur . . . utitur *F*: utatur . . . utitur *PM vulgo*: ac censu R^3: accessu $PMFR^1$.
36 alius: *quaero an scribendum* aliud.

quia Ego et pater unum sumus. haec erit προβολὴ veritatis, custos unitatis, qua prolatum dicimus filium a patre sed non separatum. protulit enim deus sermonem, quemadmodum etiam paracletus docet, sicut radix fruticem et fons fluvium et sol radium: nam et istae species προβολαὶ sunt earum substantiarum ex quibus prodeunt. nec dubitaverim filium dicere et radicis fruticem et fontis fluvium et solis radium, quia omnis origo parens est et omne quod ex origine profertur progenies est, multo magis sermo dei qui etiam proprie nomen filii accepit: nec frutex tamen a radice nec fluvius a fonte nec radius a sole discernitur, sicut nec a deo sermo. igitur secundum horum exemplorum formam profiteor me duos dicere deum et sermonem eius, patrem et filium ipsius: nam et radix et frutex duae res sunt sed coniunctae, et fons et flumen duae species sunt sed indivisae, et sol et radius duae formae sunt sed cohaerentes. omne quod prodit ex aliquo secundum sit eius necesse est de quo prodit, nec ideo tamen est separatum. secundus autem ubi est, duo sunt, et tertius ubi est, tres sunt. tertius enim est spiritus a deo et filio, sicut tertius a radice fructus ex frutice et tertius a fonte rivus ex flumine et tertius a sole apex ex radio: nihil tamen a matrice alienatur a qua proprietates suas ducit. ita trinitas per consertos et connexos gradus a patre decurrens et monarchiae nihil obstrepit et oeconomiae statum protegit.

9. Hanc me regulam professum, qua inseparatos ab alterutro patrem et filium et spiritum testor, tene ubique, et ita quid quomodo dicatur agnosces. ecce enim dico alium esse patrem et alium filium et alium spiritum (male accepit idiotes quisque aut perversus hoc dictum, quasi diversitatem sonet et ex diversitate separationem protendat patris et filii et spiritus: necessitate autem hoc dico cum eundem patrem et filium et spiritum contendunt, adversus oeconomiam monarchiae adulantes) non tamen diversitate alium filium a patre sed distributione, nec divisione alium sed distinctione, quia non sit idem pater et filius, vel modulo alius ab alio. pater enim tota substantia est, filius vero derivatio totius et portio, sicut ipse profitetur, Quia pater maior me est: a quo et minoratus canitur in psalmo, Modicum quid citra angelos. sic et pater alius a filio, dum filio maior, dum alius qui generat

27-31 *parenthesim indicavit K.*
36 minoratus R^3 : minor natu $PMFR^1$.

alius qui generatur, dum alius qui mittit alius qui mittitur, dum alius qui facit alius per quem fit. bene quod et dominus usus hoc verbo in persona paracleti non divisionem significavit sed dispositionem: Rogabo enim, inquit, patrem et alium advocatum mittet vobis, spiritum veritatis. sic alium a se paracletum, quomodo et nos a patre alium filium, ut tertium gradum ostenderet in paracleto, sicut nos secundum in filio, propter oeconomiae observationem. ipsum quod pater et filius dicuntur nonne aliud ab alio est? utique omnia quod vocantur hoc erunt, et quod erunt hoc vocabuntur, et permiscere se diversitas vocabulorum non potest omnino, quia nec rerum quarum erunt vocabula. Est est, non non: nam quod amplius est hoc a malo est.

10. Ita aut pater aut filius est, et neque dies eadem et nox neque pater idem et filius, ut sint ambo unus et utrumque alter, quod vanissimi isti monarchiani volunt. ipse se, inquiunt, filium sibi fecit. atquin pater filium facit et patrem filius: et qui ex alterutro fiunt a semetipsis sibi fieri nullo modo possunt, ut pater se sibi filium faciat et filius se sibi patrem praestet. quae instituit deus etiam ipse custodit. habeat necesse est pater filium ut pater sit, et filius patrem ut filius sit. aliud est autem habere, aliud esse: verbi gratia, ut maritus sim habeam oportet uxorem, non ipse mihi ero uxor. sic etiam ut pater sim filium habeo, non ipse mihi ero filius: et ut filius sim patrem habeo, non ipse mihi ero pater. quae enim me faciunt si habuero tunc ero, pater si filium habeam, filius ero si patrem. porro si ipse ero quid eorum, iam non habeo quod ipse ero, nec patrem quia ipse ero pater, nec filium quia ipse ero filius. in quantum autem alterum ex his habere me oportet, alterum esse, in tantum, si utrumque fuero, alterum non ero dum alterum non habeo. si enim ipse ero filius qui et pater, iam non habeo filium sed ipse sum filius. non habendo autem filium dum ipse sum filius, quomodo pater ero? habere enim filium debeo ut pater sim: non sum ergo filius, quia patrem non habeo qui facit filium. aeque si ipse sum pater qui et filius, iam non habeo patrem sed ipse sum pater. non habendo autem patrem dum ipse sum pater, quomodo filius ero? habere enim patrem debeo ut filius sim: non ergo ero pater, quia

12 *edd. post* est *virgula interpunxerunt, cum potius post* hoc *distinguendum fuerit.*
22, 23 habeo (*bis*) *PMF*: habebo (*bis*) *K.*
25 *pro* ero *suspicor* vero *esse scribendum, ut legas* filius vero si patrem.

filium non habeo qui facit patrem. hoc erit totum ingenium diaboli, alterum ex altero excludere dum utrumque in unum sub monarchiae favore concludens neutrum haberi facit, ut et pater non sit qui scilicet filium non habet, et filius non sit qui aeque patrem non habet: dum enim pater est filius non erit. sic monarchiam tenent qui nec patrem nec filium continent. sed nihil deo difficile. quis hoc nesciat? et impossibilia apud saeculum possibilia apud deum quis ignoret? et Stulta mundi elegit deus, ut confundat sapientia. legimus omnia. ergo, inquiunt, difficile non fuit deo ipsum se et patrem et filium facere adversus traditam formam rebus humanis: nam et sterilem parere contra naturam difficile deo non fuit, sicut nec virginem. plane nihil deo difficile: sed si tam abrupte in praesumptionibus nostris hac sententia utamur, quidvis de deo confingere poterimus quasi fecerit, quia facere potuerit. non autem, quia omnia potest facere, ideoque credendum est illum fecisse etiam quod non fecerit, sed an fecerit requirendum. potuit, si voluisset, deus pennis hominem ad volandum instruxisse, quod et milvis praestitit: non tamen quia potuit statim et fecit. potuit et Praxean et omnes pariter haereticos statim extinxisse: non tamen quia potuit extinxit. oportebat enim et milvos esse et haereticos, oportebat et patrem crucifigi. hac ratione erit aliquid et difficile deo, id scilicet quodcunque non fecerit non quia non potuerit sed quia noluerit. dei enim posse velle est, et non posse nolle: quod autem voluit, et potuit et ostendit. ergo quia si voluit semetipsum sibi filium facere potuit, et quia si potuit fecit, tunc probabis illum et potuisse et voluisse si probaveris illum fecisse.

11. Probare autem tam aperte debebis ex scripturis, quam nos probamus illum sibi filium fecisse sermonem suum. si enim filium nominat, filius autem non alius erit quam qui ex ipso prodiit, sermo autem prodiit ex ipso, hic erit filius, non ipse de quo prodiit: non enim ipse prodiit ex semetipso. porro qui eundem patrem dicis et filium, eundem et protulisse ex semetipso facis et prodisse quod deus est. si potuit fecisse, non tamen fecit. aut exhibe probationem quam expostulo meae similem, id est sic scripturas eundem filium et patrem ostendere

13 sed si R^{3}: sensi $PMFR^{1}$.
15 ideoque *PMF*: ideo quoque *Oeh.*
17 *post* si voluisset *add.* ita salvus sim PM^{mg}.
34 prodisse: quod deus et si potuit *et q. s., scripsit K, forsan recte.*

quemadmodum apud nos distincte pater et filius demonstrantur: distincte inquam, non divise. sicut ego profero dictum a deo, Eructavit cor meum sermonem optimum, haec tu contra opponas alicubi dixisse deum, Eructavit me cor meum sermonem optimum, ut ipse sit qui et eructavit et quod eructavit, et ipse qui protulerit et qui prolatus sit, si ipse est et sermo et deus. ecce ego propono patrem filio dixisse, Filius meus es tu, ego hodie generavi te: si velis ut credam ipsum esse patrem et filium, ostende sic pronuntiatum alibi, Dominus dixit ad se, Filius meus sum ego, ego hodie generavi me; proinde et, Ante luciferum generavi me; et, Dominus condidi me initium viarum in opera mea, ante omnes autem colles generavi me; et si qua alia in hunc modum sunt. quem autem verebatur deus dominus universitatis ita pronuntiare, si ita res erat? an verebatur ne non crederetur si simpliciter se et patrem et filium pronuntiasset? unum tamen veritus est, mentiri verit*ati*s au*ctor*em semetipsum et suam veritatem. et ideo veracem deum credens, scio illum non aliter quam disposuit pronuntiasse nec aliter disposuisse quam pronuntiavit. tu porro eum mendacem efficias et fallacem, et deceptorem fidei huius, si cum ipse esset sibi filius alii dabat filii personam, quando scripturae omnes et demonstrationem et distinctionem trinitatis ostendant: a quibus et praescriptio nostra deducitur, non posse unum atque eundem videri qui loquitur et de quo loquitur et ad quem loquitur, quia neque perversitas neque fallacia deo congruat, ut cum ipse esset ad quem loquebatur, ad alium potius et non ad semetipsum loqu*at*ur. accipe igitur et alias voces patris de filio per Esaiam: Ecce filius meus quem elegi, dilectus meus in quem bene sensi; ponam spiritum meum super ipsum et iudicium nationibus annuntiabit. accipe et ad ipsum: Magnum tibi est ut voceris filius meus ad statuendas tribus Iacob et ad convertendam dispersionem Israelis; posui te in lucem nationum, ut sis salus in extremum terrae. accipe nunc et filii voces de patre: Spiritus domini super me, quapropter unxit me ad evangelizandum hominibus. item in psalmo ad patrem de eodem: Ne dereliqueris me, donec annuntiem brachium tuum nativitati universae venturae. item in alio: Domine quid multiplicati sunt qui comprimunt me? sed et omnes paene psalmi qui Christi personam sustinent filium

3 haec *PMF* : sic *Urs.* : aeque *Oeh.*, *quem secutus K.*
16 veritatis auctorem *Turner* : veritus autem *libri et edd.*
26 loquatur R^{3} : loquebatur $PMFR^{1}$: loqueretur *Jun.* : *scribere tentarim* loqui videatur.

ad patrem, id est Christum ad deum, verba facientem repraesentant. animadverte etiam spiritum loquentem ex tertia persona de patre et filio: Dixit dominus domino meo, Sede ad dexteram meam donec ponam inimicos tuos scabellum pedum tuorum. item per Esaiam: Haec dicit dominus domino meo Christo. item per eundem ad patrem de filio: Domine, quis credidit auditui nostro et brachium domini cui revelatum est? annuntiavimus de illo sicut puerulus, sicut radix in terra sitienti, et non erat forma eius nec gloria. haec pauca de multis: nec enim affectamus universas scripturas evolvere, cum et in singulis capitulis plenam maiestatem et auctoritatem contestantes maiorem congressum in retractatibus habeamus. his itaque paucis tamen manifeste distinctio trinitatis exponitur: est enim ipse qui pronuntiat spiritus, et pater ad quem pronuntiat, et filius de quo pronuntiat. sic et cetera, quae nunc *a* patr*e* de filio vel ad filium, nunc *a* fili*o* de patre vel ad patrem, nunc *a* spirit*u* pronuntiantur, unamquamque personam in sua proprietate constituunt.

12. Si te adhuc numerus scandalizat trinitatis quasi non connexae in unitate simplici, interrogo quomodo unicus et singularis pluraliter loquitur, Faciamus hominem ad imaginem et similitudinem nostram, cum debuerit dixisse, Faciam hominem ad imaginem et similitudinem meam, utpote unicus et singularis. sed et in sequentibus, Ecce Adam factus est tanquam unus ex nobis, fallit aut ludit, ut cum unus et solus et singularis esset numerose loqueretur. aut numquid angelis loquebatur, ut Iudaei interpretantur, quia nec ipsi filium agnoscunt? an quia ipse erat pater filius spiritus, ideo pluralem se praestans pluraliter sibi loquebatur? immo quia iam adhaerebat illi filius, secunda persona, sermo ipsius, et tertia, spiritus in sermone, ideo pluraliter pronuntiavit Faciamus et Nostram et Nobis. cum quibus enim faciebat hominem, et quibus faciebat similem? filio quidem qui erat induturus hominem, spiritu vero qui erat sanctificaturus hominem, quasi cum ministris et arbitris ex unitate trinitatis loquebatur. denique sequens scriptura distinguit inter personas: ⟨Et fecit⟩ deus hominem, ad imaginem dei fecit illum. cur non suam, si unus qui faciebat et non erat

15, 16 *ita scribendum docuit Turner*: ad patrem de filio vel ad filium, nunc ad filium de patre vel ad patrem, nunc ad spiritum *libri et edd.*
36 et fecit *add. Pam.*

ad cuius faciebat? erat autem ad cuius imaginem faciebat, ad filii scilicet, qui homo futurus certior et verior imaginem suam fecerat dici hominem qui tunc de limo formari habebat, imago veri et similitudo. sed et in antecedentibus operibus mundi quomodo scriptum est? primum quidem, nondum filio apparente: Et dixit deus Fiat lux, et facta est. ipse statim sermo lux vera quae illuminat hominem venientem in hunc mundum, et per illum mundialis quoque lux. exinde autem in sermone, Christo adsistente et administrante, deus voluit fieri et deus fecit: Et dixit deus Fiat firmamentum, et fecit deus firmamentum; Et dixit deus Fiant luminaria, et fecit deus luminare maius et minus. sed et cetera utique idem fecit qui et priora, id est sermo dei per quem omnia facta sunt et sine quo factum est nihil. qui si ipse deus est secundum Ioannem—Deus erat sermo—habes duos, alium dicentem ut fiat, alium facientem. alium autem quomodo accipere debeas iam professus sum, personae non substantiae nomine, ad distinctionem non ad divisionem. ceterum ⟨etsi⟩ ubique teneo unam substantiam in tribus cohaerentibus, tamen alium dicam oportet ex necessitate sensus eum qui iubet et eum qui facit. nam nec iuberet, si ipse faceret dum iuberet fieri. per eum tamen iubebat, haud sibi iussurus si unus esset, aut sine iussu facturus; quia non expectasset ut sibi iuberet.

13. Ergo, inquis, si deus dixit et deus fecit, si alius deus dixit et alius fecit, duo dii praedicantur. si tam durus es, puta interim. et ut adhuc amplius hoc putes, accipe et in psalmo duos deos dictos: Thronus tuus, deus, in aevum, ⟨virga directionis⟩ virga regni tui; dilexisti iustitiam et odisti iniquitatem, propterea unxit te deus, deus tuus. si ad deum loquitur, et unctum deum a deo, affirmat et hic duos deos †pro virga regni tui†. inde et Esaias ad personam Christi, Et Seboin, inquit, viri elati, ad te transibunt et post te sequentur vincti manibus et te adorabunt, quia in te deus est; tu enim es deus noster et nesciebamus, deus Israelis. et hic enim dicendo Deus in te, et Tu deus, duos proponit, qui er*at* in Christo et *Chris*tum ipsum. plus est quod in

7 *quaero an scribendum* omnem hominem.
17 etsi *add. Rig.*: teneo *PM*: teneam *F.*
21 fieri. per eum *ita punxi*: fieri per eum *Oeh.*
26 virga directionis *supplendum censet* $K^{mg.}$
29 pro virga regni tui *forsan eicienda.*
34 qui erat in Christo et Christum ipsum *Turner* (*ego*): erant *PMF*: in Christum *PM*: in Christo *F*: spiritum ipsum *MF*: spiritum *P.*

evangelio totidem invenies: In principio erat sermo et sermo erat apud deum et deus erat sermo: unus qui erat, et alius penes quem erat. sed et nomen domini in duobus lego: Dixit dominus domino meo, Sede ad dexteram meam. et Esaias haec dicit: Domine, quis credidit auditui nostro, et brachium domini cui revelatum est? brachium enim *t*uum, non ⟨domini⟩ dixisset, si non dominum patrem et dominum filium intellegi vellet. etiam adhuc antiquior Genesis: Et pluit dominus super Sodomam et Gomorram sulphur et ignem de caelo a domino. haec aut nega scripta, aut quis es ut non putes accipienda quemadmodum scripta sunt, maxime quae non in allegoriis et parabolis sed in definitionibus certis et simplicibus habent sensum? quodsi ex illis es qui tunc dominum non sustinebant dei se filium ostendentem ne eum dominum crederent, recordare tu cum illis scriptum esse, Ego dixi, Vos dii estis et filii altissimi; et, Stetit deus in ecclesia deorum: ut si homines per fidem filios dei factos deos scriptura pronuntiare non timuit, scias illam multo magis vero et unico dei filio ⟨dei⟩ et domini nomen iure contulisse. ergo, inquis, provocabo te ut hodie quoque ex auctoritate istarum scripturarum constanter duos deos et duos dominos praedices. absit. nos enim, qui et tempora et causas scripturarum per dei gratiam inspicimus, maxime paracleti non hominum discipuli, duos quidem definimus, patrem et filium, et iam tres cum spiritu sancto, secundum rationem oeconomiae quae facit numerum, ne, ut vestra perversitas infert, pater ipse credatur natus et passus, quod non licet credi quoniam non ita traditum est. duos tamen deos et duos dominos nunquam ex ore nostro proferimus: non quasi non et pater deus et filius deus et spiritus sanctus deus, et deus unusquisque, sed quoniam retro et duo dii et duo domini praedicabantur, ut, ubi venisset Christus, et deus agnosceretur et dominus vocaretur quia filius dei et domini. si enim una persona et dei et domini in scripturis inveniretur, merito Christus non esset admissus ad nomen dei et domini—nemo enim alius praeter unus deus et unus dominus praedicabatur—et futurum erat ut ipse pater descendisse videretur quia unus deus et unus dominus legebatur, et tota oeconomia eius obumbraretur quae in materiam fidei prospecta atque dispensata est. at ubi venit

6 tuum *R*: suum *PMF*: domini *suppl. Rig.*
18 dei et domini *scribendum censui*: et domini *MF*: domini *P.*
33 *parenthesim indicavit K.*

Christus et cognitus est a nobis quod ipse ⟨sit⟩ qui numerum retro fecerat factus secundus a patre et cum spiritu tertius, etiam pater per ipsum plenius manifestatus, redactum est iam nomen dei et domini in unionem: *ut*, quia nationes a multitudine idolorum transirent ad unicum deum, *et* differentia constitueretur inter cultores unius et plurimae divinitatis. nam et lucere in mundo Christianos oportebat ut filios lucis, lumen mundi unum et deum et dominum colentes et nominantes. ceterum si ex conscientia qua scimus dei nomen et domini et patri et filio et spiritui convenire deos et dominos nominaremus, extinxissemus faces nostras etiam ad martyria timidiores, quibus evadendi quaque pateret occasio iurantibus statim per deos et dominos, ut quidam haeretici quorum dei plures. itaque deos omnino non dicam nec dominos, sed apostolum sequar ut si pariter nominandi fuerint pater et filius deum patrem appellem et Iesum Christum dominum nominem. solum autem Christum potero deum dicere, sicut idem apostolus: Ex quibus Christus, qui est, inquit, deus super omnia, benedictus in aevum omne. nam et radium solis seorsum solem vocabo: solem autem nominans cuius est radius, non statim et radium solem appellabo. nam etsi soles duos faciam, tamen et solem et radium eius tam duas res et duas species unius et indivisae substantiae numerabo quam deum et sermonem eius, quam patrem et filium.

14. Adhuc et illa nobis regula adsistit duos vindicantibus patrem et filium, quae invisibilem deum determinavit. cum enim Moyses in Aegypto desiderasset domini conspectum dicens, Si ergo inveni gratiam coram te, manifesta mihi te ut cognoscenter videam te: Non potes videre, inquit, faciem meam; non enim videbit homo faciem meam et vivet—id est morietur qui viderit. invenimus enim et a multis deum visum et neminem tamen eorum qui eum viderant mortuum: visum quidem deum secundum hominum capacitates, non secundum plenitudinem divinitatis. nam patriarchae deum vidisse referuntur ut Abraham et Iacob, et prophetae ut Esaias, ut Ezechiel, et tamen mortui non sunt. igitur aut mori debuerant si eum viderant—deum enim nemo videbit et vivet; aut si deum viderunt et mortui non sunt, scriptura

1 sit *suppl. Urs.*
4, 5 ut . . . et *Urs.*: et . . . ut *PMF.*
20 etsi *P*: et *MF*: non faciam *Urs.* (*parum recte*).

mentitur deum dixisse, Faciem meam homo si viderit non vivet; aut scriptura mentitur [cum invisum aut] cum visum deum profert. iam ergo alius erit qui videbatur, quia non potest idem invisibilis definiri qui videbatur: et consequens erit ut invisibilem patrem intellegamus pro plenitudine maiestatis, visibilem vero filium agnoscamus pro modulo derivationis, sicut nec solem nobis contemplari licet quantum ad ipsam substantiae summam quae est in caelis, radium autem eius toleramus oculis pro temperatura portionis quae in terram inde porrigitur. hic ex diverso volet aliquis etiam filium invisibilem contendere, ut sermonem, ut spiritum, et dum unam condicionem patris et filii vindicat unum potius atque eundem confirmare patrem et filium. sed diximus scripturam differentiae patrocinari per visibilis et invisibilis distinctionem. nam et illud adiciunt ad argumentationem, quod si filius tunc ad Moysen loquebatur, ipse faciem suam nemini visibilem pronuntiaret, quia scilicet ipse invisibilis pater fuerit in filii nomine. ac per hoc sic eundem volunt accipi et visibilem et invisibilem, quomodo eundem patrem et filium, quoniam et paulo supra, antequam faciem Moysi negasset, scriptum sit dominum ad Moysen locutum coram velut si quis loquatur ad amicum suum, non minus quam et Iacob, Ego vidi, inquit, dominum facie ad faciem: ergo visibilis et invisibilis idem: et quia idem utrumque, ideo et ipse pater invisibilis, qua et filius, visibilis. quasi non expositio scripturae quae fit a nobis filio competat, patre seposito, in sua visibilitate. dicimus enim et filium suo nomine eatenus invisibilem, qua sermo et spiritus dei, ex substantiae condicione iam nunc, [et qua deus et sermo et spiritus dei] visibilem autem fuisse ante carnem eo modo quo dicit ad Aaron et Mariam, Etsi fuerit prophetes in vobis, in visione cognoscar illi et in somnio loquar illi, non quomodo Moysi os ad os loquar illi in specie (id est in veritate) et non in aenigmate (id est non in imagine): sicut et apostolus, Nunc videmus tanquam per speculum in aenigmate, tunc autem facie ad faciem. igitur cum Moysi servat conspectum suum et colloquium facie ad faciem in futurum (nam hoc postea adimpletum est in montis secessu, sicut legimus in evangelio visum cum illo Moysen

2 cum invisum aut *seclusi*: *totus locus in libris mire turbatur.*
16 pronuntiarit *scr. K* (*forsan recte*).
25 patre seposito *ita pungendum censet Eng.*: visibilitate *libri omnes*: invisibilitate *Harris, quem secuti Pam. Rig. Oeh.*
27, 28 et qua . . . spiritus dei *seclusi*.

colloquentem), apparet retro semper in speculo et aenigmate et visione et somnio deum (id est filium dei) visum tam prophetis et patriarchis quam et ipsi adhuc Moysi: et ipse quidem dominus si forte coram ad faciem loquebatur, non tamen ut est homo faciem eius videret, nisi forte in speculo et in aenigmate. denique si sic Moysi locutus est dominus ut et Moyses faciem eius cominus sciret, quomodo statim atque ibidem desiderat faciem eius videre, quam quia viderat non desideraret? quomodo aeque et dominus negat videri faciem suam posse, quam ostenderat, si tamen ostenderat? aut quae est facies dei cuius conspectus negatur? si erat quae visa est—Vidi, inquit Iacob, deum facie ad faciem et salva facta est anima mea—alia debet esse facies quae si videatur occidit. aut numquid filius quidem videbatur—etsi facie, sed ipsum hoc in visione et somnio et speculo et aenigmate, quia sermo et spiritus nisi imaginaria forma videri non potest—faciem autem suam dicit invisibilem patrem? quis enim pater? num facies erit filii, nomine auctoritatis quam genitus a patre consequitur? non enim et de aliqua maiore persona congruit dicere, Facies mea est ille homo, et, Faciem mihi praestat? Pater, inquit, maior me est: ergo facies erit filii pater. nam et scriptura quid dicit? Spiritus personae eius Christus dominus. ergo si Christus personae paternae spiritus est, merito spiritus cuius persona erat, id est patris eius, faciem suam ex unitate scilicet pronuntiavit. mira res plane an facies filii pater accipi possit qui est caput eius: caput enim Christi deus.

15. Si hunc articulum quaestionibus scripturae veteris non expediam, de novo testamento sumam confirmationem nostrae interpretationis, ne quodcunque in filium reputo in patrem proinde defendas. ecce enim et in evangeliis et in apostolis visibilem et invisibilem deum deprehendo sub manifesta et personali distinctione condicionis utriusque. exclamat quodammodo Ioannes, Deum nemo vidit unquam: utique nec retro: ademit enim temporis quaestionem dicendo deum nunquam visum. confirmat et apostolus de deo Quem nemo vidit hominum, sed nec videri potest: scilicet quia morietur qui videbit. idem ipsi apostoli et vidisse se Christum et contrectasse testantur.

11 negatur? *et quae sequuntur, ita punxit K.*
14 facie *K, qui et parenthesim indicavit*: facies sed *PM*: facies et *F.*
17 num *PMF*: non (=nonne) *Urs.* (*perperam*).
22, 23 *ita libri omnes*: *edd. alius aliud sine causa mutaverunt.*

porro si ipse est Christus et pater et filius, quomodo et visus est et invisus? ad hanc diversitatem visi et invisi in unum conferendam qu*i* ex diverso no*bis* argumentabitur recte utrumque dictum, visibilem quidem in carne, invisibilem vero ante carnem, ut idem sit pater invisibilis ante carnem qui et filius visibilis in carne. atquin si idem ante carnem invisibilis, quomodo visus etiam retro invenitur ante carnem? aeque si idem post carnem visibilis, quomodo et nunc invisibilis pronuntiatur ab apostolis, nisi quia alius quem et retro visum in aenigmate plenius visibilem caro effecit, sermo scilicet qui et caro factus est, alius quem nunquam quisquam vidit, [nisi] pater scilicet cuius est sermo? denique inspiciamus quem apostoli viderint. Quod vidimus, inquit Ioannes, quod audivimus, oculis nostris vidimus, et manus nostrae contrectaverunt de sermone vitae. sermo enim vitae caro factus, et auditus et visus et contrectatus quia caro, qui ante carnem sermo tantum in primordio apud deum patrem, non pater apud se*metipsu*m. nam etsi deus sermo, sed apud deum, quia ex deo deus, quia cum patre apud patrem. Et vidimus gloriam eius tanquam unigeniti a patre, utique filii scilicet visibilis, glorificati a patre invisibili. et ideo, quoniam sermonem dei deum dixerat, ne adiuvaret adversariorum praesumptionem quasi patrem ipsum vidisset, ad distinguendum inter invisibilem patrem et filium visibilem superdicit ex abundanti, Deum nemo vidit unquam. quem deum? sermonem? atquin, Vidimus et audivimus et contrectavimus de sermone vitae, praedictum est. sed quem deum? scilicet patrem, apud quem deus erat sermo unigenitus filius, qui sinum patris ipse disseruit. ipse et auditus et visus, et ne phantasma crederetur etiam contrectatus. hunc et Paulus conspexit, nec tamen patrem vidit: Nonne, inquit, vidi Iesum? Christum autem et ipse deum cognominavit: Quorum patres, et ex quibus Christus secundum carnem, qui est super omnia deus, benedictus in aevum. ostendit et ipse visibilem dei filium, id est sermonem dei, quia qui caro factus est Christus dictus est. de patre autem ad Timotheum: Quem nemo vidit hominum, sed nec videre potest; exaggerans amplius: Qui solus habet immortalitatem et lucem habitat inaccessibilem; de quo et supra dixerat: Regi autem saeculorum immortali invisibili soli deo; ut et

3 qui ex diverso nobis *Turner*: quis . . . non *libri et edd.*
11 nisi *secl. K.*
16 semetipsum *Turner*: sermonem *libri et edd. excepto K qui* apud sermonem *seclusit.*

contraria ipsi filio adscriberemus, mortalitatem accessibilitatem. quem mortuum contestatur secundum scripturas et a se novissime visum, per accessibilem utique lucem: quanquam et illam neque ipse sine periculo luminis expertus est, neque Petrus et Ioannes et Iacobus sine rationis et amentia, qui si non passuri filii gloriam sed patrem vidissent ⟨essent⟩ credo morituri ibidem: deum enim nemo videbit et vivet. si haec ita sunt, constat eum semper visum ab initio qui visus fuerit in fine, et eum nec in fine visum qui nec ab initio fuit visus, et ita duos esse, visum et invisum. filius ergo visus est semper et filius conversatus est semper et filius operatus est semper, ex auctoritate patris et voluntate, quia Filius nihil a semetipso potest facere nisi viderit patrem facientem —in sensu scilicet facientem. pater enim sensu agit, filius vero qu*od* in patris sensu est videns perficit. sic omnia per filium facta sunt et sine illo factum est nihil.

16. Nec putes sola opera mundi per filium facta sed et quae a deo exinde gesta sunt. pater enim qui diligit filium et omnia tradidit in sinu eius, utique a primordio diligit et a primordio tradidit. ex quo a primordio sermo erat apud deum et deus erat sermo, cui data est omnis potestas a patre in caelis et in terra, non iudicat pater quemquam sed omne iudicium tradidit filio, a primordio tamen: omnem enim dicens potestatem, et omne iudicium, et omnia per eum facta, et omnia tradita in manu eius, nullam exceptionem temporis permittit, quia omnia non erunt si non omnis temporis fuerint. filius itaque est qui ab initio iudicavit, turrem superbissimam elidens linguasque disperdens, orbem totum aquarum violentia puniens, pluens super Sodomam et Gomorram ignem et sulphurem dominus a domino. ipse enim et ad humana semper colloquia descendit, ab Adam usque ad patriarchas et prophetas, in visione in somnio in speculo in aenigmate ordinem suum praestruens ab initio semper quem erat persecuturus in finem. ita semper ediscebat et deus in terris cum hominibus conversari, non alius quam sermo qui caro erat futurus. ediscebat autem ut nobis fidem sterneret, ut facilius crederemus filium dei descendisse in saeculum ⟨si⟩ et retro tale

6 essent *supplendum docuit Eng.*
14 quod *Urs.*: qui *libri.*
18 *pro* sinu *forsan scribendum* manu, *ut infra.*
28 dominus a domino *Pam.*: deus a deo *libri.*
35 si *suppl.* R^3.

quid gestum cognosceremus. propter nos enim sicut scripta sunt ita et gesta sunt in quos aevorum fines decucurrerunt. sic etiam adfectus humanos sciebat iam tunc, suscepturus etiam ipsas substantias hominis carnem et animam, interrogans Adam quasi nesciens, Ubi es, Adam? paenitens quod hominem fecisset quasi non praesciens, temptans Abraham quasi ignorans quid sit in homine, offensus reconciliatus eisdem, et si qua haeretici adprehendunt quasi deo indigna ad destructionem creatoris, ignorantes haec in filium competisse qui etiam passiones humanas et sitim et esuriem et lacrimas et ipsam nativitatem ipsamque mortem erat subiturus, propter hoc minoratus a patre modicum citra angelos. sed haeretici quidem nec filio dei deputabunt convenire quae tu ipsi patri inducis quasi ipse se deminoraverit propter nos, cum scriptura alium dicat ab alio minoratum, non ipsum a semetipso. quid si et alius qui coronabatur gloriam et honorem, alius qui coronabat, utique filium pater? ceterum quale est ut deus omnipotens ille invisibilis quem nemo vidit hominum nec videre potest, ille qui inaccessibilem lucem habitat, ille qui non habitat in manu factis, a cuius conspectu terra contremiscit montes liquescunt ut cera, qui totum orbem manu adprehendit velut nidum, cui caelum thronus et terra scabellum, in quo omnis locus, non ipse in loco, qui universitatis extrema linea est, ille altissimus, in paradiso ad vesperam deambulaverit quaerens Adam, et arcam post introitum Noe clauserit, et apud Abraham sub quercu refrigeraverit, et Moysen de rubo ardenti vocarit, et in fornace Babylonii regis quartus apparuerit—quanquam filius hominis est dictus? †et in imagine et speculo et aenigmate† scilicet et haec nec de filio dei credenda fuissent si scripta non essent, fortasse non credenda de patre licet scripta, quem isti in vulvam Mariae deducunt et in Pilati tribunal imponunt et in monumento Ioseph reconcludunt. hinc igitur apparet error illorum. ignorantes enim a primordio omnem ordinem divinae dispositionis per filium decucurrisse, ipsum credunt patrem et visum et congressum et operatum, et sitim et esuriem passum, adversus prophetam dicentem, Deus aeternus non sitiet nec esuriet omnino —quanto magis nec morietur nec sepelietur—et ita unum deum semper egisse, id est patrem, quae per filium gesta sunt.

17. Facilius existimaverunt patrem in filii nomine egisse quam

27 †† *eicienda suspicor.*

filium in patris, dicente ipso domino, Ego veni in patris mei nomine; item ad ipsum patrem, Nomen tuum manifestavi hominibus; condicente etiam scriptura, Benedictus qui venit in nomine domini—utique filius in patris nomine. et nomen patris Deus omnipotens, Altissimus, Dominus virtutum, Rex Israelis, Qui est. quatenus ita scripturae docent, haec dicimus et in filium competisse, et in his filium venisse et in his semper egisse et sic ea in se hominibus manifestasse. Omnia, inquit, patris mea sunt: cur non et nomina? cum ergo legis Deum omnipotentem et Altissimum et Deum virtutum et Regem Israelis et Qui est, vide ne per haec filius etiam demonstretur suo iure Deus ⟨omnipotens⟩ qua sermo Dei omnipotentis quaque omnium accepit potestatem, Altissimus qua dextera dei exaltatus sicut Petrus in Actis contionatur, Dominus virtutum quia omnia subiecta sunt illi a patre, Rex Israelis quia illi proprie excidit sors gentis istius, item Qui est quoniam multi filii dicuntur et non sunt. si autem volunt et Christi nomen patris esse, audient suo loco. interim hic mihi promptum sit responsum adversus id quod et de Apocalypsi Ioannis proferunt, Ego dominus qui est et qui fuit et venit, omnipotens, et sicubi alibi dei omnipotentis appellationem non putant etiam filio convenire: quasi qui venturus sit ⟨non sit⟩ omnipotens, cum et filius omnipotentis tam omnipotens sit quam deus dei filius.

18. Sed hanc societatem nominum paternorum in filio ne facile perspiciant perturbat illos scriptura si quando unicum deum statuit, quasi non eadem et deos et dominos duos proposuerit, ut supra ostendimus. ergo quia duos et unum, inquiunt, invenimus, ideo ambo unus, atque idem et filius et pater. porro non periclitatur scriptura ut illi de tua argumentatione succurras ne sibi contraria videatur: habet rationem et cum unicum deum statuit et cum duos patrem et filium ostendit, et sufficit sibi. filium nominari ab ea constat: salvo enim filio recte unicum deum potest determinasse cuius est filius. non enim desinit esse qui habet filium ipse unicus, suo scilicet nomine quotiens sine filio nominatur. sine filio autem nominatur cum principaliter determinatur ut prima persona, quae ante filii nomen erat proponenda, quia pater ante cognoscitur et post patrem filius nominatur.

12 omnipotens *suppl.* R^3.
22 non sit *supplenda docuit Eng.* (*ego*).

igitur unus deus pater, et absque eo alius non est: quod ipse inferens non filium negat sed alium deum: ceterum alius a patre filius non est. denique inspice sequentia huiusmodi pronuntiationum, et invenies fere ad idolorum factitatores atque cultores definitionem earum pertinere ut multitudinem falsorum deorum unio divinitatis expellat, habens tamen filium, quanto individuum et inseparatum a patre, tanto in patre reputandum etsi non nominatum. atquin si nominasset illum separasset, ita dicens, Alius praeter me non est nisi filius meus: alium enim etiam filium fecisset quem de aliis excepisset. puta solem dicere, Ego sol, et alius praeter me non est nisi radius meus: nonne denotasses vanitatem, quasi non et radius in sole deputetur? itaque praeter semetipsum non esse alium deum, hoc propter idololatriam tam nationum quam Israelis: etiam propter haereticos, qui sicut nationes manibus ita et ipsi verbis idola fabricantur, id est alium deum et alium Christum. igitur et cum se unum pronuntiabat filio pater procurabat, ne ab alio deo Christus venisse credatur sed ab illo qui praedixerat, Ego deus et alius absque me non est, qui se unicum sed cum filio ostendit cum quo caelum solus extendit.

19. Quin et hoc dictum eius in argumentum singularitatis arripient: Extendi, inquit, caelum solus: quantum ad ceteras virtutes, solus, praestruens adversus coniecturas haereticorum, qui mundum ab angelis et potestatibus diversis volunt structum, qui et ipsum creatorem aut angelum faciunt aut ad alia quae extrinsecus, ut opera mundi, ignorantem quoque subornatum. aut si sic solus caelum extendit, quomodo isti praesumunt in perversum haeretici quasi singularis non admittatur sophia illa dicens, Cum pararet caelum ego aderam illi? et si dixit, Quis cognovit sensum domini et quis illi consilio fuit? utique praeter sophiam *a*it quae illi aderat. in ipso tamen et cum illo universa compingebat non ignorante quid faceret. Praeter sophiam autem Praeter filium dicit, qui est Christus sophia et virtus dei, secundum apostolum, solus sciens sensum patris: quis enim scit quae sunt in deo nisi spiritus qui in ipso est?—non qui extra ipsum. erat ergo qui non solum deum faceret, nisi a ceteris solum. sed et evangelium recusetur quod dicat omnia per sermonem a deo

29 et si dixit: *add.* apostolus *Urs.*: Esaias *Eng.*
31 ait *Urs.*: fuit *PM*: non fuit *F.*

facta esse et sine eo nihil factum. nisi enim fallor et alibi scriptum est: Sermone eius caeli firmati sunt, et spiritu eius omnes virtutes eorum. et sermo autem, virtus et sophia, ipse erit dei filius. ita si per filium omnia, caelum quoque per filium extendens non solus extendit, nisi illa ratione qua a ceteris solus. atque adeo statim de filio loquitur: Quis alius deiecit signa ventriloquorum et divinationes a corde, avertens sapientes retrorsum et consilium eorum infatuans, sistens verba filii sui?—dicendo scilicet, Hic est filius meus dilectus, hunc audite. ita filium subiungens ipse interpretator est quomodo caelum solus extenderit, scilicet cum filio solus, sicut cum filio unum. proinde et filii erit vox, Extendi caelum solus, quia sermone caeli confirmati sunt. quia sophia in sermone adsistente paratum est caelum, et omnia per sermonem sunt facta, competit et filium solum extendisse caelum quia solus operationi patris ministravit. idem erit dicens, Ego primus, et in superventura ego sum. primum scilicet omnium sermo: In principio erat sermo, in quo principio prolatus a patre est. ceterum pater, non habens initium, ut a nullo prolatus, ut innatus, ⟨primus⟩ non potest videri: qui solus fuit semper, ordinem habere non potuit. igitur si propterea eundem et patrem et filium credendum putaverunt ut unum deum vindicent, salva est unio eius qui cum sit unus habet et filium, aeque et ipsum eisdem scripturis comprehensum. si filium nolunt secundum a patre reputari ne secundus duos faciat deos dici, ostendimus etiam duos deos in scriptura relatos et duos dominos: et tamen ne de isto scandalizentur, rationem reddimus qua dei non duo dicantur nec domini sed qua pater et filius duo, et hoc non ex separatione substantiae sed ex dispositione, cum individuum et inseparatum filium a patre pronuntiamus, nec statu sed gradu alium, qui etsi deus dicatur quando nominatur singularis, non ideo duos deos faciat sed unum, hoc ipso quod et deus ex unitate patris vocari habeat.

20. Sed argumentationibus eorum adhuc retundendis opera praebenda est si quid de scripturis ad sententiam suam excerpent, cetera nolentes intueri quae et ipsa regulam servant, et quidem salva unione divinitatis et monarchiae sonitu. nam sicut in

19 primus *add. K.*
34 *quaero an scribendum* de novis scripturis.
36 *pro* sonitu *scripsit K* statu (*forsan recte*).

veteribus nihil aliud tenent quam, Ego deus et alius praeter me non est, ita in evangelio responsionem domini ad Philippum tuentur, Ego et pater unum sumus, et Qui me viderit vidit et patrem, et Ego in patre et pater in me. his tribus capitulis totum instrumentum utriusque testamenti volunt cedere, cum oporteat secundum plura intellegi pauciora. sed proprium hoc est omnium haereticorum. nam quia pauca sunt quae in silva inveniri possunt, pauca adversus plura defendunt et posteriora adversus priora suscipiunt. regula autem omni rei semper ab initio constituta in prioribus et in posteriora praescribit, utique et in paucioribus.

21. Aspice itaque quanta praescribant tibi etiam in evangelio ante Philippi consultationem et ante omnem argumentationem tuam. et in primis ipsa statim praefatio Ioannis evangelizatoris demonstrat quid retro fuerit qui caro fieri habebat: In principio erat sermo et sermo erat apud deum et deus erat sermo; hic erat in principio apud deum; omnia per ipsum facta sunt et sine ipso factum est nihil. nam si haec non aliter accipi licet quam quomodo scripta sunt, indubitanter alius ostenditur qui fuerit a principio, alius apud quem fuit: alium sermonem dei, alium deum—licet et deus sermo, sed qua dei filius non qua pater—alium per quem omnia, alium a quo omnia. alium autem quomodo dicamus saepe iam edidimus. quo alium dicamus, necesse est non eundem: ⟨non eundem⟩ autem non quasi separatum, dispositione alium non divisione. hic ergo factus est caro, non ipse cuius erat sermo. huius gloria visa est tanquam unici a patre, non tanquam patris. hic uni*c*us sinum patris disseruit, non sinum suum pater: praecedit enim, Deum nemo vidit unquam. inde et si agnus dei ab Ioanne designatur, non ipse cuius est dilectus. certe filius dei semper, sed non ipse cuius est filius. hoc eum Nathanael statim sensit, sicut et alibi Petrus: Tu es filius dei. hoc et ipse recte sensisse illos confirmat, Nathanaeli quidem respondens, Quia dixi Vidi te sub ficu, ideo credis; Petrum vero beatum adfirmans cui non caro neque sanguis revelasset quod et patrem senserat, sed pater qui in caelis est. quo dicto utriusque personae constituit distinctionem, et filii in terris, quem Petrus agnoverat dei filium,

11 paucioribus *libri*: pauciora *Urs.*: *totam clausulam secludendam censet Eng.*
24 non eundem *suppl. Oeh.*
27 unicus *Eng.* (*ego*): unius *libri.*

et patris qui in caelis, qui Petro revelaverat quod Petrus agnoverat, dei filium Christum. cum in templum introiit, aedem patris appellat, ut filius. cum ad Nicodemum dicit, Ita, inquit, dilexit deus mundum ut filium suum unicum dederit, in quem omnis qui crediderit non pereat sed habeat vitam sempiternam: et rursus, Non enim misit deus filium suum in mundum ut iudicet mundum, sed ut salvus sit mundus per eum; qui crediderit in illum non iudicatur; qui non crediderit in illum iam iudicatus est, quia non credidit in nomine unici filii dei. Ioannes autem cum interrogaretur quid de Iesu *cum* tingeret, Pater, inquit, dilexit filium et omnia tradidit in manu eius; qui credidit in filium habet vitam aeternam; qui non credidit in filio dei non videbit deum sed ira dei manebit super eum. quem vero Samaritidi ostendit? si Messiam qui dicitur Christus, filium utique se, non patrem, demonstravit, quia et alibi Christus dei filius, non pater, dictus est. exinde discipulis, Meum est, inquit, ut faciam voluntatem eius qui me misit, ut consummem opus eius. et ad Iudaeos de paralytici sanitate, Pater meus usque modo operatur et ego operor: Pater et ego, filius dicit. denique propter hoc magis Iudaei illum interficere volebant, non tantum quod solveret sabbatum sed quod patrem suum deum diceret, aequans se deo. tunc ergo dicebat ad eos, Nihil filius facere potest a semetipso nisi videat patrem facientem; quae enim ille facit eadem et filius facit: pater enim diligit filium, et omnia demonstravit illi quae ille fecit, et maiora istis opera demonstra*b*it illi, ut vos miremini; quomodo enim ⟨pater⟩ suscitat mortuos et vivificat, ita et filius quos vult vivificat. neque enim pater iudicat, sed omne iudicium dedit filio, uti omnes honorent filium sicut honorant patrem: qui non honorat filium, non honorat patrem qui filium misit. amen amen dico vobis, quod qui audit sermones meos et credit ei qui me misit habet vitam aeternam, et in iudicium non veniet sed transit de morte in vitam. amen dico vobis, quod veniet hora qua mortui audient vocem filii dei et cum audierint vivent: sicut enim pater habet vitam aeternam a semetipso, ita et filio dedit vitam aeternam habere in semetipso, et iudicium dedit illi facere in potestate quia filius hominis est— per carnem scilicet, sicut et filius dei per spiritum eius. adhuc adicit, Ego autem habeo maius quam Ioannis testimonium;

10 cum tingeret *Eng.*: contingeret *libri.*
25 demonstrabit *K*: demonstravit *libri.*
26 pater *suppl. K.*

opera enim quae pater mihi dedit consummare, illa ipsa de me testimonium perhibent quod me pater miserit; et qui me misit pater, ipse testimonium dixit de me. subiungens autem, Neque vocem eius audistis unquam neque formam eius vidistis, confirmat retro non patrem sed filium fuisse qui videbatur et audiebatur. denique dicit, Ego veni in patris mei nomine et non me recepistis—adeo semper filius erat in dei et regis et domini omnipotentis et altissimi nomine. interrogantibus autem quid facere debeant respondit, Ut credatis in eum quem deus misit. panem quoque se adfirmat quem pater praestaret de caelo; ergo omne quod ei daret pater ad se venire, nec reiecturum se, quia de caelo descendisset non ut suam sed ut patris faceret voluntatem; voluntatem autem patris esse uti qui viderit filium et crediderit in eum vitam et resurrectionem consequatur; neminem porro ad se venire posse nisi quem pater adducat; omnem qui a patre audisset et didicisset, venire ad se: Non quasi patrem aliquis viderit, adiciens et hic, ut ostenderet patris esse sermonem per quem docti fiant. at cum discedunt ab eo multi et apostolis suis offert si velint discedere et ipsi, quid respondit Simon Petrus? Quo discedimus? verba vitae habes, et nos credimus quod tu sis Christus: patrem illum esse an patris Christum?

22. Cuius autem doctrinam dicit ad quam mirabantur? suam an patris? aeque ambigentibus inter se ne ipse esset Christus, utique non pater sed filius, *M*eque scitis, inquit, ⟨et scitis⟩ unde sim, et non veni a me ipso, sed est verus qui me misit, quem vos non nostis; ego novi illum, quia apud illum sum. non dixit, Quia ipse sum, et, Ipse me misi, sed, Ille me misit. item cum misissent ad invadendum eum pharisaei, Modicum adhuc tempus, ait, vobiscum sum, et vado ad eum qui me misit. at ubi se negat esse solum—Sed ego, inquit, et qui me misit pater—nonne duos demonstrat, tam duos quam inseparatos? immo totum erat hoc quod docebat, inseparatos duos esse: siquidem et legem proponens duorum hominum testimonium confirmantem, subiungit, Ego testimonium dico de me, et testimonium dicit de me qui me misit pater. quodsi unus esset, dum idem est et filius et pater, non uteretur legis patrocinio fidem imponentis non unius testimonio sed duorum. item interrogatus ubi esset pater, neque se neque

17 *quaero an scribendum* esse se sermonem.
24 meque *K*: neque me *PMF*: et scitis *supplenda censui.*

patrem notum esse illis respondens, duos dixit ignotos, quod si ipsum nossent patrem nossent: non quidem quasi ipse esset pater et filius, sed quia per individuitatem neque agnosci neque ignorari alter sine altero potest. Qui me, ait, misit verax est, et ego quae ab eo audivi ea et loquor in mundum: interpretante extrinsecus scriptura non cognovisse illos quod de patre dixisset, cum scilicet cognoscere debuissent sermones patris in filio esse, legendo apud Hieremiam, Et dixit mihi dominus, Ecce dedi sermones meos in os tuum; et apud Esaiam, Dominus dat mihi linguam disciplinae ad cognoscendum quando oporteat dicere sermonem; sicut ipse rursus, Tunc, inquit, cognoscetis quod ego sim, et a memetipso nihil loquar, sed sicut me docuit ita et loquor, quia et qui me misit mecum est. et hoc ad testimonium individuorum duorum. item in altercatione Iudaeorum, exprobrans quod occidere eum vellent, Ego, inquit, quae vidi penes patrem meum loquor, et vos quod vidistis penes patrem vestrum id facitis; et nunc vultis occidere hominem veritatem vobis locutum quam audivit a deo: et, Si deus esset pater vester dilexissetis me; ego enim ex deo exivi et veni (et tamen non separantur, licet exisse dixerit, ut quidam arripiunt huius dicti occasionem: exivit autem a patre ut radius ex sole, ut rivus ex fonte, ut frutex ex semine): ⟨et⟩, Ego daemonium non habeo, sed honoro patrem meum: et, Si ego me ipse glorificem, nihil est gloria mea; est qui me glorificet pater, quem vos dicitis deum esse vestrum nec nostis illum; at ego novi eum, et si dicam Non novi, ero similis vestri mendax; sed novi illum et sermonem eius servo. at cum subiungit, Abraham diem meum vidit et laetatus est, nempe demonstrat filium Abrahae retro visum, non patrem. item super caecum illum patris opera dicit se facere oportere: cui post restitutionem luminum, Tu, inquit, credis in filium dei? et interroganti quis esset iste, ipse se demonstrans utique filium demonstravit quem credendum esse dixerat. dehinc cognosci se profitetur a patre et patrem a se, et ideo se diligi a patre quod animam suam ponat, quia hoc praeceptum accepisset a patre. et interrogatus a Iudaeis si ipse esset Christus (utique dei, nam usque in hodiernum Iudaei Christum dei, non ipsum patrem, sperant, quia nunquam Christus pater scriptus est venturus), Loquor, inquit, vobis et non creditis; opera quae ego facio in

4 *sqq.* potest etc. *ita fere punxit K.*
22 et *add. K.*

nomine patris, ipsa de me testimonium dicunt. quod testimonium? ipsum scilicet esse de quo interrogabant, id est Christum dei. de ovibus etiam suis, quod nemo illas de manu eius eriperet, Pater enim, ⟨inquit⟩, quod mihi dedit maius est omnibus; et, Ego et pater unum sumus. hic ergo iam gradum volunt figere stulti, immo caeci, qui non videant, primo, Ego et pater, duorum esse significationem; dehinc in novissimo, Sumus, non ex unius esse persona, quod pluraliter dictum est; tum quod Unum sumus, non Unus sumus ⟨dicit⟩. si enim dixisset Unus sumus, potuisset adiuvare sententiam illorum: unus enim singularis numeri significatio videtur. adhuc cum duo masculini generis unum dicit neutrali verbo—quod non pertinet ad singularitatem, sed ad unitatem, ad similitudinem, ad coniunctionem, ad dilectionem patris qui filium diligit, et ad obsequium filii qui voluntati patris obsequitur—Unum sumus, dicens, ego et pater, ostendit duos esse quos aequat et iungit. adeo addit etiam multa se opera a patre ostendisse, quorum nihil lapidari mereretur. et ne putarent ideo se illum lapidare debere quasi se deum ipsum, id est patrem, voluisset intellegi quia dixerat Ego et pater unum sumus, qua filium dei deum ostendens, non qua ipsum deum, Si in lege, inquit, scriptum est, Ego dixi Vos dii estis, et non potest solvi scriptura, quem pater sanctificavit et misit in mundum vos eum blasphemare dicitis quia dixerat, Filius dei sum? si non facio opera patris mei, nolite credere; si vero facio et mihi credere non vultis, vel propter opera credite, et scitote quod ego in patre sim et pater in me. per opera ergo erit pater in filio et filius in patre, et ita per opera intellegimus unum esse patrem ⟨et filium⟩. adeo totum hoc perseverabat inducere, ut duo tamen crederentur in una virtute, quia aliter filius credi non posset nisi duo crederentur.

23. Post haec autem Mar*th*a filium dei eum confessa non magis erravit quam Petrus et Nathanael: quanquam et si errasset statim didicisset. ecce enim ad suscitandum fratrem eius a mortuis ad caelum et ad patrem dominus suspiciens, Pater, inquit

4 inquit *supplendum censui: cetera habent PM*: qui maior est omnibus mihi dedit *F*.
9 dicit *suppl. K.*
11 videtur etc. *ita fere pungenda docuit Eng.*
28 et filium *add. Urs.*
31 Martha *Pam.*: Maria *libri* (*et forsan ipse Septimius*).

utique filius, gratias ago tibi quod me semper exaudias; propter istas turbas circumstantes dixi, ut credant quod tu me miseris. sed et in conturbatione animae: Et quid dicam? pater, salvum me fac de ista hora? atquin propter hoc veni in istam horam; verum, pater, glorifica nomen tuum. in quo erat filius: Ego, inquit, veni in patris mei nomine. inde—scilicet suffecerat filii ad patrem vox—ecce ex abundantia respondet de caelo pater filio contestatus, Hic est filius meus dilectus in quo bene sensi, audite illum: ita et in isto, Glorificavi, et glorificabo rursus. quot personae tibi videntur, perversissime Praxea, nisi quot et voces? habes filium in terris, habes patrem in caelis. non est separatio ista, sed dispositio divina. ceterum scimus deum etiam intra abyssos esse et ubique consistere, sed vi et potestate: filium quoque, ut individuum, cum ipso ubique. tamen in ipsa oeconomia pater voluit filium in terris haberi, se vero in caelis. quo et ipse filius suspiciens et orabat et postulabat a patre quo et nos erectos docebat orare, Pater noster qui es in caelis, cum sit et ubique. hanc sedem suam voluit pater: ⟨Caelum, inquit, mihi thronus. hinc et⟩ minoravit filium modico citra angelos ad terram dimittendo, gloria tamen et honore coronaturus illum in caelos resumendo. haec iam praestabat illi dicens, Et glorificavi et glorificabo. postulat filius de terris, pater promittit a caelis. quid mendacem facis et patrem et filium? si aut pater de caelis loquebatur ad filium cum ipse esset filius apud terras, aut filius ad patrem precabatur cum ipse esset *pater* apud caelos, quale est ut filius item postularet a semetipso postulando a patre si filius erat pater, iterum pater sibi ipse promitteret promittendo filio si pater erat? ut sic duos divisos diceremus quomodo iactitatis, tolerabilius erat duos divisos quam unum deum versipellem praedicare. itaque ad istos nunc dominus pronuntiavit, Non propter me ista vox venit sed propter vos, ut credant et hi et patrem et filium in suis quemque nominibus et personis et locis. sed adhuc exclamat Iesus et dicit, Qui credit in me, non in me credit sed in eum credit qui me misit, quia per filium in patrem creditur et auctoritas credendi filio pater est: Et qui conspicit me conspicit eum qui me misit: quomodo? quoniam

6 inde etc. *ita punxi.*
8 contestatus *ego*: contestatur *libri*: contestaturus *Oeh.*
18 *ita fere scribendum indicavit K*: voluit pater: minoravit *PM*: voluit pater mihi thronus minoravit *F.*
25 pater *K*: filius *PMF.*

scilicet, A memetipso non sum locutus, sed qui me misit pater ipse mihi mandatum dedit quid dicam et quid loquar—Dominus enim dat mihi linguam disciplinae ad cognoscendum quando oporteat dicere—sermonem quem ego loquor, sicut mihi pater dixit ita et loquor. haec quomodo dicta sunt, evangelizator et utique tam carus discipulus Ioannes magis quam Praxeas noverat: ideoque ipse de suo sensu, Ante autem sollemnitatem paschae, inquit, sciens Iesus omnia sibi tradita a patre esse, et se ex deo esse et ad deum vadere. sed Praxeas ipsum vult patrem de semetipso exisse et ad semetipsum abisse, ut diabolus in cor Iudae non filii traditionem sed patris ipsius inmiserit: nec diabolo bene nec haeretico, quia nec in filio bono suo diabolus operatus est traditionem. filius enim traditus est dei qui erat in filio hominis, sicut scriptura subiungit: Nunc glorificatus est filius hominis et deus glorificatus est in illo. quis deus? utique non pater, sed sermo patris qui erat in filio hominis, id est in carne: in qua et glorificatus iam, virtute vero et sermone, et ante Iesu*s*, Et deus, inquit, glorifica*b*it illum in semetipso—id est pater filium, quem in semetipso habens etsi porrectum ad terram, mox per resurrectionem ⟨glorificavit⟩ morte devicta.

24. Erant plane qui et tunc non intellegerent: quoniam et Thomas aliquamdiu incredulus, Domine, inquit, non scimus quo eas, et quomodo viam novimus? et Iesus, Ego sum via, veritas et vita; nemo venit ad patrem nisi per me; si cognovissetis me cognovissetis et patrem; sed abhinc nostis illum et vidistis illum. et pervenimus iam ad Philippum, qui spe excitatus videndi patris nec intellegens quomodo visum patrem audisset, Ostende, inquit, nobis patrem, et sufficit nobis: et dominus, Philippe, tanto tempore vobiscum sum et non cognovistis me? quem dicit cognosci ab illis debuisse ⟨se⟩? hoc enim solum discuti oportet. quasi patrem an quasi filium? si quasi patrem, doceat Praxeas tanto tempore Christum cum eis conversatum patrem aliquando non dico intellegi verum vel aestimari potuisse. nobis omnes scripturae et veteres Christum dei et novae filium dei praefiniunt. hoc et retro praedicabatur, hoc et ab ipso Christo pronuntiabatur, immo iam et ab ipso patre coram de caelis filium

2 *sqq.* quid loquar, etc. *ita fere pungendum indicavit K.*
17 Iesus *Jun.*: Iesum *PMF.*
18 glorificabit *Jun.*: glorificavit *PMF.*
20 glorificavit *suppl. Urs.*
30 se *supplendum docuit Eng.*

profitente et filium glorificante: Hic est filius meus; et, Glorificavi et glorificabo. hoc et a discipulis credebatur, hoc et a Iudaeis non credebatur: hoc se volens credi ab illis omni hora patrem nominabat et patrem praeferebat et patrem honorabat. si ita est, ergo non patrem tanto tempore secum conversatum ignoraverant sed filium: et dominus, eum se ignorari exprobrans quem ignoraverant, eum utique agnosci volebat quem tanto non agnosci tempore exprobraverat, id est filium. et apparere iam potest quomodo dictum sit, Qui me videt videt et patrem: scilicet quo et supra, Ego et pater unum sumus. quare? quia, Ego ex deo exivi et veni; et, Ego sum via, nemo ad patrem venit nisi per me; et, Nemo ad me venit nisi pater eum adduxerit; et, Omnia mihi pater tradidit; et, Sicut pater vivificat, ita et filius; et, Si me cognovistis et patrem cognovistis. secundum haec enim vicarium se patris ostenderat, per quem pater et videretur in factis et audiretur in verbis et cognosceretur in filio facta et verba patris administrante: quia invisibilis pater, quod et Philippus didicerat in lege et meminisse debuerat—Deum nemo videbit et vivet. et ideo suggillatur patrem videre desiderans quasi visibilem, et instruitur visibilem eum in filio fieri ex virtutibus non ex personae repraesentatione. denique si patrem eundem filium vellet intellegi dicendo, Qui me videt patrem videt, quomodo subicit, Non credis quia ego in patre et pater in me? debuerat enim subiunxisse, Non credis quia ego sum pater? aut quo exaggeravit, si non illud manifestavit quod voluerat intellegi, se scilicet filium esse? porro dicendo, Non credis quia ego in patre et pater in me, propterea potius exaggeravit ne, quia dixerat, Qui me vidit et patrem vidit, pater existimaretur: quod nunquam existimari se voluit, qui semper se filium et a patre venisse profitebatur. igitur et manifestam fecit duarum personarum coniunctionem, ne pater seorsum quasi visibilis in conspectu desideraretur et ut filius repraesentator patris haberetur. et nihilominus hoc quoque interpretatus est, quomodo pater esset in filio et filius in patre: Verba, inquit, quae ego loquor vobis non sunt mea—utique quia patris—pater autem manens in me facit opera. per opera ergo virtutum et verba doctrinae manens in filio pater, per ea videtur per quae manet et per eum in quo manet, ex hoc ipso apparente proprietate utriusque personae dum dicit, Ego sum in patre et pater in me. atque adeo Credite ait. quid? me patrem esse? non puto scriptum esse, sed, Quia ego in patre et pater in me, si quo minus vel propter opera credite, ea utique opera per quae pater in filio non visu sed sensu videbatur.

25. Post Philippum et totam substantiam quaestionis istius, quae in finem evangelii perseverant in eodem genere sermonis, quo pater et filius in sua proprietate distinguuntur. paracletum quoque a patre se postulaturum, cum ascendisset ad patrem, et missurum repromittit, et quidem alium. sed iam praemisimus quomodo alium. ceterum, De meo sumet, inquit, sicut ipse de patris. ita connexus patris in filio et filii in paracleto tres efficit cohaerentes alterum ex altero. qui tres unum sunt, non unus, quomodo dictum est, Ego et pater unum sumus, ad substantiae unitatem non ad numeri singularitatem. percurre adhuc, et invenies quem patrem credis vi*tem* patris dictum et patrem agricolam, uti que*m* in terra tu putas fuisse hunc rursus in caelis a filio agnosci cum illuc respiciens discipulos suos patri tradidit. sed etsi in isto evangelio non est revelatum, Deus meus ad quid me dereliquisti? et, Pater in tuis manibus depono spiritum meum, tamen post resurrectionem et devictae gloriam mortis, exposita necessitate omnis humilitatis, cum iam patrem se posset ostendere tam fideli feminae, ex dilectione non ex curiositate nec ex incredulitate Thomae tangere eum adgressae, Ne, inquit, contigeris me, nondum ascendi ad patrem meum, vade autem ad fratres meos (quin et in hoc filium ostendit, filios enim appellasset illos si pater fuisset) et dices eis, Ascendo ad patrem meum et patrem vestrum, deum meum et deum vestrum. pater ad patrem et deus ad deum? an filius ad patrem et sermo ad deum? ipsa quoque clausula evangelii propter quid consignat haec scripta nisi, Ut credatis, inquit, Iesum Christum filium dei? igitur quaecunque ex his putaveris ad demonstrationem eiusdem patris et filii proficere tibi posse, adversus definitivam evangelii sententiam niteris: non ideo enim scripta sunt ut patrem credas Iesum Christum, sed ut filium.

26. Propter unum Philippi sermonem et domini responsionem ad eum videmur Ioannis evangelium decucurrisse, ne tot manifeste pronuntiata et ante et postea unus sermo subvertat, secundum

4 perseverant *PMF*: perseverat *Latinius* (*perperam*).
13 vitem *K*: vice *PMF* (*manifesto errore*).
14 uti quem *edit. Leopoldi*: utique *PMF*.

omnia potius quam adversus omnia, etiam adversus suos sensus, interpretandus. ceterum ut alia evangelia non interponam quae nativitate dominica fidem confirmant, sufficit eum qui nasci habebat ex virgine ab ipso annuntiari angelo filium dei determinatum: Spiritus dei superveniet in te et virtus altissimi obumbrabit te, propterea quod nascetur ex te sanctum vocabitur filius dei. volent quidem et hic argumentari, sed veritas praevalebit. nempe, inquiunt, filius dei deus est, et virtus altissimi altissimus est: nec pudet illos inicere quod, si esset, scriptum fuisset. quem enim verebatur ut non aperte pronuntiaret, Deus superveniet et altissimus obumbrabit te? dicens autem, Spiritus dei, etsi spiritus de*us*, tamen non directo deum nominans portionem totius intellegi voluit quae cessura erat in filii nomen. hic spiritus dei idem erit sermo. sicut enim Ioanne dicente, Sermo caro factus est, spiritum quoque intellegimus in mentione sermonis, ita et hic sermonem quoque agnoscimus in nomine spiritus. nam et spiritus substantia est sermonis et sermo operatio spiritus, et duo unum sunt. ceterum alium Ioannes profitebitur carnem factum, alium angelus carnem futurum, si non et spiritus sermo est et sermo spiritus. sicut ergo sermo dei non est ipse cuius est, ita nec spiritus, etsi deus dictus est, non tamen ipse est cuius est dictus. nulla res alicuius ipsa est cuius est. plane cum quid ex ipso est, et sic eius est dum ex ipso sit, potest tale quid esse quale et ipse ex quo est et cuius est: et ideo spiritus deus et sermo deus, quia ex deo, non tamen ipse ex quo est. quod*si spiritus* dei, tamquam substantiva res, non erit ipse deus sed hactenus deus qua ex ipsius dei substantia, qu*a* et substantiva res est et ut portio aliqua totius, multo magis virtus altissimi non erit ipse altissimus, quia nec substantiva res est quod est spiritus, sicut nec sapientia nec providentia: et haec enim substantiae non sunt sed accidentia uniuscuiusque substantiae. virtus spiritui accidit, nec ipsa erit spiritus. his itaque rebus, quodcunque sunt, spiritu dei et sermone et virtute, conlatis in virginem, quod de ea nascitur filius dei est. hoc se et in istis evangeliis ipse testatur statim a puero:

4 annuntiari *PMF*: annuntiali *K* (*forsan recte*)

8 *post* filius dei deus est *lacunam indicavit K tanquam exciderit* et spiritus dei deus est (*forsan recte*).

12 etsi spiritus deus *ego*: etsi spiritus dei *PMF*: etsi spiritus dei deus *Urs.*

21 etsi deus dictus est *libri et editores*: etsi dei dictus est *K* (*forsan recte*).

25 quodsi spiritus dei *ego*: quod deus dei *PMF*: quodsi deus dei *Urs.*

27 qua et *Urs.*: quae et *libri.*

Non scitis, inquit, quod in patris mei me esse oportet? hoc et satanas eum in temptationibus novit: Si filius dei es. hoc et exinde daemonia confitentur: Scimus qui sis, filius dei. patrem et ipse adorat. Christum se dei a Petro agnitum non negat. insultans in spiritu ad patrem, Confiteor, inquit, tibi pater quod absconderis haec a sapientibus. hic quoque patrem nemini notum nisi filio affirmat, et patris filium confessurum confessores et negaturum negatores suos apud patrem, inducens parabolam filii, non patris, in vineam missi post aliquot servos et occisi a malis rusticis et a patre defensi, ignorans et ipse diem et horam ultimam soli patri notam, disponens regnum discipulis quomodo et sibi dispositum dicit a patre, habens potestatem legiones angelorum postulandi ad auxilium a patre si vellet, exclamans quod se deus reliquisset, in patris manibus spiritum ponens, et post resurrectionem spondens missurum se discipulis promissionem patris, et novissime mandans ut tinguerent in patrem et filium et spiritum sanctum, non in unum: nam nec semel sed ter, ad singula nomina in personas singulas, tinguimur.

27. Et quid ego in tam manifestis morabor, cum ea aggredi debeam de quibus manifesta obumbrare quaerunt? undique enim obducti distinctione patris et filii, quam manente coniunctione disponimus ut solis et radii et fontis et fluvii, per individuum tamen numerum duorum et trium, aliter eam ad suam nihilominus sententiam interpretari conantur, ut aeque in una persona utrumque distinguant, patrem et filium, dicentes filium carnem esse, id est hominem id est Iesum, patrem autem spiritum, id est deum id est Christum. et qui unum eundemque contendunt patrem et filium iam incipiunt dividere illos potius quam unare. si enim alius est Iesus alius Christus, alius erit filius alius pater, quia filius Iesus et pater Christus. talem monarchiam apud Valentinum fortasse didicerunt, duos facere Iesum et Christum. sed et haec iniectio eorum ex praetractatis iam retusa est, quod sermo dei vel spiritus dei et virtus altissimi dictus sit quem patrem faciunt: non enim ips*e* sunt cuius dicuntur, sed ex ipso et ipsius. et aliter tamen in isto capitulo revincentur. ecce, inquiunt, ab angelo praedicatum est, Propterea quod nascetur sanctum vocabitur filius dei: caro itaque nata est, caro itaque erit filius dei. immo

25 dicentes *MF*: discentes *P vulgo* (*manifesto errore*).
34 ipse *K*: ipsae *PMF*.

de spiritu dei dictum est. certe enim de spiritu sancto virgo concepit, et quod concepit id peperit. id ergo nasci habebat quod erat conceptum et pariundum, id est spiritus, cuius et vocabitur nomen Emmanuel, quod est interpretatum Nobiscum deus. caro autem deus non est ut de illa dictum sit, Vocabitur sanctum filius dei, sed ille qui in ea natus est deus, de quo et psalmus, Quoniam deus homo natus est in illa et aedificavit eam voluntate patris. quis deus in ea natus? sermo et spiritus qui cum sermone de patris voluntate natus est. igitur sermo in carne: dum et de hoc quaerendum, quomodo sermo caro sit factus, utrumne quasi transfiguratus in carne an indutus carnem. immo indutus. ceterum deum inmutabilem et informabilem credi necesse est, ut aeternum. transfiguratio autem interemptio est pristini: omne enim quodcunque transfiguratur in aliud desinit esse quod fuerat et incipit esse quod non erat. deus autem neque desinit esse neque aliud potest esse. sermo autem deus, et sermo domini manet in aevum, perseverando scilicet in sua forma. quem si non capit configurari, consequens est ut sic caro factus intellegatur dum fit in carne et manifestatur et videtur et contrectatur per carnem, quia et cetera sic accipi exigunt. si enim sermo ex transfiguratione et demutatione substantiae caro factus est, una iam erit substantia Iesus ex duabus, ex carne et spiritu, mixtura quaedam, ut electrum ex auro et argento, et incipit nec aurum esse, id est spiritus, neque argentum, id est caro, dum alterum altero mutatur et tertium quid efficitur. neque ergo deus erit Iesus; sermo enim desiit esse, qui caro factus est: neque homo caro; caro enim non proprie est, quia sermo fuit. ita ex utroque neutrum est: aliud longe tertium est quam utrumque. sed enim invenimus illum directo et deum et hominem expositum, ipso hoc psalmo suggerente, Quoniam deus homo natus est in illa aedificavit eam voluntate patris: certe usquequaque filium dei et filium hominis, cum deum et hominem sine dubio secundum utramque substantiam in sua proprietate distantem, quia neque sermo aliud quam deus neque caro aliud quam homo. sic et apostolus de utraque eius substantia docet: Qui factus est, inquit, ex semine David—hic erit homo et filius hominis; Qui definitus est filius dei secundum spiritum—hic erit deus, et sermo dei filius: videmus duplicem statum, non confusum sed coniunctum, in una persona deum et hominem Iesum. de Christo autem differo. et adeo salva est utriusque proprietas substantiae, ut et spiritus res suas egerit in illo, id est virtutes et opera et signa, et caro passiones suas functa sit, esuriens sub diabolo, sitiens sub Samaritide, flens Lazarum, anxia usque ad mortem, denique et mortua est. quodsi tertium quid esset ex utroque confusum, ut electrum, non tam distincta documenta parerent utriusque substantiae; sed et spiritus carnalia et caro spiritalia egisset ex translatione, aut neque carnalia neque spiritalia sed tertiae alicuius formae ex confusione: immo aut sermo mortuus esset aut caro mortua non esset, si sermo conversus esset in carnem; aut caro enim immortalis fuisset aut sermo mortalis. sed quia substantiae ambae in statu suo quaeque distincte agebant, ideo illis et operae et exitus sui occurrerunt. disce igitur cum Nicodemo quia quod in carne natum est caro est, et quod de spiritu spiritus est. neque caro spiritus fit neque spiritus caro: in uno plane esse possunt. ex his Iesus constitit, ex carne homo ex spiritu deus, quem tunc angelus ex ea parte qua spiritus erat dei filium pronuntiavit, servans carni filium hominis dici. sic et apostolus etiam dei et hominum appellans sequestrem utriusque substantiae confirmavit. novissime, qui filium dei carnem interpretaris, exhibe qui sit filius hominis: aut numquid spiritus erit? sed spiritum patrem ipsum vis haberi, quia deus spiritus: quasi non et dei spiritus, sicut et sermo deus, et dei sermo.

28. Itaque Christum facis patrem, stultissime, qui nec ipsam vim inspicias nominis huius, si tamen nomen est Christus et non appellatio potius: unctus enim significatur. unctus autem non magis nomen est quam vestitus, quam calceatus, accidens nomini res. an tu, si ex aliquo argumento vestitus quoque vocaretur Iesus, quomodo Christus ab unctionis sacramento, aeque Iesum filium dei diceres, vestitum vero patrem crederes? nunc de Christo. si pater Christus est pater unctus est, et utique ab alio: aut si a semetipso, proba. sed non ita docent Acta Apostolorum in illa exclamatione ecclesiae ad deum, Convenerunt enim universi in ista civitate adversus sanctum filium tuum quem unxisti, Herodes et Pilatus cum nationibus. ita et filium dei Iesum contestati sunt et filium a patre unctum: ergo Iesus idem erit Christus qui a patre unctus est, non pater qui filium unxit. sic et Petrus: Firmissime itaque cognoscat omnis domus Israel quod et dominum et Christum, id est unctum, fecerit eum deus, hunc Iesum quem vos crucifixistis. Ioannes autem etiam

mendacem notat eum qui negaverit Iesum esse Christum, contra de deo natum omnem qui crediderit Iesum esse Christum: propter quod et hortatur ut credamus nomini filii eius Iesu Christi, ut scilicet communio sit nobis cum patre et filio eius Iesu Christo. sic et Paulus ubique deum patrem ponit et dominum nostrum Iesum Christum: cum ad Romanos scribit, gratias agit deo per dominum nostrum Iesum Christum; cum ad Galatas, non ab hominibus se apostolum praefert nec per hominem, sed per Iesum Christum et deum patrem. et habes ⟨per⟩ totum instrumentum eius quae in hunc modum pronuntiant et duos proponunt deum patrem et dominum nostrum Iesum Christum filium patris, et Iesum ipsum esse Christum, in altero quoque nomine dei filium. nam exinde eo iure quo utrumque nomen unius est, id est dei filii, etiam alterum sine altero eiusdem est: et sive Iesus tantummodo positum est, intellegitur et Christus quia Iesus unctus est, sive solummodo Christus, idem est et Iesus quia unctus est Iesus. quorum nominum alterum est proprium quod ab angelo impositum est, alterum accidens quod ab unctione convenit, dum tamen Christus filius sit, non pater. postremo quam caecus est qui nec in Christi nomine intellegit alium deum portendi si Christi nomen patri adscribat. si enim Christus pater deus est qui dicit, Ascendo ad patrem meum et patrem vestrum et deum meum et deum vestrum, utique alium patrem super se et deum ostendit. si item pater Christus est, alius est qui solidat tonitruum et condit spiritum et adnuntiat in homines Christum suum. et si Adstiterunt reges terrae et archontes congregati sunt in unum adversus ⟨dominum et adversus⟩ Christum ipsius, alius erit dominus contra cuius Christum congregati sunt reges et archontes. et si Haec dicit dominus domino meo Christo, alius erit dominus qui loquitur ad patrem Christ*um*. et cum apostolus scribit, Ut deus domini nostri Iesu Christi det vobis spiritum sapientiae et agnitionis, alius erit deus Christi Iesu, charismatum spiritalium largitor. certe, ne per omnia evagemur, qui suscitavit Christum, suscitaturus [est] et mortalia corpora nostra, tanquam alius erit suscitator quam pater mortuus et pater suscitatus, si Christus qui est mortuus pater est.

9 per *suppl. K*: totum instrumentum *PMFR*^{1}: tota instrumenta *R*^{3} *vulgo*.
11 deum patrem *libri*: deum et patrem *R*^{1}.
27 dominum et adversus *suppl. K.*
30 Christum *K*: Christi *libri*.
34 est *secl. K.*
35 tanquam *PMF*: iamque *Rig.*

29. Obmutescat, obmutescat ista blasphemia. sufficiat Christum filium dei mortuum dici, et hoc quia ita scriptum est. nam et apostolus, non sine onere pronuntians Christum mortuum, adicit Secundum scripturas, ut duritiam pronuntiationis scripturarum auctoritate molliret et scandalum auditori everteret. quanquam cum duae substantiae censeantur in Christo Iesu, divina et humana, constet autem immortalem esse divinam, ut mortalem quae humana sit, apparet quatenus eum mortuum dicat, id est qua carnem et hominem et filium hominis, non qua spiritum et sermonem et dei filium. dicendo denique, Christus mortuus est—id est unctus—id quod unctum est mortuum ostendit, id est carnem. ergo, inquis, et nos eadem ratione dicentes qua vos filium non blasphemamus in dominum deum; non enim ex divina sed ex humana substantia mortuum dicimus. atquin blasphematis, non tantum quia mortuum dicitis patrem sed et quia crucifixum. maledictio*ne* enim crucifixi quae ex lege in filium competit, quia Christus pro nobis maledictio factus est, non pater, Christum in patrem convertentes in patrem blasphematis. nos autem, dicentes Christum crucifixum, non maledicimus illum sed maledictum legis referimus, quia nec apostolus hoc dicens blasphemavit. sicut autem de quo quid capit dici sine blasphemia dicitur, ita quod non capit blasphemia est si dicatur. ergo nec compassus est pater filio. scilicet directam blasphemiam in patrem veriti, diminui eam hoc modo sperant, concedentes iam patrem et filium duos esse, si filius sic quidem patitur pater vero compatitur. stulti et in hoc. quid est enim compati quam cum alio pati? porro si impassibilis pater utique et incompassibilis; aut si compassibilis utique passibilis. nihil ei vel hoc timore tuo praestas. times dicere passibilem quem dicis compassibilem. tam autem incompassibilis pater est quam impassibilis etiam filius ex ea condicione qua deus est. sed quomodo filius passus est si non compassus est et pater? separatur a filio, non a deo. nam et fluvius si aliqua turbulentia contaminatur, quanquam una substantia de fonte decurrat nec secernatur a fonte, tamen fluvii iniuria non pertinebit ad fontem; et licet aqua fontis sit quae patiatur in fluvio, dum non in fonte patitur sed in fluvio non fons patitur sed fluvius qui ex fonte est. ita et

16 maledictione R^3 *vulgo*: maledictio $PMFR^1$: maledictionem *K qui postea* Christum *omittit*.

22 quod *PMF*: de quo *K* (*forsan recte*).

spiritus dei qui pati possit in filio? quia non in patre pateretur sed in filio, pater passus non videretur? sed sufficit nihil spiritum dei passum suo nomine: quia si quid passus est in filio ⟨possibile⟩ quidem erat ut pater cum filio pateretur in carne. qui*n* hoc retractatum, nec quisquam negabit: quando nec nos pati pro deo possumus nisi spiritus dei sit in nobis, qui et loquitur de nobis quae sunt confessionis, non ipse tamen patiens sed pati posse praestans.

30. Alioquin si ultra perg*es*, potero tibi durius respondere et te cum ipsius domini pronuntiatione committere, uti dicam, quid de isto quaeris? habės ipsum exclamantem in passione, Deus meus, deus meus, ut quid me dereliquisti? ergo aut filius patiebatur a patre derelictus, et pater passus non est qui filium dereliquit: aut si pater erat qui patiebatur, ad quem deum exclamabat? sed haec vox carnis et animae, id est hominis, non sermonis nec spiritus, id est non dei, propterea emissa est ut impassibilem deum ostenderet qui sic filium dereliquit dum hominem eius tradidit in mortem. hoc et apostolus sensit scribens, Si pater filio non pepercit. hoc et Esaias prior pronuntiavit: Et dominus eum tradidit pro delictis nostris. sic reliquit dum non parcit, sic reliquit dum tradit. ceterum non reliquit pater filium, in cuius manibus filius spiritum suum posuit. denique posuit, et statim obiit: spiritu enim manente in carne caro omnino mori non potest. ita relinqui a patre mori fuit filio. filius igitur et moritur et resuscitatur a patre secundum scripturas. filius ascendit in superiora caelorum, qui et descendit in interiora terrae. hic sedet ad dexteram patris, non pater ad suam. hunc videt Stephanus, cum lapidatur, adhuc stantem ad dexteram dei, ut exinde sessurum donec ponat illi pater omnes inimicos sub pedibus suis. hic et venturus est rursus super nubes caeli talis qualis et ascendit. hic interim acceptum a patre munus effudit spiritum sanctum, tertium nomen divinitatis et tertium gradum maiestatis, unius praedicatorem monarchiae sed et oeconomiae interpretatorem si quis sermones novae prophetiae eius admiserit, et deductorem omnis veritatis quae est in patre et filio et spiritu sancto secundum Christianum sacramentum.

1-4 *locum paene conclamatum ita punxi et* possible *addere ausus sum.*
4 quin *scripsi*: quia *libri.* retractatum *G*: retractatus *PMF.*
9 perges *K*: pergens *libri*: pergas R^3 *vulgo.*

31. Ceterum Iudaicae fidei ista res, sic unum deum credere ut filium adnumerare ei nolis et post filium spiritum. quid enim erit inter nos et illos nisi differentia ista? quod opus evangelii, quae est substantia novi testamenti statuens legem et prophetas usque ad Ioannem, si non exinde pater et filius et spiritus, tres crediti, unum deum sistunt? sic deus voluit novare sacramentum ut nove unus crederetur per filium et spiritum, ut coram iam deus in suis propriis nominibus et personis cognosceretur qui et retro per filium et spiritum praedicatus non intellegebatur. viderint igitur antichristi, qui negant patrem et filium: negant enim patrem dum eundem filium dicunt, et negant filium dum eundem patrem credunt, dando illis quae non sunt, auferendo quae sunt. qui vero confessus fuerit Christum filium dei, non patrem, deus in illo manet et ipse in deo. nos credimus testimonio dei quo testatus est de filio suo: Qui filium non habet, nec vitam habet. non habet autem filium qui eum alium quam filium credit.

14 nos *PM*: non *FR* (*manifesto errore*).

AGAINST PRAXEAS

1. In divers ways has the devil shown hostility to the Truth. At times he has tried to shake it by pretending to defend it. He is the champion of the one Lord, the Almighty, the creator of the world, so that he may make a heresy out of the unity. He says that the Father himself came down into the virgin, himself was born of her, himself suffered, in short himself is Jesus Christ. The serpent has forgotten himself: for when he tempted Jesus Christ after the baptism of John it was as Son of God that he attacked him, being assured that God has a son at least from those very scriptures out of which he was then constructing the temptation : *If thou art the Son of God, command that these stones be made bread*[1]*:* again, *If thou art the Son of God cast thyself down from hence, for it is written that he*—the Father, of course—*hath given his angels charge concerning thee, that in their hands they should bear thee up, lest in any place thou dash thy foot against a stone.*[2] Or will he accuse the gospels of lying, and say, "Let Matthew and Luke see to it: I for my part approached God himself, I tempted the Almighty hand to hand: that was the reason for my approach, that was the reason for the temptation: otherwise, if it had been ⟨only⟩ God's son, perhaps I should not have demeaned myself ⟨to tempt⟩ him"? Nay but he himself rather is a liar from the beginning,[3] and so is any man whom he has suborned with his own ⟨coin⟩, like Praxeas. For this person was the first to import to Rome out of Asia this kind of wrong-headedness—a man generally of restless character, and moreover puffed up with boasting of his confessorship on account of nothing more than a mere short discomfort of imprisonment: though even if he had given his body to be burned he would have profited nothing, since he had not the love of God,[4] whose spiritual gifts he also drove out by assault. For at that time the bishop of Rome was on the point of recognising the prophecies of Montanus and Prisca and Maximilla, and as a result of that recognition was offering peace to the churches of Asia and Phrygia; but this man, by false assertions concerning the prophets themselves and their churches, and by insistence on the decisions of the bishop's predecessors, forced him both to recall the letters of peace already

[1] Matt. 4. 3.
[2] Matt. 4. 6 : Ps. 91. 11, 12.
[3] Cf. John 8. 44.
[4] 1 Cor. 13. 3.

issued and to desist from his project of receiving the spiritual gifts. Thus Praxeas at Rome managed two pieces of the devil's business: he drove out prophecy and introduced heresy: he put to flight the Paraclete and crucified the Father. Praxean tares [1] were sown above ⟨the wheat⟩ and had germinated here also, while many were asleep in simplicity of doctrine. Thereafter they were brought to light, by whom God would, and seemed even to have been rooted up. In fact the teacher gave security for amendment by return to his former opinions, and his bond remains in the custody of the natural men,[2] in whose presence the transaction was then carried out. After that, silence. I for my part was subsequently separated from the natural men by my acknowledgement and defence of the Paraclete. But those tares had at that time scattered their seed everywhere, and so for a time it lay hid, deceptively dissembling its life, and has now burst forth anew. But it shall also be plucked up anew, if the Lord will, in the time now at my disposal: if not, then in its due time all counterfeit grain will be gathered and, along with other offences, be burned up in unquenchable fire.

2. And so, after ⟨all this⟩ time, a Father who was born, a Father who suffered, God himself the Lord Almighty, is preached as Jesus Christ. We however as always, the more so now as better equipped through the Paraclete, that leader into all truth,[3] believe (as these do) in one only God, yet subject to this dispensation (which is our word for "economy") that the one only God has also a Son, his Word who has proceeded from himself, by whom all things were made and without whom nothing has been made:[4] that this ⟨Son⟩ was sent by the Father into the virgin and was born of her both man and God, Son of man and Son of God, and was named Jesus Christ: that he suffered, died, and was buried, according to the scriptures,[5] and, having been raised up by the Father and taken back into heaven, sits at the right hand of the Father[6] and will come to judge the quick and the dead[7]: and that thereafter he, according to his promise,[8] sent from the Father the Holy Spirit the Paraclete, the sanctifier of the faith of those who believe in the Father and the Son and the Holy Spirit. That this Rule has come down from the beginning

[1] Matt. 13. 24 ff.
[2] 1 Cor. 2. 14.
[3] John 16. 13.
[4] John 1. 1-3.
[5] 1 Cor. 15. 3, 4.
[6] Mark 16. 19.
[7] Acts 10. 42.
[8] John 16. 7.

of the Gospel, even before all former heretics, not to speak of Praxeas of yesterday, will be proved as well by the comparative lateness of all heretics as by the very novelty of Praxeas of yesterday. So equally against all heretics let it from now on be taken as already proven that whatever is earliest is true and whatever is later is counterfeit. Still, saving that demurrer, yet everywhere, for the offensive and defensive equipment of certain persons, place must be granted also for further discussions, if for no other reason lest each several piece of wrong-headedness seem to be condemned not after examination but by previous judgement—and in particular this one which supposes itself to possess truth unadulterated while it thinks it impossible to believe in one God unless it says that both Father and Son and Holy Spirit are one and the same: as though the one ⟨God⟩ were not all ⟨these things⟩ in this way also, that they are all of the one, namely by unity of substance, while none the less is guarded the mystery of that economy which disposes the unity into trinity, setting forth Father and Son and Spirit as three, three however not in quality but in sequence, not in substance but in aspect, not in power but in ⟨its⟩ manifestation, yet of one substance and one quality and one power, seeing it is one God from whom those sequences and aspects and manifestations are reckoned out in the name of the Father and the Son and the Holy Spirit. How they admit of plurality without division the discussion will show as it proceeds.

3. For all the simple people, that I say not the thoughtless and ignorant (who are always the majority of the faithful), since the Rule of the Faith itself brings ⟨us⟩ over from the many gods of the world to the one only true God, not understanding that while they must believe in one only ⟨God⟩ yet they must believe in him along with his economy, shy at the economy. They claim that the plurality and ordinance of trinity is a division of unity—although a unity which derives from itself a trinity is not destroyed but administered by it. And so ⟨people⟩ put it about that by us two or even three ⟨gods⟩ are preached, while they, they claim, are worshippers of one God—as though unity irrationally summed up did not make heresy and trinity rationally counted out constitute truth. "We hold", they say, "to the monarchy": and even Latins so expressively frame the sound, and in so masterly a fashion, that you would think they understood monarchy as

well as they pronounce it: but while Latins are intent to shout out "monarchy", even Greeks refuse to understand the economy. But if I have gathered any small knowledge of both languages, I know that monarchy indicates neither more nor less than a single and sole empire, yet that monarchy because it belongs to one man does not for that reason make a standing rule that he whose it is may not have a son or must have made himself his own son or may not administer his monarchy by the agency of whom he will. Nay more, I say that no kingdom is in such a sense one man's own, in such a sense single, in such a sense a monarchy, as not to be administered also through those other closely related persons whom it has provided for itself as officers: and if moreover he whose the monarchy is has a son, it is not *ipso facto* divided, does not cease to be a monarchy, if the son also is assumed as partner in it, but it continues to belong in first instance to him by whom it is passed on to the son: and so long as it is his, that continues to be a monarchy which is jointly held by two who are so closely united. Therefore if also the divine monarchy is administered by the agency of so many legions and hosts of angels (as it is written, *Ten thousand times ten thousand stood before him and thousand thousands ministered unto him*),[1] yet has not therefore ceased to belong to one, so as to cease to be a monarchy because it has for its provincial governors so many thousand authorities, how should God be thought, in the Son and in the Holy Spirit occupying second and third place, while they are to such a degree conjoint of the Father's substance, to experience a division and a dispersion such as he does not experience in the plurality of all those angels, alien as they are from the Father's substance? Do you account provinces and family connexions and officials and the very forces and the whole trappings of empire to be the overthrow of it? You are wrong if you do. I prefer you to busy yourself about the meaning of a fact rather than the sound of a word. Overthrow of monarchy you should understand as ⟨taking place⟩ when there is superimposed another kingship of its own character and its own quality, and consequently hostile, when another god is introduced to oppose the Creator, as with Marcion, or many gods according to people like Valentinus and Prodicus: then is it for the overthrow of the monarchy when it is for the destruction of the Creator.

[1] Dan. 7. 10.

4. Yet how can I, who derive the Son from no alien ⟨source⟩, but from the Father's substance, ⟨who say⟩ he does nothing without the Father's will [1] and that he has received from the Father all authority [2]—how can I in the matter of the faith be destroying that monarchy which I say has been delivered by the Father to the Son and is conserved in the Son? Let this be taken to apply also to the third sequence, for I reckon the Spirit from nowhere else than from the Father through the Son. Beware therefore lest you rather are destroying the monarchy, who are overthrowing that ordinance and dispensation of it which consists in as many names as God would. But to such a degree does it abide in its own quality, though a trinity be introduced, that it has even to be restored to the Father by the Son, inasmuch as the apostle writes concerning the last end, *When he shall have delivered up the kingdom to the God and Father. For he must reign until* God *put all his enemies under his feet,*[3] evidently according to the psalm, *Sit thou at my right hand until I make all thine enemies the footstool of thy feet.*[4] *But when all things have been made subject to him*, except him *who hath subjected all things to him, then also* he *himself will be subjected to him who hath subjected all things to him, that God may be all things in all.*[5] We see then that the Son is not prejudicial to the monarchy, although today it is in the Son's hands, because it is both in its own quality in the Son's hands, and retaining its own quality will be restored to the Father by the Son. Thus no one will on this account destroy it by admitting a Son, when it is agreed both that it has been delivered to him by the Father and that sometime it is to be restored by him to the Father. By this one passage of the apostolic epistle we have already been able to show that Father and Son are two, besides ⟨by deduction⟩ from the names Father and Son, also from the fact that he who has delivered the kingdom and he to whom he has delivered it, as also he who has subjected it and he to whom he has subjected it, must of necessity be two.

5. But seeing they will have it that the two are one, so that the Father and the Son are to be considered identical, we must also examine the whole ⟨question⟩ concerning the Son, whether he is, and who he is, and in what manner he is, and thus the fact itself will establish its own legality by the advocacy of the scriptures

[1] John 5. 19. [2] Matt. 28. 18. [3] 1 Cor. 15. 24 ff.
[4] Ps. 110. 1. [5] 1 Cor. 15. 27, 28.

and the interpretations of them. Certain people affirm that in Hebrew Genesis begins, *In the beginning God made for himself a son.*[1] Against the ratification of this I am persuaded by other arguments from God's ordinance in which he was before the foundation of the world until the generation of the Son. For before all things God was alone, himself his own world and location and everything—alone however because there was nothing external beside him. Yet not even then was he alone: for he had with him that Reason which he had in himself—his own, of course. For God is rational, and reason is primarily in him, and thus from him are all things: and that Reason is his consciousness. This the Greeks call *Logos*, by which expression we also designate discourse: and consequently our people are already wont, through the artlessness of the translation, to say that *Discourse was in the beginning with God,*[2] though it would be more appropriate to consider Reason of older standing, seeing that God is [not] discursive from the beginning but is rational even before the beginning, and because discourse itself, having its ground in reason, shows reason to be prior as being its substance. Yet even so it makes no difference. For although God had not yet uttered his Discourse, he always had it within himself along with and in his Reason, while he silently thought out and ordained with himself the things which he was shortly to say by the agency of Discourse: for while thinking out and ordaining them in company of his Reason, he converted into Discourse that ⟨Reason⟩ which he was discussing in discourse. And that you may understand this the more easily, observe first from yourself, as from the image and likeness of God,[3] how you also have reason within yourself, who are a rational animal not only as having been made by a rational Creator but also as out of his substance having been made a living soul.[4] See how, when you by reason argue silently with yourself, this same action takes place within you, while reason accompanied by discourse meets you at every movement of your thought, at every impression of your consciousness: your every thought is discourse, your every consciousness is reason: you must perforce speak it in your mind, and while you speak it you experience as a partner in conversation that discourse which has in it this very reason by which you speak when you think in company of that ⟨discourse⟩ in speaking by means of

[1] Gen. 1. 1. [2] John 1. 1, 2. [3] Gen. 1. 26. [4] Gen. 2. 7.

which you think. So in a sort of way you have in you as a second ⟨person⟩ discourse by means of which you speak by thinking and by means of which you think by speaking: discourse itself is another ⟨than you⟩. How much more completely therefore does this action take place in God whose image and similitude you are authoritatively declared to be, that even while silent he has in himself reason, and in ⟨that⟩ reason discourse. So I have been able without rashness to conclude that even then, before the establishment of the universe, God was not alone, seeing he continually had in himself Reason, and in Reason Discourse, which he made another beside himself by activity within himself.

6. This function and this ordinance of the divine consciousness is in the scriptures also displayed under the name of Wisdom. For what is wiser than the Reason or Discourse of God? So listen also to Wisdom, established as a second person. First, *The Lord created me as the beginning of his ways for his works' sake, before he made the earth, before the mountains were set in their places; yea, before all the hills he begat me*[1]—establishing and begetting, of course, in his own consciousness. Afterwards observe her, by the fact of being separate, standing by him: *When he was preparing the heaven*, she says, *I was present with him, and as he made strong above the winds the clouds on high, and as he made safe the fountains of ⟨the earth⟩ which is under heaven, I was with him as a fellow-worker, I was she in whose presence he delighted; for daily did I delight in his person.* For when first God's will was to produce in their own substances and species those things which in company of Wisdom and Reason and Discourse he had ordained within himself, he first brought forth Discourse, which had within it its own inseparable Reason and Wisdom, so that the universe of things might come into existence by the agency of none other than him by whose agency they had been thought out and ordained, yea even already made as far as concerns the consciousness of God: for this ⟨only⟩ they lacked, to be openly also recognised and apprehended in their own species and substances.

7. At that point therefore Discourse also itself receives its manifestation and equipment, namely sound and voice, when God says, *Let there be light.*[2] This is the complete nativity of Discourse, when it comes forth from God: ⟨it was⟩ first established by him

[1] Prov. 8. 22 ff. [2] Gen. 1. 3.

for thought under the name of Wisdom—*The Lord established me as the beginning of his ways*[1]: then begotten for activity—*When he prepared the heaven I was present with him*[2]: thereafter causing him to be his Father by proceeding from whom he became Son, the first-begotten as begotten before all things,[3] the only-begotten as alone begotten out of God in a true sense from the womb of his heart, according as the Father himself testifies, *My heart hath disgorged a good Discourse*[4]: and to him thenceforth as he rejoices in his person ⟨the Father⟩ himself rejoicing ⟨says⟩, *Thou art my Son, this day have I begotten thee,*[5] and, *Before the daystar I begat thee.*[6] So also the Son in his own person, under the name of Wisdom, confesses the Father, *The Lord established me as the beginning of his ways for his works' sake, yea before the hills he begat me.*[7] For if in this place it appears that Wisdom says she was established by the Lord for the sake of his works and ways, but elsewhere it is revealed that by Discourse were all things made and without him was not anything made,[8] as also again *By the Discourse of the Lord were the heavens confirmed, and all their host by his Spirit*[9]—that Spirit of course which was present in Discourse—it is clear that it is one and the same function, now under the name of Wisdom, now under the designation of Discourse, which received the beginning of ways for God's works' sake, which confirmed the heaven, by which all things were made and without which nothing was made. And enough of that, for evidently under the name of Wisdom and of Reason and of the whole divine mind and spirit ⟨we are to understand⟩ Discourse, who became Son of God when by proceeding from him he was begotten. "So", you say, "you postulate that Discourse is a sort of substance, consisting of spirit and wisdom and reason." Certainly. For you refuse to consider him substantive in objectivity, as being a substance which is himself, that ⟨thus⟩ he may be seen to be an object and a person, and so may be capable, inasmuch as he is another beside God, of causing there to be two, the Father and the Son, God and the Word[10]: for what, you will say, is a word except voice and oral sound and (as the grammarians' tradition has it) smitten air intelligible in the hearing, for the rest an empty

[1] Prov. 8. 22. [2] Prov. 8. 27. [3] Col. 1. 15: John 1. 18.
[4] Ps. 45. 1. [5] Ps. 2. 7. [6] Ps. 110. 3.
[7] Prov. 8. 22. [8] John 1. 3. [9] Ps. 33. 6.
[10] From now onwards we translate *sermo*, which we have hitherto represented by "discourse", by its usual English equivalent, "the Word".

something, void and incorporal? But I affirm that from God nothing void and empty can have come forth—for he is not void and empty from whom it has been brought forth: and that that cannot lack substance which has proceeded from so great a substance and is the maker of such great substances—for he himself is the maker of things which were made through him. How can he be nothing without whom no thing was made, so that one void should have wrought solid things, and one empty full things, and one incorporal corporal things? For although at times something can be made which is the opposite of that whereby it is made, yet by what is empty and void nothing can be made. ⟨Can you describe as⟩ an empty and void object that Word of God whom scripture calls the Son, who also is designated God—*And the Word was with God and the Word was God*?[1] It is written, *Thou shalt not take the name of God for an empty thing.*[2] Certainly this is he who, *being in the form of God, thought it not robbery to be equal with God.*[3] In what form of God? Evidently in some form, not in none: for who will deny that God is body, although *God is a spirit*?[4] For spirit is body, of its own kind, in its own form. Moreover if those invisible things,[5] whatever they are, have in God's presence both their own body and their own shape by which they are visible to God alone, how much more will that which has been sent forth from his substance not be devoid of substance. Whatever therefore the substance of the Word was, that I call a Person, and for it I claim the name of Son: and while I acknowledge him as Son I maintain he is another beside the Father.

8. If anyone thinks that hereby I introduce some "projection", that is, prolation of one thing from another, as Valentinus does who produces æon from æon one after another, in the first place I shall say to you, "The Truth does not abstain from using that word and the fact and the origin represented by it, on the ground that heresy uses it: nay rather, heresy has taken over from the Truth that which it might build up into its own lie". Was the Word of God brought forth, or not? Meet me on that ground. If he was brought forth, acknowledge "projection" as the Truth understands it, and let heresy beware what it has copied from the

[1] John 1. 1. [2] Exod. 20. 7. [3] Phil. 2. 6.
[4] John 4. 24. [5] Rom. 1. 20.

Truth. The question now before us is who uses, and in what sense he uses, any fact and the term that denotes it. Valentinus secludes and separates his "projections" from their originator, and places them so far from him that an æon is ignorant of its father: at length it desires to know him and is unable, in fact it is almost consumed and dissolved into residuary substance. But with us the Son alone knows the Father,[1] and himself has declared the bosom of the Father,[2] and has both heard and seen all things in the Father's presence[3]: and whatsoever things he has been commanded by the Father, those he also speaks[4]: and has accomplished not his own will but the Father's,[5] which he knew intimately, yea from the beginning. For who knows the things which be in God, except the Spirit who is in him?[6] But the Word consists of spirit, and (so to speak) spirit is the body of the Word. Therefore the Word is always in the Father, as he says, *I am in the Father*[7]: and always with God, as it is written, *And the Word was with God*[8]: and never separate from the Father or other than the Father, because, *I and the Father are one.*[9] This will be the Truth's "projection", the guardian of unity, ⟨that projection⟩ by which we say that the Son was brought forth from the Father, but not made separate. For God brought forth the Word, as also the Paraclete teaches, as a root brings forth the ground shoot, and a spring the river, and the sun its beam: for these manifestations also are "projections" of those substances from which they proceed. You need not hesitate to say that the shoot is son of the root and the river son of the spring and the beam son of the sun, for every source is a parent and everything that is brought forth from a source is its offspring—and especially the Word of God, who also in an exact sense has received the name of Son: yet the shoot is not shut off from the root nor the river from the spring nor the beam from the sun, any more than the Word is shut off from God. Therefore according to the precedent of these examples I profess that I say that God and his Word, the Father and his Son, are two: for the root and the shoot are two things, but conjoined; and the spring and the river are two manifestations, but undivided; and the sun and its beam are two aspects, but they cohere. Everything that

[1] Matt. 11. 27.
[2] John 1. 18.
[3] John 8. 38.
[4] Cf. John 14. 31.
[5] John 6. 38.
[6] Cf. 1. Cor. 2. 11.
[7] John 14. 11.
[8] John 1. 1.
[9] John 10. 30.

proceeds from something must of necessity be another beside that from which it proceeds, but it is not for that reason separated ⟨from it⟩. But where there is a second ⟨one⟩ there are two, and where there is a third there are three. For the Spirit is third with God and ⟨his⟩ Son, as the fruit out of the shoot is third from the root, and the irrigation canal out of the river third from the spring, and the illumination point out of the beam third from the sun: yet in no respect is he alienated from that origin from which he derives his proper attributes. In this way the Trinity, proceeding by intermingled and connected degrees from the Father, in no respect challenges the monarchy, while it conserves the quality of the economy.

9. Remember at every point that I have professed this rule, by which I testify that Father and Son and Spirit are unseparated from one another, and in that case you will recognise what I say and in what sense I say it. For look now, I say that the Father is one, and the Son another, and the Spirit another (every unlearned or self-willed person takes this statement in bad part, as though it proclaimed diversity and because of diversity threatened a separation of Father and Son and Spirit: but I am bound to make it, so long as they maintain that Father and Son and Spirit are identical, favouring the monarchy at the expense of the economy), not however that the Son is other than the Father by diversity, but by distribution, not by division but by distinction, because the Father is not identical with the Son, they even being numerically one and another. For the Father is the whole substance, while the Son is an outflow and assignment of the whole, as he himself professes, *Because my Father is greater than I*[1]: and by him, it is sung in the psalm, he has also been made less, *a little on this side of the angels.*[2] So also the Father is other than the Son as being greater than the Son, as he who begets is other than he who is begotten, as he who sends is other than he who is sent, as he who makes is other than he through whom a thing is made. It suits my case also that when our Lord used this word regarding the person of the Paraclete, he signified not division but ordinance: for he says, *I will pray the Father and he will send you another advocate, the Spirit of truth.*[3] Thus ⟨he calls⟩ the Paraclete other than himself, as we say

[1] John 14. 28. [2] Ps. 8. 6. [3] John 14. 16.

the Son is other than the Father, so as to display the third sequence in the Paraclete as we the second in the Son, and so to preserve the economy. Is not the very fact that they are spoken of as Father and Son ⟨a statement that they are⟩ one thing beside another? Surely all facts will correspond with their designations, and diversity of designation can by no means be confused, since neither can ⟨the diversity⟩ of the things of which they are the designations. "*Is*" *is* "*is*", *and* "*not*" *is* "*not*": *for what is more than this is on the side of evil.*[1]

10. Thus ⟨one⟩ "is" either father or son, and day is not identical with night, nor is the Father identical with the Son in the sense that both are one ⟨person⟩ and each is both ⟨terms of the relationship⟩, as those very silly monarchians will have it. He himself, say they, made himself his own son. Nay, but father makes son, and son makes father, and those who become what they are by relationship with one another cannot by any means so become by relationship with themselves, as that a father should make himself his own son or a son cause himself to be his own father. The rules God has made, he himself observes. A father must have a son so as to be a father, and a son must have a father so as to be a son. For to have is one thing, to be is another: for example, to be a husband I must have a wife, I shall not be my own wife. So also, that I may be a father I have a son, I shall not be my own son: and that I may be a son I have a father, I shall not be my own father. For if I have those things that make me ⟨what I am⟩ I shall be ⟨what I am⟩, a father if I have a son, a son if I have a father. Moreover, whatever of those I am, I have not that which I myself am, no father since I shall be the father, no son since I shall be the son. To what degree I must have one of these things so as to be the other, to that degree if I am both I cease to be the one because I have not the other. For if I am son who also am father, I already have no son but am myself son. But as not having a son because I am myself the son, how shall I be a father? For I must have a son so as to be a father, and consequently I am no son, because I have no father and father makes son. Equally, if I am father who also am son, already I have no father but am myself father. But as not having a father because I myself am the father, how shall I

[1] Matt. 5. 37.

be a son? For I must have a father so as to be a son, and consequently I shall be no father, because I have no son and son makes father. This will be the sum of the devil's ability, to make the two mutually destructive, while by locking up both in one to please the monarchy he causes neither ⟨father nor son⟩ to be had, with the result that ⟨God⟩ is no father as not having a son, and ⟨the Son⟩ is no son as equally having no father: for so long as he is the Father he will not be the Son. This is how these maintain the monarchy, who retain neither the Father nor the Son. "But", ⟨they say⟩, "to God nothing is difficult." Who does not know it? and who is not aware that *things impossible with the world are possible with God*?[1] Also *God hath chosen the foolish things of the world to confound the things that are wise.*[2] We have read it all. "Consequently", they say, "it was not difficult for God to make himself both father and son, contrary to the law traditional in human affairs: for it was not difficult for God, contrary to nature, to cause the barren woman to bear—or even the virgin." Certainly nothing is difficult for God: but if in our assumptions we so rashly make use of this judgement, we shall be able to invent any manner of thing concerning God, as that he has done it, on the ground that he was able to do it. But we must not, on the ground that he can do all things, for that reason believe that he has done even what he has not done, but must enquire whether he has done it. God could, if he had wished, have equipped men with wings for flying—a faculty he has also provided kites with: yet, because he could, he did not as a matter of course also do it. He could at once have blotted out of existence both Praxeas and all heretics alike: yet he has not, because he could, blotted them out. For there had to be kites, and heretics,[3] and the Father had to be crucified. On this reckoning there will be something even difficult for God, that in fact which he has refrained from doing, not because he could not but because he would not. For God's power is his will, and his inability is his absence of will: and what his will was, that was in his power, and he has shown ⟨what it was⟩. Therefore, because if he wished he could have made himself his own son, and because if he could he did it, you will prove that he could have done it and wished to do it only when you have proved that he did do it.

[1] Matt. 19. 26. [2] 1 Cor. 1. 27. [3] 1 Cor. 11. 19.

11. But it will be your duty to prove it as openly from the scriptures as we prove that he made his own Word his Son. For if he calls him Son, while the Son will be no other than he who came forth from him, and the Word came forth from him, this ⟨Word⟩ will be the Son, not he from whom ⟨the Word⟩ came forth: for he did not himself come forth from himself. Further, you who identify Father and Son, cause the same one both to have brought forth from himself that which is God, and as such to have come forth. If he could have done so, yet he did not do so. Or else display the proof which I demand, like mine, that is that the scriptures so represent the Son as identical with the Father as among us the Father and the Son are demonstrated in distinction: in distinction, I say, not in division. Just as I allege as spoken by God, *My heart hath disgorged a good Word*,[1] against this do you object that God somewhere said, My heart hath disgorged myself as a good word, so that he himself may be both he who disgorged and what he disgorged, himself both he who brought forth and he who was brought forth, if he himself is Word and God. Look now, I allege that the Father said to the Son, *Thou art my Son, this day have I begotten thee*[2]: if you will have me believe that the Father himself is also the Son, show me that it is stated elsewhere in this form, The Lord said to himself, I am my son, today have I begotten myself: consequently also, Before the daystar have I begotten myself[3]: and, I the Lord have established myself as the beginning of ways for my works' sake, yea before all the hills have I begotten myself[4]: and any others there are in this fashion. Before whose disapproval was God, the Lord of the universe, afraid of so stating it, if so the fact was? Or was he afraid of not being believed if he plainly stated that he was both the Father and the Son? One thing however he was afraid of, to belie himself the author of truth, and to belie his own truth.[5] And so, believing that God is true, I know that his statements are consonant with his ordinance, and his ordinance consonant with his statements. You however would make him a liar and a deceiver,[6] a disappointer of this faith ⟨of mine⟩, if being himself his own son he assigned the role of son to another, since all the scriptures display both the demonstration and the distinctness of the Trinity: and from them is derived also our standing

[1] Ps. 45. 1. [2] Ps. 2. 7. [3] Cf. Ps. 110. 3.
[4] Cf. Prov. 8. 22. [5] Rom. 3. 4. [6] 1 John 1. 10.

rule, that speaker and person spoken of and person spoken to cannot be regarded as one and the same, for as much as neither wilfulness nor deception befits God as that, being himself the one spoken to, he should prefer to speak to another and not to himself. Hear therefore also other words of the Father concerning the Son, ⟨spoken⟩ through Isaiah: *Behold my son whom I have chosen, my beloved in whom I am well pleased; I will place my spirit upon him and he will announce judgement to the gentiles.*[1] Hear also ⟨what he says⟩ to him: *It is a great thing for thee to be called my son for the establishment of the tribes of Jacob and the conversion of the dispersion of Israel; I have set thee for a light of the gentiles, that thou mayest be salvation unto the end of the earth.*[2] Hear next also the Son's words concerning the Father: *The Spirit of the Lord is upon me, wherefore he hath anointed me to preach the gospel to men.*[3] Also in a psalm ⟨he speaks⟩ to the Father concerning the same ⟨Spirit⟩: *Forsake me not, until I announce thy arm to the whole generation to come.*[4] Also in another ⟨psalm⟩: *Lord, why are they increased that repress me?*[5] Nay but almost all the psalms which sustain the role of Christ represent the Son as speaking to the Father, that is, Christ as speaking to God. Observe also the Spirit speaking in the third person concerning the Father and the Son: *The Lord said unto my lord, Sit thou at my right hand until I make thine enemies the footstool of thy feet.*[6] Again, through Isaiah: *Thus saith the Lord to my lord Christ.*[7] Also through the same ⟨prophet⟩ ⟨the Spirit speaks⟩ to the Father concerning the Son: *Lord, who hath believed our report, and to whom is the arm of the Lord revealed? We have announced concerning him like a young boy, like a root in a thirsty land, and there was no beauty or glory of his.*[8] These are a few out of many: for we make no pretence of turning up the whole of the Scriptures, since even in one passage at a time we bring to witness their plenary majesty and authority, and thus have the advantage in argument in ⟨these⟩ discussions. So in these ⟨texts⟩, few though they be, yet the distinctiveness of the Trinity is clearly expounded: for there is the Spirit himself who makes the statement, the Father to whom he makes it, and the Son of whom he makes it. So also the rest, which are statements made sometimes by the Father concerning the Son or to the Son, sometimes by the Son

[1] Is. 42. 1. [2] Is. 49. 6. [3] Is. 61. 1.
[4] Ps. 71. 18. [5] Ps. 3. 1. [6] Ps. 110. 1.
[7] Is. 45. 1. [8] Is. 53. 1: John 12. 38: Rom. 10. 16.

concerning the Father or to the Father, sometimes by the Spirit, establish each several Person as being himself and none other.

12. If you are still offended by the plurality of the Trinity, on the ground that it is not combined in simple unity, I ask you how it is that one only single ⟨person⟩ speaks in the plural, *Let us make man after our image and likeness*,[1] when he ought to have said, Let me make man after my image and likeness, as being one only single ⟨person⟩. Also in what follows, *Behold, Adam is become as one of us*,[2] he is deceptive or joking in speaking in the plural while being one and alone and singular. Or was he speaking to the angels, as the Jews explain it, because they, like you, do not recognise the Son? Or, because he was himself father-son-spirit, did he for that reason make himself plural and speak to himself in the plural? Nay rather, because there already was attached to him the Son, a second Person, his Word, and a third Person, the Spirit in the Word, for that reason he spoke in the plural, *Let us make*, and *Our*, and *Of us*. For in whose company was he making man, and like whom was he making him? He was speaking with the Son who was to assume manhood, and the Spirit who was to sanctify man, as with ministers and mediators in consequence of the unity of the Trinity. Then again the scripture that follows distinguishes between the Persons: *And God made man, in the image of God made he him*.[3] Why not "his own image", if the maker was one, and there was none in whose image he was making him? But there was one in whose image he was making him, the Son's in fact, who because he was to be the surer and truer man caused that man to be called his image who at that time had to be formed of clay, as the image and similitude of the true.[4] But also in the preceding works of the world, how is it written? At first, while the Son is not yet on the scene, *And God said, Let there be light, and it was made*.[5] The Word himself is in first instance *the true light that lighteneth* the *man that cometh into this world*,[6] and through him also the mundane light ⟨comes to be⟩. But from then on in the Word, ⟨that is⟩, with Christ as assistant and minister, God wished things to be made, and God made them: *And God said, Let a firmament be made, and God made a firmament*[7]: *And God said, Let lights be made, and God made the greater*

[1] Gen. 1. 26.
[2] Gen. 3. 22.
[3] Gen. 1. 27.
[4] Heb. 9. 24.
[5] Gen. 1. 3.
[6] John 1. 9.
[7] Gen. 1. 6, 7.

and the lesser light.[1] So also the rest of things the very same one made as made the earlier, that is, the Word of God *by whom all things were made and without whom nothing was made.*[2] And if he himself is God, as John says—*the Word was God*[3]—you have two, one commanding a thing to be made, another making it. But how you must understand "another" I have already professed, in the sense of person, not of substance, for distinctiveness, not for division. Yet although I always maintain one substance in three who cohere, I must still, as a necessary consequence of the meaning ⟨of the passage⟩, say that he who commands is other than he who makes. For he would not be commanding if he himself were making while commanding things to be made. Yet he did command ⟨them to be made⟩ by him, since he would not have commanded himself if he had been one ⟨alone⟩: or he would have made them without command, for he would not have waited to command himself.

13. "Consequently", you say, "if God spake and God made, if one God spake and another made, two gods are preached." If you are so stubborn, keep on thinking so for a time. And, to give you more cause to think it, hear how also in a psalm two are called gods: *Thy throne, O God, is for ever, a sceptre of direction is the sceptre of thy kingdom; thou hast loved righteousness and hatest iniquity, wherefore God, even thy God, hath anointed thee.*[4] If he is speaking to God, and to God anointed by God, here also he affirms that two are gods. Concerning this also Isaiah ⟨speaks⟩, regarding the person of Christ, *And the Sabæans, men of stature, shall come over unto thee and shall follow after thee with their hands in chains and shall worship thee because God is in thee; for thou art our God and we knew it not, O God of Israel.*[5] For here also, by saying *God is in thee*, and *Thou O God*, he sets forth two, him who was in Christ, and Christ himself. It is of more moment that in the Gospel you will find the same number: *In the beginning was the Word and the Word was with God and the Word was God*[6]: there is one who "was", and another "within whom" he was. Also I read the name Lord applied to two: *The Lord said unto my Lord, Sit thou at my right hand.*[7] And Isaiah says this: *Lord, who hath believed our report, and to whom is the arm of the Lord*

[1] Gen. 1. 14, 16. [2] John 1. 2. [3] John 1. 1.
[4] Ps. 45. 6, 7. [5] Is. 45. 14. [6] John 1. 1.
[7] Ps. 110. 1.

revealed?[1] For he would have said "thy arm", not "arm of the Lord", unless he had wished us to understand Lord the Father and Lord the Son. Also Genesis, of still older date: *And the Lord rained upon Sodom and Gomorrah brimstone and fire out of heaven from the Lord.*[2] Either deny that these things are written, or who are you that you should think they must not be accepted as they are written, especially those which have their meaning not in allegories and parables but in clearly defined and simple statements? But if you are of those who on one occasion did not tolerate our Lord when he showed himself to be the Son of God, for fear of having to believe that he is the Lord,[3] recollect along with them that it is written, *I said, Ye are gods and sons of the Most High*[4]; and, *God standeth in the congregation of the gods*[5]: so that, if scripture has not been afraid to pronounce to be gods those men who by faith have been made sons of God, you may know that much more has it by right applied the name of God and Lord to the true and only Son of God. "Therefore", you say, "I will challenge you, today also by the authority of those scriptures consistently to preach two gods and two lords." God forbid. For we, who by the grace of God examine both the occasions and the intentions of the scriptures, especially as being disciples not of men but of the Paraclete, do indeed specify two, the Father and the Son, and even three with the Holy Spirit, according to that calculation of the economy which makes plurality, lest, as your selfwill imports, the Father himself be believed to have been born and to have died—which is not lawful to be believed, seeing it has not been so delivered. Yet "two gods" or "two lords" we never let issue from our mouth: not but that both the Father is God and the Son is God and the Holy Spirit is God, and each several one ⟨of them⟩ is God; but that of old time two were preached as Gods and two as Lords, so that when Christ came he should both be recognised as God and have the name of Lord, because he is the son of ⟨him who is⟩ God and Lord. For if there were found in the scriptures one Person both of God and of the Lord, rightly would Christ not have been admitted to the name of God and Lord (because none other besides one God and one Lord was preached), and it would have come about that the Father himself would have seemed to have come down

[1] Is. 53. 1. [2] Gen. 19. 24. [3] John 10. 33.
[4] Ps. 82. 6. [5] Ps. 82. 1.

⟨from heaven⟩ (because we were reading of one God and one Lord), and darkness would have fallen upon his whole economy which was designed and administered for material of faith. But when Christ came and was known by us as being he who of old time had caused plurality by being made a second beside the Father, and a third along with the Spirit, and now that through him the Father was more fully made manifest, the name of God and of Lord was reduced again to union: with the result that, since the gentiles were passing over from a multitude of idols to the one only God, a difference was established between worshippers of one divinity and worshippers of many. For it was necessary also that Christians should shine in the world as sons of light,[1] while worshipping and calling upon the name of the light of the world,[2] one God as also one Lord. Otherwise, if as a result of the private knowledge by which we know that the name of God and of Lord is applicable to both Father and Son and Spirit, we had been calling upon the name of gods and lords, we should have put out our candle [3] by being also less bold in face of martyrdom; for at every turn opportunity would lie open for us to escape by immediately swearing by gods and lords, as do certain heretics whose gods are more than one. Consequently I shall in no case say either "gods" or "lords", but shall follow the apostle, with the result that if the Father and the Son are to be mentioned together, I call the Father "God" and name Jesus Christ "the Lord".[4] But Christ by himself I shall be able to call God, as does the same apostle ⟨when⟩ he says, *Of whom is Christ, who is God over all, blessed for evermore.*[5] For also the sun's beam, when by itself, I shall call "the sun": but when naming the sun, whose the beam is, I shall not immediately call the beam "the sun". For though I make two suns, yet the sun and its beam I shall count as two objects, and two manifestations of one undivided substance, in the same sense as ⟨I count⟩ God and his Word, the Father and the Son.

14. Once more, we have the support, in our vindication of the duality of the Father and the Son, of that rule which has defined God as invisible. For when Moses in Egypt had expressed a desire for the sight of God, saying, *If therefore I have found grace in thy sight shew thyself to me that I may knowledgeably see thee,*[6]

[1] Eph. 5. 8.
[2] John 8. 12.
[3] Cf. Ps. 18. 28.
[4] Rom. 1. 7.
[5] Rom. 9. 5.
[6] Exod. 33. 13.

⟨God⟩ said, *Thou canst not see my face, for a man will not see my face and live* [1]—that is, he who sees it will die. For we find that God was seen, even by many, yet that none of those who had seen him died—that God was seen, of course, according to men's capacity, not according to the fulness of his divinity. For patriarchs are related to have seen God, as Abraham and Jacob, and prophets, as Isaiah, as Ezekiel, yet they did not die. Therefore they either ought to have died, if they had seen him—for no man will see God and live: or, if they saw God and did not die, the scripture says falsely that God said, *If a man sees my face he shall not live* [2]: or else the scripture speaks falsely when it alleges that God was seen. So then it will be another who was seen, for it is impossible for the same one who was seen, to be characterised as invisible: and it will follow that we must understand the Father as invisible because of the fulness of his majesty, but must acknowledge the Son as visible because of the enumeration of his derivation, just as we may not look upon the sun in respect of the total of its substance which is in the sky, though we can with our eyes bear its beam because of the moderation of the assignment which from thence reaches out to the earth. Here one of our adversaries will wish to contend that the Son also is invisible as Word and as Spirit, and, maintaining that the Father and the Son are in like case, to affirm rather that Father and Son are one and the same. But we have deposed that the scripture, by its distinguishing of visible and invisible, advocates a difference. For they also add this to their quibbling, that if on that occasion it was the Son speaking to Moses,[3] he pronounced his own face visible to no man, because of course he was the invisible Father himself under the name of Son. And consequently they wish the visible one and the invisible one to be taken as identical, in the same way as ⟨they wish⟩ Father and Son ⟨to be taken as⟩ identical, because also a little earlier, before he refused Moses ⟨the sight of⟩ his face, it is written that the Lord spake to Moses face to face as a man speaks to his friend,[4] and furthermore that Jacob says, *I have seen the Lord face to face* [5]: consequently the same one is visible and invisible: and because the same one has both attributes, therefore also the invisible Father is himself visible, as being also Son. As though the explanation of the scripture which we offer

[1] Exod. 33. 20.
[2] Exod. 33. 20.
[3] Exod. 33. 20.
[4] Exod. 33. 11.
[5] Gen. 32. 30.

did not, leaving the Father out of question, befit the Son in his own visibility. For we say that the Son also on his own account is, as Word and Spirit, invisible even now by the quality of his substance, but that he was visible before the incarnation in the manner in which he says to Aaron and Miriam, *Although there be a prophet among you, I shall become known to him in a vision and shall speak to him in a dream; not as with my servant Moses shall I speak to him mouth to mouth in manifestation*[1]—that is, in truth—*and not in an enigma*—that is, not in imagination: as also says the apostle, *Now we see as in a mirror in an enigma, but then face to face.*[2] Therefore since for Moses he reserves for the future the sight of himself and conversation with himself face to face (for this was fulfilled afterwards when he withdrew into a mountain, as we read in the Gospel that Moses was seen talking with him),[3] it is clear that always aforetime God—that is, the Son of God—was seen in a mirror and an enigma and a vision and a dream, both by prophets and patriarchs and Moses himself till that time: and if perchance the Lord did speak in visual presence, yet a man would not see his face as he really is, but only perchance in a mirror and in an enigma. Lastly, if the Lord spoke to Moses in such sort that Moses knew his face from near to, why does he immediately at the same moment ask to see his face, which if he had seen he would not ask to see? Equally, why does the Lord deny that his face can be seen,[4] though he had let him see it, if indeed he had let him see it? Or what face of God is that, the sight of which is refused? If there was ⟨a face⟩ which was seen—*I have seen*, says Jacob, *God face to face and my life is preserved*[5]—there must be another face which slays if it is seen. Or is it that the Son indeed was seen—albeit in face, yet even this in a vision and a dream and a mirror and an enigma, because Word and Spirit cannot be seen except in imaginary aspect—yet by his face he means the invisible Father? For who is the Father? Shall he be the Son's face, on account of the authority which he obtains as begotten of the Father? For is it not of some greater personage that it befits one to say, "That man is my face", or "He gives me face"? *The Father*, he says, *is greater than I*[6]: therefore the Father will be the Son's face. For also what says the scripture? *The spirit of his countenance, Christ the Lord.*[7] Therefore if Christ

[1] Num. 12. 6. [2] 1 Cor. 13. 12.
[3] Matt. 17. 3: Mark 9. 4: Luke 9. 30. [4] Exod. 33. 20.
[5] Gen. 32. 30. [6] John 14. 28. [7] Lam. 4. 20.

is the spirit of the Father's countenance, rightly has the Spirit pronounced him whose the countenance is, namely his Father, to be his face—evidently because of their unity. Can you be surprised if the Father can be understood to be the Son's face, when he is his head? For *the head of Christ is God.*[1]

15. If I do not clear this point by enquiries made of the old scriptures, I shall take from the New Testament confirmation of our interpretation, lest whatever I account to the Son you immediately claim for the Father. For both in the gospels and in the apostles I discover God visible and invisible, with an evident personal distinction betwen these two qualities. John as it were cries out, *No man hath seen God at any time* [2]—clearly not in the past, for he has precluded question of time by saying that God was never seen. The apostle also confirms this, 〈speaking〉 of God *whom no man hath seen, nor can he be seen* [3]—obviously because he who sees him will die. Those very same apostles testify both that they have seen Christ and that they have handled him.[4] Consequently if Christ is himself both Father and Son, how is he both seen and unseen? So as to confer upon one 〈Person〉 this diversity of "seen" and "unseen", our adversary will argue that both are rightly spoken, 〈since he was〉 visible in the incarnation but invisible before the incarnation; and that consequently the Father, invisible before the incarnation, is the same 〈Person〉 as the Son, visible in the incarnation. And yet, if the same 〈Person〉 was invisible before the incarnation, how is it he is found to have been seen also aforetime before the incarnation? Equally, if the same 〈Person〉 is visible after the incarnation, how is he even now pronounced invisible by the apostles, unless there is one whom, aforetime seen in an enigma, the incarnation has made more fully visible—the Word in fact, who also *was made flesh* [5]—and another whom *no one hath ever seen* [6]—the Father in fact, whose the Word is? Once for all let us examine who it was the apostles saw. *That which we have seen*, says John, *which we have heard, have seen with our eyes, and our hands have handled, of the Word of life.*[7] For the Word of life was made flesh, and was heard and seen and handled because 〈he was〉 flesh, 〈the same〉 who before the incarnation as Word only was in the beginning in the presence of

[1] 1 Cor. 11. 3.
[2] John 1. 18.
[3] 1 Tim. 6. 16.
[4] 1 John 1. 1: 1 Cor. 9. 1.
[5] John 1. 14.
[6] 1 Tim. 6. 16.
[7] 1 John 1. 1.

God the Father, not the Father in the presence of himself. For although the Word was God, yet he was ⟨God⟩ in the presence of God, because he was God from God, because he was along with the Father, in the Father's presence. *And we beheld his glory, ⟨the glory⟩ as of the only-begotten of the Father* [1]—evidently of course ⟨the glory⟩ of the visible Son, glorified by the invisible Father. And consequently, because he had said that the Word of God was God, so as not to assist our adversaries' assumption as that he had seen the Father himself, but so as to distinguish between the invisible Father and the visible Son, he adds of superfluity, *No one hath seen God at any time.*[2] Which God? The Word? Nay but, it was said before, *We have seen and heard and handled, of the Word of life.*[3] But which God? Evidently the Father, in whose presence the Word, the only-begotten Son, who *himself hath declared the bosom* [4] of the Father, was God. He himself was both heard and seen, and lest he should be taken for a phantom was even handled. Him also Paul had sight of, yet he saw not the Father: *Have I not*, he says, *seen Jesus?* [5] But he also has applied to Christ the name of God: *Whose are the fathers, and out of whom is Christ according to the flesh, who is God over all, blessed for ever.*[6] He also presents as visible the Son of God, that is, the Word of God, because he who was made flesh is called Christ.[7] But of the Father ⟨he says⟩ to Timothy, *Whom no man hath seen nor can see* [8]: and he piles it up even more, *Who alone hath immortality and dwelleth in light unapproachable* [8]: and of him he had previously said, *To the king eternal, immortal, invisible, the only God,*[9] so that to the Son we might ourselves also ascribe the contrary, mortality and approachability. Him also he testifies to have died according to the scriptures, and to have been seen of himself last of all [10]—evidently by means of approachable light: though even that he did not experience without danger to his sight,[11] as neither did Peter and John and James without danger to their reason and without astonishment,[12] and if they had seen, not the glory of the Son who was to suffer, but the Father, I think they would have died on the spot: for no one will see God and live. As this is so, our case stands, that from the beginning he always was seen who was seen at the end, and that he was not

[1] John 1. 14.
[2] John 1. 18.
[3] 1 John 1. 1.
[4] John 1. 18.
[5] 1 Cor. 9. 1.
[6] Rom. 9. 5.
[7] Gal. 3. 1.
[8] 1 Tim. 6. 16.
[9] 1 Tim. 1. 17.
[10] 1 Cor. 15. 3, 8.
[11] Acts 9. 8.
[12] Matt. 17. 6.

seen at the end who from the beginning had not been seen, and that thus there are two, one seen and one unseen. Therefore it was the Son always who was seen and the Son always who conversed and the Son always who wrought, by the authority and will of the Father, because *The Son can do nothing of himself, unless he have seen the Father doing it* [1]—doing it, of course, in his consciousness. For the Father acts by consciousness, whereas the Son sees and accomplishes that which is in the Father's consciousness. Thus all things were made by the Son, and without him nothing was made.

16. And think not that solely the works of the world were made by the Son, but those also which from then on were performed by God. For the Father, who *loveth the Son and hath delivered all things into his bosom*,[2] right from the beginning loves him, and from the beginning has delivered them. Ever since from *the beginning the Word was with God and the Word was God*,[3] and to him was given by the Father *all power in heaven and in earth*,[4] *The Father judgeth no man, but hath delivered all judgement to the Son*,[5] yes, from the beginning: for when he says "all power" and "all judgement", and that all things were made by him, and that all things are delivered into his hand, he allows no exception of time, for they will not be "all" unless they have been of all time. And so it is the Son who from the beginning has judged, smashing down the tower of pride and confounding the tongues,[6] punishing the whole world by the violence of the waters,[7] raining down upon Sodom and Gomorrah fire and brimstone [8]—the Lord ⟨raining it down⟩ from the Lord. For he it always was who came down to converse with men, from Adam even to the patriarchs and prophets,[9] always from the beginning preparing beforehand in dream and in a mirror and in an enigma that course which he was going to follow out to the end. Thus he was always also learning how as God to company with men, being none other than the Word who was to be flesh. But he was learning with the purpose of laying a foundation of faith for us, that we might the more easily believe that the Son of God has come down into the world, if we knew that something of the sort had previously been done. For, as things were written, so also they were done,

[1] John 5. 19. [2] John 3. 35. [3] John 1. 1.
[4] Matt. 28. 18. [5] John 5. 22. [6] Gen. 11. 7.
[7] Gen. 6. 17. [8] Gen. 19. 24. [9] Bar. 3. 37.

for our sake *upon whom the ends of the world are come.*[1] Thus also he already at that time knew human affections, as he was going to take upon himself also man's substances, flesh and soul, asking Adam a question as though he did not know—*Adam, where art thou?*[2]—repenting that he had made man,[3] as though he had no foreknowledge; tempting Abraham,[4] as though ignorant what is in a man[5]; angry, and reconciled with the same persons; and all those things which heretics, for the destruction of the Creator, seize upon as unworthy of God, ignorant that these things befitted the Son, who was also going to undergo human passions, both thirst and hunger and tears and nativity itself and death itself, for this purpose made by the Father *a little lower than the angels.*[6] But the heretics indeed will refuse to count proper even for the Son things with which you becloud the Father himself, as though he had himself made himself lower for our sakes, though the scripture says that one was made lower by another, not himself by himself. Moreover it is one who was crowned with glory and honour, and it is another who crowned him, evidently the Father ⟨crowning⟩ the Son. Besides, how can it be that God Almighty, that invisible one whom none of men hath seen nor can see, he who dwelleth in light unapproachable,[7] he who dwelleth not in things made with hands,[8] before whose aspect the earth trembleth,[9] and the mountains melt as wax,[10] who graspeth the whole world in his hand like a nest,[11] whose throne is the heaven and the earth his footstool,[12] in whom is all space but he not in space, who is the boundary line of the universe, he the Most High, should have walked in paradise in the evening looking for Adam,[13] should have shut up the ark after Noah had gone in,[14] should have rested under an oak with Abraham,[15] should have called to Moses from the burning bush,[16] and should have appeared with three others in the Babylonian king's furnace[17]—although it says he was a son of man? Certainly these things ought not to have been believed of the Son of God unless they had been written, and perhaps not to have been believed of the Father though they had been written: yet these people bring him down into Mary's womb,

[1] 1 Cor. 10. 11.
[2] Gen. 3. 9.
[3] Gen. 6. 6.
[4] Gen. 22. 1.
[5] John 2. 25.
[6] Ps. 8. 5.
[7] 1 Tim. 6. 16.
[8] Acts 17. 24.
[9] Joel 2. 10.
[10] Ps. 97. 5.
[11] Is. 10. 14.
[12] Is. 66. 1.
[13] Gen. 3. 8.
[14] Gen. 7. 16.
[15] Gen. 18. 4.
[16] Exod. 3. 4.
[17] Dan. 3. 25.

and set him at Pilate's judgement seat, and shut him up in Joseph's sepulchre. Hence therefore it is evident that they are astray. For not knowing that from the beginning the whole course of the divine ordinance has come down through the Son, they believe that the Father himself both was seen and conversed and wrought, and suffered thirst and hunger, in spite of the prophet who says *The eternal God shall never thirst nor hunger at all* [1]—and how much more shall he neither die nor be buried—and that thus the one God, that is, the Father, has always done those things which ⟨in fact⟩ have been performed by ⟨the agency of⟩ the Son.

17. They have found it easier to think that the Father has acted in the Son's name than the Son in the Father's, though the Lord himself says, *I am come in my Father's name* [2]: and again, to the Father himself ⟨he says⟩, *I have manifested thy name to men* [3]: and the scripture also agrees, *Blessed is he that cometh in the name of the Lord* [4]—evidently the Son in the name of the Father. And the Father's name is God Almighty, the Most High, the Lord of hosts, the King of Israel, I am. In as much as the scriptures so teach, we say that these also have applied to the Son, and that in these the Son came, and in these always acted, and thus in himself manifested them to men. *All things that the Father hath*, he says, *are mine* [5]: and why not also the names? When therefore you read of God Almighty, and the Most High, and the God of hosts, and the King of Israel, and I am, beware lest by these the Son also is shown to be of his own right God Almighty as being the Word of God Almighty and as having received power over all [6]; and the Most High as having been *by the right hand of God exalted,* [7] as Peter preached in the Acts; and the Lord of Hosts because all things are subjected to him by the Father [8]; and the King of Israel because to him especially has fallen the lot of that nation [9]; and also "I am" because there are many that are called sons and art not.[10] But if they will have it that Christ's name also is the Father's, they will hear ⟨my answer⟩ in its proper place. Meantime let this be my ready response against that which they allege from the Revelation of John, *I am the Lord, who is and who was and is to come, the Almighty,* [11]

[1] Is. 40. 28.
[2] John 5. 43.
[3] John 17. 6.
[4] Ps. 118. 26.
[5] John 16. 15.
[6] Matt. 28. 18.
[7] Acts 2. 33.
[8] 1 Cor. 15. 27.
[9] Deut. 32. 9.
[10] Cf. Rev. 2. 9.
[11] Rev. 1. 8.

and wherever else they think the designation "Almighty" not appropriate to the Son: as if he who is to come were not the Almighty, when the Son of the Almighty is no less almighty than the Son of God is God.

18. But they are thrust out of the way of easily seeing in the Son this partnership in the Father's names by those occasions when the scripture has stated that God is one alone—as though the same scripture had not set before us two Gods and Lords, as we have already shown. Therefore, say they, because we find two as well as one, consequently both are one ⟨Person⟩, and the same one is both Son and Father. Surely the scripture is not in such jeopardy that you have to come to its rescue by your quibbling to prevent it from appearing to be contrary to itself: it is correct both when it states that God is one only and when it reveals Father and Son as two, and it needs no help but its own. It is agreed that by it the name of the Son is mentioned: for without prejudice to the Son it can be right in having defined as one only, God whose ⟨son⟩ the Son is. For he who has a son does not cease to be one only, on his own account of course as often as he is named without his son: and he is named without his son when he is primarily defined as the first person who must needs be premised before the name of the son, because the father is first recognised, and after the father the son is named. Therefore there is one God, the Father,[1] and *besides him there is no other*,[2] and he himself who introduces this ⟨statement⟩ is denying, not the Son, but another god: whereas the Son is not another ⟨god⟩ than the Father. Finally, look at the contexts of statements like this, and you will find that their pronouncement has an eye to makers and worshippers of idols, so that a multitude of false gods may be ejected by the unity of the divine, ⟨the one God⟩, who yet has a Son who, precisely because he is indivisible and inseparable from the Father, must be accounted as in the Father even when his name is not mentioned. And moreover, if he had mentioned him he would have made him separate—if he had spoken in this manner, Beside me there is none other except my Son: for he would have made the Son another ⟨god⟩ by excepting him from those others ⟨who are no gods⟩. Imagine the sun saying, I am the sun and beside me there is none other except my beam:

[1] 1 Cor. 8. 6. [2] Is. 45. 5.

would you not have remarked adversely upon his futility, as though the beam were not accounted in the sun? And so ⟨the statement⟩ that besides himself there is no other god is ⟨made⟩ on account of the idolatry both of the gentiles and of Israel: also on account of the heretics, who manufacture idols with words as the gentiles do with their hands—that is, another God and another Christ. Therefore even when pronouncing himself one the Father was serving the Son's interest, lest Christ should be believed to have come from any other God than him who had already said, *I am God, and other beside me there is not*,[1] ⟨God⟩ who reveals himself as one only, yet ⟨one only⟩ with the Son, with whom also he alone has spread out the heaven.[2]

19. Yes, and also this saying of his they will seize upon for a proof of his singularity. *I alone*, he says, *have spread out the heaven* [3]—alone in respect of the other powers, erecting a barrier against the guesses of the heretics, who will have it that the world was built by angels and hostile powers, ⟨heretics⟩ who make the creator himself either an angel or one suborned for other external acts, like the making of the world, and ignorant at that. Or if in their sense he alone spread out the heaven, why do these ⟨present⟩ heretics perversely assume the exclusion of that singular Wisdom who says, *When he prepared the heaven I was present with him?* [4] And if one has said, *Who hath known the mind of the Lord and who hath been his counsellor?*,[5] evidently he means "besides Wisdom who was present with him". In him, however, and with him she fashioned all things, seeing he was not ignorant what he was doing. But "besides Wisdom" means "besides the Son", who is *Christ the Wisdom and the Power of God*,[6] as the apostle says, he who alone knoweth the mind of the Father: for who knoweth the things which be in God, except the Spirit which is in him? [7]—not which is outside him. There was then one who made God not alone, except as alone in respect of other gods. But also let the Gospel be refused ⟨a hearing⟩ because it says that all things were made by God through the Word, and that without him was nothing made.[8] For, if I mistake not, it is also elsewhere written, *By his Word were the heavens established, and all their powers by his Spirit.*[9] But the Word also, the Power and the

[1] Is. 45. 5 : 44. 6.
[2] Is. 44. 24.
[3] Is. 44. 24.
[4] Prov. 8. 27.
[5] Is. 40. 13 : Rom. 11. 34.
[6] 1 Cor. 1. 24.
[7] Cf. 1 Cor. 2. 11.
[8] John 1. 3.
[9] Ps. 33. 6.

Wisdom, will himself be the Son of God. Thus if all things are by the Son, when he spreads out the heaven also by the Son he is not alone in spreading it out, except on that reckoning that he is alone in respect of the other ⟨gods⟩. And consequently he immediately speaks concerning the Son: *Who else hath cast down the tokens of the ventriloquists, and divinations away from the heart, turning the wise backward and making their counsel foolish, establishing the words of his Son?* [1]—by saying, of course, *This is my beloved Son, hear him.*[2] By thus subjoining the Son, he himself is the interpreter of how he alone has spread out the heaven, that is, alone with his Son, even as he is one thing with his Son. And further, it will be the Son's voice ⟨which says⟩ *I alone have spread out the heaven,*[3] because by the Word were the heavens established: because with the assistance of Wisdom in the Word the heaven was prepared, and because all things were made by the Word, it is feasible for the Son also alone to have spread out the heaven, because he alone ministered to the Father's operation. He also it will be who says, *I am the first, and unto things that are to come after, I am he.*[4] Evidently the Word is the first thing of all: *In the beginning was the Word,*[5] and in that beginning he was brought forth by the Father: whereas the Father, having no beginning, as having been brought forth by none, as being unborn, cannot be regarded as first: he who was always alone could have no ⟨numerical⟩ order. Therefore if their reason for thinking they must believe the identity of the Father and the Son has been that they may prove their case for the unity of God, the unity is safe of him who, being one, has also a Son himself also no less ⟨than the Father⟩ included in the same scriptures. If they are unwilling for the Son to be accounted a second beside the Father, lest the second give rise to the expression "two gods", we have shown that even two Gods are referred to in scripture, and two Lords: and yet, that they be not offended at that, we are rendering an account how the expressions "two gods" or "two lords" are not used, but how the Father and the Son are two, and this not as a result of separation of substance, but as a result of ordinance, while we declare the Son indivisible and inseparable from the Father, another not in quality but in sequence, who, although he is called God when he is named by himself, yet does

[1] Is. 44. 25, 26. [2] Luke 9. 35. [3] Is. 44. 24.
[4] Is. 41. 4. [5] John 1. 1.

not for that reason make a duality of gods, but one God, by this very fact that he has to be called God as a result of his unity with the Father.

20. But for the further rebutment of their quibblings we must pay attention to whatever they will glean from the ⟨new⟩ scriptures to support their opinion, while they refuse to look at the other ⟨places⟩ which themselves also observe the rule, and that while safeguarding the divine unity and the impressiveness of the monarchy. For as in the old ⟨scriptures⟩ they retain nothing else but, *I am God and other beside me there is not*,[1] so in the Gospel they uphold the Lord's answer to Philip, *I and the Father are one*,[2] and, *He that hath seen me hath also seen the Father*, and, *I am in the Father and the Father in me.*[3] To these three citations they wish the whole appurtenance of both testaments to yield, though the smaller number ought to be understood in accordance with the greater. But this is the characteristic of all heretics. For because there are a few ⟨instances⟩ which can be found among the undergrowth, they maintain the cause of ⟨these⟩ few against the many and become advocates of the later against the earlier. But the rule determined for every subject in earlier instances ever since the beginning, makes a precedent for the later also—and the same in the case of the fewer.

21. See therefore how many ⟨instances⟩ set the precedent for you even in the Gospel, before Philip's consultation and before all your quibbling. And to begin with, the very preface of John the Evangelist shows what he who had to be made flesh had aforetime been: *In the beginning was the Word and the Word was with God and the Word was God; the same was in the beginning with God; all things were made through him, and without him was nothing made.*[4] For if this may not otherwise be received than as it is written, undoubtedly one is revealed who was from the beginning, and another with whom he was: ⟨he reveals⟩ one the Word of God, and God another—though the Word also is God, but as God's Son, not as the Father: one through whom are all things, another by whom are all things. But what we mean by "another" we have already often explained. When we say "another" we necessarily mean "not the same": "not the same"

[1] Is. 45. 5. [2] John 10. 30. [3] John 14. 9, 10, 11. [4] John 1. 1-3.

however not as separated, another by ordinance, not by division. He therefore it was who was made flesh, not he whose Word he was. His was the glory seen, *as of the only one of the Father*,[1] not as of the Father. He, the only one, has revealed the bosom of the Father, not the Father his own bosom: for there comes first, *No one hath seen God at any time.*[2] Therefore even if he is pointed out by John as the Lamb of God [3] ⟨he is⟩ not ⟨pointed out as⟩ he whose beloved he is. Certainly he is always God's Son, not he whose Son he is. Nathanael immediately perceived this of him, as also did Peter elsewhere: *Thou art the Son of God.*[4] And that this they rightly perceived he himself confirms, replying to Nathanael, *Because I said I saw thee under the fig tree, therefore thou believest* [5]; and affirming the blessedness of Peter, to whom not flesh or blood had revealed what he had perceived, the Father as well ⟨as the Son⟩, but the Father who is in heaven.[6] And by this saying he determined the distinction of both Persons, the Son on earth whom Peter had recognised as God's Son, and the Father in heaven who had revealed to Peter what Peter had recognised, that Christ is God's Son. When he has entered into the Temple he calls it his Father's house,[7] as a son ⟨would⟩. When he speaks to Nicodemus he says, *God so loved the world that he gave his only Son that every one who believeth in him should not perish but have everlasting life* [8]: and again, *For God sent not his Son into the world to judge the world, but that the world may be saved through him; he that believeth in him is not judged; he that believeth not in him is judged already, because he hath not believed in the name of the only Son of God.*[9] When John moreover was being asked what ⟨he thought⟩ of Jesus when he was baptizing, he said, *The Father hath loved the Son and hath delivered all things into his hand; he that believeth in the Son hath eternal life; he that believeth not in the Son of God shall not see* God, *but the wrath of God shall abide upon him.*[10] Whom moreover did he reveal to the Samaritan woman? If it was *the Messiah who is called Christ*,[11] evidently he showed himself to be the Son, not the Father, for elsewhere also Christ is called the Son of God, not the Father. Thereafter to the disciples he says, *Mine it is to do the will of him that sent me, that I may accomplish his work.*[12] And to the Jews concerning the healing of the paralytic

[1] John 1. 14. [2] John 1. 18. [3] John 1. 29, 36.
[4] John 1. 49: Matt. 14. 33: 16. 6. [5] John 1. 50. [6] Matt. 16. 17.
[7] John 2. 16. [8] John 3. 16. [9] John 3. 17, 18.
[10] John 3. 35, 36. [11] John 4. 25. [12] John 4. 34.

<he says>, *My Father worketh hitherto, and I work* [1]: "my father and I" is what a son says. At length *for this cause the Jews the more sought to kill him, not only because he relaxed the sabbath, but because he called God his Father, making himself equal with God.*[2] Then therefore he said to them, *The Son can do nothing of himself, except he see the Father doing it; for the things which he doeth, the same also the Son doeth; for the Father loveth the Son and hath shewn him all things which he hath done, and greater works than these shall he shew him, that ye may marvel; for as the Father raiseth up the dead and quickeneth them, so also the Son quickeneth whom he will. For neither doth the Father judge, but hath given all judgement to the Son, that all may honour the Son as they honour the Father; he that honoureth not the Son honoureth not the Father who sent him. Verily, verily, I say unto you, that he who heareth my words and believeth him that sent me, hath eternal life, and shall not come into judgement but hath passed from death into life. Verily I say unto you, that the hour will come in which the dead shall hear the voice of the Son of God, and when they have heard shall live; for as the Father hath* eternal *life in himself so also hath he given to the Son to have* eternal *life in himself, and hath given him to do judgement with authority, because he is the Son of Man* [3]—through the flesh of course, as he is also Son of God through God's Spirit. Again he adds, *But I have a greater witness than John's; for the works which the Father hath given me to accomplish, themselves bear witness concerning me that the Father hath sent me; and the Father who hath sent me, himself hath borne witness concerning me.*[4] But when he adds, *Ye have neither heard his voice at any time nor seen his form,*[5] he confirms <our position> that aforetime it was not the Father but the Son who was seen and heard. At length he says, *I am come in my Father's name and ye have not received me* [6]—consequently the Son always was in the name of God and King and Lord Almighty and Most High. To those moreover who asked him what they must do he replied, *To believe in him whom God hath sent.*[7] He affirms also that he is the bread which the Father was providing from heaven: consequently that everything which the Father gave him was coming to him, and that he would not cast it out, because he had come down from heaven not to do

[1] John 5. 17. [2] John 5. 18. [3] John 5. 19-27.
[4] John 5. 36, 37. [5] John 5. 37. [6] John 5. 43.
[7] John 6. 29.

his own will but the Father's; and that the Father's will was that he who hath seen the Son and believeth in him may obtain life and resurrection: further, that no one can come to him except him whom the Father draweth, and that everyone who had heard and had learned from the Father was coming to him [1]: adding at this point also, *Not that anyone hath seen the Father*,[2] that he might show that ⟨he⟩ was the Father's Word by whom men become taught. But when many go away from him, and he gives his disciples the chance of going away if they wish, what did Simon Peter answer? *Whither go we? Thou hast the words of life, and we believe that thou art Christ.*[3] ⟨Does he mean⟩ that he is the Father, or the Father's Christ?

22. But whose doctrine does he say it was at which they marvelled? His own, or the Father's? [4] Likewise when they were in doubt among themselves whether he were not the Christ—evidently not the Father but the Son—he says, *Ye both know me and ye know whence I am, and I am not come of myself, but he is true that hath sent me, whom ye know not: I know him because I am with him.*[5] He says not, Because I am he, or, I have sent myself, but, *He hath sent me.*[6] Also when the Pharisees had sent to attack him, he said, *Yet a little time I am with you, and I go to him that sent me.*[7] But when he says he is not alone—*But I*, he says, *and the Father that sent me* [8]—does he not point to two, as much two as inseparable? Yea, this was the whole of his teaching, that there are two, inseparable: since also while citing the law which confirms the witness of two men, he adds, *I bear witness concerning myself, and the Father who sent me beareth witness concerning me.*[9] But if there had been but one ⟨Person⟩, the same one being both Son and Father, he would not have made use of the advocacy of the law which demands belief in the witness not of one but of two.[10] Also when asked where was the Father, when he replied that neither he nor the Father was known to them, he spoke of two unknown, though if they had known him they would have known the Father: not indeed as though he were himself Father and Son, but because through their indivisibility the one can neither be known nor unknown without the other. *He that sent me*, he says,

[1] John 6. 32-44.
[2] John 6. 46.
[3] John 6. 66-69.
[4] John 7. 15, 16.
[5] John 7. 26-29.
[6] John 7. 32, 33.
[7] John 7. 33.
[8] John 8. 16.
[9] John 8. 18.
[10] John 8. 19.

is true, and the things which I have heard from him, those also I speak unto the world[1]: and the scripture in a digression explains that they knew not that he had spoken to them of the Father[2]; though of course they ought to have known that the Father's words are in the Son, by reading in Jeremiah, *And the Lord said to me, Behold I have put my words in thy mouth*[3]; and in Isaiah, *The Lord giveth me the tongue of discipline to know when it is right to speak a word*[4]; as he himself again says, *Then shall ye know that I am he, and that of myself I speak nothing, but as he hath taught me so also I speak, because also he is with me that hath sent me.*[5] So much concerning the witness of two ⟨who are⟩ indivisible. Also in the dispute with the Jews, when chiding them because they wished to kill him, he says, *I speak those things which I have seen with my Father, and ye do that which ye have seen with your father; and now ye wish to kill me, a man who hath spoken to you the truth which he hath heard from God*[6]: and, *If God were your father ye would have loved me, for I came forth and am come from God*[7] (howbeit they are not separated, though he said he was come forth, as some seize upon the chance which this saying gives them: for he came forth from the Father like the beam from the sun, like the stream from the spring, like the groundshoot from the seed): and, *I have not a devil, but I honour my Father*[8]: and, *If I glorify myself my glory is nothing; there is one that glorifieth me, the Father, who ye say is your God and ye do not know him; but I know him, and if I shall say, I know him not, I shall be a liar like unto you; but I know him and I keep his word.*[9] But when he adds, *Abraham saw my day and rejoiced,*[10] he surely shows that aforetime the Son was seen by Abraham, not the Father. Again, regarding that blind man he says he must do the Father's works[11]: and after the restoration of his eyes he says to him, *Dost thou believe in the Son of God?*[12] And when he asked who was he and he pointed out himself, he evidently pointed out the Son, who he had told him must be believed in. Thereafter he claims that he is known by the Father and the Father by him, and that he is loved by the Father because he lays down his life, because he had received this commandment from the Father.[13] And when asked by the Jews whether he were

[1] John 8. 26.
[2] John 8. 27.
[3] Jer. 1. 9.
[4] Is. 50. 4.
[5] John 8. 28.
[6] John 8. 38, 40.
[7] John 8. 42.
[8] John 8. 49.
[9] John 8. 54, 55.
[10] John 8. 56.
[11] John 9. 4.
[12] John 9. 35.
[13] John 10. 15, 17.

himself the Christ (evidently ⟨the Christ⟩ of God,[1] for even to the present day the Jews are hoping for the Christ of God, not the Father himself, for it is nowhere written that Christ the Father will come), he says, *I speak to you and ye believe not; the works which I do in the Father's name themselves bear witness concerning me.*[2] What witness? That he of course was he concerning whom they were asking, that is, the Christ of God. And concerning his sheep, that no one would snatch them from his hand, he says, *For what the Father hath given me is greater than ⟨they⟩ all*; and, *I and the Father are one.*[3] Here then they wish to make a stand, these fools, yea blind, who see not, first, that "I and the Father" is an indication of two; secondly, at the end ⟨of the sentence⟩, that "are" is not from the person of one, because it is spoken in the plural; and then, that he says "are one ⟨thing⟩", not "are one ⟨person⟩". For if he had said "are one ⟨person⟩" he would have been able to assist their case: for "one ⟨person⟩" is apparently an indication of the singular number. Yet when he says that two, of the masculine gender, are one ⟨thing⟩, in the neuter—which is not concerned with singularity but with unity, with similitude, with conjunction, with the love of the Father who loveth the Son, and with the obedience of the Son who obeys the Father's will—when he says, *One ⟨thing⟩ are I and the Father,*[4] he shows that those whom he equates and conjoins are two. Consequently he adds that he has shown them also many works from the Father, none of which deserved stoning.[5] And so that they should not think they ought to stone him on the ground that he had wished himself to be taken for God himself, that is, the Father, because he had said *I and the Father are one*, by way of showing that he is God, the Son of God, not by way of ⟨showing⟩ that he is God himself, he says, *If it is written in the law, I said, Ye are gods, and the scripture cannot be relaxed, say ye of him whom the Father hath sanctified and sent into the world, that he blasphemeth, because he said, I am the Son of God? If I do not the works of my Father, believe not; but if I do ⟨them⟩ and ye will not believe me, believe even for the works' sake, and know that I am in the Father and the Father in me.*[6] By means of the works, then, the Father will be in the Son and the Son in the Father, and thus by means of the works we understand that the Father and the Son are one. With

[1] John 10. 24.
[2] John 10. 25.
[3] John 10. 28, 29, 30.
[4] John 10. 30.
[5] John 10. 32.
[6] John 10. 34-38.

such insistence did he bring all this to light, to the intent that we should believe there are two, albeit in one act of power, because it would be impossible to believe there is a Son otherwise than if we believe there were two.

23. After this Martha, confessing him to be the Son of God,[1] was no more astray than Peter and Nathanael: though also if she had been astray she would at once have learned ⟨the truth⟩. For the Lord, for the raising up of her brother from the dead, looked up to heaven and to the Father and said, *Father*—evidently a son ⟨speaks⟩—*I thank thee that thou hearest me always: for the sake of these multitudes that stand by I said it, that they may believe that thou hast sent me.*[2] Also at the troubling of his soul: *And what shall I say? Father, save me from this hour? Yet for this cause came I unto this hour. But, Father, glorify thy name.*[3] And the Son was in that ⟨name⟩: *I am come*, he says, *in my Father's name.*[4] Thereafter—of course the Son's word to the Father would have been enough—behold, of superfluity the Father answers the Son from heaven; and as he had already testified, *This is my beloved Son in whom I am well pleased, hear him,*[5] so here again ⟨he says⟩, *I have both glorified it and will glorify it again.*[6] How many Persons do you think there are, self-opinionated Praxeas, if not as many as there are voices? You have the Son on earth, you have the Father in heaven. That is no separation, but a divine ordinance. Yet we know that God is even within the depths, and takes up his position everywhere [7]—though in function and power—and that the Son also, as inseparable, is with him everywhere. Yet in the economy itself it was the Father's will that the Son should be regarded as on earth, but himself in heaven. And thither also the Son looked up and prayed and made request of the Father [8]—where also he taught us to lift ourselves up and pray, *Our Father which art in heaven* [9]—though he is also everywhere. This the Father would have for his abode: *The heaven*, he says, *is my throne.*[10] From this also he made the Son a little less than the angels by sending him down to earth, yet with the intention of crowning him with glory and honour by taking him back into heaven.[11] This he was already granting him when he said, *I have*

[1] John 11. 27. [2] John 11. 41-42. [3] John 12. 27, 28.
[4] John 5. 43. [5] Matt. 17. 5. [6] John 12. 28.
[7] Ps. 139. 8. [8] John 11. 41. [9] Matt. 6. 9.
[10] Is. 66. 1. [11] Ps. 8. 5.

both glorified it and will glorify it.[1] The Son makes request from earth, the Father makes a promise from heaven. Why do you make both Father and Son a liar? If it is the case that either the Father was speaking to the Son from heaven while being himself the Son upon earth, or that the Son was praying to the Father while being himself the Father in heaven, how is it that the Son should also, by making request of the Father, make request of himself, ⟨as he would do⟩ if the Father were the Son, or again that the Father should, by making a promise to the Son, make a promise to himself, ⟨as he would do⟩ if ⟨the Son⟩ were the Father? Though it were the case that we spoke of two divided ⟨from each other⟩, as you put it about that we do, yet it were more tolerable to preach two divided than one chameleon god. And so with reference to those people the Lord next stated, *This voice came not for my sake but for your sakes,*[2] that these ⟨monarchians⟩ also may believe in both the Father and the Son, each in his own name and person and location. But once more Jesus cries and says, *He that believeth in me believeth not in me but believeth in him that sent me*—because through the Son does one believe in the Father, and the Father is the authority for believing the Son: *And he that beholdeth me beholdeth him that sent me*—how? surely because, *I have not spoken of myself, but the Father that sent me himself hath given me commandment what I shall say and what I shall speak* [3]—for, *The Lord giveth me the tongue of learning, to know when I ought to speak* [4]—*The word which I speak, even as the Father hath said unto me, so also I speak.*[5] In what sense this is said the evangelist, as being that dear disciple John, knew better than Praxeas: and consequently, himself of his own mind he says, *But before the feast of the Passover Jesus, knowing that all things were delivered to him by the Father and that he was from God and was going to God.*[6] But Praxeas will have it that the Father himself came forth from himself and went away to himself, with the result that the devil put into the heart of Judas the betrayal [8] not of the Son but of the Father himself—with no benefit either to the devil or to the heretic, since not even in respect of the Son did the devil contrive the betrayal with advantage to himself. For he who was betrayed was the Son of God who was in the Son of Man, as the

[1] John 12. 28.
[2] John 12. 30.
[3] John 12. 44-49.
[4] Is. 50. 4.
[5] John 12. 50.
[6] John 13. 1, 3.
[7] John 13. 2.

scripture adds: *Now is the Son of Man glorified, and God is glorified in him.*[1] What God? Evidently not the Father, but the Word of the Father who was in the Son of Man, that is, in the flesh: and Jesus, who had already been glorified in that ⟨flesh⟩, though but by power and word, ⟨now⟩ says, *And God will glorify him in himself*[2]—that is, the Father ⟨will glorify⟩ the Son, whom, because he had him in himself though brought low to earth, he did shortly afterwards by the conquest of death glorify through the resurrection.

24. Clearly there were some who even then did not understand: for Thomas, for a while unbelieving, says, *Lord, we know not whither thou goest, and how know we the way?* And Jesus ⟨said⟩, *I am the way, the truth, and the life: no one cometh unto the Father but by me: if ye had known me ye would have known the Father also: but from henceforth ye know him and have seen him.*[3] And now we come to Philip, who, bestirred by the hope of seeing the Father, and not understanding in what sense he had been told that the Father had been seen, says, *Shew us the Father and it sufficeth us*: and the Lord (said⟩, *Philip, am I so long time with you and ye do not know me?*[4] ⟨As⟩ who does he say he ought to have been known by them? For this alone calls for discussion. As the Father, or as the Son? If as the Father, let Praxeas tell us how Christ, having companied so long time with them, could ever, I say not be understood to be the Father, but even be thought to be. To us all the scriptures predetermine, the old the Christ of God, the new the Son of God. This was preached aforetime, this was stated also by Christ himself, yea now also by the Father himself openly from heaven confessing the Son and glorifying the Son—*This is my Son,*[5] and, *I have glorified and will glorify.*[6] This also was believed by the disciples, this also was not believed by the Jews. Wishing them to believe him to be this he at every hour named the Father and set forth the Father and honoured the Father. If that is so, it was not the Father who they did not know had companied so long time with them, but the Son: and the Lord, upbraiding them for not knowing himself as him whom they had not known, clearly wished to be recognised as he whom he had upbraided them for not recognising in so long a time, namely the Son. And now it can appear in what sense

[1] John 13. 31. [2] John 13. 32. [3] John 14. 5-7.
[4] John 14. 8, 9. [5] Matt. 17. 5. [6] John 12. 28.

it was said, *He that seeth me seeth the Father also*[1]: of course in the same sense as above, *I and the Father are one.*[2] Why? Because, *I came forth and am come from God*[3]; and, *I am the way, no one cometh unto the Father but by me*[4]; and, *No one cometh unto me except the Father have drawn him*[5]; and, *All things hath the Father delivered to me*[6]; and, *As the Father quickeneth, so also the Son*[7]; and, *If ye know me ye know the Father also.*[8] For according to these ⟨texts⟩ he had revealed himself as the deputy of the Father, by means of whom the Father was both seen in acts and heard in words and known in the Son ministering the Father's acts and words: because the Father is invisible, a fact which Philip also had learned in the Law and ought to have remembered —*No one shall see God and live.*[9] And consequently he is chidden for desiring to see the Father as though he were visible, and is informed that he becomes visible in the Son, in consequence of acts of power, not in consequence of actual manifestation of his Person. Further, if by saying *He that seeth me seeth the Father,*[10] he wished the identity of Father and Son to be understood, why does he add, *Believest thou not that I am in the Father and the Father in me?*[11] For he ought to have added, Believest thou not that I am the Father? Or why did he enlarge upon it, except that he made that clear which he wished them to understand, namely that he was the Son? Further, in saying *Believest thou not that I am in the Father and the Father in me,*[12] he enlarged upon it for this reason rather, lest, on the ground that he had said *He that hath seen me hath seen the Father also,*[13] he might be thought to be the Father: and this he never wished to be thought to be, for he always professed to be the Son, and to have come from the Father. Therefore he also made manifest the conjunction of the two Persons, so that the Father separately might not, as though visible, be asked for in open view, and that the Son might be accepted as he who makes the Father present. And no less did he explain this also, in what manner the Father was in the Son and the Son in the Father: *The words*, he says, *that I speak unto you are not mine*—evidently because they are the Father's—*but the Father abiding in me doeth the works.*[14] Therefore the

[1] John 14. 9.
[2] John 10. 30.
[3] John 16. 27.
[4] John 14. 6.
[5] John 6. 44.
[6] Matt. 11. 27.
[7] John 5. 21.
[8] John 14. 7.
[9] Exod. 33. 20.
[10] John 14. 9.
[11] John 14. 10.
[12] John 14. 10.
[13] John 14. 9.
[14] John 14. 10.

Father, abiding in the Son through works of power and words of doctrine, is seen through those things through which he abides, and through him in whom he abides: and from this very fact it is apparent that each Person is himself and none other, while he says, *I am in the Father and the Father in me*. And so he says, *Believe*. What? That I am the Father? I think it is not so written, but, *That I am in the Father and the Father in me, or if not, believe for the very works' sake* [1]—those works in fact through which the Father was seen in the Son, not with the eyes but with the mind.

25. After Philip and the whole context of that question, the things which ⟨follow⟩ down to the end of the gospel continue in the same kind of discourse, in which the Father and the Son are distinguished as being each himself. He promises that when he has ascended to the Father he will also request of the Father the Paraclete, and will send him, ⟨specifying⟩ *another*.[2] But we have already explained in what sense ⟨he means⟩ "another". Moreover he says, *He will take of mine*,[3] as I myself have taken of the Father's. So the close series of the Father in the Son and the Son in the Paraclete makes three who cohere, the one attached to the other. And these three are one ⟨thing⟩, not one ⟨person⟩, in the sense in which it was said, *I and the Father are one*,[4] in respect of unity of substance, not of singularity of number. Take a further quick glance, and you will find that he whom you believe to be the Father is called the Father's vine,[5] and the Father the husbandman, just as ⟨you will find⟩ that he who you think was on earth was by the Son acknowledged to be in heaven when he lifted up his eyes there and commended his disciples to the Father.[6] But although in this gospel there is no revelation of *My God, why hast thou forsaken me*? [7] or of *Father, in thy hands I lay down my spirit*,[8] yet after the resurrection and the glory of the conquest of death, when he has put off from him the necessity of any humility and now could show himself as the Father to that faithful woman who attempted to touch him as a result of affection and not of curiosity nor of Thomas's unbelief, he says, *Touch me not, for I am not yet ascended to my Father, but go to my brethren*—and even in this he shows himself the Son, for

[1] John 14. 11. [2] John 14. 16. [3] John 16. 14.
[4] John 10. 30. [5] John 15. 1. [6] John 17. 1.
[7] Matt. 27. 46 : Mark 15. 34. [8] Luke 23. 46.

he would have called them his sons if he had been the Father—*and tell them, I ascend to my Father and your Father, my God and your God.*[1] Father to Father, and God to God? Or Son to Father, and Word to God? Also what reason does the very conclusion of the gospel set as the seal upon *these things* that *are written*, except, *That ye may believe that Jesus Christ is the Son of God*? [2] Therefore whatever of these things you have thought were able to be of advantage to you for the demonstration of the identity of Father and Son, you are striving against the express judgement of the gospel: for the things were written, not that you may believe that Jesus Christ is the Father, but that ⟨you may believe that he is⟩ the Son.

26. On account of Philip's one remark and the Lord's reply to it we seem to have made a complete study of John's gospel, so that so many things clearly stated both before it and after it may not be overturned by one remark, which ought to be interpreted in accordance with them all, not in contradiction with them all and even in contradiction with its own meaning. But, so as not to lodge ⟨as evidence⟩ other gospels which by ⟨relating⟩ the Lord's nativity confirm our faith, it is enough that he who was to be born of the virgin was by the angel messenger himself defined as the Son of God: *The Spirit of God shall come upon thee and the power of the Most High shall overshadow thee, wherefore that which shall be born of thee shall be called holy, the Son of God.*[3] They will wish to quibble even here, but the truth will prevail. "Doubtless", say they, "the Son of God is God, and the power of the Most High is the Most High", and they are not ashamed to assume that which, if it had been so, would have been so written. For, consideration for whom prevented him from openly stating, God shall come upon thee and the Most High shall overshadow thee? For when he said *The Spirit of God*,[4] although God is spirit, yet since he did not mention God in the nominative case he wished there to be understood an assignment of the whole which was to go to the Son's account. This Spirit of God will be the same as the Word. For as, when John says *The Word was made flesh*,[5] we understand also Spirit at the mention of the Word, so also here we recognise also the Word under the name of the Spirit. For spirit is the substance of the Word, and word

[1] John 20. 17. [2] John 20. 31. [3] Luke 1. 35.
[4] Luke 1. 35. [5] John 1. 14.

is an operation of the Spirit, and the two are one ⟨thing⟩. Otherwise there will be one whom John declares to have been made flesh, and another who the angel says will be flesh, if it is not the case that both the Spirit is the Word and the Word is the Spirit. As therefore the Word of God is not ⟨God⟩ himself whose ⟨Word⟩ he is, so the Spirit also, though he is called God, is yet not ⟨God⟩ himself whose ⟨Spirit⟩ he is called. Nothing in genitive dependence is that on which it is dependent. Clearly when a thing is "from him", and is "his" in the sense that it is from him, it can be a thing which is like him from whom it is and whose it is: and consequently the Spirit is God and the Word is God, because he is from God, yet is not ⟨God⟩ himself from whom he is. But if the Spirit of God, as being a substantive thing, will not ⟨be found to⟩ be God himself, but in that sense God as being from the substance of God himself, in that it is a substantive thing and a certain assignment of the whole, much more so the power of the Most High will not be the Most High himself, because it is not even a substantive thing as the Spirit is, any more than wisdom or providence: for these are not substances, but attributes of each several substance. Power is an attribute of spirit, and will not itself be spirit. Since then these, whatever they are, the Spirit of God and his Word and his power, were conferred upon the virgin, that which is born of her is the Son of God. This in these gospels he himself testifies that he is, immediately, as a boy: *Know ye not*, he says, *that I must be in my Father's ⟨house⟩?* [1] This also Satan knew at the temptations: *If thou art the Son of God.*[2] This also later the devils confess: *We know thee who thou art, the Son of God.*[3] He himself prays to the Father.[4] When Peter recognises him as the Christ of God he does not deny it.[5] When he rejoices in the Spirit he says to the Father, *I thank thee, Father, that thou hast hid these things from the wise.*[6] In the same passage also he affirms that the Father is known to none but the Son,[7] and that the Son of the Father will in the presence of the Father confess them that confess him and deny them that deny him,[8] while he introduces the parable of a son, not a father, who was sent into a vineyard after a number of servants ⟨had been sent⟩ and was killed by wicked rustics and

[1] Luke 2. 49. [2] Matt. 4. 3, 6. [3] Mark. 1. 24. [4] Mark 1. 35. [5] Luke 9. 20. [6] Luke 10. 21. [7] Luke 10. 22. [8] Matt. 10. 32.

avenged by his father [1]: and he even himself knows not the last day or hour, which is known to the Father alone [2]: and he ordains for his disciples a kingdom even as he says one has been ordained for him by his Father [3]: and he has power to ask his Father for legions of angels to help him, if he wished [4]: and he cries aloud that God has forsaken him,[5] and places his spirit in the Father's hands,[6] and after the resurrection pledges himself to send to his disciples the promise of the Father,[7] and, lastly, commands them to baptize unto the Father and the Son and the Holy Spirit,[8] not unto one ⟨only⟩: for not once, but thrice, are we baptized, unto each several Person at each several name.

27. But why shall I delay over things so evident, when I ought to be attacking those ⟨arguments⟩ by which they seek to cast darkness over ⟨these⟩ evident things? For, convicted on all sides by the distinctness of the Father and the Son, which we say is ordained without disturbing the permanence of the union as of the sun and the beam and of the spring and the river, they attempt to interpret this ⟨distinctness⟩ in another way, not less in accordance with their opinion, so as no less ⟨than before⟩ to distinguish Father and Son both in one person, while they say that the Son is the flesh, that is, the Man, Jesus, while the Father is the Spirit, that is, God, Christ. These who contend that the Father and the Son are one and the same, now begin to divide them rather than to call them one. For if Jesus is one and Christ is another, the Son will be one and the Father another, because Jesus is the Son and Christ is the Father. This sort of monarchy they perhaps learned of from Valentinus, to make two of Jesus and Christ. But this assumption of theirs has already had its point blunted by our previous discussion, because he whom they make the Father is described as the Word of God, or the Spirit of God and the power of the Most High: for these are not he to whom they are described as belonging, but are from him and belong to him. Yet they will be refuted also in another way in that text. "Behold", they say, "it was announced by the angel, *Therefore that which shall be born of thee shall be called holy, the Son of God* [9]: and so it was flesh that was born, and so the flesh will be the Son of God." And yet the statement was made con-

[1] Matt. 21. 33-41. [2] Mark 13. 32. [3] Luke 22. 29.
[4] Matt. 26. 53. [5] Matt. 27. 46: Mark 15. 34. [6] Luke 23. 46.
[7] Luke 24. 49. [8] Matt. 28. 19. [9] Luke 1. 35.

cerning the Spirit of God. For certainly it was of the Holy Spirit that the virgin conceived, and what she conceived that she brought to birth. Therefore that must have been born which was conceived and was to be brought to birth, that is, the Spirit, whose name also shall be called *Emmanuel, which is interpreted, God with us.*[1] But flesh is not God, that of it should be said, *It shall be called holy, the Son of God*; but he who as God was born in it, of whom also the psalm ⟨speaks⟩, *Because God as man was born in her and hath builded her by the will of the Father.*[2] Who, being God, was born in her? The Word, and the Spirit who with the Word was born by the Father's will. Therefore the Word is in flesh; while we must also enquire about this, how the Word was made flesh, whether as transformed into flesh or as having clothed himself with flesh. Certainly as having clothed himself. God however must necessarily be believed to be immutable and untransformable, as being eternal. But change of form is a destruction of what was there first: for everything that is transformed into something else ceases to be what it was and begins to be what it was not. But God neither ceases to be, nor can be anything else. And the Word is God, and *the Word of God abideth for ever,*[3] evidently by continuing in his own form. And if it is not feasible for him to be conformed ⟨to something else⟩, it follows that he must be understood to have been made flesh in the sense that he comes to be in flesh, and is manifested and seen and handled by means of the flesh[4]: because the other considerations also demand this acceptation. For if the Word was made flesh as the result of a transformation or mutation of substance, Jesus will then be one substance ⟨composed⟩ of two, flesh and spirit, a kind of mixture, as electrum is ⟨composed⟩ of gold and silver: and he begins to be neither gold (that is, spirit) nor silver (that is, flesh), seeing that the one thing is changed by the other and a third thing is brought into being. In that case Jesus will not be God, for he has ceased to be the Word, since it has become flesh: neither will his manhood be flesh, for it is not properly flesh, seeing it has been the Word. Thus out of both things there is neither: there is some third thing far other than both. Yet we find that he is, not in genitive dependence, set forth as both God and Man, the psalm itself making this suggestion, *Because God as man was born*

[1] Matt. 1. 23. [2] Ps. 87. 5. [3] Is. 40. 8.
[4] 1 John 1. 1, 2.

in her, he hath builded her by the will of the Father [1]: certainly ⟨we find him set forth⟩ as in every respect Son of God and Son of man, since ⟨we find him⟩ as both God and Man, without doubt according to each substance as it is distinct in what itself is, because neither is the Word anything else but God nor the flesh anything else but man. Thus also the apostle teaches of both his substances: *Who was made*, he says, *of the seed of David*—here he will be man, and Son of Man: *Who was defined as Son of God according to the Spirit* [2]—here he will be God, and the Word, the Son of God: we observe a double quality, not confused but combined, Jesus in one Person God and Man. I postpone ⟨the consideration⟩ of "Christ". And to such a degree did there remain unimpaired the proper being of each substance, that in him the Spirit carried out its own acts, that is powers and works and signs, while the flesh accomplished its own passions, hungering in company of the devil,[3] thirsting in company of the Samaritan woman,[4] weeping for Lazarus,[5] sore troubled unto death [6]—and at length it also died. But if there had been some third thing, a confusion of both, like electrum, there would not be in evidence such distinct proofs of both substances; but the Spirit would have performed the functions of the flesh and the flesh the functions of the Spirit, by interchange, or else neither those of the flesh nor those of the Spirit but those of some third form, by confusion: yes, either the Word would have died or the flesh would not have died, if the Word had been converted into flesh, for either the flesh would have been immortal or the Word mortal. But because both substances acted distinctively each in its own quality, therefore to them accrued both their own activities and their own destinies. Learn therefore with Nicodemus that *what is born in the flesh is flesh and what is born of the Spirit is spirit.*[7] Flesh does not become spirit nor spirit flesh: evidently they can ⟨both⟩ be in one ⟨person⟩. Of these Jesus is composed, of flesh as Man and of spirit as God: and on that occasion the angel, in respect of that part in which he was spirit, pronounced him the Son of God, reserving for the flesh the designation Son of Man. Thus also the apostle, in calling him even the mediator of God and of man,[8] confirms ⟨the fact that he is⟩ of both substances. Lastly,

[1] Ps. 87. 5.
[2] Rom. 1. 3, 4.
[3] Matt. 4. 2.
[4] John 4. 7.
[5] John 11. 35.
[6] Matt. 26. 38.
[7] John 3. 6.
[8] 1 Tim. 2. 5.

you who interpret "Son of God" as the flesh, show me who the Son of Man may be. Or is he to be the Spirit? But you wish the Spirit to be taken to be the Father himself, since God is spirit: as though, just as the Word is God, God's Spirit might not also be God's Word.

28. And so you make Christ into the Father, you great fool, because you do not even examine the very force of this name, if indeed "Christ" is a name and not rather a title: for it signifies "anointed". Yet "anointed" is no more a name than "clothed" or "shod", but is something attributive to a name. If as a result of some quibbling Jesus were also called "clothed", as he is called Christ from the sacrament of anointing, would you, as you do here, call Jesus the Son of God but believe "clothed" to be the Father? Now concerning "Christ". If the Father is Christ, the Father is anointed, and by some one else at that: or if by himself, prove it. But that is not the teaching of the Acts of the Apostles in that cry of the church to God, *For in this city have all assembled together, Herod and Pilate with the gentiles, against thy holy Son whom thou hast anointed.*[1] Thus they testified both that Jesus is the Son of God and that the Son was anointed by the Father: consequently Jesus will be the same as Christ who was anointed by the Father, not ⟨the same as⟩ the Father who anointed the Son. So also Peter: *Therefore let all the house of Israel know assuredly that God hath made both Lord and Christ*—that is, anointed—*this Jesus whom ye crucified.*[2] But John even brands as a liar him who has denied that Jesus is Christ,[3] and in contrast ⟨says⟩ that every one who believes that Jesus is Christ is born of God[4]: for which reason he also exhorts us to believe in the name of his Son Jesus Christ, so that, he says, we may have fellowship with the Father and with his Son Jesus Christ.[5] Thus also Paul in every place puts *God the Father and our Lord Jesus Christ*: when he writes to the Romans he gives thanks to God through our Lord Jesus Christ[6]; when to the Galatians, he represents himself as an apostle, not from men nor through man, but through Jesus Christ and God the Father.[7] And you have, throughout all his collected works, ⟨texts⟩ which make statements in this manner and set forth as two God the Father and our Lord Jesus Christ

[1] Acts 4. 27. [2] Acts 2. 36. [3] 1 John 2. 22.
[4] 1 John 5. 1. [5] 1 John 1. 3. [6] Rom. 1. 8.
[7] Gal. 1. 1.

the Son of the Father, and ⟨say⟩ that Jesus himself is Christ, and, under another name also, the Son of God. For continually, by that right by which both names belong to one, that is, the Son of God, one even without the other belongs to the same one: and if "Jesus" alone is written "Christ" also is understood because Jesus was anointed; while if only "Christ" is written, the same is also Jesus because the anointed is Jesus. And of these names one is a proper name which was conferred by the angel, while the other as an attributive accrues from the anointing, yet only so long as Christ is the Son and not the Father. Finally, how blind is the man who does not understand that if he ascribes the name of Christ to the Father the presage of another god is implied in the name of Christ. For if Christ the Father is God who says, *I ascend to my Father and your Father and my God and your God,*[1] evidently he reveals another father and god above himself. Also if the Father is Christ, there is another *who stablisheth the thunder and createth the spirit and announceth unto men his Christ.*[2] And if *the kings of the earth are stood up and the rulers are gathered together into one against the Lord and against his Christ*[3] there will be another lord against whose Christ the kings and rulers are gathered together. And if *Thus saith the Lord to my Lord Christ,*[4] there will be another lord who is speaking to Christ the Father. And when the apostle writes, *That the God of our Lord Jesus Christ may give you the Spirit of wisdom and knowledge,*[5] there will be another god of Jesus Christ, the bestower of spiritual gifts. Certainly, so as not to wander over the whole ground, he who raised up Christ and is also to raise up our mortal bodies,[6] will be as it were another raiser up than the Father who died and the Father who was raised up, if it is the case that Christ who died is the Father.

29. Let this blasphemy be silent, be silent. Let it be enough to say that Christ the Son of God died, and this ⟨only⟩ because it is so written. For the apostle, while stating not without risk that Christ died, adds *According to the scriptures,*[7] so as by the authority of the scriptures to soften the hardness of the statement[8] and avert offence to the hearer. And yet, since in Christ Jesus there are assessed two substances, a divine and a human, and it is admitted that the divine is immortal, as that that which is

[1] John 20. 17. [2] Amos 4. 13. [3] Ps. 2. 2.
[4] Is. 45. 1. [5] Eph. 1. 17. [6] Rom. 8. 11.
[7] 1 Cor. 15. 3. [8] John 6. 60.

human is mortal, it is evident in what respect he says he died, namely in that he is flesh and man and Son of Man, not in that he is spirit and Word and Son of God. By saying then that Christ —that is, the anointed—died, he makes it clear that that which was anointed died, that is, the flesh. "So", you say, "we also who, by the same reasoning as you, say that the Son ⟨died⟩, do not blaspheme against the Lord God; for we say that he died not in respect of his divine but of his human substance." Yet you do blaspheme, not only because you say the Father died but also because ⟨you say he was⟩ crucified. For by converting Christ into the Father you blaspheme against the Father with that curse upon one crucified [1] which by the Law accrues to the Son, because it was Christ, not the Father, who was *made a curse for us.*[2] Whereas we, when we say that Christ was crucified, curse him not, but relate the curse of the Law, because neither did the apostle blaspheme when he said this. But just as a thing said of anyone of whom it may appropriately be said is said without blasphemy, so what is not appropriate is blasphemy if it is said. Consequently neither did the Father suffer with the Son. In fact because they are ashamed of direct blasphemy against the Father, they hope it may in this manner be mitigated, while they now admit that Father and Son are two if indeed in this fashion the Son suffers while the Father suffers with ⟨him⟩. In this also are they fools. For what is "compassion" except "suffering with" another? Further, if the Father is impassible he is of course incompassible: or if he is compassible he is of course passible. So you do him no benefit by this fear of yours. For you fear to call passible him whom you do call compassible. But the Father is just as incompassible as the Son also is impassible as regards that state in which he is God. "But in what way did the Son suffer, if the Father also did not suffer with him?" The difference begins from the Son, not from the Father. For also if a river is defiled by some muddying, although the one substance comes down from the spring and there is no interruption at the spring, yet the malady of the river will not attach to the spring: and though the water which suffers ⟨injury⟩ belongs to the spring, so long as it suffers not in the spring but in the river it is not the spring that suffers, but the river which ⟨has come⟩ from the spring. So also how could the Spirit of God suffer in the Son? On the ground

[1] Deut. 21. 23. [2] Gal. 3. 13.

that ⟨the Spirit⟩ was suffering not in the Father but in the Son, would it seem that the Father had not suffered? But it is enough that the Spirit of God suffered nothing on his own account: because if he did suffer anything in the Son there was a possibility of the Father suffering with the Son, in the flesh. But this has ⟨already⟩ been discussed, and no one will deny ⟨our conclusion⟩: since neither can we suffer on behalf of God except there be in us the Spirit of God, who also speaks concerning us the things which belong to ⟨our⟩ confessorship, while himself not suffering, but granting us the ability to suffer.

30. Otherwise, if you will persist further, I shall be able to give you a harder answer and to put you in conflict with the statement of the Lord himself, so as to say, Why do you ask questions about that ⟨answer⟩? You have him crying aloud at his passion, *My God, my God, why hast thou forsaken me?* [1] Consequently either the Son was suffering, forsaken by the Father, and the Father did not suffer, seeing he had forsaken the Son: or else, if it was the Father who was suffering, to what God was he crying aloud? But this utterance of flesh and soul (that is, of the manhood), not of the Word and Spirit (that is, not of God), was sent forth with the express purpose of showing the impassibility of God who thus forsook the Son when he delivered his manhood to death. This was in the apostle's mind when he wrote, *If the Father spared not his Son.*[2] This also Isaiah, an earlier ⟨authority⟩ stated: *And the Lord hath delivered him for our iniquities.*[3] He forsook in that he did not spare, he forsook in that he delivered. Yet the Father did not forsake the Son, since the Son placed his own spirit in the Father's hands.[4] He placed it ⟨there⟩ in short, and straightway died: for while the spirit remains in the flesh the flesh cannot die at all. Thus, to be forsaken by the Father was to the Son death. The Son therefore both dies and is raised up again by the Father according to the scriptures.[5] The Son ascended into the higher parts of heaven, as he did also descend into the inner parts of the earth.[6] This is he who sitteth at the right hand of the Father,[7] not the Father at his own right hand. This is he whom Stephen sees, when he is being stoned, still standing at the right hand of God,[8] as thenceforth to sit, until the Father do put all

[1] Matt. 27. 46. [2] Rom 8. 32. [3] Is. 53. 6.
[4] Luke 23. 46. [5] 1 Cor. 15. 3. [6] Eph. 4. 9.
[7] Mark 16. 19. [8] Acts 7. 55.

enemies under his feet.[1] This is he who is also to come again above the clouds of heaven in like fashion as also he ascended.[2] This is he who meanwhile has poured forth the gift which he has received from the Father, the Holy Spirit, the third name of the deity and the third sequence of the majesty, the preacher of one monarchy and also the interpreter of the economy for those who admit the words of his new prophecy, and the leader into all the truth [3] which is in the Father and the Son and the Holy Spirit according to the Christian mystery.

31. Moreover this matter is of Jewish faith, so to believe in one God as to refuse to count in with him the Son, and after the Son the Spirit. For what ⟨difference⟩ will there be between us and them except that disagreement? What need is there of the Gospel, what is that confidence of the New Testament which establishes the Law and the Prophets until John,[4] unless thereafter Father and Son and Spirit, believed in as three, constitute one God? It was God's will to make a new covenant for the very purpose that in a new way his unity might be believed in through the Son and the Spirit, so that God who had aforetime been preached through the Son and the Spirit without being understood might now be known in his own proper names and persons. Therefore let them beware, these antichrists who deny the Father and the Son [5]: for they do deny the Father while they identify him with the Son, and they deny the Son while they identify him with the Father, granting them things they are not and taking away things they are. But *he who shall confess that Christ is the Son of God*—not the Father—*God abideth in him and he in God.*[6] We believe *the testimony of God by which he hath testified concerning his Son: He that hath not the Son hath not life.*[7] But he has not the Son who believes him to be other than the Son.

[1] Ps. 110. 1.
[2] Acts 1. 11 : Luke 21. 27.
[3] John 16. 13.
[4] Matt. 11. 13.
[5] 1 John 2. 22.
[6] 1 John 4. 15.
[7] 1 John 5. 9, 12.

COMMENTARY AND NOTES

TERTULLIANI ADVERSUS PRAXEAN LIBER

1. *It is a habit of the devil to attack the truth by pretending to defend it. He champions the divine unity, but only to make a heresy of it. He says that the Father himself was incarnate. But he has forgotten himself, for when he was tempting Christ he approached him as Son of God, ⟨thus admitting a distinction between the Father and the Son⟩: unless perchance he alleges that Matthew and Luke have wrongly reported him, and have falsified the Gospel narrative. On the contrary: he himself is the falsifier, along with underlings of his such as Praxeas. This person was the first to import this heresy from Asia to Rome, where he also prevailed upon the Roman bishop to desist from his project of recognising the new prophecy. The tares sown by Praxeas bore fruit in Africa also: I had them brought to light and they had apparently been pulled up, the teacher having signed a document admitting his error. But they had seeded themselves, and having lain hid for a time are now beginning to grow again. Consequently they again need to be rooted up: and that is the purpose of this treatise.*

For the historical circumstances here summarised see the Introduction, p. 10, and for the monarchianist theology, p. 11.

Aemulatus est,

"has shown hostility". So always in Tertullian. Rivalry may begin as competitive striving towards a good end, but it is prone to develop into personal enmity: the word has suffered the fate of the moral process which it describes. Cf. *adv. Marc.* i. 26, *quia aemulum sit necesse est* (sc. *eius*) *quod noluit admitti et nolendo prohibuit . . . qui non alias plene bonus sit nisi mali aemulus: ibid.* ii. 11, *nihil enim aemulum mali non bonum sicut et boni aemulum nihil non malum: de anima,* 2, *quia et ex aemulis* (our adversaries) *nonnunquam testimonium necessarium, si non aemulis prosit*: *ibid.* 57, *quid novi aemulatio veritatis in spiritu immundo? de carne Christi*, 4, *in aemulationem sapientiae saecularis* (in contrast with).

Adfectavit,

which means "pretend" in both the older and the newer sense of the English word, here appears to distribute those senses between *defendendo* and *concutere*, i.e. "he has tried to shake by pretending to defend".

Ipsum . . . patrem descendisse.

On the interpretation of Luke 1. 35 see the Introduction, p. 63.

Coluber,

the serpent, which is the devil and Satan: Gen. 3. 15: Rom. 16. 20: Rev. 20. 2.

Ex ipsis scripturis: Ps. 91. 11, 12: cf. Matt. 4. 6: Luke 4. 10, 11.

Viderit M. et L.

Cf. *de anima*, 2, *sed viderit utriusque* (sc. *medicinae et philosophiae*) *praestantiae ambitio: adv. Prax.* 31, *viderint igitur antichristi.*

Ad ipsum deum . . . ipsum omnipotentem.

Tertullian's own practice follows the New Testament in applying the designation *deus* rarely, and in a derivative sense or predicatively, to God the Son: less infrequently than the New Testament he applies it to the Holy Spirit. There is in Tertullian's mind a sense in which the Father is God, so to speak, in first instance, while the Son is *derivatio totius substantiae deitatis.* In the Church Service, as a rule, though there are exceptions, prayers addressed to our Lord begin not with *Deus* but with *Domine.* There is however a certain irony in the present sentence, which is supposedly spoken by the devil, and need not of necessity represent Tertullian's own view. See a note on § 9, and cf. § 13.

Nunquam illum, etc.

"perhaps I should not have demeaned myself ⟨to tempt⟩ him". The conjecture of Ursinus seems unnecessary: brevity by omission is quite in Tertullian's style.

Praxeas

is not mentioned by other anti-heretical writers, except pseudo-Tertullian (*adv. omn. haer.* 8), Augustine, and Gennadius, who are too late to be regarded as first-hand authorities. The silence of Hippolytus is remarkable, for he must have been in Rome at the presumed time of Praxeas' visit there. Consequently it has been suggested (see the Introduction, p. 10) that the name was invented by Tertullian to cover some important person, such as

Zephyrinus or Callistus. The reference to confessorship would suit either of these, though there is no evidence that they came from Asia. Tertullian does not say that Praxeas was ever in Africa: the common opinion that he was is deduced from a false reading *Roma* in the next sentence, and *doctor* later in this chapter need not be Praxeas.

Romam, homo.

This is Oehler's emendation, and on general grounds seems likely to be correct: though he is wrong in suggesting that it means the provinces near Rome, for it means the city itself. *Romanae humo*, of the earlier editions, was intended to give the same meaning. But *romana humus* could only mean imperial territory, in which Asia is already included. Also the dative is the wrong case, and without *homo* or some such word the succeeding epithets are left lame. Engelbrecht, whose suggestions are usually good, would read *romanae humo, homo*: but again "soil" has no point, unless (which is unlikely) there is a reference by anticipation to the parable of the Tares.

Episcopum romanum.

The tract *adv. omn. haer.* (preserved in the same MS. as Tertullian, *de praescr. haer.*, but possibly by Victorinus of Petavio, a martyr in Diocletian's persecution) gives this bishop's name as Victorinus. This seems like a conflation of an original reading "Victor" with a scribal correction "Zephyrinus". Zephyrinus (202-219) is perhaps too late to suit Tertullian's narrative: Victor (192-202) is more probable. But there is a remarkable coincidence of language between Tertullian's words here, *pacem ecclesiis Asiae et Phrygiae inferentem*, and those of Eusebius (*H.E.* v. 3), who says that the brethren in Gaul, hearing of the various opinions held concerning the prophecies of Montanus, Alcibiades, and Theodotus, sent letters expressing their own judgement, and expounding letters written in prison by their own martyrs, to the brethren in Asia and Phrygia and to Eleutherus bishop of Rome (177-192), τῆς τῶν ἐκκλησιῶν εἰρήνης ἕνεκα πρεσβεύοντες. According to Tertullian, Eleutherus condemned the prophets: Victor, ignorant of his predecessor's policy, or preferring to disregard it, was inclined to approve of the movement, until Praxeas arrived in Rome and (*a*) gave him information discreditable to the prophets, and (*b*) reminded him of his predecessor's ruling.

Falsa de ipsis prophetis, etc.

For contemporary estimates of Montanism and strictures upon the character of Montanus and his associates see the Introduction, p. 78. It is hard to believe that Tertullian would have approved either of moral disorder or of that type of enthusiasm which is described as "involuntary madness of the soul": and we must surmise (*a*) that in Africa the more fanatical manifestations of the movement were rarely or never produced, and (*b*) that Tertullian had heard of, but did not credit, some of the other objectionable features of Phrygian Montanism.

Praecessorum eius auctoritates.

Praecessorum may be a rhetorical plural, and refer only to Eleutherus (177-192). There is no evidence independent of this passage that he or Soter (168-177) condemned Montanism: but they may have done so, and provoked the martyrs of Lyons to remonstrance. The appeal to a previous decision would have had some weight at Rome, and in all catholic Churches, but none whatever with Tertullian, who would have replied, *dominus noster Christus veritatem se, non consuetudinem, cognominavit* (*de virg. vel.* 1).

Fruticaverant avenae Praxeanae hic quoque superseminatae,

"Here ⟨in Africa⟩ also Praxean tares were sown over ⟨the good seed⟩ and germinated": cf. *de anima*, 16, *avenarum superseminatorem et frumentariae segetis nocturnum interpolatorem*, and Hippolytus, *philos.* ix. 7 (a passage treating of the same subject as the present), Ἐπίγονός τις τοὔνομα, ὃς τῇ Ῥώμῃ ἐπιδημήσας ἐπέσπειρε τὴν ἄθεον γνώμην. Tertullian does not say that Praxeas himself came to Africa: his doctrines were taught there by some person unnamed, referred to below as "the teacher". "While men slept" in simplicity of doctrine, they obtained some vogue: afterwards they were brought to light (*traductae*, a late use of the word, cf. Petronius, 17, *neve traducere velitis tot annorum secreta*: *de anima*, 1, *nondum enim Christianae potestatis documenta processerant, quae vim istam perniciosissimam . . . sola traducit*); "by whom God would", i.e. by Tertullian himself, probably the only man in Africa with sufficient theological acumen to be aware of the danger. The teacher *caverat pristinum*—a legal expression meaning that he gave security for his return to his former opinions [1]: he signed a written document to that effect, which when Tertullian was writing was still in the archives of the Church: and there is no reason to think that he went back on his word. That being so, if he were now a person of note, only harm would be done by publishing his name. The tares appeared to have been rooted up, and it seemed as if the trouble were at an end. But not so: they had been allowed to grow long enough to make seed, which was self-sown over the land, and for a time lay dormant (*subdola vivacitate latitavit*) because those infected with it dissembled their views (*per hypocrisin*): it had now germinated afresh, and called for a fresh uprooting. *Avenae* stood in the Old Latin version for *ζιζάνια* (so, e.g., Prudentius, *hamartigenia*, 217, *malignus ager . . . triticeam vacuis segetem violavit avenis*): the Vulgate retains the Greek word.

Apud psychicos, apud quos tunc gesta res est.

St Paul (1 Cor. 2. 14-3. 3) distinguishes between the carnal man, the natural man (ψυχικός, *animalis*), and the spiritual man. All men, he would say, are endowed with the three constituents, body, soul, and spirit: the distinction depends on whether body, soul, or spirit is the ruling factor in one's outlook and conduct; and that depends on the grace of God and one's use of it. See a masterly exposition of these terms in St Augustine, *de fide et symbolo*, 23. The gnostics, and afterwards the Manichees, made the distinction absolute: the carnal man was so constituted that he could not help being carnal, and likewise the natural man, and the spiritual man. The spiritual man was the gnostic, certain of salvation; the carnal man the pagan, incapable of salvation; the natural man the ordinary Christian, capable of a limited salvation but not of reception within the "fulness of the godhead". Tertullian uses the terms in a Pauline sense, but with a difference. To him the psychic or animal or natural man is the ordinary Christian; the spiritual man is the Montanist, who has received or who acknowledges the *χαρίσματα* of the Holy Spirit in the "new prophecy". The *psychici* therefore in the present passage

[1] A note by Fr. Junius, quoted by Oehler, suggests that *caverat pristinum* is equivalent to τὸ ἀρχαῖον ἠσφαλίζετο, which he says (though he produces no evidence) has the meaning given in the note. C. H. Turner (*J.T.S.* vol. xiv. p. 556), disregarding this suggestion, objects that there is no adverb *pristinum*, and offers an emendation *caverat presbyter istorum doctor*. But if Junius is right, *pristinum* is not an adverb, but a cognate or adverbial accusative.

are the Catholic Church of Africa. The question had arisen in Asia, Gaul, and Rome, whether Montanists could be retained within the Church. The Asiatic bishops, with nearer knowledge of their irregularities, after some consideration decided that they could not. There are indications that the African Churches would have been disposed to look more favourably upon them: probably Felicity and Perpetua were Montanists (see Armitage Robinson, *The Passion of S. Perpetua*, pp. 6, 51 sqq.), and neither the African nor the Roman Church has ever counted this to their discredit. The impediment in Tertullian's case was not in the Church, but in that schismatical temper which, along with the acknowledgement and defence of the Paraclete, led him to despise his fellow Christians as merely "psychic": he separated from them, not they from him, and even so (such was their reasonableness) within thirty years of his death they had forgotten that he was not one of themselves.

In isto commeatu,

"in the time at my disposal". *Commeatus* is regularly used by Tertullian for a *time* of opportunity: *de fuga*, 9, *si redimendum tempus dicit quia dies nequam sunt, non per fugam, per sapientiam conversationis lucrari nos vult commeatum* (where *lucrari commeatum* seems to be a paraphrase of *redimere tempus*, which is hardly a satisfactory translation of ἐξαγοράζεσθαι τὸν καιρόν, Eph. 5. 16; both *tempus* and *commeatus* connote extent of time, which καιρός excludes): *de anima*, 30, *commeatus hic vitae*, "the usual length of human life": *ibid.* 34, *in primo quoque vitae huius commeatu*, "in each soul's first allowance of this life" [i.e. on the supposition of metempsychosis]. *Iste*, equivalent to *hic talis* or *hic tantus*, and without any suggestion of contempt or depreciation, is common in late Latin. The reference to the parable of the Tares, Matt. 13. 24, is evident, though Tertullian prefers to anticipate the time of harvest.

II. *Praxeas says that it was the Father who was born and who suffered, that God himself, the Lord Almighty, is Jesus Christ. We also believe that there is one God, yet in the divine unity we acknowledge an economy: the one God has also a Son, his Word, who has proceeded from him, and was the agent of creation. He it was who was born, being God and man, who suffered and died and was buried and was raised up again and was taken up again into heaven and will come again in judgement. He has also sent from the Father the promised Paraclete. The truth of this Rule of the Faith is shown by its antiquity, for it is older than all the heresies: and all heresies alike are judged beforehand on the principle that what came first is genuine and what comes after is debased. So long as this claim is allowed, there is room for further exposition, so that certain persons may be armed and fortified, and lest heresy appear to be condemned by prejudice, without examination. This new heresy thinks the divine unity can only be maintained by the identification of Father and Son and Holy Spirit: we reply that the unity is a unity of substance, but that the mystery of the economy must be guarded, which distributes the unity into a trinity, the Son and the Holy Spirit deriving their being from the Father. The purpose of this treatise is to show how there can be plurality without division.*

This chapter contains (1) a summary statement of the monarchian position: (2) the Rule of the Faith which Tertullian claims is as old as Christianity and has the right to be considered true because primitive: and (3) a statement in technical terms of the trinitarian doctrine which the treatise is intended to expound and defend. The monarchianist doctrine, and the meaning of Tertullian's terminology, have been discussed in the Introduction, pp. 6 and 38, *q.v.*

The Rule of the Faith, *regula fidei*, κήρυγμα τῆς ἀληθείας, is not the same thing as the Creed. The Creed is a liturgical document, whose proper use is in the immediate preparation for and in the administration of Baptism: its other uses are subsequent and secondary to this. It was a jealously guarded form of words: in different Churches, though the general sense was the same, verbal details might differ; but in the same Church verbal accuracy was insisted on. It was a very brief document, consisting in Tertullian's day of no more than five or six clauses, referring to each several Person of the Holy Trinity, to the Passion and Resurrection of Christ, and to little more (see Badcock, *History of the Creeds* (2nd ed.), p. 24). The Rule of the Faith is not a form of words but a series of ideas, a guide for teachers rather than a test of the neophyte's faith. It is thrice rehearsed by Tertullian, and once by Irenaeus (*haer.* i. 2), in varying forms comprising substantially the same matter: it is the *regula* rather than the Creed from which Novatian seems to be quoting (*de trin.* 1, 9, 29).

A comparison of Tertullian's three forms gives results of some interest:

REGULA FIDEI A TERTULLIANO ADHIBITA

de praesc. haer. 13	*de virg. vel.* 1	*adv. Prax.* 2
Regula est autem fidei	Regula quidem fidei una omnino est . . .	
qua creditur	credendi scilicet	
unum omnino deum esse nec alium praeter mundi conditorem,	in unicum deum omnipotentem mundi conditorem:	Unicum quidem deum credimus,
		sub hac tamen dispensatione, quam οἰκονομίαν dicimus, ut unici dei sit et filius, sermo ipsius qui ex ipso processerit,
qui universa de nihilo produxerit per verbum suum primo omnium demissum:		per quem omnia facta sunt et sine quo factum est nihil:
id verbum filium eius appellatum, in nomine dei visum esse a patriarchis, in prophetis semper auditum,		
postremo delatum ex spiritu patris dei et virtute in virginem Mariam, carnem factum in utero eius et ex ea natum egisse Iesum Christum:	et filium eius Iesum Christum, natum ex virgine Maria,	hunc missum a patre in virginem et ex ea natum
		hominem et deum, filium hominis et filium dei, et cognominatum Iesum Christum:
exinde praedicasse novam legem et novam promissionem regni caelorum, virtutes fecisse,		
crucifixum	crucifixum sub Pontio Pilato	hunc passum, hunc mortuum et sepultum secundum scripturas,
tertia die resurrexisse,	tertia die resuscitatum a mortuis,	et resuscitatum a patre
in caelos ereptum	receptum in caelis,	et in caelo resumptum
sedisse ad dexteram patris,	sedentem nunc ad dexteram patris,	sedere ad dexteram patris
misisse vicariam vim spiritus sancti qui credentes agat:		
venturum cum claritate ad sumendos sanctos in vitae aeternae et promissionum fructum et ad profanos iudicandos igni perpetuo,	venturum iudicare vivos et mortuos	venturum iudicare vivos et mortuos:
facta utriusque partis resuscitatione		

de praesc. haer. 13	*de virg. vel.* 1	*adv. Prax.* 2
cum carnis restitutione.	per carnis etiam resurrectionem.	
		qui exinde miserit, secundum promissionem suam, a patre spiritum sanctum paracletum, sanctificatorem fidei eorum qui credunt in patrem et filium et spiritum sanctum.

From this it appears that:

(*a*) The constant elements are those which refer to one God the Creator; his Son Jesus Christ, born of the Virgin Mary; the death, resurrection, ascension, and heavenly session of Christ, and his coming again to judgement; and (in two cases explicitly, in the other by implication) the resurrection of the dead.

(*b*) In the later works, *adv. Prax.* and *de virg. vel.*, the reference to the Holy Spirit seems to have been affected by Tertullian's Montanism. In the earlier work, *de praescr. haer.*, there is no identification of the Word and the Holy Spirit in the account of the Incarnation: the Word indeed is said to have been sent down upon the Virgin, but "the Spirit and power of God the Father" was the operative agent in that demission. Also in that work there is a statement of the mission of the Holy Spirit after the heavenly session, which can most naturally be referred to Pentecost. In the later works the references to the Holy Spirit at the Incarnation and at Pentecost are omitted: when Luke 1. 35 has to be referred to, "the Spirit and power of the Most High" is identified with the Word: and *adv. Prax.* has at the end of the *regula fidei* a reference to the mission of the Holy Spirit the Paraclete which by its position and phrasing seems to disregard Pentecost in favour of something more recent. In *de virg. vel.* the Rule omits all reference to the Holy Spirit: but the rest of that work is a claim that he was then at work in reforming church discipline, but had hardly been operating until the Montanist movement began.

(*c*) *De praescr. haer.* and *adv. Prax.* expressly state that the Word was the agent of creation: the former adds that it was the Word or Son who as God appeared to the patriarchs and spake in the prophets, a contention which forms the basis of a great deal of the argument of *adv. Prax.*

Tertullian has nothing corresponding to the statement of

Irenaeus that the Holy Spirit announced beforehand in the prophets "the economies and the comings, the virginal birth and the passion, the resurrection from the dead and the corporal assumption into heaven of the beloved Christ Jesus our Lord, and his coming from heaven in the glory of the Father to recapitulate all things and to raise up all flesh of all mankind . . . so that he may do judgement upon all". The rule in this shape, basing the facts connected with the Incarnation on Old Testament prophecy rather than on the New Testament narrative, was known also to Justin; *apol.* I. 61, καὶ ἐπ' ὀνόματος πνεύματος ἁγίου ὃ διὰ τῶν προφητῶν προεκήρυξε τὰ κατὰ τοῦ Ἰησοῦ πάντα.

Post tempus

might possibly be construed with *natus et passus*, not with *praedicatur*, i.e. "in time" as contrasted with "in eternity", and perhaps with a reminiscence of the Pauline phrase "in the fulness of time".

Ut instructiores per paracletum.

Concerning Montanism and its bearing on Tertullian's theology see the Introduction, p. 75.

Dispensatione, quam οἰκονομίαν dicimus.

Dispensatio, *de anima*, 43, *dispensatio ciborum*, means digestion: in this treatise and elsewhere, e.g. *adv. Marc.* v. 18 (a quotation of Eph. 3. 8, 9) it is a translation of οἰκονομία. In St Paul ἡ οἰκονομία τοῦ μυστηρίου τοῦ ἀποκεκρυμμένου is the dispensation, the carrying into activity in the temporal sphere, of the eternal purposes of God. In Irenaeus οἰκονομία means the dispensation of the Old or the New Testament, which is sufficiently near the Pauline sense, as is also the common patristic usage by which ἡ οἰκονομία means the Incarnation: cf. Ignatius, *ad Eph.* 18, Ἰησοῦς ὁ Χριστὸς ἐκυοφορήθη ὑπὸ Μαρίας κατ' οἰκονομίαν θεοῦ: Athenagoras, *suppl.* 21, κἂν σάρκα θεὸς κατὰ θείαν οἰκονομίαν λαμβάνῃ. In Origen οἰκονομίαι μυστικαί are those Old Testament histories (e.g of Abraham and his two wives) which are best treated as allegories. Tertullian, followed by Hippolytus, regularly uses it of the Holy Trinity: Hippolytus, *c. Noet.* 8, ὅσον δὲ κατὰ τὴν οἰκονομίαν τριχῆς ἡ ἀπόδειξις: *ibid.* 14, δύο μὲν οὐκ ἐρῶ θεοὺς ἀλλ' ἢ ἕνα, πρόσωπα δὲ δύο, οἰκονομίαν (*fortasse* οἰκονομίᾳ, Routh) δὲ τρίτην τὴν χάριν τοῦ ἁγίου πνεύματος: *ibid.*, οἰκονομίᾳ συμφωνίας συνάγεται εἰς ἕνα θεόν. Tatian had already used the word in this connexion: *orat.* 5, τὸ δὲ μερισθὲν οἰκονομίας τὴν αἵρεσιν προσλαβὸν οὐκ ἐνδεᾶ τὸν ὅθεν εἴληπται πεποίηκεν (but μερισθὲν involves a conception which Tertullian summarily rejects: cf. §§ 8, 9). At first sight it might appear that Tertullian had misunderstood the word, for he certainly does not mean that the Holy Trinity is a temporal or in any sense temporary manifestation of the divine being; but further consideration will show what he does mean by the term. In § 4 *dispensatio* is a synonym of *dispositio: vide ergo ne tu potius monarchiam destruas, qui dispositionem et dispensationem eius evertis in tot nominibus constitutam in quot deus voluit*: and so frequently throughout the treatise. But *dispositio* is regularly used of a divine ordinance: *apol.* 22, *dispositiones etiam dei et tunc prophetis contionantibus excerpunt* ("they make excerpts from the law"): *ibid.* 41, *admittite prius dispositiones eius et non retorquebitis: adv. Marc.* iii. 21, *nec enim dispositio expuncta inveniretur si non ille venisset post quem habebat evenire* ("for you would not find an ordinance fulfilled unless he had come whose coming was a condition of it being fulfilled"). Οἰκονομία therefore, with its Latin equivalents, used with reference to the Holy Trinity, means nothing temporary: it refers to the law of God's being, which (from the nature of that being) must be an eternal law, the expression of an eternal fact. [In our translation we have represented οἰκονομία and *dispensatio* by their English derivatives, and *dispositio* by "ordinance", which (as in the English marriage service) implies something more fundamental than "law", a fact inherent in the very nature of things.]

Filius, sermo ipsius.

For the term λόγος and its theological history see the Introduction, p. 31, and the note on § 5. *Processerit* is more appropriate to *sermo* than to *filius*: cf. Matt. 4. 4, ἐν παντὶ ῥήματι ἐκπορευομένῳ διὰ στόματος θεοῦ. Later theologians, who thought more readily of the Son than of the Word, preferred *genitus* to express his relation to the Father and reserved ἐκπορεύεσθαι for the Holy Spirit, of whom this verb is used at John 15. 26, *τὸ πνεῦμα τῆς ἀληθείας ὃ παρὰ τοῦ πατρὸς ἐκπορεύεται*, and in the figure of the River of Life, Rev. 22. 1.

Posteritas

in classical authors means either "futurity" or "posterity"—the latter as a collective noun: in Tertullian it means "the fact of being later" or, if there were such a word, "subsequency": cf. *de praesc. haer.* 31 (quoted below) and *adv. Marc.* v. 19, *soleo in praescriptione adversus haereses omnes de testimonio temporum compendium figere, priorem vindicans regulam nostram omni haeretica posteritate*, "earlier than any heresy, for these are all of later emergence".

Salva ista praescriptione, etc.,

"though we lodge this protest, yet we must, for the accoutrement and protection of certain persons, be prepared to discuss matters again". *Praescribere* in legal language is to enter a demurrer claiming that certain aspects of a case have been already decided and ought not to be argued again as part of the present suit. Tertullian claims that the contents of the Rule are beyond argument, on the principle *id esse verum quodcunque primum*: cf. *de praesc. haer.* 31, *principalitas veritatis et posteritas mendacitatis*. **Retractatus** (in the singular) is found in the sense of doubt or hesitation, e.g. *de res. carn.* 2, *animae autem salutem credo retractatu carere*, by direct derivation from one of the senses of *retracto*. Here, and in some other places, it seems to be a compound of *re* and *tractatus*, tractate (cf. Pliny, xiv. 4, 5, § 45), and its natural meaning would be a second or subsidiary discussion of a subject, the concrete result of the process of *retractatio*, reconsideration. But cf. *de anima*, 22, *itaque iam ab isto dispositionis retractatu recedam*, "I will leave that discussion of its characteristics": *de carne Christi*, 11, *prius retractemus an isto modo ostendenda fuerit anima*, "consider": from which it appears that there is no particular force in the prefix *re*, and that *retractatus* are simply discussions. For the scope and limits and limitations of discussion of the faith see *de praescr. haer.* 13, 14.

Non alias putat credendum.

Rönsch, *Itala und Vulgata*, p. 433, gives examples of the gerundive as equivalent to the future infinitive passive, but no parallel to the present instance, where *credendum* seems to mean *credi posse*.

Quasi non sic, etc.

For a discussion of this sentence see the Introduction, p. 50.

Omnia

"all three things", viz. the things implied by the three names.

Quia unus Deus, ex quo . . . deputantur.

If Tertullian means what he says, this sentence would have given some countenance to what Athanasius (admitting his ignorance of the facts) surmised to have been the sophistry of Paul of Samosata: *de synodis*, 45, τοῦ Παύλου σοφίζεσθαί τε θέλοντος καὶ λέγοντος, Εἰ μὴ ἐξ ἀνθρώπου γέγονεν ὁ χριστὸς θεός, οὐκοῦν ὁμοούσιός ἐστι τῷ πατρί, καὶ ἀνάγκη τρεῖς οὐσίας εἶναι, μίαν μὲν προηγουμένην τὰς δὲ δύο ἐξ ἐκείνης. [Athanasius], *Orat. c. Arian.* iv. 13, refers to two forms of the Sabellian heresy: according to one of them the Father is the monad who expands into Son and Holy Spirit; according to the other the monad is anterior to the Father and the Son and the Holy Spirit. If this sentence of Tertullian's is taken literally it means something dangerously like the second of these; but that this is not his meaning is shown by the whole tenor of the treatise and by the similes of the tree, the river, and the light in § 8. Evidently he means that it is the Father who is the source of the being of the Son and the Holy Spirit, and in him the Trinity has its unity: if he had written *in quo* and not *ex quo* this meaning would have been plain. The sentence involves the truth that the Son and the Holy Spirit are not afterthoughts of the Father, but are as essential to his Being as he is to theirs. ***Deputantur*** probably means no more than "are reckoned", not "are grafted off".

Numerum patiuntur,

"admit of plurality". The ancient mathematicians regarded two as the lowest number.

III. *The Rule of the Faith recalls us from the many gods of the heathen to the one only true God. The simple and unlearned, having apprehended this unity, recoil from the dispensation of the Trinity, which they think implies division. Consequently we are accused of preaching a plurality of gods. They reiterate the word "monarchy", but have not understood its meaning. Monarchy signifies a single* imperium*: but there is nothing to prevent an emperor from sharing his* imperium *with his son, or administering it through agents. The divine monarchy is administered through innumerable multitudes of angels, but is not thereby divided. Far less is it divided because of the Son and the Holy Spirit, since they are* consortes substantiae patris, *equal possessors of the Father's substance. If the meaning of the word is considered, and not its mere sound, a subversion of monarchy only takes place when an alien and independent authority is introduced, like the god of Marcion or the many gods of the gnostics.*

This first stage of the argument (intended primarily for the unlearned) merely skirts the fringe of the subject. It is not a sufficient characterisation of the Son and the Holy Spirit to compare them with the *officiales* of an emperor. The contrast between the angels who are God's ministers, and the Son and the Holy Spirit who are *consortes substantiae patris* comes nearer to the point. Monarchy is only subverted by the interpolation of an alien and independent authority: and *consortes substantiae patris* can never be alien or independent, nor can the primary Authority be alien to or independent of them.

Ad unicum et verum deum.

In his rehearsal of the Rule, Tertullian has, *de virg. vel.* 1, *in unicum deum omnipotentem: de praescr. haer.* 13, *unum omnino deum esse, nec alium praeter mundi conditorem: adv. Prax.* 2, *unicum quidem deum.* Irenaeus, *haer.* I. ii. has εἰς ἕνα θεὸν πατέρα παντοκράτορα. The Creed of the *Egyptian Church Order*, which is possibly the Roman creed of the second century, has "in one God the Father almighty". ***Verum***, ἀληθινόν, occurs in Creeds of Cappadocian origin in the fourth century (Badcock, *Creeds* (2nd ed.), pp. 49-50) and the idea is introduced, also in contrast with the supposed gods of the heathen, by Justin Martyr, *apol.* i. 6, τοῦ ἀληθεστάτου (sc. θεοῦ) καὶ πατρὸς δικαιοσύνης καὶ σωφροσύνης καὶ τῶν ἄλλων ἀρετῶν. Eastern baptismal creeds almost invariably had εἰς ἕνα θεόν: the clause stood so in the Creed of Caesarea, from which it was transferred to the Faith of Nicaea, which in its original form was not a creed but a *regula fidei.*

Unitas ex semetipsa derivans trinitatem.

Derivare is to draw off a stream from a main stream through a sluice: cf. § 8 for the figure of the source and the stream, and § 9, *pater enim tota substantia est, filius vero derivatio totius et portio*. In the present passage the language, if taken strictly temporally, is open to the same objection as *unus deus ex quo* in § 2: but (1) the *derivatio* must be understood to be not a temporal process but an eternal fact, and (2) it is not the work of any outside agent but of the *unitas* itself.

Administretur

= οἰκονομεῖται, and consequently has the same sense of permanency which Tertullian implies by the term οἰκονομία.

Duos et tres iam iactitant a nobis praedicari.

In origin the monarchian controversy arose from the necessity of justifying the Christian practice of offering to the Lord Jesus Christ those prayers and praises which can properly be offered to God alone. That practice can be justified only if our Lord is himself personally God: for Christianity has never treated with anything but scorn the heathen deifications of men either dead or living. The question then arises, what is the relation between our Lord, and God to whom he prayed and to whom he referred as "my Father". Primarily it is a question of the relation between *two* divine Persons: and those of the school of Theodotus and Artemas hardly took it further than that, finding it easy enough to regard the Holy Spirit as an impersonal divine attribute or function. But with Noetus and his successors there was always question of *three* divine Persons, even when, as often happens, only two are being discussed: for the controversy with the patripassians is always a trinitarian controversy, and no such word as *dyad* is known to the Church writers or their opponents. Translate: "They have for long been casting hints that we preach two, or even three", and cf. below, *secundum et tertium sortitis locum*: § 4, *monarchiam quam a patre filio traditam in filio servo: hoc mihi et in tertium gradum dictum sit*: Athenagoras, *suppl.* 10, where also αὐτὸ τὸ ἐνεργοῦν τοῖς ἐκφωνοῦσι προφητικῶς ἅγιον πνεῦμα is mentioned only after some discussion of the Son, but is immediately acknowledged as equal with the Father and the Son, and (not as in the much discussed passage of Justin, *apol.* i. 6 —but cf. *ibid.* 13) as in a different sphere from the πλῆθος ἀγγέλων καὶ λειτουργῶν, who are next mentioned as a rebuttal of the charge of atheism: τίς οὖν οὐκ ἂν ἀπορήσαι *λέγοντας θεὸν πατέρα καὶ υἱὸν θεὸν καὶ πνεῦμα ἅγιον, δεικνύντας αὐτῶν καὶ τὴν ἐν τῇ ἑνώσει δύναμιν καὶ τὴν ἐν τῇ τάξει διαίρεσιν, ἀκούσας ἀθέους καλουμένους;* The subject of *iactitant* is no longer the *imprudentes et idiotae* but the main movers of the controversy.

Trinitas rationaliter expensa.

One might suspect that *expensa* is written for *expansa*, which seems to make a more objective contrast with *collecta*. [So C. H. Turner, who remarks that *extensa* is more likely than *expansa*.] But an objective contrast is not needed: it is subjective thoughts, not objective facts, that make heresy.

Et ita sonum ipsum, etc.

The MSS. read *solium*, changed by Rhenanus in his third edition to *sonum*, which has become the accepted reading. I suspect that *solium* may be right, as being Tertullian's equivalent of ἀρχή, and I wonder if we should not read: *Monarchiam, inquiunt, tenemus—et ita solum solium* [or perhaps *solisolium*] *vocaliter exprimunt etiam Latini—et tam opifice, etc.* "The monarchy, say they, is what we are upholding (for even Latins say 'monarchy' when they mean a single throne), and they pronounce the word in so masterly a fashion that you would think they understood monarchy as well as they pronounce it." C. H. Turner suggests *etiam Latini, etiam opifices* (in which Rigaltius had anticipated him), remarking that there is no adverb *opifice*: that would not have prevented Tertullian from inventing one, though the suggestion is otherwise attractive. *Sonare* means "make to sound impressive": see the note on *sonitu*, § 20.

Singulare et unicum imperium.

For the previous history of the term μοναρχία, see the Introduction, p. 6, footnote.

Officiales,

a post-classical word, first quoted from Appuleius, *metam.* i. 25, in the sense of apparitor: the same is perhaps the meaning in Tertullian, *adv. Marc.* i. 25, *proinde enim aemulationi occurrant* (i.e. *praesto sint*) *necesse est officiales suae in ea quae aemulatur, ira, discordia, odium, dedignatio, indignatio, bilis, violentia, offensa: de idol.* 17, *quid facient officiales sacrificantibus dominis?* Here, however, it seems that more important officials are intended. It would be an unsatisfactory parallel if it were meant that God has looked out or provided for himself, ***prospexerit sibi***, the Son and the Holy Spirit to act as his subordinates in administration: it is, however, little more than a passing phrase, an illustration rather than an argument.

Principaliter,

"in the first instance and as the origin of the rest": cf. *scorp.* 2, *nec aliud primum tam principaliter denuntiantis quam ab omni factura atque cultura idolorum cavere: apol.* 6, *ipsum adhuc quod videmini fidelissime tueri a patribus traditum, in quo principaliter reos transgressionis Christianos destinastis, studium dico deorum colendorum. Princeps* is the first of a series, not the ruler of it: Eusebius is *princeps historicorum ecclesiasticorum* because he is the first of them, and Peter is *princeps apostolorum* for the same reason.

A duobus tam unitis. The MSS. read *unicis*, by an obvious error.

Divisionem et dispersionem.

Divisio, division into two or more substantive things: *dispersio*, dispersion into unrecognisable elements: cf. *de res. carn.* 31, *si et populus allegorice mussitaret ossa sua arefacta et spem suam perditam, dispersionis exitu querulus : adv. Hermog.* 39, *si et materia eadem aeternitate censetur, neque initium habens neque finem, eadem ratione non poterit pati dispertitionem* (v.l. *dispersionem*) *et demutationem, qua nec deus.*

Secundum et tertium sortitis locum,

"who occupy the second place and the third": cf. *de anima*, 8, *ceterum etsi invisibilis anima, est pro condicione corporis sui et pro proprietate substantiae et pro natura etiam eorum quibus invisibilis esse sortita est: de res. carn.* 26, *proinde et in paradisum restitutio carni videbitur repromissa quae eum incolare et custodire sortita est, ut talis illuc homo revocetur qualis inde pulsus est.* In both cases the reference is to a quality or prerogative conceded from above, not by chance or lot, but by deliberate assignment, and involving permanent possession. Cf. JUVENAL XV. 144, *venerabile soli|sortiti ingenium divinorumque capaces.*

Tam consortibus substantiae patris.

Cf. Athenagoras, *suppl.* 18, ἑνὶ τῷ θεῷ καὶ τῷ παρ' αὐτοῦ λόγῳ υἱῷ νοουμένῳ ἀμερίστῳ. **Consortes** are joint possessors, not mere sharers (*participes*).

Et quidem tam, etc.

The MSS. read *et quidem tam a substantia patris membra*, for which it is hard to find any meaning. Gangneius and Gelenius read *et quidem tam* ⟨*alienorum*⟩ *a substantia patris. membra et pignora*, etc., which gives a good sense and involves very little interference with the MSS. The sentence, *membra . . . deputas eius*, is easier to interpret if it applies not to the divine monarchy but to monarchy in general.

Membra, pignora, instrumenta, vim, censum.

Conceivably the Son and the Holy Spirit could be designated *patris membra* by a figurative interpretation of expressions such as "the eyes of the Lord", "the hands of the Lord", or the two branches of the olive tree (Zech. 4. 14), though such fancifulness is not in Tertullian's manner; but *membra monarchiae* (following the other punctuation) gives a better sense, as it naturally means the provinces of the empire, cf. Seneca, *ep.* 21. 6, *membra et partes alienae potentiae.* **Pignora**, in its secondary senses, means (*a*) children, *ad nat.* i. 15, *vestra pignora extinguitis*; (*b*) any near relations, *de idol.* 12, *pignora et artificia et negotia propter dominum relinquenda* (where see Oehler's note): *ad nat.* ii. 9, *qui pro salute principum et domus eorum adversus liberos et coniuges et omne pignus suum deierant*: Quintilian, *inst. orat.* vi. 1. 24, *affert in his momentum et aetas et sexus et pignora, liberi dico et parentes et propinqui.* In this broader sense the Son and the Holy Spirit might be described as *pignora patris*; but it is better to construe *pignora monarchiae*, as referring to the sons and colleagues of Severus. *Instrumenta* is frequently used by Tertullian for the holy Scriptures or some part of them, e.g. *de res. carn.* 33, *instrumentum Ioannis.* It would not be easy to assign any intelligible meaning to *patris instrumenta*; but *instrumenta monarchiae* would mean the officials through whom the empire was administered. *Ipsa vis monarchiae* therefore means the army, and **census** (which frequently means "origin" and more naturally "rank") is here used for *apparatus*, i.e. the court officials.

"Do you account provinces, and the emperor's sons and officials, and the very forces and trappings of the empire, as destructive of its unity?"

Suae condicionis et proprii status, etc.,

"when there is introduced another lordship, self-established and of independent quality, and consequently hostile". *Condicio* and *conditio* appear to be frequently confused, though the former strictly means attributes or circumstances, the latter creation or establishment: *de carne Christi*, 5, *proprietas conditionum divinae et humanae* (where *conditio divina* cannot imply creation or anything fortuitous): *ibid.* 6, *nec tamen infringitur semel separata conditio dominicae carnis ex causa alterius dispositionis*, i.e. the corporal appearances of angels are without prejudice to the conditions of the Incarnation: *ibid.* 22, *eadem conditio substantiae*, the same sort of substance: *de anima*, 40, *caro . . . res est alterius plane substantiae et alterius condicionis, addicta tamen animae ut supellex* (where *altera condicio* apparently means another act of creation). *Status, natura, condicio* (or *conditio* in the sense of *condicio*) appertain to the same set of facts: the first two are permanent, as dependent on *substantia*: *condicio* refers more to external circumstances, and is capable of change, cf. *de res. carn.* 57, *permitte hanc et deo potestatem per vim demutationis illius* (sc. the Pauline *omnes demutabimur*) *conditionem non naturam reformandi, dum et passiones auferuntur et munitiones conferuntur.*

Cum Marcione

is Oehler's conjecture. The MSS. read *tunc male*, which Engelbrecht would correct to *tunc mage*, the chief objection to which is that Tertullian seems always to write *magis*. ***Valentinos et Prodicos:*** the plurals are contemptuous. Valentinus is well known as one of the most famous gnostic teachers: cf. *adv. Val.* passim. Prodicus is mentioned at *scorp.* 15 (again in company with Valentinus) as *suggerens non in terris esse confitendum apud homines*. The writer of the article *Prodicus* in *D.C.B.* (George Salmon) refers to Clem. Alex., *strom.* i. 15, where the school of Prodicus are said to possess the books of Zoroaster: *ibid.* iii. 4, they are said to have justified and practised licentious living: *ibid.* vii. 7, to have objected to the practice of prayer. Theodoret, *haer. fab.* i. 6, says that Prodicus was the founder of the sect of the

Adamites: but Salmon remarks that Theodoret could only have learned of this sect from Epiphanius, who acknowledges that he had never met any of them, and so his connexion of them with Prodicus can be no more than a guess.

IV. *That being so, we introduce no such subversion in the matter of the faith, for the Son is of the substance of the Father, does nothing without the Father's will, and from the Father has received all authority. The same also holds good of the Holy Spirit. There is more danger of a subversion of the divine monarchy by these false teachers who set themselves up as independent authorities against the revelation which God has made of himself. That the kingdom remains a single one is shown by the fact that it has been committed in its integrity to the Son* (Ps. 110. 1), *who will at the last deliver it in its integrity to the Father* (1 Cor. 15. 24-28). *That the Father and the Son are two is evident both from the names Father and Son, and from the fact that he who delivers up the kingdom must be another than he to whom it is delivered, as he who puts it in subjection is another than he to whom it is put in subjection.*

In the first sentence, monarchy is still considered in a subjective sense, of the authority inherent in, or possessed by, the monarch. In what follows, Tertullian (apparently unconsciously) passes over to the objective sense, of the persons over whom (or the sphere in which) the authority is exercised. It cannot be denied that this form of the problem is easier to discuss, and that the transition amounts to a shelving of the real question. Tertullian's excuse could be that the political theme had been introduced not by him but by his opponents, and that in such a case a forensic victory is good enough. He has now finished with this aspect of the matter, and with the *simpliciores*: the rest of the treatise approaches the doctrine of the Holy Trinity from other sides.

Ceterum qui filium, etc.

This sentence balances the last sentence of the previous chapter. The Christian doctrine of God introduces none of those factors which produce subversion of monarchy: the Son is *de substantia patris*, i.e., *non proprii status*; we acknowledge him as *nil facientem sine patris voluntate*, i.e., *non aemulum*; as *omnem a patre consecutum potestatem*, i.e. *non suae condicionis*.

De fide destruere monarchiam

"overthrow the monarchy in respect of the faith": *de fide* reintroduces the theological question after the preceding secular illustrations. C. H. Turner remarks, "I cannot translate in this connexion the words 'de fide': perhaps 'quomodo possum videri destruere monarchiam' "—which is certainly attractive.

A patre filio traditam.

Matt. 11. 27=Luke 10. 22, πάντα μοι παρεδόθη ὑπὸ τοῦ πατρός μου. The whole authority is delivered to the Son, and is preserved by the Son, in singularity: hence ***in filio servo***, a pregnant expression for "which I affirm is preserved in the Son".

Spiritum non aliunde puto, etc.

Puto, reckon: Kroymann reads *deputo*, plausibly but needlessly. There seem to be no precedents for this statement of the "double procession": it may have been suggested to Tertullian by the images in § 8, where observe, *tertius enim est spiritus a deo et filio, sicut tertius a radice fructus ex frutice et tertius a fonte rivus ex flumine et tertius a sole apex ex radio. De praescr. haer.* 13, *misisse vicariam vim spiritus sancti* (quoted by Tixeront in this connexion), refers to the temporal mission of the Holy Spirit. In JUSTIN the question of procession does not arise. THEOPHILUS, *ad Autol.* i. 10, πνεῦμα ἐὰν εἴπω ἀναπνοὴν αὐτοῦ λέγω, occurs in too rhetorical a context for the meaning to be pressed: but *ibid.* ii. 10, while the double procession is not clearly stated, the strict sense of the preposition μετὰ perhaps involves it—ἔχων οὖν ὁ θεὸς τὸν ἑαυτοῦ λόγον ἐν τοῖς ἰδίοις σπλάγχνοις ἐγέννησεν αὐτὸν μετὰ τῆς ἑαυτοῦ σοφίας ἐξερευξάμενος πρὸ τῶν ὅλων.—God generates the Word endowed with, not merely accompanied by, the Wisdom, which thus proceeds from God through the Word. ATHENAGORAS seems to consider only a single procession of the Holy Spirit, parallel with the generation of the Word: *suppl.* 10, καίτοι καὶ αὐτὸ τὸ ἐνεργοῦν τοῖς ἐκφωνοῦσι προφητικῶς ἅγιον πνεῦμα ἀπόρροιαν εἶναί φαμεν τοῦ θεοῦ, ἀπορρέον καὶ ἐπαναφερόμενον ὡς ἀκτῖνα ἡλίου: *ibid.* 24, νοῦς λόγος σοφία ὁ υἱὸς τοῦ πατρὸς καὶ ἀπόρροια ὡς φῶς ἀπὸ πυρὸς τὸ πνεῦμα. TERTULLIAN, applying to the Son the relation ὡς ἀκτῖνα ἡλίου, *solis radium*, is logically led to the further relation *apex ex radio*, and so to the doctrine of the double procession in the form in which it appeared in the fourth century and in which (apart from reserves due to later controversy) the Greek theologians would still apparently be prepared to accept it: see Tixeront, *Histoire des Dogmes*, vol. ii. pp. 89-93, vol. iii. pp. 198-202.

Dispositionem et dispensationem, etc.

Διάθεσιν καὶ οἰκονομίαν: the words are practically synonymous, and διάθεσις, ***dispositio***, has a sense of permanency and essentiality. The Trinity is not merely administrative, not a mere assignment of functions, but a permanent and essential διάθεσις of the Godhead. Consequently the divine activity in the temporal sphere corresponds with the essential facts of the divine nature; and as e.g. the Holy Spirit is *a patre per filium* (see the preceding note), so it is the Son who sent *vicariam vim spiritus sancti*. ***Nominibus***=*personis* (see the Introduction, p. 48): but below *hoc nomine* means "on this account": ***constitutam***, ὑπάρχουσαν, *existentem*. ***Voluit*** has here no special significance, and no bearing on the question whether the Son is begotten "by the will" of the Father: "you, who deny the three names, are the subverter of the monarchy, for by that denial you set yourself in opposition to the will of God who has declared that three there are". Nor has Justin, *dial.* 61, ἔχει γὰρ πάντα (sc. ταῦτα τὰ ὀνόματα) προσονομάζεσθαι ἔκ τε τοῦ ὑπηρετεῖν τῷ πατρικῷ βουλήματι καὶ ἐκ τοῦ ἀπὸ τοῦ πατρὸς θελήσει γεγενῆσθαι, any bearing on that question: nor does it, as Otto's note suggests, refer to the Incarnation; the meaning is that the Son served the Father's will by willingly (θελήσει) appearing to or presenting himself to (γεγενῆσθαι = παραγεγενῆσθαι) the patriarchs. When Origen says (*de princ.* iv. 4. 1) that the Son ἐκ θελήματος τοῦ πατρὸς ἐγενήθη, the scriptural images with which he supports that statement (Col. 1. 15: Heb. 1. 3) show that he intends this not in the sense in which the Arians afterwards claimed his support, and it seems possible that he used the expression in implied opposition to the gnostic supposition of spontaneous or unconscious emanation.

Ut etiam restitui habeat, etc.

This is the earliest patristic discussion of 1 Cor. 15. 24-28 and it is to be observed that, whereas Origen and Eusebius discovered in the passage difficulties which called for explanation,

Tertullian finds it entirely to his purpose. He welcomes it as indicating that the Son, who holds the kingdom, is not the same as the Father to whom he will deliver it up, and argues that the monarchy is safeguarded by the fact that only one Person holds it at a time: the Father has delivered it to the Son, who now possesses it, and the Son will in due course surrender it to the Father. Evidently he can only say this by regarding the monarchy entirely in an objective sense (as do Origen and Eusebius), not as the kingly authority but as those who acknowledge it, the domain over which the Son is now ruling. This is perhaps less than St Paul's words would naturally mean. Even so, Tertullian's position seems to be hardly more than verbally different from that of his adversaries: it is not easy to see why the severalness of the three Persons should be so anxiously maintained if in the process it has to be allowed that only one at a time is in active authority.

ORIGEN offers two explanations to smooth away difficulties which the text of St Paul had already suggested:

(a) *de princ.* iii. 5. 6, that the final subjection of Christ is the climax of his redemptive work, and consists of the subjection of all those of whom he is the Head and who find their salvation in him: *quia ergo non solum regendi vel regnandi verum etiam oboediendi, ut diximus, reparare venerat disciplinam, in semetipso prius complens quod ab aliis volebat impleri, idcirco non solum usque ad mortem crucis patri oboediens factus est, verum etiam in consummatione saeculi in semetipso complectens omnes quos subicit patri et qui per eum veniunt ad salutem, cum ipsis et in ipsis quoque subiectus dicitur patri, dum omnia in ipso constant et ipse est caput omnium et in ipso est salutem consequentium plenitudo. hoc ergo est quod de eo dicit apostolus, Cum autem omnia ei fuerint subiecta, etc.* With this Koetschau compares *in Levit. hom.* vii. 2, *cum vero consummaverit opus suum et universam creaturam suam ad summam perfectionis adduxerit, tunc ipse dicetur subiectus in his quos subdidit patri et in quibus opus quod ei pater dederat consummavit, ut sit deus omnia in omnibus.* The words *dicitur*, *dicetur*, might suggest that Origen regards the subjection of the Son as merely putative, the reality being the subjection of those over whom he has authority: but this is not the case: he regards the Son's subjection, in the sense indicated, as not less than real, and *dicitur*, *dicetur*, introduce apostolic authority for his inference.

(b) *de princ.* iii. 5, 7, *verum nescio quo pacto haeretici non intellegentes apostoli sensum . . . subiectionis in filio nomen infamant: cuius appellationis si proprietas requiritur, ex contrario facile poterit inveniri. nam si subiectum esse non est bonum, restat ut illud quod contrarium est bonum sit, id est non esse subiectum.* Who the heretics were is not clear: certain theologians, whom Origen would hardly have stigmatised as heretics, tended to repudiate any idea not only of subjection but even of subordination, and *infamant* would in that case mean "repudiate as false": or *subiectionis nomen infamant* may mean "give the term 'subjection' a bad name", by overpressing it, in which case the people in question would be Sabellians anticipating the interpretation ascribed to Marcellus of Ancyra. Origen proceeds: It is precisely because Christ is already subject that it is possible for all things in him to be made subject: and since subjection is a good thing it is for the good of those who are to be subject, *ut sicut cum dicitur filius patri subiectus perfecta universae creaturae restitutio declaratur, ita cum filio dei inimici dicuntur esse subiecti, subiectorum salus in eo intellegatur et reparatio perditorum.*

Marcellus of Ancyra, unless Eusebius misrepresents him, argued from this text in a Sabellian and Nestorian sense: *apud* Euseb. *de eccl. theol.*, ii. 9 (p. 113 *a*), καὶ διὰ τοῦτο οὐχ υἱὸν θεοῦ ἑαυτὸν ὀνομάζει, ἀλλὰ πανταχοῦ υἱὸν ἀνθρώπου ἑαυτὸν λέγει, ἵνα διὰ τῆς τοιαύτης ὁμολογίας θέσει τὸν ἄνθρωπον διὰ τῆς πρὸς αὐτὸν κοινωνίας υἱὸν θεοῦ γένεσθαι παρασκευάσῃ, καὶ μετὰ τὸ τέλος τῆς πράξεως αὖθις ὡς λόγος ἑνωθῇ τῷ θεῷ, πληρῶν ἐκεῖνο τὸ ὑπὸ τοῦ ἀποστόλου εἰρημένον, Τότε αὐτὸς ὑποταγήσεται τῷ ὑποτάξαντι αὐτῷ τὰ πάντα ἵνα ᾖ πάντα καὶ ἐν πᾶσιν ὁ θεός. The same passage is quoted *c. Marc.* ii. 2 (p. 42 *a*) with some variations of which the only one of any significance is Χριστός for ὁ θεός.

Eusebius, *de eccl. theol.* iii. 15 (p. 183 sqq.), argues as follows: (*a*) ὑποταγή is not the same as ἕνωσις: (*b*) ἀλλ' ὥσπερ οὐχ ἕνωσιν ὁ ἀπόστολος ἐδήλου . . . ἀλλὰ τὴν ἐξ αὐθεκουσίου προαιρέσεως ὑπακοὴν καὶ τὴν δόξαν καὶ τὴν τιμὴν ἣν ἀποδώσει αὐτῷ τὰ πάντα οἷα σωτῆρι καὶ βασιλεῖ τῶν ὅλων, τὸν αὐτὸν τρόπον καὶ τὸ αὐτὸν ὑποταγήσεσθαι τῷ πατρὶ οὐδὲν ἕτερον σημαίνοι ἂν ἢ τὴν δόξαν καὶ τὴν τιμὴν καὶ τὸ σέβας τήν τε μεγαλοπρέπειαν τήν τε *αὐθεκουσίαν ὑπακοὴν ἣν καὶ αὐτὸς ἀποδώσει τῷ θεῷ καὶ πατρὶ ἐπειδὰν τοὺς πάντας ἀξίους τῆς πατρικῆς θεότητος εἶναι παρασκευάσῃ.* This could bear the sense indicated by Origen, though it is expressed in language which betrays a sympathy with Arianism. (*c*) For the present, Christ exercises a corrective office: but this task will be completed when death, the last enemy, is destroyed, *ὧν ὧδε εὐτρεπισθέντων τῷ υἱῷ τοῦ θεοῦ σωτήριον ὑποταγὴν πάντες οἱ ἅγιοι ὑποταγήσονται . . . οὐδὲ τῆς θεότητος αὐτοῖς φθονήσει . . . καὶ σώμασιν οὐρανίοις ἡλίῳ καὶ σελήνῃ καὶ ἄστροις χρήσονται παραπλησίοις*: therefore Marcellus is wrong in suggesting that the Word will discard his body, but rather it *καταποθήσεται, οὐχ ὑπὸ μόνης τῆς ζωῆς ὁμοίως τῷ ἡμετέρῳ, ἀλλὰ καὶ ὑπὸ τῆς αὐτοῦ θεότητος . . . καὶ τοιαύτην τινὰ τὴν σωτήριον ὑποταγὴν χρὴ νοεῖν καθ' ἣν καὶ αὐτὸς ὁ υἱὸς ὑποταγήσεται τῷ ὑποτάξαντι αὐτῷ τὰ πάντα, ἄλεκτόν* (*v.l.* *ἄληκτόν*) *τινα καὶ ἄρρητον καὶ μόνῳ αὐτῷ πρέπουσαν ὑποταγὴν ποιησόμενος, ὅτε τοὺς ὑπ' αὐτοῦ πάντας χοροῦ δίκην περιστοιχισάμενος τῷ θεῷ καὶ πατρὶ προσάξει.* Here again the general sense is derived from Origen. (*d*) There follows an exposition of *ἵνα ᾖ ὁ θεὸς τὰ πάντα ἐν πᾶσιν*, and (p. 187*d*) *οὐ γὰρ παύσεσθαι μὲν τῆς βασιλείας τὸν υἱὸν τὸν δὲ θεὸν βασιλεύσειν ἔφη ὁ ἀπόστολος, ἀλλὰ τὸν μὲν υἱὸν τῷ θεῷ καὶ πατρὶ τὴν βασιλείαν παραδώσειν, σῴαν τὴν παραθήκην καὶ πρὸς τὴν τοῦ πατρὸς λατρείαν τε καὶ ἱερωσύνην ἐπαρκοῦσαν ἐνδεικνύμενον*, which is probably what Tertullian means in the present passage.

The treatise known as ATHANASIUS, *contra Arianos* iv, surprisingly does not discuss this text.

Sede ad dexteram meam.

Ps. 110 is cited by JUSTIN, *dial.* 56 (p. 277 *b*, note), to prove *ὅτι καὶ παρὰ τὸν νοούμενον ποιητὴν τῶν ὅλων ἄλλος τις κυριολογεῖται ὑπὸ τοῦ ἁγίου πνεύματος.* IRENAEUS, *haer.* iii. 6. 1, quotes this and the other passages adduced by Justin, with the comment: *patrem enim filio collocutum ostendit, qui dedit ei haereditatem gentium et subiecit ei omnes inimicos. vere igitur cum pater sit dominus et filius vere sit dominus, merito spiritus sanctus domini appellatione signavit eos.* Our Lord cited the same text (Matt. 22. 44) to indicate that the Messiah, though David's son, is David's lord, and therefore to suggest that the Jews must look to find in Messiah something nobler even than descent from David, which can only be divine Sonship: the text is an unexpressed statement of Christ's divinity. The psalm is quoted for the same purpose in Heb. I. 13.

In suo statu . . . cum suo statu.

Cf. above, *adeo autem manet in suo statu.* It is not easy to find a consistent translation for *status*: the former phrase might well mean "in its real quality", while the latter would naturally mean "with its appurtenances". Possibly *cum* is an insignificant variation for *in*.

Hoc uno capitulo, etc.

The argument that the delivery of the kingdom from one to the other implies the existence of two, and that the two cannot be identical is a matter of common sense and cannot be impugned: the further statement, that the mention of Father and Son involves there being two, though sound here, will not hold in all cases, as is observed by [ATHAN.] *c. Arian.* iv. 33, ἔθος δὲ τοῦτο τῇ γραφῇ, ἀπεριέργως καὶ ἁπλῶς τὰς λέξεις ἐκφράζειν. *Capitulum* means neither "chapter" nor "section" in any conventional sense, but "passage", i.e. the text under discussion, whether long or short: cf. below, § 20.

v. *Our opponents affirm that the Father and the Son are one and the same. We have therefore to examine the question of the Son's existence, personality, and relation to the Father. The facts, as established from the Scriptures, will provide their own justification. It is alleged by some that Gen.* I. I *reads in the Hebrew, "In the beginning God made for himself a son". That this is not true appears, among other arguments, from the following considerations. Before all things, when God alone existed, he was not alone: for he had with him his* Λόγος *or Reason. This Greek word is commonly translated by* sermo, *"speech"; but wrongly, for reason precedes speech. God was rational before the beginning: speech begins at the beginning. Yet even so, reason when it is articulate involves a kind of unspoken speech, as may be seen in ourselves who are of God's image and likeness. The mind, active within itself, holds a conversation with its speech. Thought is reason: articulate thought is speech. Speech therefore is a kind of second self: and if this is*

true of man, the more so is it true of God. We thus arrive at a presumption that before the world was made God was not alone, but had with him his Reason and Speech.

An sit et qui sit et quomodo sit.

The next few chapters will prove (*a*) that there is a Son of God (§ 5): (*b*) that he is the divine Person revealed in the Scriptures as the Word or Wisdom of God, the Son of God, Jesus Christ (§§ 6, 7): (*c*) that his relation to the Father is such as to involve no separation or division of the divine unity (§ 8).

Res ipsa formam suam . . . vindicabit.

Forma is habitually used by Tertullian to mean a rule of law, prescript, warrant, contract (the classical *formula*): see the Introduction, p. 54.

Aiunt quidam, etc.

The MSS. reading *quidem* can hardly be right: if it were, the subject of *aiunt* would be the monarchians, the least of all people likely to approve of the suggestion that "in the beginning God made for himself a son". *Quidam* introduces, for one sentence only, a different set of persons. Tertullian must have misunderstood his informant: among many comments on the alleged Hebrew of Gen. I. I this particular piece of fancifulness seems not to recur. The Armenian translator of Irenaeus, *praed. apost.* 43, mistook the first syllable of *bara* for "the Son"—"The Son in the beginning: afterwards God established the heaven and the earth": the mistake may go back to Irenaeus, who however, *adv. haer.* ii. 2. 4, quotes the text correctly. Certain gnostics (*ibid.* i. 11. 1) interpreted ἀρχή as ἡ μητὴρ τῶν ὅλων. A typical comment is the following:

Hilar. Pictav., *tract. in psalm.* ii. 2: "Ambiguitatis autem linguae Hebraicae unum afferemus exemplum, ex quo caetera istius modi esse atque ita ut sunt intelligantur. *Bresith*, verbum hebraicum est. Id tres significantias in se habet, id est, *in principio*, et *in capite*, et *in filio*. Sed translatores LXX *in principio* ediderunt, caeteris diverse transferentibus: et secundum hanc ambiguitatem haec ab illis in omni translatione est facta confusio."

On which the Benedictine editors have the following note:

Hunc Hilarii locum notasse videtur Hieronymus, Quaest. Hebr. in Genesim, dicens: "Plerique existimant, sicut in altercatione Jasonis et Papisci scriptum est, et Tertullianus in libro contra Praxeam disputat, necnon Hilarius in expositione cujusdam psalmi affirmat, in Hebraeo haberi, *In Filio fecit Deus caelum et terram*: quod falsum esse ipsius rei veritas comprobat: nam et LXX interpretes et Symmachus et Theodotion *In principio* transtulerunt, et in Hebraeo scriptum est *Beresith*, quod Aquila interpretatur *In capitulo*, et non *Baben*, quod interpretatur *In filio*. Magis itaque secundum sensum quam secundum verbi translationem de Christo est."

Ita tamen in Hebraeo haberi *In filio* affirmat Hilarius ut huic interpretationi neque adhaereat ipse neque adhaerendum putet. De Tertulliano obiter observamus eam in ipsius libro contra Praxeam nusquam reperiri, sed hoc dumtaxat num. 5 de Praxeae sectariis, "Aiunt quidem [*sic*] et Genesim in Hebraeo ita incipere etc." Quanquam hunc Tertulliani locum ex Hieronymo emendandum esse facile concedamus. Ipse vero Tertullianus legere solet *In primordio*, et libro contra Hermogenem n. 20 juxta vim vocis graecae permittit ut legatur *In principatu et potestate*.

The passage referred to is this (*adv. Hermog.* 19 *ad fin.*):

Possum et aliter principium interpretari, non ab re tamen: nam et in Graeco principii vocabulum, quod est ἀρχή, *non tantum ordinativum sed et potestativum capit principatum, unde et* ἄρχοντας *dicunt principes et magistratus. Ergo secundum hanc quoque significationem principium pro principatu et potestate sumetur: in principatu enim et potestate fecit caelum et terram.*

But the preceding statement is not entirely correct: *adv. Hermog.* 3, 22, 26, Tertullian reads *In principio*: *In primordio* occurs *de bapt.* 3 and (from John 1. 1) *adv. Prax.* 5.

For the interpretation ἐν ἀρχῇ=*in filio*, cf. THEOPHILUS, *ad Autol.* ii. 10, οὗτος (sc. ὁ λόγος) λέγεται ἀρχή, ὅτι ἄρχει καὶ κυριεύει πάντων τῶν δι' αὐτοῦ δεδημιουργημένων.

Hoc ut firmum non sit, etc.

Elliptical for *ut firmum non esse censeam*. ***Deducere*** is used for *movere, persuadere*, cf. *de anima*, 43, *inde deducimur etiam imaginem mortis iam tunc eum* (sc. *somnum*) *recensere*. ***Alia argumenta:*** for *a priori* reasons Tertullian is unable to approve of the suggestion: it cannot be reconciled with his inherited conception of the relation between the Father and the Son: for the Son is the Word or Reason of God and it is impossible to think of God having made for himself his own reason and thereby to have made himself for the first time rational. It would probably not have occurred to Tertullian to ask a Jewish scholar for light on the Hebrew: one does not consult an unbeliever on matters connected with Christian theology—though Origen did.

Ad usque filii generationem.

Tertullian does not really think that the Father ever existed without the Son: as he says almost immediately, *ceterum ne tunc quidem solus.* But he is unable to rid himself of the idea of a priority of the Father, at least in thought, or to dissociate it from some sort of time sequence. Hence, e.g. in § 7, the statement, which he alleges to have a scriptural basis, that God made the Word into his Son, *sibi filium fecisse sermonem suum.* Hence also the verbs in the preterite, *prodiit*, *protulisse*, as though the generation of the Son was an event which took place, albeit before the beginning of time, and is not rather (as Origen says) an eternal fact of the divine Being. The thought is on the lines of that involved in the contrast λόγος ἐνδιάθετος, λόγος προφορικός, which seems to appear first in THEOPHILUS, *ad Autol.* ii. 10, ἔχων οὖν ὁ θεὸς τὸν ἑαυτοῦ λόγον ἐνδιάθετον ἐν τοῖς ἰδίοις σπλάγχνοις, ἐγέννησεν αὐτὸν μετὰ τῆς ἑαυτοῦ σοφίας (i.e. the Holy Spirit) ἐξερευξάμενος (Ps. 45. 1) πρὸ τῶν ὅλων: see below on § 7. IRENAEUS, who had found something akin to this idea in gnostic teachings, points out its difficulties, *haer.* ii. 16. 1, 2, where he argues that if the "emission" is outward it involves separation, while if it is inward it is otiose and ineffective: elsewhere, *haer.* ii. 42. 4, he accepts the term prolation, but prefers not to discuss its mysteries: *si quis itaque nobis dixerit, Quomodo ergo filius prolatus a patre est? dicimus ei quia prolationem istam sive generationem sive nuncupationem sive adapertionem aut quolibet quis nomine vocaverit generationem eius inenarrabilem exsistentem nemo novit . . . quoniam enim ex cogitatione et sensu verbum emittitur, hoc utique sciunt omnes homines,* and consequently those who have thought of this contrast have not made any great discovery, nor have they (says Irenaeus) been very wise in transferring human analogies to God. See below on § 8.

Ante omnia enim deus erat solus.

Tertullian does not say that the Father was alone, but that

God was alone: i.e. the created world did not exist. Even when God was alone in this sense, he was not alone in himself, as having always with him his λόγος: cf. ATHENAGORAS, *suppl.* 10, ἐξ ἀρχῆς γὰρ ὁ θεὸς, νοῦς ἀίδιος ὤν, εἶχεν αὐτὸς ἐν ἑαυτῷ τὸν λόγον, ἀιδίως λογικὸς ὤν. See also TATIAN, *orat. ad Graecos*, 5, quoted in the Introduction, p. 35.

Ipse sibi et mundus et locus et omnia.

ATHENAGORAS, *suppl.* 16, ὁ δὲ κόσμος οὐχ ὡς δεομένου τοῦ θεοῦ γέγονεν· πάντα γὰρ ὁ θεός ἐστιν αὐτὸς αὐτῷ, φῶς ἀπρόσιτον, κόσμος τέλειος, πνεῦμα, δύναμις, λόγος. THEOPHILUS, *ad Autol.* ii. 10, αὐτὸς ἑαυτῷ τόπος ὢν καὶ ἀνενδεὴς ὤν: *ibid.* i. 3, πατέρα ἐὰν εἴπω τὰ πάντα αὐτὸν λέγω (a sentence which has received many apparently needless suggestions for emendation: see Otto's note).

Rationalis enim deus, etc.

The MSS. reading seems to give a tolerable meaning, though Turner's suggestion *et ab ipso in omnia* gives a balanced sentence which is at first sight attractive. *In ipsum*, and not the more obvious *in ipso*, was no doubt deliberately written in view of the Johannine *apud deum* (soon to be quoted), and to indicate that the relation of God's reason to God himself is fundamentally a relation of person with person and not that of a mere faculty or function within a person. Reason is primarily in relation with God, *et ita ab ipso omnia*, i.e. because of that relationship all things come to be and are.

Quae ratio sensus est.

Sensus varies its meaning as widely as its English derivative or its German equivalent *Sinn*, from sense-perception to mental impression, from feeling to consciousness, with an extension upwards to "mind" and downwards to "sensuality". According to *de anima*, 18, *sensus* is concerned with *corporalia*, *intellectus* with *spiritalia*: so *ibid.* 43, the Stoics say that sleep is *resolutionem sensualis vigoris, quia corporis solius quietem procuret, non et animae*: but *ibid.* 40, *sensus* (plural) are thoughts as distinguished from acts, *sensus delictorum etiam sine effectibus imputari solent animae*, "the soul is blamed for thoughts of sin even if they are not brought into effect". Cf. *de carne Christi*, 5, *an ideo passiones a Christo non rescidisti quia ut phantasma vacabat a sensu earum*, "feeling", "perception": *de res. carn.* 46, *si vero sine anima ⟨caro⟩ nullius est sensus intellege sensum carnis ad animam esse referendum*, "if without the soul the flesh is void of perception, 'the mind of the flesh' must be referred to the soul" (*sensus*=φρόνημα): but *ibid.* 45, quoting Eph. 4. 23, *renovari spiritu sensus, sensus*=νοῦς. *De carne Christi*, 12, *animae anima sensus est: igitur cum omnibus anima sentire praestet et ipsa sentiat omnium etiam sensus nedum qualitates, cui veri simile est ut ipsa sensum sui ab initio sortita non sit?* "the soul perceives not only the attributes of things but also the perception of the attributes: therefore it must from the beginning have possessed perception of itself"—i.e. there was no need for Christ to turn soul into flesh so as to make it perceptible to itself. *De res. carn.* 40, *Ephesiis scribens in interiorem hominem habitare Christum sensibus utique intimandum dominum significavit*, "the mind": so *ibid.* 15, *principalitas sensuum quod* ἡγεμονικὸν *appellatur . . . animae cogitatorium* (in this passage *sensus* seems to mean impressions, *cogitatus* thoughts): *ibid.* 3, *communes enim sensus simplicitas ipsa commendat*, "common impressions", "opinions". But *ibid.* 47, *per totam hanc sensuum seriem*, "this whole series of thoughts": and *de carne Christi*, 20, *nunc ad sensus ipsos decertemus*, the actual meanings of the texts under discussion. In the present passage the meaning apparently is that reason is the divine consciousness, or self-consciousness: cf. § 6, *in sensu suo condens et generans . . . immo et facta iam quantum in dei sensu.*

Quia sermonalis a principio.

The MSS. read *non sermonalis*: but the meaning seems to be that since reason precedes speech, and "from the beginning" God has been articulate (*sermonalis* a word apparently coined by Tertullian in imitation of *rationalis*), therefore even before the beginning he was rational. Even so, the argument continues, there is no real thinking without a sort of unspoken speech, and the priority of reason to speech is no more than theoretic. The sentence gives two reasons why *ratio* is preferable to *sermo* as a translation of λόγος: (1) the theoretical priority of reason: (2) the metaphysical priority, in that speech is founded on reason and reason is the substance of speech.

Cum ratione enim sua, etc.

God made reason into speech by making it articulate. Tertullian seems to be struggling to avoid the contrast ἐνδιάθετος, προφορικός: *ratio* did not become *sermo* by being emitted as speech at any point of time, but λόγος is always *sermo* because it is always articulate *ratio*.

Ante recognosce . . . quo habeas.

The text is doubtful (see critical note) but the sense is sufficiently clear. Oehler comments, *Quo, id est quorsum, in quem usum*; but the point remarked on is not the purpose of human reason but the manner of it, and if *quo* is correct it stands for *quomodo*. For the comparison with the human voice see the references in the Introduction, § IV, to Justin, Tatian, Theophilus, and Irenaeus: but Tertullian's treatment of the analogy guards against those suggestions of impermanence to which Irenaeus objects.

Factus . . . animatus.

Gen. 1. 27: 2. 7: *ex substantia ipsius* because the substance of God is spirit, and that spirit, as the breath of life, was breathed into man.

Quodcunque cogitaveris, etc.,

"Your articulate thought is speech; your instinctive thought is reason. You must perforce speak that ⟨thought⟩ in your mind: and while you are speaking ⟨it⟩ you have in conversation with you Speech, which comprises this very Reason by which, while thinking, you converse with that ⟨Speech⟩ by means of which, while speaking, you think. So there is in you Speech, as it were another ⟨besides yourself⟩, by means of which, while thinking, you speak, and by means of which, while speaking, you think: Speech itself is someone else."

Imago et similitudo censeris,

"whose image and similitude you are authoritatively declared to be". *Censeri* is invariably used by Tertullian with the idea of a census in his mind, the object of a census being (1) to count numbers, (2) to ascertain a person's rank or position as determined by his origin, or (3) to assign to him a new rank in view of his present office or possessions. The verb never means "is thought to be", for the census deals not with mere opinion but is the public acknowledgement of what is already, or what is henceforth to be, an objective fact. The following quotations illustrate this contention. (1) Arithmetical numbering: *de anima*, 31, *iam nunc de tanto Graeciae censu quattuor solae animae recensentur*, where *census*=population, and *recensentur* means "are counted a second time", i.e. make a second appearance by metempsychosis: *ibid.* 32, *maiorem piscium censum*, "the greater number", "the majority": *ibid.*, *in tam contraria unicuique substantiae animalia reformari et censum eis de sua translatione conferre*, "increased numbers". (2) Origin: *de carne Christi*, 8, *peccatrix de peccatorio censu*, i.e. on the heretical supposition that the creation of the world was a sin, the flesh of Christ, from whatever element it were taken, would be sinful by reason of its sinful origin: *de anima*, 21, *quodsi nec spiritale nec quod dicitur materiale proprium in illo* (sc. Adam) *fuit . . . superest ut solum in illo et unicum fuerit naturale quod censetur animale, quod statu simplex et uniforme defendimus*, "the one and only natural property in him would be that which in its origin pertains to the soul": *ibid.* 38, *praestruximus omnia naturalia animae ipsi substantiae inesse . . . ex ingenito animae censu*, "its inherited quality" (almost in the now obsolete social sense of the word "quality"): *de res. carn.* 6, *licet et caro audiat, Terra es, etc., origo recensetur, non substantia revocatur*, "its rank is referred to its origin, but it is not denied to be what it is": *ibid.*, *excusato censu*, "removing the reproach of its origin". (3) Rank or class: *de anima*, 8, *abruptum alioquin et absurdum idcirco quid de corporalium eximere censu quia ceteris corporalibus exemplis non adaequet*: *ibid.* 40, *ita omnis anima eo usque in Adam censetur donec in Christo recenseatur, tamdiu immunda quamdiu recenseatur*, "takes its rank from Adam until it receives a new rank in Christ" (*quamdiu* apparently=*donec*). Moreover, the active verb *censere* does not mean "think" or "suppose", but "decide" or "authoritatively determine": *de anima*, 39, *ut huius spei pignore matrimoniis, quae retinenda censuerat, patrocinaretur*, "marriage, which he decreed must be retained": *adv. Hermog.* 7, *ambo ex pari magna, ex pari sublimia, ex pari solidae et perfectae felicitatis quae censetur aeternitas*, "both equally great, equally sublime, equally possessing that entire and perfect felicity which is authoritatively designated eternity"—which is closely parallel with the present passage. Finally, if the meaning of *censeri* is as we have suggested, the much discussed sentence, *de orat.* 6 (*corpus eius in pane censetur: Hoc est corpus meum*) will mean "his body is authoritatively declared to be in the bread": i.e. it is not a mere matter of repute or supposition, for what the censor decides is either an acknowledgement of an already existent fact or the establishment of a new fact from now on—in this case the latter, for the censorial *aestimatio* is represented by the dominical words, which for that reason are quoted without preamble or explanation.

Proinde.

Cf. § 7, *gaudens proinde gaudentem,* "each rejoicing in view of the other's joy": so here, there is *ratio* because there is *sermo,* and there is *sermo* because there is *ratio.*

Quem secundum a se faceret, etc.,

"which he made another besides himself by activity within himself": cf. § 7 *ad fin., secundum a patre,* "another besides the Father": JUSTIN, *dial.* 128, ἀριθμῷ ἕτερόν τί ἐστι. *De anima,* 6, *secundum sit necesse est quod ex alio est: nihil porro ex alio est nisi dum gignitur: sed tunc duo sunt.*

VI. *The Reason or Speech of God is referred to in holy Scripture as Wisdom. Wisdom itself, in Prov.* 8, *speaks first* (*verse* 22) *of its own establishment, creation, or generation, before the foundation of the world: and then* (*verse* 27) *it represents itself as distinct from God, yet present with him, at the creation. As soon as God determined to create in their own substances and forms the things which he had already, in company with Wisdom's reason and speech, ordained within himself, he first produced Speech, with the reason and the wisdom which are inseparable from it, to the end that all things might come into existence by the agency of it by which they had been thought out and ordained, nay even already made, in the mind of God. The only thing they lacked was to be perceived and apprehended in forms and substances of their own.*

Tertullian adduces selections from this passage of Proverbs, *adv. Hermog.* 18, in support of his argument that the world was not made of pre-existent matter. If, he says, God had needed material *ad opera mundi,* he had such material at hand as philosophers cannot take account of, but prophets can understand, namely his Wisdom, which alone knows the mind of the Lord. Paraphrasing 1 Cor. 2. 11, *Quis enim scit quae sunt dei et quae in ipso, nisi spiritus qui in ipso?,* he identifies Wisdom with that Spirit: and he quotes Prov. 8. 27 sqq. (*cum pararet caelum, etc.*) to prove that Wisdom was in fact operative in the creation of the world. This Wisdom he declares to be *omnium fontem et originem . . . materiam materiarum, non fini subditam, non statu diversam, non motu inquietam, non habitu informem, sed insitam et propriam et compositam et decoram, quali deus potuit eguisse, sui magis quam alieni egens.* He proceeds: *denique ut necessariam sensit ad opera mundi, statim eam condit et generat in semetipso: Dominus, inquit, condidit me . . . prior autem abysso genita sum.* Hermogenes must observe that even the Wisdom of God is declared to have been born and established, for the express purpose that we should not believe that anything exists *innatum et inconditum* except God alone. For if, within the Lord, that which is of him and in him was not without beginning, namely, his Wisdom which was born and established from ⟨the time⟩ when (*ex quo*) in the mind of God it began to be set in motion for purposes of creation, *a fortiori* there cannot be anything outside God which is without beginning. If there were, that something would be more ancient and therefore more noble, and indeed stronger, than the Son of God himself. Moreover, if evil is *innatum*, while the Word was begotten (quoting Ps. 45. 1 *Eructavit, etc.*), then evil could never have been brought under control by good. Hermogenes gives matter precedence of God, by giving it precedence of the Son (quoting John 1. 1: 10. 30).

Evidently Tertullian is somewhat carried away by his argument: to say that Wisdom was *condita et generata* within God is to say that God was originally ἄλογος, which he certainly cannot have intended to say. In the present passage (*adv. Prax.* 6) he interprets even this primary generation as a generation not of Wisdom itself but of the projected world *in dei sensu*, so anxious is he to maintain that Wisdom itself is coeternal with God.

Again, *adv. Hermog.* 20, having identified Wisdom and *principium* (substantified from *in principio fecit deus*), he says: *in sophia enim primo fecit, in qua cogitando et disponendo iam fecerat . . . quia cogitatio et dispositio prima sophiae fit operatio, de cogitatu viam operibus instituens.* This agreement with his later work shows what was his settled opinion, when not carried away by disputation. The previous interpretation recurs in the summary of his argument, *adv. Hermog.* 45: *at enim prophetae et apostoli non ita tradunt mundum a deo factum apparente solummodo et adpropinquante materiae, quia nec materiam ullam nominaverunt, sed primo sophiam conditam, initia viarum in opera ipsius, dehinc et sermonem prolatum, per quem omnia facta sunt et sine quo factum est nihil: denique sermone eius caeli confirmati sunt et spiritu ipsius universae virtutes eorum.*

Tertullian was not the first to use Prov. 8, as the following note shows; but he was the first to interpret it with such attention to detail. He is almost the last to make *positive* use of it: later writers needed to interpret it apologetically. None of them saw that their difficulties arose from the fact that it has no real application to their purpose.

Among the second-century expositors of Prov. 8. 22 sqq. and similar texts there was some uncertainty as to whether the divine Wisdom is the Son or the Holy Spirit. JUSTIN identifies σοφία with the Word or Son of God: *dial.* 61, μαρτυρήσει δέ μοι ὁ λόγος τῆς σοφίας, αὐτὸς ὢν οὗτος ὁ θεὸς ἀπὸ τοῦ πατρὸς τῶν ὅλων γεννηθείς, καὶ λόγος καὶ σοφία καὶ δύναμις καὶ δόξα τοῦ γεννήσαντος ὑπάρχων, quoting Prov. 8. 21-36: *ibid.* 129, quoting verses 21-25, νοεῖτε, ὦ ἀκροαταί, εἴ γε καὶ τὸν νοῦν προσέχετε, καὶ ὅτι γεγεννῆσθαι ὑπὸ τοῦ πατρὸς τοῦτο τὸ γέννημα πρὸ πάντων ἁπλῶς τῶν κτισμάτων ὁ λόγος ἐδήλου, καὶ (*suppl.* ὅτι) τὸ γεννώμενον τοῦ γεννῶντος ἀριθμῷ ἕτερόν ἐστι πᾶς ὁστισοῦν ὁμολογήσειε. ATHENAGORAS likewise identifies Word, Son, Wisdom: *suppl.* 10 νοοῦμεν γὰρ καὶ υἱὸν τοῦ θεοῦ. καὶ μή μοι γελοῖόν τις νομίσῃ τὸ υἱὸν εἶναι τῷ θεῷ. οὐ γὰρ ὡς ποιηταὶ μυθοποιοῦσιν οὐδὲν βελτίους τῶν ἀνθρώπων δεικνῦντες τοὺς θεοὺς ἢ περὶ τοῦ θεοῦ καὶ πατρὸς ἢ περὶ τοῦ υἱοῦ πεφρονήκαμεν. ἀλλ' ἔστιν ὁ υἱὸς τοῦ θεοῦ λόγος τοῦ πατρὸς ἐν ἰδέᾳ καὶ ἐνεργείᾳ· πρὸς αὐτὸν γὰρ καὶ δι' αὐτοῦ πάντα ἐγένετο, ἑνὸς ὄντος τοῦ πατρὸς καὶ τοῦ υἱοῦ. ὄντος δὲ τοῦ υἱοῦ ἐν πατρὶ καὶ πατρὸς ἐν υἱῷ ἑνότητι καὶ δυνάμει πνεύματος, νοῦς καὶ λόγος τοῦ πατρὸς ὁ υἱὸς τοῦ θεοῦ . . . συνᾴδει δὲ τῷ λόγῳ καὶ τὸ προφητικὸν πνεῦμα, Κύριος γάρ φησιν ἔκτισέ με ἀρχὴν ὁδῶν αὐτοῦ εἰς ἔργα αὐτοῦ: *ibid.* 24, νοῦς λόγος σοφία ὁ υἱὸς τοῦ πατρὸς καὶ ἀπόρροια ὡς φῶς ἀπὸ πυρὸς τὸ πνεῦμα. IRENAEUS on the other hand, *praed. apost.* 5, interpreting Ps. 33. 6, "By the Word of the Lord . . . by the Breath of his mouth", says that the Word is the Son, and the Spirit is the Wisdom: "Therefore, because the Word constitutes, that is, gives substance and confers the power of existence, but the Spirit forms and shapes the different forces, rightly and properly the Word is called the Son, and the Spirit the Wisdom of God": *adv. haer.* iv. 34. 2, *quoniam autem et sapientia, quae est spiritus, erat apud eum ante omnem constitutionem, per Salomonem ait, Deus sapientia fundavit terram, etc.* (Prov. 3. 19-20): *et rursus autem, Dominus creavit me, etc.* (Prov. 8. 22-25, 27-31). THEOPHILUS for the most part is of the same opinion: *ad Autol.* i. 7, ὁ θεὸς, ὁ θεραπεύων καὶ ζωοποιῶν διὰ τοῦ λόγου καὶ τῆς σοφίας. ὁ θεὸς διὰ τοῦ λόγου αὐτοῦ καὶ τῆς σοφίας ἐποίησε τὰ πάντα (quoting Ps. 33. 6): *ibid.* 15, ὡσαύτως καὶ αἱ τρεῖς ἡμέραι πρὸ τῶν φωστήρων γεγονυῖαι τύποι εἰσὶν τῆς τριάδος, τοῦ θεοῦ καὶ τοῦ λόγου αὐτοῦ καὶ τῆς σοφίας αὐτοῦ: and, a little later, θεός, λόγος, σοφία: *ibid.* 18, οὐκ ἄλλῳ δέ τινι εἴρηκεν Ποιήσωμεν ἀλλ' ἢ τῷ ἑαυτοῦ λόγῳ καὶ τῇ ἑαυτοῦ σοφίᾳ: but *ibid.* ii. 10 he seems to identify Word and Spirit and Wisdom, οὗτος οὖν, ὢν πνεῦμα θεοῦ καὶ ἀρχὴ καὶ σοφία καὶ δύναμις ὑψίστου, κατήρχετο εἰς τοὺς προφήτας: *ibid.* i. 3 (in a rhetorical context), σοφίαν ἐὰν εἴπω, γέννημα αὐτοῦ λέγω. ORIGEN agrees with Justin and Athenagoras: *de princ.* i. 2 . . . *unigenitus filius dei, qui multis quidem et diversis nominibus pro rebus vel opinionibus appellantium nuncupatur* (cf. *comm. in Joa.* i. 21 sqq.): *sapientia namque dicitur, sicut et Salomon dixit ex persona sapientiae, Dominus creavit me, etc.* There follows a discussion of the theological implications of this title. Later authors accept this identification, which, with Prov. 8. 22 sqq., is much to the fore in the discussions of the fourth century.

Haec vis et haec divini sensus dispositio.

Vis is apparently the equivalent of δύναμις, as in Justin's paraphrase of λόγος, δύναμις λογική: cf. Otto's note 6 on Theophilus, ii. 10, which quotes a remark of Ziegler that to Theophilus λόγος and σοφία are *Kräfte und Eigenschaften Gottes*—which is something less than the truth. Here *vis* seems to mean "function": cf. § 7, *apparet unam eandemque vim esse nunc in nomine sophiae nunc in appellatione sermonis.* ***Dispositio*** at *de res. carn.* 35, *dispositio corporalis*, means attitude or posture: at *adv Hermog.* 20, *cogitatio et dispositio prima sophiae fit operatio*, it has the active sense "ordaining": cf. *cogitata et disposita* at the end of this chapter. ***Divini sensus dispositio*** apparently means something like "posture of the divine consciousness", and as such a "posture" has about it nothing either fortuitously assumed or imposed from without it may perhaps be best represented by "ordinance": see the note on *οἰκονομία*, § 2. ***Sensus:*** see the note on § 5.

Conditam . . . condens.

This is apparently an attempt to soften the meaning of *creavit* in the quotation: "establish" is a possible meaning of *κτίζειν*, as Eusebius remarked (see below): Tertullian tacitly slurs over the difficulty.

Primo . . . dehinc

divide the quotation into two parts, the first describing the establishment of Wisdom as another by the side of God, the second describing the creation of the world with Wisdom as assistant.

Dominus creavit me, etc.

These sentences from Prov. 8. 22 sqq. are selections only, translated from the LXX. This and the other passages cited, many of them only by strong allegorism brought to bear on the subject under discussion, had become common form from Justin onwards, and do not seem to have been new even to him. The LXX translate as follows: *Κύριος ἔκτισέν με ἀρχὴν ὁδῶν αὐτοῦ εἰς ἔργα αὐτοῦ . . . πρὸ τοῦ τὴν γῆν ποιῆσαι . . . πρὸ τοῦ ὄρη ἑδρασθῆναι, πρὸ δὲ πάντων βουνῶν γεννᾷ με. ἡνίκα ἡτοίμαζεν τὸν οὐρανὸν συνπαρήμην αὐτῷ . . . καὶ ὡς ἰσχυρὰ ἐποίει τὰ ἄνω νέφη, καὶ ὡς ἀσφαλεῖς ἐτίθει πηγὰς τῆς ὑπ' οὐρανόν . . . ἤμην παρ' αὐτῷ ἁρμόζουσα, ἐγὼ ἤμην ᾗ προσέχαιρεν, καθ' ἡμέραν δε εὐφραινόμην ἐν προσώπῳ αὐτοῦ.* According to Tertullian's exposition, the first half of the quotation, as far as *generavit me*, represents the premundane establishment of Wisdom as another Person, *secundam personam*, by the side of the Lord: the second half, from *cum pararet*, represents her as *ipsa separatione* distinct from him, yet *adsistentem* (=*aderam illi*), present with him and assistant to him at the creation. But, he adds, the first sentence represents not the establishment of Wisdom herself, but the establishment in her of the world as proposed for creation in the mind of God: the second sentence, assuming that Reason and Wisdom have meantime been emitted as Speech, describes the creation of the actual sensible world through Speech as God's agent. Tertullian is only partly aware of the difficulties caused by deriving Christian theology from a Hebrew scripture not primarily intended for that purpose. Following (as he thinks) his text, he seems to indicate that the Λόγος only obtained separate personal existence for the purpose of being the agent of creation. But if the doctrine of the Holy Trinity is true it must always have been true, and must represent an essential fact of the divine being. ORIGEN was aware of that: *de princ.* iv. 4. 1 (quoted by ATHANASIUS, *de decret.* 27), *ἀλλ᾽ οὐ θέμις ἐστὶν οὐδὲ ἀκίνδυνον διὰ τὴν ἀσθένειαν ἡμῶν τὸ ὅσον ἐφ᾽ ἡμῖν ἀποστερεῖσθαι τὸν θεὸν τοῦ ἀεὶ συνόντος αὐτῷ λόγου μονογενοῦς, σοφίας ὄντος ᾗ προσέχαιρεν· οὕτω γὰρ οὐδὲ χαίρων ἀεὶ νοηθήσεται.* He therefore, following up the implications of this text, which seems to connect the generation of the Word with the creation, supposes the creation, along with the Word, to be an eternal fact of the mind of God: *de princ.* i. 4, 4, *haec ergo ipsa est sapientia cui semper adgaudebat deus orbe perfecto, ut per hoc etiam semper laetari intellegatur deus. in hac igitur sapientia, quae semper erat cum patre, descripta semper et formata conditio, et nunquam erat quando eorum quae futura erant praefiguratio apud sapientiam non erat.* See the notes in Koetschau, *Origenes Werke*, vol. v. p. 67.

Creavit, ἔκτισεν,

provoked much discussion, both before and after Eusebius of Caesarea had exhaustively treated the subject: e.g. DIONYSIUS of Rome (*ap.* Routh, *R.S.*, vol. iii. p. 376), *οὐ μία γὰρ ἡ τοῦ Ἔκτισεν, ὡς ἴστε, σημασία· Ἔκτισε γὰρ ἐνταῦθα ἀκουστέον ἀντὶ τοῦ Ἐπέστησε τοῖς ὑπ᾽ αὐτοῦ γεγονόσιν ἔργοις, γεγονόσιν δὲ δι᾽ αὐτοῦ τοῦ υἱοῦ· οὐχὶ δέ γε τὸ Ἔκτισε νῦν λέγοιτ᾽ ἂν ἐπὶ τοῦ Ἐποίησε· διαφέρει γὰρ τοῦ ποιῆσαι τὸ κτίσαι . . . καὶ πολλαχοῦ δὲ τῶν θείων λογίων γεγεννῆσθαι ἀλλ᾽ οὐ γεγονέναι τὸν υἱὸν λεγόμενον εὕροι τις ἄν.* The Arians pressed the word to prove that the Son of God is a created being inferior to and of a different kind from the Father: their opponents for the most part alleged that the text refers to the created nature which the Word took upon him at the Incarnation. EUSEBIUS of Caesarea, *c. Marcell.* ii. 3, complains that Marcellus, applying this text to the Incarnation, infers that the Word only became the Son at the Incarnation: *de eccl. theol.* i. 10 (a notable passage as against both Sabellians and

Arians), he complains that Marcellus and others, once in Scripture finding the word ἔκτισε, base upon it a denial of the generation of the Son. He discusses the text fully, *de eccl. theol.* iii. 2, saying: (1) κτίζειν is often used metaphorically for καθιστάναι, κατατάσσειν: (2) in the text before us its sense is qualified by the secondary object, "the beginning of his ways": (3) the correct translation of the Hebrew word קנה is not ἔκτισεν but ἐκτήσατο, as witness Aquila, Symmachus, and Theodotion: he quotes other texts of the Old Testament where the Hebrew verb has this sense, and adds, τὸ γὰρ μέγα κτῆμα τοῦ θεοῦ ὁ μονογενὴς υἱὸς ἦν, καθὸ μὲν ἐξ αὐτοῦ γεγέννητο υἱὸς ὢν αὐτοῦ, καθὸ δὲ τοῖς πᾶσιν κοινωφελὴς καὶ σωτήριος καθέστηκε τὸ μέγιστον καὶ τιμιώτατον κτῆμα τοῦ πατρὸς ὑπάρχων τε καὶ ὠνομασμένος· οὐδὲ γὰρ ἄλλο τι γένοιτ' ἂν πατέρι υἱοῦ τιμιώτερον κτῆμα: and again, ὁμοῦ καὶ τὴν προΰπαρξιν αὐτοῦ ἐδήλου καὶ τὴν ἰδιάζουσαν πρὸς τὸν πατέρα οἰκειότητα, ὁμοῦ καὶ τὸ χρήσιμον καὶ ἀναγκαῖον τῆς οἰκείας περὶ τὰ πατρῷα ἔργα προνοίας τε καὶ διοική-σεως. ATHANASIUS, *orat. c. Arian.* ii. 43 sqq., still unacquainted with the Hebrew, says (1) this text must be interpreted in the light of Prov. 9. 1, ἡ σοφία ᾠκοδόμησεν ἑαυτῇ οἶκον, which means τὸ ἡμέτερον σῶμα ὅπερ ἀναλαβὼν γέγονεν ἄνθρωπος: and (2) κτίζειν in holy Scripture often means not the creation of something new but the making of something into something else.

Ipsa separatione,

an instrumental ablative: it is by the very fact of being distinct that Wisdom "stands by", for otherwise it would not stand by but coincide. This is the evident meaning of Tertullian's text as it stands: the difficulty is that he is elsewhere insistent that the Son is *individuus et inseparatus*, and consequently Kroymann substituted *in ipsa operatione*, which Turner improved on with *ipsius operationi*. There is however just a possibility that the inconsistency is due to Tertullian: at this point he is concerned to prove duality, and only later becomes anxious to defend himself against the charge that duality involves division.

Et quomodo fortia, etc.

The MSS. read *quomodo* (twice), which must be restored to the text: LXX has ὡς, of which *quomodo* is a literal translation. It is possible that ὡς was intended to mean "how", or it may be a device for avoiding the repetition of ἡνίκα and ὅτε (like the French *que* which picks up the sense of a preceding conjunction, or the "that" which takes up "forasmuch as" in the preface to the English baptism service). Editors from Rhenanus onwards have substituted *quum*. ***Super ventos*** has slipped in from the preceding sentence (omitted by Tertullian), καὶ ὅτε ἀφώριζεν τὸν ἑαυτοῦ θρόνον ἐπ' ἀνέμων: CYPRIAN, *test.* ii. 1, translates this, *cum super ventos validas faceret desuper nubes*: English R.V. "when he set a circle upon the face of the deep". ***Eius quae*** represents the Greek τῆς, sc. οἰκουμένης.

In substantias et species suas,

"in their own substances and species": so again at the end of this chapter.

Individuas,

"inseparable": *de pat.* 15, *cum ergo spiritus dei descendit, individua patientia comitatur eum.* Reason and Wisdom are essential attributes of the Word, of his very substance, and no activity of his is conceivable without them.

VII. *The nativity of the Word becomes complete when he proceeds from the Father in the expression, Let there be light. Established already for thought, he is now begotten for action, and from henceforth stands to God in the relation of Son to Father, being first-begotten and only-begotten. The texts which speak of creation by Wisdom, combined with those which speak of creation by the Word, and with those which identify the Word and the Son, prove that Wisdom, Word, and Son are one and the same. Moreover, the Word is not empty sound, but is substantial. Nothing which proceeds from God can be less than substantial, nor could anything unsubstantial be the maker of substances: and the Word is himself the maker of the things which were made through him. The designations Son and God, applied in holy Scripture to the Word, imply substantiality, for the name God cannot be taken in vain, that is, for an empty thing. The Son's being in the form of God has the same implication; for God is corporeal, though he is spirit, since spirit is body, of its own kind and in its own form. And if the invisible things of God have their body and form, in which they are visible to God alone, how much more must that which proceeds from his substance not be devoid of substance. This substance of the Word I denominate a Person, claiming for him the name of Son, as being another besides the Father.*

Speciem et ornatum,

"manifestation and equipment", immediately explained as *sonum et vocem*, "sound and articulation".

Cum dicit deus, Fiat lux.

Probably the repeated καὶ εἶπεν ὁ θεός of Gen. 1, preceded by the reference to the Spirit of God moving (ἐπεφέρετο) above the waters, suggested the verse of the Ps. 33. 6, τῷ λόγῳ τοῦ κυρίου οἱ οὐρανοὶ ἐστερεώθησαν, καὶ τῷ πνεύματι τοῦ στόματος αὐτοῦ πᾶσα ἡ δύναμις αὐτῶν and this in turn suggested to the evangelist the designation ὁ Λόγος, without any dependence upon Philo or the Greek philosophers. The sublimity of the conception was observed by the heathen author of the tract περὶ ὕψους (9. 9), who writes: ταύτῃ καὶ ὁ τῶν Ἰουδαίων θεσμοθέτης, οὐχ ὁ τυχὼν ἀνήρ, ἐπειδὴ τὴν τοῦ θείου δύναμιν κατὰ τὴν ἀξίαν ἐχώρησε κἀξέφηνεν, εὐθὺς ἐν τῇ εἰσβολῇ γράψας τῶν νόμων, Εἶπεν ὁ θεός, φησί· τί; Γενέσθω φῶς, καὶ ἐγένετο· γενέσθω γῆ, καὶ ἐγένετο. [The passage has been suspected as possibly an interpolation; but rashly, since Longinus (if he is the author of the book) could have had his attention drawn to the Scriptures by Paul of Samosata.]

Haec est nativitas perfecta sermonis.

Prov. 8. 22 sqq. having been interpreted (§ 6) as falling into two parts, in the first part Tertullian takes the key-word to be *creavit* (now paraphrased as *condidit, conditus*), which he refers to God's plan or project for creation, *ad cogitatum:* in the second part the key-word is *generavit*, referring to the external expression of Wisdom as the Word of creation. Wisdom and Word are identical: but, says Tertullian, there was a prior generation, creation, establishment, as Wisdom, and afterwards that same Wisdom received expression as the Word. This is *nativitas perfecta sermonis;* not that *sermo* is more perfect than *sophia*, but that his generation as *sermo* is now complete. Further, as *conditus primum ad cogitatum* represents the first stage, and

dehinc generatus ad effectum the second, ***exinde eum patrem sibi faciens*** declares the permanence of the οἰκονομία thus evolved in two stages. The monarchians regarded the Son as a temporary manifestation of the Father in the work of redemption: Tertullian not only refers the manifestation of the Son back to the creation, but denies also that that manifestation is temporary or that it is a manifestation of the Father in person, for the Son, once begotten, is a second Person by the side of the Father. But, though the Son's existence does not come to an end when redemption is completed, Tertullian cannot rid himself of the thought that the *ratio dei*, itself eternal, had in some sense a beginning of its existence as Son. This, of course, has nothing in common with the Arian position that "there was once when he was not", for the Arians maintained that there are two λόγοι, one an eternal attribute of God, the other (which afterwards was incarnate) created for the purpose of creating the world. For Tertullian Wisdom, Word, and Son are identical, as eternal as God himself, though Wisdom only becomes completely the Word when expressed in the word of creation.

Conditus, condidit.

The substitution of ***condidit*** removes the ambiguity involved in *creavit:* cf. AUGUSTINE, *de fide et symbolo*, 5, *nam idem est condere quod creare: quanquam in latinae linguae consuetudine dicatur aliquando creare pro eo quod est gignere; sed graeca discernit. hoc enim dicimus creaturam quod illi κτίσμα vel κτίσιν vocant: et cum sine ambiguitate loqui volumus non dicimus creare sed condere.* For all that, Tertullian does not say that the Word was created, but that Prov. 8. 22 means that the projected world was created in him, as the actual world was afterwards created by him.

Exinde eum patrem sibi faciens, etc.

Patrem is, as Kroymann discovered, the reading of *M*, and is obviously right: cf. § 10, *patrem . . . qui facit filium, filium . . . qui facit patrem.* ***Primogenitus***, Col. 1. 15: ***unigenitus***, John 1. 18: 1 John 4. 9: ***ut solus ex deo genitus***, because other things, though they are sometimes by a misuse of the word said to have been begotten, were not begotten of God but created out of nothing: cf. § 17, *multi filii dicuntur et non sunt.* ***Proprie*** depends on *solus ex deo genitus*, "alone begotten from God in the strict sense of the word", *de vulva cordis ipsius*, "from the womb of his heart". The next quotation is brought in to justify *cordis ipsius*: *vulva* comes from Ps. 110. 3, ἐκ γαστρὸς πρὸ ἑωσφόρου ἐξεγέννησά σε, which is quoted in part below, *ante luciferum genui te*.

Eructavit cor meum sermonem optimum.

Ps. 45. 1, where LXX reads ἐξηρεύξατο ἡ καρδία μου λόγον ἀγαθόν, "my heart hath disgorged a good word". Driver translates, "my heart is astir with a goodly matter". This is another of the texts, having even in Greek no immediate bearing on the subject, which are constantly adduced in this connexion: cf. below, § 11, and *adv. Marc.* ii. 4, *adhibet operi bono optimum etiam ministrum, sermonem suum: Eructavit, inquit, cor meum sermonem optimum: agnoscat hinc primum fructum optimum utique optimae arboris Marcion: ibid.* iv. 14, *iam hoc ipsum quod a benedictionibus coepit* (sc. Lk. 6. 20 *beati mendici*) *creatoris est qui universa prout edidit nulla alia voce quam benedictionis dedicavit: Eructavit enim, inquit, cor meum sermonem optimum: adv. Hermog.* 18, *proinde si malum quidem innatum est, natus autem sermo dei—Eructavit enim, inquit, sermonem optimum—non scio an a bono malum possit adduci, validius ab infirmo, ut innatum a nato.* The citation was perhaps originally suggested by Heb. 1. 8, 9, where verses 7, 8 of this psalm (ὁ θρόνος σου, ὁ θεὸς, κτέ.) are quoted as proof of the greatness of the Son of God, and the words ἔχρισέ σε ὁ θεός justify a Messianic interpretation. JUSTIN, *dial.* 38, quotes the whole psalm, and promises the Christian interpretation later: *ibid.* 56, he adduces ὁ θρόνος σου, ὁ θεὸς, κτέ. to prove that καὶ παρὰ τὸν νοούμενον ποιητὴν τῶν ὅλων ἄλλος τις κυριολογεῖται ὑπὸ τοῦ ἁγίου πνεύματος: *ibid.* 63, quoting verses 6-12, he comments, ὅτι γοῦν καὶ προσκυνητός ἐστι καὶ θεὸς καὶ χριστὸς (*suppl.* ὁ) ὑπὸ τοῦ ταῦτα ποιήσαντος μαρτυρούμενος καὶ οἱ λόγοι οὗτοι διαρρήδην σημαίνουσι· καὶ ὅτι τοῖς εἰς αὐτὸν πιστεύουσιν, ὡς οὖσι μιᾷ ψυχῇ καὶ μιᾷ συναγωγῇ καὶ μιᾷ ἐκκλησίᾳ, ὁ λόγος τοῦ θεοῦ ὡς θυγατρὶ (*suppl.* παραινεῖ *vel simile quid*) τῇ ἐκκλησίᾳ, τῇ ἐξ ὀνόματος αὐτοῦ γενομένῃ καὶ μετασχούσῃ τοῦ ὀνόματος αὐτοῦ—Χριστιανοὶ γὰρ πάντες καλούμεθα—ὁμοίως φανερῶς οἱ λόγοι κηρύσσουσι διδάσκοντες ἡμᾶς καὶ τῶν *παλαιῶν πατρῴων ἐθῶν ἐπιλάθεσθαι*: *ibid.* 76 and 86 he quotes *ἔχρισέ σε ὁ θεός*. IRENAEUS, *haer.* iv. 55. 1, quotes verses 3, 8, 4, and 5, as proof that the prophets foresaw the glory of Christ: *ibid.* iii. 6. 1, quoting verses 7, 8, he comments, *utrosque enim dei appellatione signavit spiritus, et eum qui ungitur filium et eum qui ungit, id est patrem: ibid.* iii. 32. 1 he quotes verse 17, *pro patribus nati sunt tibi filii* in a discussion of the Lucan genealogy: *ibid.* iv. 9. 2 he cites the same verse to prove that the fathers, i.e. Abraham, Isaac, and Jacob, are God's sons: *praed. apost.* 47, quoting verses 6, 7, he comments, "For the Son, since he is God, receives from the Father who is God, the throne of eternity and the oil of anointing more than his fellows. And the oil of anointing is the Spirit with which he is anointed, and his fellows are the prophets and righteous men and apostles and all who receive the communication of his kingdom, that is, who are His disciples." Thus far the comment is within the limits of Heb. 1. 8, 9 and may claim scriptural authority. Doubtful exegesis begins when THEOPHILUS mistakes the "good word", by which the psalmist means the subject-matter of his ode, for the Word or Son of God: *ad Autol.* ii. 10, *ἔχων οὖν ὁ θεὸς τὸν ἑαυτοῦ λόγον ἐνδιάθετον ἐν τοῖς ἰδίοις σπλάγχνοις ἐγέννησεν αὐτὸν μετὰ τῆς ἑαυτοῦ σοφίας ἐξερευξάμενος πρὸ τῶν ὅλων*: Otto's note gives the following references: Tertullian, *adv. Prax.* 7. 11; Cyprian, *test.* ii. 3; Alexander Alexandrinus, *ap.* Socr. *H.E.* i. 6; Athanasius *de decret.* tom. 1, p. 227, *al.* The orthodox fathers insist that *ἐξηρεύξατο* means *ἐγέννησεν* and cannot possibly be made to imply creation: it does not seem to have occurred to their adversaries to reply that the quotation has no bearing on the theological question. ORIGEN, *comm. in Ioa.* i. 24 (p. 25), remarks that certain persons are always quoting this text, *οἰόμενοι προφορὰν πατρικὴν οἱονεὶ ἐν συλλαβαῖς κειμένην εἶναι τὸν υἱὸν τοῦ θεοῦ, καὶ κατὰ τοῦτο ὑπόστασιν αὐτῷ, εἰ ἀκριβῶς αὐτῶν πυνθανοίμεθα, οὐ διδόασιν, οὐδὲ οὐσίαν αὐτοῦ σαφηνίζουσιν, οὐδέπω φαμὲν τοιάνδε, ἀλλ' ὅπως ποτὲ οὐσίαν.* He claims that the title *λόγος*, equally with other titles such as door, vine, way, must be subjected to examination in search of its intended meaning: apparently his suggestion is that *λόγος* is no more a proper name than any of these others. Tertullian always reads *sermonem optimum*: Cyprian, *l.c.*, *verbum bonum*.

Ad quem deinceps, etc.

For ***proinde*** see the note on § 5 *ad fin.* ***In persona illius:*** see a further note on *filius ex sua persona*, p. 229 : here the phrase might mean that the Father, in Ps. 2. 7, addresses the Son as a person, or possibly the meaning is that as Ps. 2 is spoken throughout by the Son, in verse 7 the Father "in the Son's role" or "as quoted by the Son" speaks to the Son as Son. The sentence then seems to mean, "And immediately thereafter (i.e. after the disgorging of the good word) the Father rejoicing, as the Son himself relates, addresses the Son, equally rejoicing". ***Filius meus es tu***, etc., is quoted at Acts 13. 33 (with reference to the Resurrection of Christ) and at Heb. 1. 5 (as proving the Son's superiority to the angels, to whom such a thing was never said): and no doubt the words spoken from heaven at the Baptism and the Transfiguration were understood to be a reference to the psalm. Hence certain of the school of Theodotus maintained that the Baptism or the Resurrection marked the beginning of the divine Sonship.

Ante luciferum genui te.

Oehler's punctuation needs correction, to mark a new quotation: Ps. 110. 3, *ἐκ γαστρὸς πρὸ ἑωσφόρου ἐξεγέννησά σε*, where Driver translates, "from the womb of the dawn thine is the dew of thy young men", and comments, "The verse describes how the king is enabled to carry into effect the commission, 'Rule thou in the midst of thine enemies': . . . fresh and numerous as the dewdrops in the early dawn, his young warriors press forward in his service". This text also has a long exegetical and controversial history. That the psalm was, in pre-Christian Jewish circles, regarded as Messianic is shown by the quotation of the first verse, *Εἶπεν ὁ κύριος τῷ κυρίῳ μου*, at Matt. 22. 41-46 and Luke 20. 41-44: the fourth verse, *σὺ ἱερεὺς εἰς τὸν αἰῶνα κατὰ τὴν τάξιν* Μελχισεδέκ, is cited at Heb. 5. 6. The present verse is again quoted by Tertullian, *adv. Marc.* v. 9, where he remarks that Marcion says it refers to Hezekiah (see below), whereas it evidently means Christ's nativity, which took place at night before the dawn, as is proved by the appearance of the star, and by the angels appearing to the shepherds by night, and by its taking place at an inn, a place where people go only at night: further, he says, *ex utero* can only apply to a real (not a putative) son, unless perhaps it signifies the virgin birth, *ex solo utero sine viri semine*. JUSTIN, *apol.* i. 45, quotes verses 1-3 as a prophecy of the Ascension, without particular comment on verse 3: *dial.* 32, 33, he quotes the whole psalm, and contests in detail the Jewish exegesis which refers it to Hezekiah: *ibid.* 83, he quotes verses 1-3, with the same explanation: *ibid.* 45, Χριστὸν τοῦτον τοῦ θεοῦ υἱόν, ὃς πρὸ ἑωσφόρου καὶ σελήνης ἦν, where ἑωσφόρος means not the dawn but the planet itself (cf. *ibid.* 76, καὶ Δαβὶδ δὲ πρὸ ἡλίου καὶ σελήνης ἐκ γαστρὸς γεννηθήσεσθαι αὐτὸν κατὰ τὴν τοῦ πατρὸς βουλὴν ἐκήρυξε): *ibid.* 63, καὶ τὰ ὑπὸ Δαβὶδ εἰρημένα, Ἐν ταῖς λαμπρότησι . . . κατὰ τὴν τάξιν Μελχισεδέκ, οὐ σημαίνει ἡμῖν ὅτι ἄνωθεν καὶ διὰ γαστρὸς ἀνθρωπείας ὁ θεὸς καὶ πατὴρ τῶν ὅλων γεννᾶσθαι αὐτὸν ἔμελλε; [here for ἄνωθεν Otto's Latin version has *antiquitus*, but the meaning is clearly *iterum*]. Tertullian therefore, at one time interpreting the text as referring to the Incarnation, at another time to the eternal generation, follows Justin's lead: so that there is no *a priori* objection to its appearance here (*F* omits it), especially as without it *de vulva cordis ipsius* would remain unexplained. ATHENAGORAS and THEOPHILUS do not quote this psalm. IRENAEUS, *haer.*, quotes verse 1 several times: *praed. apost.* 43, he quotes verse 3 (ascribing it to Jeremiah) to show that the Son existed before the foundation of the world: *ibid.* 48, he quotes the whole psalm to prove that "he has been before all, and has conquered the heathen, and judges all men, and even kings, who now hate him and persecute his name". This is another of the texts quoted by Alexander of Alexandria in his encyclical letter, and so introduced into the Arian controversy.

Sic et filius ex sua persona, etc.

Persona here seems to combine the dramatic with the metaphysical sense: "the Son in his own person", but *in nomine sophiae* "calling himself Wisdom", acknowledges the existence of the Father (and so of the father-son relationship) by using the word *generavit*: and moreover, in the metaphysical sense, the Son, as well as the Father, is a *persona*, as being distinct from, yet in relation with, another *persona*.

Nam si hic quidem, etc.

The text of Proverbs which speaks of creation by Wisdom,

and the text of the Gospel which speaks of creation by the Word, taken together prove that the titles Wisdom and Word indicate ***unam eandemque vim***, "one and the same function" (see above, § 6): and moreover, as the Gospel identifies the Word and the Son, the three designations, Wisdom, Word, Son, signify one and the same Person. See the critical note on page 95, line 19.

Nec diutius de isto, etc.

"But enough of that matter: for evidently the Word himself is ⟨represented⟩ under the name of Wisdom and Reason and of the whole divine Mind and Spirit: and that Word became Son of God, by proceeding from whom he was begotten." ***De isto***, i.q. *de ista re.* ***Quasi non***, a common locution in Tertullian, e.g. *apol.* 49, *quasi non totum quod in nos potestis nostrum sit arbitrium*, "for evidently all that you can do against us is a matter of our own choice", seeing we can please ourselves whether we are Christians or not. ***Divini . . . spiritus:*** It is evident from § 2 and elsewhere that Tertullian does not identify the Word and the Holy Spirit; "spirit" is a common term which describes the substance of God: πνεῦμα ὁ θεός, and therefore the Word of God is spirit: the Holy Spirit is a third Person (§ 8, *tertius enim est spiritus a deo et filio*), but the same spirit. ***Filius factus est dei***, "became", not "was made": Tertullian is neither an Arian nor an adoptionist: he does not mean that Wisdom was raised to the rank of Son, but that, retaining her divine rank and substance, she became Word and Son by issuing forth from God.

Ergo, inquis, etc.

Here the argument takes a new step, justifying and reinforcing the position already assumed, that the Word of God is not, like human speech, a mere faculty or activity, but is ***aliqua substantia***, a substance of some kind (i.e. a Person, which is a particular kind of substance) possessing attributes and exercising activity. Tertullian is aware of the danger to which Irenaeus refers (*haer.* ii. 42. 3, quoted in the Introduction, p. 37), of thinking that human attributes and faculties are a sufficient illustration of the divine nature: cf. *adv. Marc.* ii. 16, *stultissimi qui de humanis divina praeiudicant . . . discerne substantias, et suos eis distribue sensus tam diversos quam substantiae exigunt, licet vocabulis communicare videantur . . . et haec ergo imago censenda est dei in homine, quod eosdem motus et sensus habeat humanus animus quos et deus, licet* *non tales quales deus: pro substantia enim et status eorum et exitus distant.* *Das* would naturally mean "concede": here it evidently means "postulate". *Constructam* does not here bear its strict sense of "composed" or "created", but means nothing more precise than "subsisting": so also *constitutus*, below. If the traditional text is correct, this sentence can only mean that that substance which is the Word is *spiritu constructa*, consists of spirit (ablative of origin), because πνεῦμα ὁ θεός, spirit is the substance of God and consequently of the Word; and is *sophiae traditione constructa*, subsists by the transference of Wisdom (ablative of means), because the divine Wisdom, when translated into speech, is the Word. But Turner's conjecture is evidently correct, and saves the awkwardness of using the ablative in two senses in the same phrase: "consisting of spirit, wisdom, and reason" (ablative of origin throughout).

Non vis enim, etc.

This seems to be the correct reading. The difficulty (which perhaps was thought to call for *novimus*, the reading of *P*) arose from failure to observe that *enim* refers back beyond *plane* to *inquis* in the preceding sentence: *novimus* would leave *enim* in the following sentence hanging in the air. Kroymann's insertion of *ne* before *ut* is unnecessary, for *videri* does not mean "seem" but "be seen" or "be acknowledged". "For you are not prepared to regard him as substantive, in objective existence, on account of his being a substance which is himself, that so he may be seen to be objectively and personally existent, and consequently, by being another beside God, may establish the existence of two, Father and Son, God and Word." *In re*, in objective existence, as a *res* and not merely an attribute or activity: Turner's *haberi in se* is then unnecessary. *Per substantiae proprietatem*, because he is a substance of his own: *proprietas* hardly means "property" for it seems invariably to look not towards the things possessed but towards the possessor: *de cor.* 10, *usque adhuc proprietatem istius habitus* (sc. *coronae*) *et ex originis censu et ex superstitionis usu idolis vindicamus*, "the true possession of that decoration": *de praesc. haer.* 35, *apostolis ubique* (leg. *ubi quid*) *non damnatur, immo defenditur, hoc erit indicium proprietatis*, "that it really belongs to them": *de bapt.* 2, *pro misera incredulitas, quae denegas deo proprietates suas, simplicitatem et potestatem*, "attributes which he alone possesses in perfection": *de fug. in pers.* 2, *vides iam et a servis dei facilius diabolum accipere potestatem—tanto abest ut eam ex proprietate possideat*, "possesses it by his own right": *de anima*, 38, *desiderabit igitur cibos anima sibi quidem ex causa necessitatis, carni vero ex natura proprietatis*, "for itself because of its relationship with the flesh (*necessitas=necessitudo*), for the flesh because food by nature belongs to it": *ibid.* 43, *omnis enim natura aut defraudatione aut enormitate rescinditur, proprietate mensurae conservatur*, "by that measure which is its own": so *adv. Prax.* 27, *utramque substantiam in sua proprietate distantem*, "in that which is properly itself": *ibid.*, *utriusque proprietas substantiae*, "that which each substance itself is": and *ibid.* 11, *unam quamque personam in sua proprietate constituunt*, "in that which he himself is". In the present passage the argument is that his being a substance of his own proves him to be, in a metaphysical sense, *res quaedam*, a substantive existence, and, in a psychological sense, *persona quaedam*, a person. ***Capiat***=ἐνδέχηται. ***Secundus a deo***, "another beside God", cf. below, *secundum a patre defendo*. ***Constitutus***=ὑφεστώς or ὑπάρχων (as below in the quotation of Phil. 2. 6), without any passive meaning. ***Efficere***, "establish by argument", not "bring into existence".

Aer offensus.

The point is now too obvious to need illustration: the ancients had doubts about it. AULUS GELLIUS, *N.A.* v. 15, *vetus atque perpetua quaestio inter nobilissimos philosophorum agitata est, corpusne sit vox an incorporeum. hoc enim vocabulum quidam finxerunt proinde quod graece dicitur ἀσώματον. corpus autem est quod aut efficiens est aut patiens: id graece definitur τὸ ἤτοι ποιοῦν ἢ πάσχον. quam definitionem significare volens Lucretius poeta ita scripsit: Tangere enim aut tangi nisi corpus nulla potest res. alio quoque modo corpus esse Graeci dicunt τὸ τριχῇ διάστατον. sed vocem Stoici corpus esse contendunt, eamque esse dicunt ictum aera, Plato autem non esse vocem corpus putat: Non enim percussus, inquit, aer sed plaga ipsa atque percussio, id vox est. Democritus ac deinde Epicurus ex individuis corporibus vocem constare dicunt, eamque, ut ipsis eorum verbis utar, ῥεῦμα ἀτόμων appellant.* STOBAEUS, *ecl.* i. 45, οἱ ἀπὸ Πλάτωνος· πλήττεσθαι τὸν ἐν τῇ κεφαλῇ ἀέρα, τοῦτον δ' ἀνακλᾶσθαι εἰς τὰ ἡγεμονικὰ καὶ γίγνεσθαι τῆς ἀκοῆς αἴσθησιν. Πλάτωνος ἐν Τιμαίῳ (p. 67 *b*)... ὅλως μὲν οὖν φωνὴν θῶμεν τὴν δι' ὤτων ὑπ' ἀέρος ἐγκεφάλου τε καὶ αἵματος μέχρι ψυχῆς πληγὴν διαδιδομένην, ⟨τὴν δ' ὑπ' αὐτῆς κίνησιν, ἀπὸ τῆς κεφαλῆς μὲν ἀρχομένην,⟩ τελευτῶσαν δὲ περὶ τὴν τοῦ ἥπατος ἕδραν, ἀκοήν: *ibid.* 46, Πλάτων τὴν φωνὴν ὁρίζεται πνεῦμα διὰ στόματος ἀπὸ διανοίας καὶ πληγὴν ὑπ' ἀέρος δι' ὤτων καὶ ἐγκεφάλου καὶ αἵματος μέχρι ψυχῆς διαδεδομένην. LUCRETIUS, iv. 524-614, takes the view that particles of speech travel from the organ of speech to the organ of hearing: *principio auditur sonus et vox omnis, in auris | insinuata suo pepulere ubi corpore sensum. | corpoream vocem quoque enim constare fatendumst | et sonitum, quoniam possunt impellere sensus.* Mayor, *ad loc.*, quotes EPIC. *in Diog.* x. 52, τὸ ἀκούειν γίνεται ῥεύματός τινος φερομένου ἀπὸ τοῦ φωνοῦντος ἢ ἠχοῦντος ἢ ψοφοῦντος ἢ ὅπως δήποτ' ἀκουστικὸν πάθος παρασκευάζοντος· τὸ δὲ ῥεῦμα τοῦτο εἰς ὁμοιομερεῖς ὄγκους διασπείρεται. [APPULEIUS] *Asclepius* 20 (which G. Boissier, *La Fin du paganisme*, vol. ii. p. 196, says is a fourth-century version of a Greek original), *si enim vox haec est, ex aere spiritu percusso sonus, declarans omnem hominis voluntatem vel sensum quem forte ex sensibus mente perceperit, etc.* C. H. Turner (*J.T.S.*, vol. xiv. p. 563) quotes *vox est aer ictus* or similar phrases from the grammarians, who he thinks represent a tradition older than Tertullian. By the fourth century the theory was sufficiently well established to find a place in the Church Service: *Cons. Apost.* viii. 12. 10 (from the preface to the anaphora), ὁ ποιήσας . . . ἀέρα ζωτικὸν πρὸς εἰσπνοὴν καὶ ἀναπνοὴν καὶ φωνῆς ἀπόδοσιν διὰ γλώττης πληττούσης τὸν ἀέρα, καὶ ἀκοὴν συνεργουμένην ὑπ' αὐτοῦ ὡς ἐπαΐειν εἰσδεχομένην τὴν προσπίπτουσαν αὐτῇ λαλιάν.

At ego nihil dico, etc.

Five considerations prove the substantiality of the divine Word: (1) That which proceeds from the divine substance must itself be substance: (2) Nothing devoid of substance could have been the creator of substances (and the Agent in creation is a creator): (3) The titles "Son" and "God", applied to the Word in Scripture, are indicative of substance: (4) The scriptural expression "in the form of God" implies substance, because (*a*) there can be no form without substance, and (*b*) since God is substance that which is in his form must be substance: (5) If the "invisible things of God", i.e. the divine attributes, have such body and form as to be visible to him, *a fortiori* that which is not a mere attribute but has been "sent forth" from him, cannot but be substance.

Scriptum est, Non sumes, etc.

THEOPHILUS, *ad Autol.* ii. 10 (quoting Gen. 1. 1), πρῶτον ἀρχὴν καὶ ποίησιν ὠνόμασεν, εἶθ' οὕτως τὸν θεὸν συνέστησεν· οὐ γὰρ ἀργῶς χρὴ καὶ ἐπὶ κενῷ θεὸν ὀνομάζειν.

In effigie dei constitutus, etc.

Phil. 2. 6, ἐν μορφῇ θεοῦ ὑπάρχων. ***Constitutus*** supplies the place of the missing participle of *esse*. Cyprian reads *in figura dei constitutus*: Augustine and the Vulgate, *qui cum in forma dei esset*. Except when quoting this text (here and *adv. Marc.* v. 20, *de res. carn.* 6), Tertullian uses ***effigies*** for what is appearance but not fact, e.g. *de anima*, 53, *paulatim et ipsa* (sc. *anima*) *migrare compulsa deducitur in diminutionis effigiem*. ***Esse se aequalem deo:*** *adv. Marc.* v. 20, *pariari deo: de res. carn.* 6, *parem esse deo.* ***Utique in aliqua:*** so Kroymann for the MSS. *utique in alia*, which seems meaningless.

Quis enim negabit deum corpus esse?

It was a Stoic fancy that all reality is corporeal: see the authorities quoted by Ritter and Preller, §§ 488-490, e.g. CICERO, *acad.* i. 39, *nullo modo arbitrabatur* ⟨Zeno⟩ *quicquam effici posse ab ea* (sc. *natura*) *quae expers esset corporis . . . nec vero aut quod efficeret aliquid aut quod efficeretur posse esse non corpus.* Consequently, according to other authorities, truth, knowledge, understanding, mind, are σώματα, because they are efficient: SENECA, *ep.* 106. 3, *quaeris bonum an corpus sit: bonum facit, prodest enim: quod facit corpus est.* So TERTULLIAN, *de anima*, 6, *bene autem quod et artes Stoici corporales affirmant: adeo sic quoque anima corporalis si et artibus ali creditur.* Tertullian can grudgingly allow, for the sake of argument, that incorporeal existence is conceivable: *adv. Hermog.* 35, *omnis res aut corporalis aut incorporalis sit necesse est—ut concedam interim esse aliquid incorporale de substantiis dumtaxat, cum ipsa substantia corpus sit rei cuiusque—certe post corporale et incorporale nihil tertium.* His real opinion is given *de carne Christi*, 11, *nihil enim habens invisibile quomodo potest ⟨anima⟩ invisibilis dici? sed ne esse quidem potest nisi habens per quod sit. cum autem sit, habeat necesse est aliquid per quod est. si habet aliquid per quod est, hoc erit corpus eius. omne quod est corpus est sui generis. nihil est incorporale nisi quod non est.* So with reference to creation *ex nihilo*, *de res. carn.* 11, *quo enim interest ex nihilo quid proferri an ex aliquo, dum quod non fuit fiat, quando etiam non fuisse nihil sit fuisse? sic et fuisse e contrario nonnihil est fuisse.* Consequently the soul is corporeal, since it really exists: *de anima*, 7, *⟨anima sub terris⟩ nihil, si non corpus: incorporalitas enim ab omni genere custodiae liber est, immunis et a poena et a fovella:* but the soul is body with a difference, *de res. carn.* 53, *anima vero etsi corpus, tamen quia ipsa est corpus non animatum sed animans potius, animale corpus non potest dici, nec fieri quod facit:* consequently the suggestion that *corpus animale* at 1 Cor. 15. 44, means the soul cannot be upheld.

According to EUSEBIUS, *H.E.* iv. 26, Melito of Sardis wrote a treatise περὶ ἐνσωμάτου θεοῦ. JEROME, who had not seen the book, did not know what the title meant, and kept it in Greek: RUFFINUS, translating *de deo corpore induto*, took it to refer to the Incarnation. ORIGEN, who apparently had seen the book, gives the impression that Melito understood literally the anthropomorphisms of the Old Testament: *Fragm. comment. in Genes.* (*ap.* THDT. *quaest. in Genes.* 20), προδιαληπτέον πρότερον ποῦ συνίσταται τὸ κατ' εἰκόνα, ἐν σώματι ἢ ἐν ψυχῇ. ἴδωμεν δὲ πρότερον οἷς χρῶνται οἱ τὸ πρῶτον λέγοντες, ὧν ἐστι καὶ Μελίτων σύγγραμμά τι (so Otto for MS. συγγράμματα) καταλελοιπὼς περὶ τοῦ ἐνσώματον εἶναι τὸν θεόν. μέλη γὰρ θεοῦ ὀνομαζόμενα εὑρίσκοντες . . . ἄντικρυς φάσκουσι ταῦτα οὐχ ἕτερόν τι διδάσκειν ἢ τὴν μορφὴν τοῦ θεοῦ. The Clementine homilies (xvii. 7) take the Old Testament anthropomorphisms literally, but soften them slightly: "He has all the members, but not for use . . . it is for man's sake, so that the pure in heart may enjoy the sight of him". See Routh, *R.S.*, vol. i. pp. 121, 143: Otto, *Corp. Apol.* ix. pp. 394 sqq.: NOVATIAN, *de trin.* 5, quoted in the Introduction, p. 53. GENNADIUS of Marseilles, *de eccl. dogm.* 4, classes Melito with Tertullian, the anthropomorphites, and Audianus, as having believed the Trinity to be corporeal: but he was unintelligent, or ill-informed, in classing Tertullian with these, seeing he insists on the fact that it is man who is in God's image, not God who is in man's: *adv. Marc.* ii. 16, *discerne substantias, et suos eis distribue sensus tam diversos quam substantiae exigunt, licet vocabulis communicare videantur: nam et dexteram et oculos et pedes dei legimus, nec ideo tamen humanis comparabuntur quia de appellatione sociantur.* When he says that God is *corpus* he means no more than that he really exists: he cannot conceive of *substantia* except as *corpus*: cf. below, § 8, *sermo autem spiritu structus est, et ut ita dixerim sermonis corpus est spiritus.*

Etsi deus spiritus est.

NOVATIAN, in what is apparently a deliberate criticism of Tertullian, remarks, *de trin.* 7, that when our Lord says "God is a spirit", spirit is no more a substantival name than *caritas* or *lux: ut merito et quando spiritus dictus est, non omne id quod est dictus est, sed ut dum mens hominum intellegendo usque ad ipsum proficit spiritum, conversa iam ipsa in spiritu aliud quid amplius per spiritum conicere deum esse possit . . . denique si acceperis spiritum substantiam dei, creaturam feceris deum: omnis enim spiritus creatura est.*

Spiritus enim corpus sui generis in sua effigie.

Genus seems to mean "kind of substance", though how it is differentiated is not explained: *effigies*, the attributes by which the substance is cognisable. Elsewhere *effigies* means mere appearance: *de anima*, 53, *deducitur in diminutionis effigiem . . . actu elanguens non statu, constantiam non substantiam decoquens, quia comparere cessat non quia esse.*

Invisibilia illa :

Rom. I. 20: cf. *adv. Hermog.* 45, *haec autem sunt invisibilia eius, quae secundum apostolum ab institutione mundi de factis eius conspiciuntur, non materiae nescioquae, sed sensualia ipsius.*

Quaecunque ergo, etc.

The *substantia* of the Λόγος, being derived from the Father, not created by him, is personal, as is the *substantia* of the Father; is also Son, because he proceeds from the Father, for sonship is the only word which will adequately describe this relationship of person derived from person; and therefore he is *secundus a patre,* "another besides the Father", not identical with him as the monarchians allege.

VIII. *The expression* quod ex ipsius substantia emissum est, "*that which has been produced from his own substance*", *may be objected to as reminiscent of the Valentinian* προβολαί, prolationes, *projections. But* (1) *the word* προβολή *is not to be rejected on the ground that heretics use it: the heretics have borrowed it from the Truth, although they use it to maintain a lie. The question for us is whether the Word did or did not proceed forth: and the answer is that he did.* (2) *Valentinus makes his æons so proceed as to be separated from and ignorant of their origin: whereas we say that the Son, who alone knows the Father, perfectly accomplishes the Father's will.* (3) *The Word, being the Spirit who is* "*in God*", *cannot be separate from him, but is one with him, as the branch is one with the root, the river one with the spring, the beam one with the sun. These are in each case two, and yet inseparable, as the Father and the Son are two, and yet inseparable: for that which proceeds from something must be another besides that from which it proceeds.* (4) *The Holy Spirit is a third ⟨proceeding⟩ from the Father and the Son, as the fruit from the root through the branch, the irrigation canal from the spring through the river, the illumination point from the sun through the beam. None of these is alienated from its origin: and likewise the Trinity, originating in the Father, safeguards the economy without gainsaying the monarchy.*

In the Valentinian theology the "fulness of the godhead" is supposed to have evolved by a succession of emissions or projections of pairs of æons from an original pair, Depth and Silence. It is essential to the system (*a*) that each emission should have taken place without conscious activity on the part of the projecting pair, and (*b*) that each pair should be ignorant of all above itself, and especially of the original unknown and unknowable Depth: for in this scheme the Fall, as enacted in the celestial sphere, consists of a passionate desire for that forbidden knowledge on the part of one of the lowest æons, and that passionate desire is substantified and becomes the semi-celestial prototype of matter—*dissolvitur in reliquam substantiam.* Christian theology does not take kindly to the non-scriptural word προβολή (see note); but Tertullian, being confronted with it, and having found it and its cognates in reputable authorities, is prepared to allow it, though with the safeguard that the προβολή of the Son and of the Holy Spirit does not separate them from the Father nor admit of their being ignorant of him. Origen, with Justin before him, adds the further safeguard that the Son was begotten "from the will of the Father" (*de princ.* iv. 4. 1, cf. i. 2. 6, quoted above), thus excluding the gnostic theory of unconscious emission: the Arians took up this phrase and twisted it to imply that the Son exists by the will of the Father, i.e. is a created being, and by the will of the Father could cease to exist.

Tertullian's three illustrations, if overpressed, would be open to both the above objections: e.g. the spring is ignorant of its act of producing a river, and the river is ignorant of its source in the spring. But these are illustrations, not proofs, of the contention that it is possible for there to be three, who yet are one: with that limitation they were regarded as reasonably satisfactory and were adopted by other expositors. AUGUSTINE, *de fide et symbolo*, 17, points out another defect in the illustration: *sane cavendum est ne quisquam ineffabilem illius maiestatis substantiam sicut fontem istum visibilem atque corporeum vel fluvium vel potionem cogitet. in his enim aqua illa quae nunc in fonte est exit in fluvium, nec in se manet: et cum de fluvio vel de fonte in potionem transit non ibi permanet unde sumitur. itaque fieri potest ut eadem aqua nunc ad fontis appellationem pertineat, nunc ad fluvii, nunc ad potionis, cum in illa trinitate dixerimus non posse fieri ut pater aliquando sit filius, aliquando spiritus sanctus.* This defect, he adds, is corrected by the other illustration, of the root, the trunk, and the branches, where there is no passing over of the one into the other: and if this image, in its turn, is open to the objection that the three parts of the tree, though all and each are wood, are of differing qualities and consistencies, it again can be corrected by the simile of the water which is of the same quality in the river and the cup as in the fountain. He concludes: *sed haec non propter illius divinae naturae similitudinem sed propter visibilium etiam unitatem corporalia exempla data sunt, ut intelligeretur fieri posse ut aliqua tria non tantum singillatim, sed etiam simul, unum singulare nomen obtineant.* HIPPOLYTUS, *c. Noet.* 10, evidently borrows from Tertullian: τῶν δὲ γιγνομένων ἀρχηγὸν καὶ σύμβουλον καὶ ἐργάτην ἐγέννα λόγον . . . καὶ οὕτως παρίστατο αὐτῷ ἕτερος. ἕτερον δὲ λέγων οὐ δύο θεοὺς λέγω ἀλλ' ὡς φῶς ἐκ φῶτος, ἢ ὡς ὕδωρ ἐκ πηγῆς, ἢ ὡς ἀκτῖνα ἀπὸ ἡλίου.

Προβολὴν *aliquam*.

Προβάλλειν means "emit" or "give out" apparently only in late writers: Liddell and Scott (8th ed.) quote from DIOSCORIDES (ὀσμήν), DIODORUS (φωνὴν, ἦχον), and JOSEPHUS (καρπόν). Προβολή in the corresponding sense is not quoted: one of its meanings is "bulwark", "protection", "pretext", and it seems possible that the Valentinians, using the word in the sense of "emission" (or better, "emanation"), were not unconscious of the idea that the æons were a series of defences of the majesty of Βῦθος. Tertullian is right in hinting that the word has respectable Christian authority: Justin used it in all good faith, and it was because of Valentinian misuse that Origen expressly rejected it. JUSTIN, *dial.* 61, ἀλλ' οὐ τοιοῦτον ὁποῖον καὶ ἐφ' ἡμῶν γιγνόμενον ὁρῶμεν; λόγον γάρ τινα προβάλλοντες λόγον γεννῶμεν, οὐ κατ' ἀποτομὴν ὡς ἐλαττωθῆναι τὸν ἐν ἡμῖν λόγον προβαλλόμενοι: *ibid.* 62, "Let us make man", was not spoken to angels, ἀλλὰ τοῦτο τὸ τῷ ὄντι ἀπὸ τοῦ πατρὸς προβληθὲν γέννημα πρὸ πάντων τῶν ποιημάτων συνῆν τῷ πατρί, καὶ τούτῳ ὁ πάτηρ προσομιλεῖ: *ibid.* 76, καὶ τὸ λίθον τοῦτον εἰπεῖν ἄνευ χειρῶν τμηθέντα ἐν μυστηρίῳ τὸ αὐτὸ κέκραγε· τὸ γὰρ ἄνευ χειρῶν εἰπεῖν αὐτὸν ἐκτετμῆσθαι, ὅτι οὐκ ἔστιν ἀνθρώπινον ἔργον ἀλλὰ τῆς βουλῆς τοῦ προβάλλοντος αὐτὸν πατρὸς τῶν ὅλων θεοῦ. THEOPHILUS does not use the word: IRENAEUS uses it only in describing gnostic tenets. ATHENAGORAS appears at first sight to come near to it: *suppl.* 10, πρῶτον γέννημα . . . τῷ πατρί, οὐχ ὡς γενόμενον . . . ἀλλὰ ὡς τῶν ὑλικῶν ξυμπάντων . . . ἰδέα καὶ ἐνέργεια εἶναι προελθών: but here the reference is not to the generation of the Word, but to his coming forth to create the world: the question of generation does not arise, since ἐξ ἀρχῆς ὁ θεὸς . . . εἶχεν αὐτὸς ἐν ἑαυτῷ τὸν λόγον. He uses the kindred idea, ἀπόρροια, of the procession of the Holy Spirit; *ibid.* 10, ἅγιον πνεῦμα ἀπόρροιαν εἶναί φαμεν τοῦ θεοῦ, ἀπορρέον καὶ ἐπαναφερόμενον ὡς ἀκτῖνα ἡλίου: *ibid.* 24, νοῦς λόγος σοφία ὁ υἱὸς τοῦ πατρός, καὶ ἀπόρροια ὡς φῶς ἀπὸ πυρὸς τὸ πνεῦμα. Athenagoras thus applies to the Holy Spirit the scriptural image of light from light, which in the first instance appertains to the Son. ORIGEN deprecates both the word προβάλλειν and the speculations of those who use it: *de princ.* i. 2. 6, *observandum namque est ne quis incurrat in illas absurdas fabulas eorum qui prolationes quasdam sibi ipsi depingunt . . . magis ergo sicut voluntas procedit e mente et neque partem aliquam mentis secat neque ab ea separatur aut dividitur, tali quadam specie putandus est pater filium genuisse: ibid.* iv. 4. 1, . . . περὶ πατρὸς ὡς ἀδιαίρετος ὢν καὶ ἀμέριστος υἱοῦ γίγνεται πατήρ, οὐ προβαλὼν αὐτὸν ὡς οἴονταί τινες· εἰ γὰρ πρόβλημά ἐστιν ὁ υἱὸς τοῦ πατρὸς καὶ γέννημα γεγεννημένον ἐξ αὐτοῦ ὁποῖα τὰ τῶν ζῴων γεννήματα, ἀνάγκη σῶμα εἶναι τὸν προβαλόντα καὶ τὸν προβεβλημένον: and, a little later, *ex invisibili et incorporeo deo verbum et sapientiam genitam dicimus absque ulla corporali passione, velut si voluntas procedat e mente* . . . οὗτος δὴ ὁ υἱὸς ἐκ θελήματος τοῦ πατρὸς ἐγενήθη. Origen is objecting as much to anthropomorphism as to gnosticism, and apparently rejects γεννᾶν as well as προβάλλειν: but ἐκ θελήματος would exclude the Valentinian theory of an involuntary self-development or self-articulation of the divine being. Cf. NOVATIAN, *de trin.* 15, *si homo tantummodo Christus, quomodo dicit: Ego ex deo prodii et veni; cum constet hominem a deo factum esse, non ex deo processisse?* Tertullian, *de anima*, 34, translates προβολή, in a gnostic sense, by *iniectio*: Simon of Samaria says that he is the most high Father, and that Helen, his companion, is his *prima iniectio.*

Non ideo utitur, etc.

Read *utitur* for the MSS. *utatur*: a statement of what Christian usage is is more to the point here than an injunction as to what one desires it to be: *utatur* (Kroymann's conjecture) at the end of the sentence, as well as being grammatically correct, may be what Tertullian wrote. ***Res vocabuli*** is the fact which the word signifies, in this case the derivation of the Son from the substance of the Father. Heretical misunderstanding does not cause the Truth to repudiate this fact but to distinguish the true from the false interpretation of it. The falsehood of gnosticism is not in using the word and the fact of προβολή, but in supposing that τὸ προβληθὲν is separate from and ignorant of its ἀρχή. ***Census vocabuli*** is the word's origin and antecedents: see Oehler's index, where *census* is equated with *origo, natura*: "nam in censuales libros referebantur cuiusque parentes atque natales, cf. *adv. Marc.* iv. 7": *ad nat.* i. 12, *omne omnino genus censum ad originem refert.* See the note on § 5. The word προβολή is of quite respectable origin, and remains respectable in spite of heretical misuse.

Iam nunc quaeritur, etc.

Delete Oehler's note of interrogation: a statement of fact is more to the point than a remonstrative question.

Valentinus.

On the Valentinian theology see *adv. Val.* 14, 15: possibly a sentence or so of summary has dropped out after *nesciat*: *denique* seems to mark the last clause of a series, and *reliquam* needs an antecedent.

Apud nos autem, etc.

This sentence is a cento of adapted scriptural phrases: Matt. 11. 27 (Luke 10. 22), *οὐδεὶς ἐπιγινώσκει τὸν υἱὸν εἰ μὴ ὁ πατήρ, οὐδὲ τὸν πατέρα τις ἐπιγινώσκει εἰ μὴ ὁ υἱός, κτέ.*: John 1. 18, *ὁ ὢν εἰς τὸν κόλπον τοῦ πατρός, ἐκεῖνος ἐξηγήσατο*, where Tertullian takes the object of *ἐξηγήσατο* to be *τὸν κόλπον* (as also § 21, *hic unicus sinum patris disseruit, non sinum suum pater:* cf. Novatian, *de trin.* 18, *qui sinum exposuit patris: ibid.* 28, *cum nondum sinum patris Christus exposuisset:* Hippolytus, *c. Noet.* 5, *μόνος ὁ παῖς καὶ τέλειος ἄνθρωπος καὶ μόνος διηγησάμενος τὴν βουλὴν τοῦ πατρός*, quoting John 1. 18): John 8. 26, *κἀγὼ ἃ ἤκουσα παρ᾽ αὐτοῦ* (*apud patrem*, as though the Greek were *παρ᾽ αὐτῷ*) *ταῦτα λαλῶ*, conflated with 8. 38, *ἃ ἐγὼ ἑώρακα παρὰ τῷ πατρί, λαλῶ*: John 14. 31, *καθὼς ἐνετείλατό μοι ὁ πατήρ, οὕτω ποιῶ*, conflated with 8. 28, *καθὼς ἐδίδαξέ με ὁ πατήρ, ταῦτα λαλῶ*: John 6, 38, *οὐχ ἵνα ποιῶ τὸ θέλημα τὸ ἐμόν, ἀλλὰ τὸ θέλημα τοῦ πέμψαντός με.* ***Immo de initio:*** Kroymann conjectures *de intimo*, which is plausible; but possibly *de initio noverat* is a reminiscence of 1 John 2. 13, *ὅτι ἐγνώκατε τὸν ἀπ᾽ ἀρχῆς*.

Quis enim scit, etc.

This misquotation of 1 Cor. 2. 11 occurs again in § 19 and *adv. Hermog.* 18. Tertullian transfers *τὸ ἐν αὐτῷ* from the spirit of man to the Spirit of God, and proceeds to interpret the apostle's words as referring to the Son: there are indications that his Montanism led him to think that the Paraclete was not operating until the rise of the prophetic movement, and that consequently all apostolic references to the Spirit (other than promises of future operation) must be interpreted of the Son: see a note on § 2. For the identification of Spirit and Word see JUSTIN, *apol.* i. 33 (quoted on § 2); TATIAN, *orat.* 7, λόγος γὰρ ὁ ἐπουράνιος, πνεῦμα γεγονὼς ἀπὸ τοῦ πατρὸς καὶ λόγος ἐκ τῆς λογικῆς δυνάμεως: *ibid.* 20, ⟨οἱ προφῆται⟩ πεπεισμένοι ὅτι πνεῦμα τὸ οὐράνιον ἐπένδυμα τῆς θνητότητος κεκτήσεται. On the former passage Otto quotes a note by Daniel: *Offenbar ist hier* πνεῦμα *generische Bezeichnung eines geistigen Wesens: es bezeichnet das Princip des hervorgegangen* λόγος. This remark is not true of the second passage quoted; but it is what Tertullian means here by *sermonis corpus est spiritus.*

Aut alius a patre.

Perhaps read *aliud.* C. H. Turner suggests *alienus*, quoting passages where it is said that the Son is *alius a patre*, and referring to *nihil . . . alienatur* later in this chapter.

Prolatum . . . sed non separatum.

JUSTIN, *dial.* 61, οὐ κατ' ἀποτομήν: *ibid.* 128, οὐ κατ' ἀποτομὴν ὡς ἀπομεριζομένης τῆς τοῦ πατρὸς οὐσίας: TATIAN, *orat.* 5, γέγονε δὲ κατὰ μερισμόν, οὐ κατὰ ἀποκοπήν· τὸ γὰρ ἀποτμηθὲν τοῦ πρώτου κεχώρισται, τὸ δὲ μερισθὲν οἰκονομίας τὴν αἵρεσιν προσλαβὸν οὐκ ἐνδεᾶ τὸν ὅθεν εἴληπται πεποίηκεν. See the note on λόγος, § 5.

Quemadmodum etiam paracletus docet.

See the note on *ut instructiores per paracletum*, § 2 and the Introduction, p. 81. Of the three similes here expounded, that of the sun and its radiance has a scriptural background in Heb. 1. 3, ἀπαύγασμα τῆς δόξης: that of the fountain and the stream is scriptural as applied to the Holy Spirit (John 7. 38, 39, ποταμοὶ ἐκ τῆς κοιλίας αὐτοῦ ῥεύσουσιν ὕδατος ζῶντος, κτέ. cf. *Apoc.* 22. 1), but as applied to the generation of the Word it seems to be new: that of the tree and the branch seems also to be new and may be due to the new prophecy. JUSTIN, *dial.* 61 and 128, and TATIAN, *orat.* 5, give as an illustration fire lighted from fire without loss to the parent fire, an illustration only valid if fire is regarded as an element in itself. DIONYSIUS ALEXANDRINUS (Routh, *R.S.*, vol. iii. pp. 390 sqq.), ἀπαύγασμα δὲ ὢν φωτὸς ἀιδίου, πάντως καὶ αὐτὸς ἀίδιος ἐστιν, κτέ. and (*ibid.* p. 398), ζωὴ ἐκ ζωῆς ἐγεννήθη, καὶ ὥσπερ ποταμὸς ἀπὸ πηγῆς ἔρρευσε, καὶ ἀπὸ φωτὸς ἀσβέστου λαμπρὸν φῶς ἀνήφθη. [ATHANASIUS] *orat. c. Arian.* iv. 10, ἔστιν δὲ παράδειγμα ἀνθρώπινον, τὸ πῦρ καὶ τὸ ἐξ αὐτοῦ ἀπαύγασμα, δύο μὲν τῷ εἶναι καὶ ὁρᾶσθαι, ἓν δὲ τῷ ἐξ αὐτοῦ καὶ ἀδιαίρετον εἶναι τὸ ἀπαύγασμα αὐτοῦ.

Quia omnis origo, etc.

The terms parent and offspring can be used in an extended sense of all originals and of that which proceeds from them: even more so does this apply to God and his Word, the Word who has in its exact sense (*proprie*) received the name of Son.

Nam et radix, etc.

Res, species, formae, are not quite synonymous: see the Introduction, p. 57. *Coniunctae, indivisae, cohaerentes* are apparently insignificant variations of the same idea.

Tertius enim est.

See the note on § 3, *secundum et tertium sortitis locum.*

Nihil tamen a matrice alienatur.

The subject of the sentence is *spiritus*, and *nihil* is an adverbial accusative. If *nihil* be taken as the subject, the statement is too general to be true. On *matrix* see *apol.* 21, quoted in the Introduction, p. 59: evidently the original physiological meaning is almost or entirely out of mind.

IX. *The inseparability of the Father, the Son, and the Holy Spirit is to be kept in mind as a standing background of all that I shall proceed to say. The Father, the Son, and the Holy Spirit are other than one another—I make this statement in spite of the objections of the unlearned or the opinionated, who pay respect to the word "monarchy" at the expense of the economy—other however not by dissimilarity but by individuality, not by division but by differentiation: for the Father is not the same as the Son, there being even a numerical difference between them. The Father is the whole substance ⟨of the Godhead⟩; the Son is an outflow and apportionment of the whole: for the Father is greater than the Son, as holy Scripture testifies. Our Lord himself uses this word "other" in reference to the Holy Spirit, with no suggestion of division but only of distribution: we are using it in reference to the Father and the Son. The very words "Father" and "Son" indicate a difference: the names cannot be confused, for the facts behind the names are not confused, since Yea is Yea, and Nay is Nay, and anything more is on the side of evil.*

Quid quomodo dicatur,

"what I say, and the meaning I attach to it."

Alium esse patrem, etc.

In view of this it is practically certain that in § 8, *nunquam separatus a patre aut alius a patre, aliud* should be read: and clearly (§ 9 *infra*) *quia non sit idem pater et filius, idem* is masculine gender.

Male accepit . . . adulantes.

Kroymann rightly makes these clauses parenthetical, so that *non tamen . . . alius ab alio* depends directly upon *dico alium esse, etc.* Delete Oehler's comma after *protendat.*

Diversitas

is used by Tertullian to indicate a fundamental unlikeness: *ad nat.* i. 20, *si nihil inter nos* (sc. Christians and pagans) *diversitas habet, si unum et eidem sumus: adv. Marc.* i. 20 (and frequently elsewhere), *diversa pars* means "the opposite party", "my opponents". Possibly "dissimilarity" is a sufficient translation, but "opposition" would not be too strong.

Distributio

appears to mean an assignment, or allocation, of functions (and so forth) among persons fundamentally alike: *ad nat.* i. 19, *sed et philosophi de animarum reciprocatione et iudicii distributione confirmant*, "concerning the return of souls to their bodies and concerning the administration of judgement". It is more or less synonymous with οἰκονομία, *dispensatio*: see below on *dispositio.*

Divisio.

See the note on § 8, *prolatum . . . sed non separatum.*

Distinctio.

Possibly a colourless word indicating a difference which the writer is not prepared to define accurately.

Quia non sit idem, etc.

Idem is masculine gender: *et* stands for *atque*. *Vel modulo alius ab alio:* Kroymann adds *alii*, which is what Tertullian means, though the addition of the word to the text is unnecessary. *Modulus* can mean the abacus, and so indicate numerical reckoning: cf. *apol.* 21, *ita et de spiritu spiritus et de deo deus modulo alternum numerum gradu non statu fecit et a matrice non recessit sed excessit*, "brought about duality in reckoning": on which passage Oehler quotes Rigaltius, *itaque modus et modulus est certarum rerum secundum sui generis rationes dispositio, ordinatio, oeconomia*, which seems like an attempt to gloze over the fact that elsewhere Tertullian does say that in some sense the Father is "greater" (if only in the sense of metaphysically "elder") than the Son: see the following note, and cf. § 14 *et consequens erit ut invisibilem patrem intellegamus pro plenitudine maiestatis, visibilem vero filium agnoscamus pro modulo derivationis.* The present sentence, *vel modulo alius ab alio*, is too concise for perfect clarity, though apparently what Tertullian means is *siquidem vel modulo sint alius ab alio alii*, and whether *modulo* means "by reckoning" or "by measure" is not yet clear: cf. *de anima*, 37, *ceterum animam substantia crescere negandum est, ne etiam decrescere substantia dicatur atque ita defectura credatur: sed vis eius, in qua naturalia peculia consita retinentur, salvo substantiae modulo quo a principio inflata est, paulatim cum carne producitur*: from which it would appear that, as substances are incapable of increase or decrease, since Father and Son are one substance there can be no difference of magnitude between them, and *modulo* will mean "by numerical reckoning".

Derivatio totius et portio.

Cf. *apol.* 21, *et cum radius ex sole porrigitur, portio ex summa: sed sol erit in radio quia solis est radius, nec separatur substantia sed extenditur* ("the substance is not divided but extended"): *ita et de spiritu spiritus et de deo deus ut lumen de lumine accensum: manet integra et indefecta materiae matrix etsi plures inde traduces qualitatis mutueris. ita et quod de deo profectum est deus est et dei filius, et unus* (sc. *deus*) *ambo*. ***Derivare*** in its literal sense is to draw water (or intransitively for water to pass) from a main stream into a side channel: and here the meaning seems to be that there is a "derivation" of the whole substance of the Deity into the Son, the whole substance remaining unimpaired in the Father: cf. *de pud.* 21, *si quia dixerit Petro dominus, Super hanc petram, etc., idcirco praesumis et ad te derivasse solvendi et alligandi potestatem . . . qualis es, evertens atque commutans manifestam domini intentionem personaliter hoc Petro conferentem?* The Roman bishop's claim appears to have been that the whole authority committed to Peter had passed down the stream to the apostle's successor for the time being. So it is tempting to suggest that ***portio*** does not mean "part" but "endowment" (as by inheritance), and that ***portio totius*** means that the Son "inherits", or is endowed with, the whole substance of deity, which yet remains entire in the Father: and so also at § 26, *dicens autem, Spiritus dei, etsi spiritus dei* (leg. *deus*), *tamen non directo deum nominans portionem totius intellegi voluit quae cessura erat in filii nomen*, "an endowment of the whole, which was to fall to the Son's account". Cf. Juvenal, ix. 128, *brevissima vitae portio* "our brief allowance of life". In that case the description of Domitian as *portio Neronis dè crudelitate* (*apol.* 5) would not mean that he was less ruthless than Nero, but that he, so to speak, inherited Nero's character: but Eusebius, *H.E.* iii. 20, translates μέρος ὢν τῆς τοῦ Νέρωνος ὠμότητος, and Tertullian, adding the remark, *sed qua et homo facile coeptum repressit*, seems to indicate that the later Emperor was less confirmed in (if not less well endowed with) ferocity than the earlier. Also it must be added that in the third century *portio* seems to be regularly used as equivalent to *pars*: e.g. Novatian, *de trin.* 11, *quoniam nec tenebit perfectam veritatem quisquis aliquam veritatis excluserit portionem*. On the other hand Tertullian, *de res. carn.* 16, remarking that the flesh is the servant of the soul, not its tool, adds, *ita et ministerium tenebitur iudicio, etsi de suo nihil sapiat, quia portio est eius quae sapit, non ministerium*: on which it is to be observed that as the body is on no showing part of the soul, *portio* cannot mean "part", but yet means something intrinsically connected, something between "part" and "possession"—perhaps "purtenance". On the whole then it seems that in his description of the Son as *derivatio totius et portio*, Tertullian is acknowledging, even pressing the acknowledgement of, a certain difference of magnitude such as (fortified by the texts which he quotes) safeguards the non-identity of Father and Son: while on the other hand he is trying to keep the question of magnitude as much as possible in the background (qualifying *portio* with *totius*, a descriptive, not a partitive, genitive), so as not to suggest an inferior grade of deity, or the exhaustion of the source by the procession of the stream. And it would appear likely that while the suggestion of minoration was forced upon him by controversy, the safeguarding of equality was a requirement of the received tradition.

Pater maior me est.

John 14. 28, quoted again § 14, *non enim et de aliqua maiore persona congruit dicere, Facies mea est ille homo, et, Faciem mihi praestat? Pater, inquit, maior me est.* [The mark of interrogation, omitted by Oehler, is necessary after *praestat*: the Son, says Tertullian, is *spiritus personae patris*, and *persona* is equivalent to *facies*, and therefore the Father is greater than the Son, and they are two Persons and not one.] IRENAEUS, *haer.* ii. 43. 3, uses the text to show that there is not, as the gnostics allege, another god greater than the Father: Why, he asks, does our Lord say that the Father alone knows the day and the hour? . . . *ut discamus per ipsum super omnia esse patrem. etenim Pater, inquit, maior me est. et secundum agnitionem itaque praepositus esse pater annuntiatus est a domino nostro, ad hoc ut et nos in quantum in figura huius mundi sumus perfectam scientiam et tales quaestiones concedamus deo, et ne forte quaerentes altitudinem patris investigare in tantum periculum incidamus uti quaeramus an super deum alter sit deus.* ORIGEN, *de princ.* iv. 4. 8, adds a superiority of the Father's knowledge to a general superiority: the passage is omitted by Rufinus but quoted by Jerome and Justinian: εἰ δὲ ὁ πατὴρ ἐμπεριέχει τὰ πάντα, τῶν δὲ πάντων ἐστὶν ὁ υἱὸς, δῆλον ὅτι καὶ τὸν υἱόν. ἄλλος δέ τις ζητήσει εἰ ἀληθὲς τὸ ὁμοίως τὸν θεὸν ὑφ' ἑαυτοῦ γινώσκεσθαι τῷ γινώσκεσθαι αὐτὸν ὑπὸ τοῦ μονογενοῦς, καὶ ἀποφανεῖται ὅτι τὸ εἰρημένον, Ὁ πατήρ μου ὁ πέμψας με μείζων μου ἐστίν, ἐν πᾶσιν ἀληθές· ὥστε καὶ ἐν τῷ νοεῖν ὁ πατὴρ μειζόνως καὶ τρανοτέρως καὶ τελειοτέρως νοεῖται ὑφ' ἑαυτοῦ ἢ ὑπὸ τοῦ υἱοῦ. Later custom interpreted the text of Christ's human nature—*minor patre secundum humanitatem*: EUSEBIUS, *de eccl. theol.* ii. 7 (p.

110 *b*, *c*), demurs to an early suggestion to that effect, and (like Tertullian) points out that inequality implies duality: δι' ὧν ἁπάντων ἕτερον ἑαυτὸν τοῦ πατρὸς δείκνυται. καὶ τὸ ὑπερέχον τῆς δόξης τοῦ πατρὸς παρίστησι διὰ τοῦ τὸν μὲν ἀπεσταλκέναι λέγειν, ἑαυτὸν δὲ ἀπεστάλθαι, καὶ ἐκ τοῦ οὐρανοῦ κατεληλυθέναι οὐχ ἵνα ποιήσῃ τὸ θέλημα τὸ ἑαυτοῦ ἀλλὰ τὸ τοῦ πέμψαντος αὐτόν. καὶ τί ἂν πρὸς ταῦτα φαίη Μάρκελλος, ἀκούων τοῦ κατεληλυθότος ἐξ οὐρανοῦ ταῦτα διδάσκοντος; οὐ γὰρ δήπου καὶ νῦν τὴν σάρκα τοῦ σωτῆρος ταῦτα φάσκειν ἐρεῖ. οὐ γὰρ ἡ σὰρξ ἐκ τοῦ οὐρανοῦ κατελήλυθε.

Minoratus . . . modicum quid citra angelos.

Ps. 8. 5, quoted Heb. 2. 5-10, where the argument is (*a*) that according to the psalmist mankind in general, and Jesus among them, are a little lower than the angels, and (*b*) that Jesus, and mankind with him, is on account of the suffering of death (διὰ τὸ πάθημα) and by means of sufferings (διὰ παθημάτων) crowned with glory and honour. Tertullian quotes the text again, § 16, where he says that the minoration of the Son consisted of those anticipations of the Incarnation, the appearances to the patriarchs, things which we believe true of the Son only because they are written, and possibly should not believe true of the Father even though they were written: cf. *adv. Marc.* ii. 27, to the same effect. Again, § 23, he refers it to the Incarnation itself: *minoravit filium modico citra angelos ad terram dimittendo, gloria tamen et honore coronaturus eum in caelos resumendo. Adv. Marc.* iv. 21: the real (as opposed to the Marcionist) Christ has never been ashamed to demean himself *pro suo homine, pro imagine et similitudine sua, non aliena*: so also *adv. Iud.* 14: *de carne Christi*, 15, adding, and so he was not ashamed to take to him our corruptible flesh: *ibid.* 14, reading *minuisti* and emphasising *citra angelos*, by which he refutes the suggestion that the Son took upon him the nature of angels. *De corona*, 14, the martyrs, like Christ, will reach glory through suffering: *nec ante rex gloriae in caelestibus salutatus est quam rex Iudaeorum proscriptus cruci, minoratus primo a patre modico quid citra angelos et ita gloria et honore coronatus.* The present passage therefore stands alone in regarding the minoration as the subordination of the Son to the Father within the Godhead. TATIAN, *orat.* 15 (p. 154 *d*), misquotes the verse, κατὰ τὸν εἰπόντα λόγον, Ἐπειδὴ βραχύ τι παρὰ ἀγγέλους ἠλαττώθησαν, in describing the condition of mankind μετὰ τὴν τῆς ἀθανασίας ἀποβολήν.

Bene quod.

Oehler, note to *de idol.* 5, gives examples of this expression from Tertullian: Mayor, note to *apol.* 7, gives references to other authors. In APPULEIUS it appears to mean "it is a good thing that . . ."; in Tertullian, in the passages cited, it means "it suits my case that". *Dispositio* is equivalent to οἰκονομία below, and the contrast with *divisio* illustrates the meaning of *distributio* and *distinctio* above: cf. note on § 2.

Propter oeconomiae observationem,

"so as to respect the economy". Cf. *de corona*, 2, where *observare* (several times) is to keep a rule, and *observatio* is a rule or custom which ought to be kept: *ergo nec nullum nec incertum videri potest delictum quod committitur in observationem suo iam nomine vindicandam et satis auctoratam consensus patrocinio.*

Ipsum quod pater et filius dicuntur.

"The very fact that Scripture uses the terms Father and Son." Diversity of terms implies diversity of facts: the admission here of *diversitas rerum quarum erunt vocabula* in a sense goes back on *non diversitate alium . . . sed distributione* earlier in this chapter, and goes to suggest that the balanced phrases of the earlier passage are rhetorical rather than accurately thought out: Tertullian perhaps would not object to *diversitas* provided it is not thought to involve *separatio* or *divisio*.

Quod amplius est hoc.

Correct Oehler's punctuation, placing the comma after *hoc*: Matt. 5. 37, τὸ δὲ περισσὸν τούτων. Cf. *de carne Christi*, 23, *Lux lux et tenebrae tenebrae et est est et non non: quod amplius hoc a malo est.*

x. *The monarchians, ignoring this distinction, allege that the Father made himself his own son. But father and son are correlatives, and each implies the existence of the other. This is one of those laws of nature which God ordained, and which God himself keeps. To be a father a man must have a son, and to be a son he must have a father. To have is not the same thing as to be. Whichever of these I am, that I have not: if I am both at once, I am neither, since I have neither. Consequently this affectation of respecting the monarchy denies both the Father and the Son. But, they say, God can do anything, and can have made himself both father and son, without regard to our human relationships: the miracles of the nativity of John and of our Lord prove it. I admit that God can do anything: but we have no right to assume that he has done any particular thing unless we have proof that he did. He could have done all manner of things which he has evidently not done. Which proves that there is something that God cannot do, namely, what it was not his will to do: for with God to will is to be able. Therefore, to prove that God could have made himself his own son, and that it was his will to do so, you will first need to prove that he did so.*

This chapter makes the transition from Tertullian's general statement of his own position to his particular discussion of the scriptural texts alleged by his adversaries in support of their case, and of those texts which he produces in proof of his.

Ita aut pater aut filius est, etc.

Kroymann reads, *ut pater et filius est*, "as there is a Father so there is a Son": C. H. Turner suggests *et pater et filius est*, "there is both a Father and a Son": Engelbrecht conjectured *et ut neque dies*, which Kroymann has printed in his text. But the traditional text makes quite good sense, when it is observed that *est* refers back to the scriptural quotation *est est*.

Qui ex alterutro fiunt,

"those whose existence depends on each other", i.e. those who are correlatives: cf. DIONYSIUS ALEXANDRINUS, *ap.* Routh, *R.S.* vol. iii. p. 391, ὄντος οὖν αἰωνίου τοῦ πατρὸς αἰώνιος ὁ υἱός ἐστι, φῶς ἐκ φωτὸς ὤν. ὄντος γὰρ γονέως ἔστι καὶ τέκνον· εἰ δὲ μὴ τέκνον εἴη, πῶς καὶ τίνος εἶναι δύναται γονεύς; ἀλλ' εἰσὶν ἄμφω, καὶ εἰσὶν ἀεί: *ibid.* p. 392, καὶ γὰρ ἀνθρωπείαν γονὴν παρεθέμην, δῆλον ὡς οὖσαν ὁμογενῆ, φήσας πάντως τοὺς γονεῖς μόνον ἑτέρους εἶναι τῶν τέκνων, ὅτι μὴ αὐτοὶ εἶεν τὰ τέκνα, ἢ μήτε γονεῖς ἀναγκαῖον ὑπάρχειν μήτε τέκνα. He mentions πλείονα τῶν συγγενῶν ὁμοιώματα, e.g. the seed (or the root) and the plant, the fountain and the river, which are correlatives and (he implies) in a sense ὁμοούσια. [ὁμοφυής is the vegetable equivalent, as ὁμογενής is the animate equivalent of ὁμοούσιος.] *Ibid.* p. 395, τῶν ὑπ' ἐμοῦ λεχθέντων ὀνομάτων ἕκαστον ἀχώριστόν ἐστι καὶ ἀδιαίρετον τοῦ πλησίον· πατέρα εἶπον, καὶ πρὶν ἐπαγάγω τὸν υἱὸν ἐσήμανα καὶ τοῦτον ἐν τῷ πατρί· υἱὸν ἐπήγαγον· εἰ καὶ μὴ προειρήκειν τὸν πατέρα, πάντως ἂν ἐν τῷ υἱῷ προείληπτο . . . οἱ δὲ οὐκ ἴσασιν ὅτι μήτε ἀπηλλοτρίωται πατὴρ υἱοῦ ᾗ πατήρ· προκαταρκτικὸν γάρ ἐστι τῆς συναφείας τὸ ὄνομα. οὔτε ὁ υἱὸς ἀπῴκισται τοῦ πατρός· ἡ γὰρ πατὴρ προσηγορία δηλοῖ τὴν κοινωνίαν.

Sic etiam ut pater sim, etc.

In this sentence Kroymann twice reads *habebo* for *habeo*, presumably to regularise the tenses—for which there is no pressing need. In the following sentence Oehler's punctuation should be corrected: and possibly the second *ero* should be deleted, or changed into *vero*.

Patrem . . . qui facit filium,

"without whom no one can be a son", as below *qui facit patrem*, "without whom no one can be a father": and cf. the corrected text of § 7, *exinde eum patrem sibi faciens*.

Hoc erit totum ingenium diaboli, etc.

Totum is evidently attributive to *ingenium*, not defined by *hoc*: "this it is that all the devil's ingenuity will amount to", i.e. it will have logical consequences on which he did not reckon. ***Alterum ex altero excludere:*** to suppress one or the other is the devil's ingenuity: to suppress each as a consequence of suppressing the other is all he gains by it. ***Dum neutrum haberi facit,*** "he suppresses 'having' in both cases", i.e. he causes neither the Father to have a son nor the Son to have a father, and consequently is driven by our logic to deny "being" in each case: ***dum enim pater est, etc.,*** for in the case we are discussing "father" and "son" are not only correlative terms but are mutually exclusive.

Impossibilia apud saeculum.

Matt. 19. 26, παρὰ ἀνθρώποις τοῦτο ἀδύνατόν ἐστι, παρὰ δὲ θεῷ πάντα δυνατά ἐστι. ***Stulta mundi elegit,*** 1 Cor.

1. 27, τὰ μωρὰ τοῦ κόσμου ἐξελέξατο ὁ θεὸς ἵνα καταισχύνῃ τοὺς σοφούς.

Adversus traditam formam rebus humanis,

"in opposition to the traditional law imposed upon human affairs". ***Traditam*** bears a double sense, "traditional in human affairs", which would have required *rerum humanarum*, and also "assigned to or imposed upon human affairs" (sc. by the Creator), which requires the dative. ***Forma*** is equivalent to *lex* or *institutum*: or perhaps an architect's or surveyor's plan. See the Introduction, p. 54.

Quasi fecerit.

The sentence might have read *quidvis deum confingere poterimus fecisse*, except that Tertullian wished to castigate such inventions as attacks on the veracity or integrity of God: so he writes *de deo confingere*, which requires the periphrasis *quasi fecerit*, and *quidvis* now serves a double purpose as the object of both *confingere* and *fecerit*.

Oportebat . . . esse et haereticos.

1 Cor. 11. 19, δεῖ γὰρ καὶ αἱρέσεις ἐν ὑμῖν εἶναι ἵνα οἱ δόκιμοι φανεροὶ γένωνται ἐν ὑμῖν. ***Oportebat et patrem crucifigi:*** unless this is a mere passing sarcasm, Tertullian's meaning is that even this patripassian heresy has its uses, in that it causes the true doctrine to receive a new and more systematic presentation.

XI. *Such proof must be derived from the Scriptures. In them God speaks of his Son, evidently meaning not himself, but the Word who came forth from him. Our adversaries make out that God brought forth, or came forth, himself from himself. The texts which refer to the generation of the Son cannot without manipulation be made to mean that. If that was what God meant, why did he not say it? By alleging that he said one thing and meant another our adversaries make him a liar. Evidently he who speaks is not the same person as he who is spoken of or he who is spoken to. There are texts in which God speaks of or to his Son, by that name. Again there are others in which the Son speaks of or to the Father, i.e. Christ speaks of or to God. And again there are others in which the Holy Spirit speaks of the Father and the Son, or to the Father of the Son: there is no need*

to quote all of them, but the few which we have quoted are sufficient to show a distinction constituting a trinity, for they specify each several Person as being himself and none other.

Of the five sets of texts quoted in this chapter, the first, concerning the generation of the Word, have already been cited in chapters 6, 7. The source of all the citations seems to be Justin, or possibly some collection of proof texts which may have been used by Justin. Those of the second set, in which the Father addresses the Son, have only been made to suit Tertullian's purpose by strained application and (in one case) by a misrepresentation of the Hebrew and the Greek. Those of the third and fourth sets, in which the Son speaks of or to the Father, are introduced by Is. 61. 1, which our Lord himself interpreted as applying to himself (Luke 4. 18): the messianic character of some of the Psalms was universally acknowledged, by Jews as well as Christians, and here Tertullian's citations would carry conviction. In the fifth set, in which the Holy Spirit speaks of the Father and the Son or to the Father of the Son, there is an underlying assumption that the Holy Spirit is the speaker of the Old Testament prophecies, and that the prophets themselves are mere mouthpieces (hence *per Esaiam loquentem*): this is contrary to the teaching of the New Testament, where Ps. 110. 1 is quoted by our Lord (Matt. 22. 43) as by David speaking in his own person, albeit under the influence of the Holy Spirit (Souter rightly prints ἐν Πνεύματι).

Porro qui eundem, etc.

The text as printed by Oehler makes good sense: "Further, you who identify the Father and the Son, make out that the same One both brought forth from himself a divine entity and proceeded forth from himself as that divine entity." Kroymann's repunctuation and slight verbal alteration (. . . *et prodiisse. quod deus etsi potuit fecisse non tamen fecit*), at first sight attractive, breaks down on examination: the admission that God could have done something which he has not in fact done, is not one that Tertullian is prepared to make (see the conclusion of § 10): the bare suggestion (*si*, not *etsi*) is all he is able to allow.

Distincte . . . non divise.

A reference to § 9, *nec divisione alium sed distinctione*: so again,

§ 12, *personae non substantiae nomine, ad distinctionem non ad divisionem.*

Quem verebatur, etc.

Quem is the object of *verebatur*, not of *pronuntiare: quem verebatur* is grammatically equivalent to *quid timebat* and so governs the infinitive *pronuntiare*. *Unum tamen veritus est, etc.* The text as Oehler prints it will just make sense: but Turner's brilliant emendation ought almost certainly to be adopted: *unum tamen veritus est, mentiri veritatis auctorem semet ipsum et suam veritatem.*

Alii dabat filii personam.

Possibly here, and twice later in this chapter, *persona* has a dramatic sense, "assigned the role of the Son to another".

Deceptorem fidei huius: i.e. the faith implied by *veracem deum credens*, above.

Praescriptio nostra.

See a note on § 2. "Our standing claim that it is not possible for speaker and person spoken of and person spoken to to be regarded as one and the same."

Perversitas.

Cf. § 9, *perversus quisque. Perversitas* is such a misdirected insistence on one's own way as would (in the present case) lead to the use of language in a sense opposed to that in which it is commonly understood.

Ecce filius meus, etc.

Is. 42. 1: LXX reads, Ἰακὼβ ὁ παῖς μου, ἀντιλήμψομαι αὐτοῦ· Ἰσραὴλ ὁ ἐκλεκτός μου, προσεδέξατο αὐτὸν ἡ ψυχή μοῦ· ἔδωκα τὸ πνεῦμά μου ἐπ' αὐτόν, κρίσιν τοῖς ἔθνεσιν ἐξοίσει. The Hebrew has nothing about Jacob and Israel, and in that respect Tertullian is more correct than Justin: but he is wrong in translating παῖς by *filius* (the Greek word will not naturally mean "son", and the Hebrew is "servant") and in putting *dilectus* for ἐκλεκτός (the Greek of Irenaeus, *haer.* iii. 2. 9, may have read ἀγαπητός: the Latin is *Ecce filius meus dilectissimus in quo bene sensi*). Justin, *dial.* 123, quotes the LXX with slight variants, remarking περὶ τοῦ χριστοῦ λέγων ὁ θεὸς

. . . Ἰακὼβ αὐτὸν καλεῖ καὶ Ἰσραήλ: again, *ibid.* 135, he quotes LXX accurately, pointing out that the executing of judgement implies kingship, and as Jacob was not a king the prophecy must be taken as looking forward to Christ who is a king.

Magnum tibi est, etc.

Is. 49. 6: Tertullian is sufficiently close to LXX, except that again he reads *filius meus* for παῖδά μου, and omits εἰς διαθήκην γένους which LXX interpolates before εἰς φῶς ἐθνῶν. JUSTIN, *dial.* 121, quotes LXX with slight variations, emphasising εἰς φῶς ἐθνῶν as marking the contrast between Christ's former coming in ignominy and his later coming in glory.

Spiritus domini super me, etc.

Is. 61. 1, Luke 4. 18. LXX has τοῖς πτωχοῖς: so Tertullian, *adv. Marc.* iv. 14, reads *pauperibus*: ***hominibus*** here is possibly a slip. IRENAEUS, *haer.* iii. 18. 1, iv. 37. 1 (referring to Luke), iii. 19. 3, with the comment, *significans et unguentem patrem et unctum filium et unctionem qui est spiritus.*

Ne dereliqueris me.

Ps. 71. 18: Tertullian follows LXX. ***De eodem:*** I suspect means "concerning the same Spirit", by that interpretation by which the "hands of the Lord" are taken to represent the Word and the Spirit. Engelbrecht's *domine* is ruled out by the fact that both the Hebrew and the Greek require *deus*: Kroymann rashly prints *Dee domine*, which is not Latin.

Domine, quid multiplicati, etc.

Ps. 3. 1: Tertullian follows LXX.

Psalmi qui Christi personam sustinent

perhaps means "the psalms which sustain the role of Christ", and a little later, *spiritum loquentem ex tertia persona* possibly means "the Spirit speaking as a third interlocutor". Oehler quite correctly points out that ***sustinere*** usually means *expectare, sperare:* so *de anima*, 56, *ceterum quam vanum ut anima corporis iusta sustineat, quasi aliquid ex illis ad inferos avehat*, "wait for the body's funeral rites": *ibid.*, *tempora constituta frustra mutilantur si iam impleri sustinentur* (*v.l. sustinent*). But the verb seems almost always to refer to irksome, not hopeful, waiting (as in the passages quoted): and once at least it has a present sense, *de*

anima*, 1, *universi orbis iniquam sententiam sustinens pro nomine veritatis*,** "bearing, suffering from, the unjust judgement of the whole world". In our present passage, if ***sustinent means "expect", ***Christi personam*** will have to mean "Christ himself" or "Christ in person"—an awkward turn of phrase: and ***loquentem ex tertia persona*** will be a grammatical term, "speaking in the third person". For "sustain the role" cf. JUVENAL iii. 93, *cum Thaida sustinet aut cum | uxorem comoedus agit vel Dorida.*

Dixit dominus, etc.

Ps. 110. 1: the latter part of the verse is quoted above, § 4, in connexion with 1 Cor. 15. 24 sqq.: the whole verse in §§ 13 and 30. The first ***dominus*** represents יהוה, the second אדני: Tertullian could not be expected to know that, and once the psalm is accepted as messianic the difference does not affect his argument. JUSTIN, *dial.* 32, interprets the psalm as a prophecy of the Ascension: *ibid.* 56, he uses it to show that besides the God and Father of all ἄλλος τις κυριολογεῖται. ***Ex tertia persona*** either goes with ***spiritum***, "as a third interlocutor" or with ***de patre et filio***, "in the third person". There appears to be no parallel to Tertullian's suggestion that the Holy Spirit refers here to the Son as "my lord".

Haec dicit dominus, etc.

Is. 45. 1, where LXX, following the Hebrew, reads οὕτως λέγει κύριος ὁ θεὸς τῷ χριστῷ μου Κύρῳ. The text is quoted again with the same misreading in § 28, and *adv. Iud.* 7 as a prophecy which the Jews must acknowledge to have been fulfilled in the conversion of the gentiles to Christianity.

Domine quis credidit, etc.

Is. 53. 1: Tertullian follows LXX, except in writing ***de illo sicut puerulus*** instead of ὡς παιδίον ἐναντίον αὐτοῦ: neither of these represents the Hebrew. The chapter was apparently not reckoned by the Jews as messianic; but it was so reckoned by Christian teachers from the episode described in Acts 8. 32 and onwards, cf. Rom. 10. 16. JUSTIN frequently quotes it: see especially *dial.* 13.

Nec enim affectamus, etc.

The text as printed by Oehler could conceivably mean: "For I make no pretence of ransacking the whole of the Scriptures, since (because in every single chapter I call into evidence their plenary majesty and authority) I have the advantage in argument in these discussions"; but the difficulty of the sentence must be admitted. Kroymann's insertion of *sunt* before *plenam* and of a period after *contestantes* hardly makes things easier.

Maiorem congressum.

Congressus, *congressio*, are used for the debate or discussion, as at *de carne Christi*, 21, *accedam adhuc cominus ad congressum*, and *maior congressus* seems to mean "the advantage in debate".

Est enim ipse, etc.

This sentence evidently refers only to the fifth group of texts quoted: hence probably the whole passage from *haec pauca* to the third *pronuntiat* must be taken as having that restricted reference.

Sic et cetera, etc.

The sentence as printed by Oehler will construe, but has no precise bearing either on the Scriptures in themselves or on the texts which Tertullian has quoted: for example, he cites no texts addressed to the Holy Spirit, and it is questionable whether there are any. C. H. Turner suggests . . . *quae nunc a patre de filio vel ad filium, nunc a filio de patre vel ad patrem, nunc a spiritu pronuntiantur*, which (when once suggested) is unquestionably right, as closely corresponding to Tertullian's five groups of texts. Kroymann had already printed *a spiritu.* The present editor (before his attention was drawn to Turner's article) was disposed to suggest *nunc ad patrem de filio vel a filio, nunc ad filium de patre vel a patre, nunc a spiritu.*

Unamquamque personam, etc.

Persona here (perhaps for the first time) appears in what afterwards became its standard theological meaning. *In sua proprietate*, "in that which is specifically himself": we have to rid ourselves of the idea that *proprietas* necessarily implies ownership —a meaning which is not found in authors earlier than Suetonius: the *proprietas* of each Person is not that which he specifically possesses but that which he specifically is: so § 27, *utramque substantiam in sua proprietate distantem*, where there is no question of "properties" either physical or metaphysical, but of each substance being referred to separately by St Paul as being itself and not the other. See note on § 7.

XII. *Those who refuse to recognise the Trinity are unable to explain the plural locutions found in the Scriptures. Such are, "Let* us *make man after* our *image and likeness", "Adam is become as one of* us". *Is it that God was speaking to the angels, as the Jews explain? or is it that being himself Father and Son and Holy Spirit, ⟨as the monarchians allege⟩, he was representing himself as plural? Rather it is that he was speaking to the Son and the Holy Spirit, the one who was to take manhood upon him, the other who was to sanctify man. Moreover the narrative continues, "God made man in the image of God", distinguishing between God who made man, and God in whose image he made him: for man is the image and likeness of the Son, who was to become the real and true Man. Also in the preceding narrative the distinction is found. At first, the Son not yet appearing, God said "Let there be light", and the light was made: for the Word is the true light, and mundane light ⟨comes into existence⟩ through him. But, in what follows, the Word is present and operative: God speaks and God makes, that is, the Word makes, since by him all things were made: and inasmuch as "the Word was God", you have two, one commanding and another making. I have already explained that by "another" I imply a distinction of Persons, not a division of substance. Yet though I maintain one substance in three inseparable ⟨Persons⟩, the text compels me to distinguish the one who gives the command from the one who carries it out: for if he had been ⟨merely⟩ one, he would not have waited for himself to command, but would have made things without a command.*

The texts here discussed were habitually interpreted in the sense indicated by Tertullian: Liddon, Bampton Lectures (4th ed.), pp. 48 sqq., gives a reference to Petavius, *de trin.* ii. 7. 6. TERTULLIAN, *de res. carn.* 6, commenting on Gen. I. 27: *recogita totum illi* (sc. *limo*) *deum occupatum ac deditum, manu sensu opere consilio sapientia providentia, et ipsa imprimis adfectione quae liniamenta dictabat. quodcunque enim limus exprimebatur, Christus cogitabatur homo futurus: quod et limus et caro sermo quod et terra tunc.*[1] *sic enim praefatio patris ad filium, Faciamus*

[1] The meaning here is far from clear, and the punctuation is doubtful: perhaps, "for whatever expression the clay took upon it, the thought was of Christ who was to become man (which is clay), and of the Word to become flesh (a thing which at that time was earth)".

hominem ad imaginem et similitudinem nostram. et fecit hominem deus. id utique quod finxit, ad imaginem dei fecit illum, scilicet Christi . . . ita limus ille iam tunc imaginem induens Christi futuri in carne non tantum dei opus erat sed et pignus. Elsewhere, contending for the unity of God and of the created world, he disregards the plural forms: *adv. Hermog.* 26, *nobis autem unus deus et una est terra, quam in principio deus fecit. cuius ordinem incipiens scriptura decurrere primo factam eam edicit, dehinc qualitatem ipsius edisserit* . . . [quoting Gen. 1. 1, 1. 7, 1. 27, 2. 7] . . . *et utique sic decet narrationem inire, primo praefari postea prosequi, nominare deinde describere.* In writing the present passage he seems to have had in mind JUSTIN (*dial.* 62), who, having quoted Prov. 8. 21-36, proceeds: καὶ τοῦτο αὐτό, ὦ φίλοι, εἶπε καὶ διὰ Μωυσέως ὁ τοῦ θεοῦ λόγος, μηνύων ἡμῖν ὃν ἐδήλωσε, τὸν θεὸν λέγειν τούτῳ αὐτῷ τῷ νοήματι ἐπὶ τῆς ποιήσεως τοῦ ἀνθρώπου, λέγων ταῦτα· Ποιήσωμεν ἄνθρωπον . . . καὶ πληρώσατε τὴν γῆν καὶ κατακυριεύσατε αὐτῆς. καὶ ὅπως μή, ἀλλάσσοντες τοὺς προλελεγμένους λόγους, ἐκεῖνα λέγητε ἃ οἱ διδάσκαλοι ὑμῶν λέγουσιν, ἢ ὅτι πρὸς ἑαυτὸν ἔλεγεν ὁ θεὸς Ποιήσωμεν, ὁποῖον καὶ ἡμεῖς μέλλοντές τι ποιεῖν πολλάκις πρὸς ἑαυτοὺς λέγομεν Ποιήσωμεν, ἢ ὅτι πρὸς τὰ στοιχεῖα, τουτέστι τὴν γῆν καὶ τὰ ἄλλα ὁμοίως ἐξ ὧν νοοῦμεν τὸν ἄνθρωπον γεγονέναι, θεὸν εἰρηκέναι (*scribere debuit* θεὸς εἴρηκε) Ποιήσωμεν, λόγους τοὺς εἰρημένους ὑπ' αὐτοῦ τοῦ Μωυσέως πάλιν ἱστορήσω ἐξ ὧν ἀναμφιλέκτως πρός τινα καὶ ἀριθμῷ ὄντα ἕτερον καὶ λογικὸν ὑπάρχοντα ὡμιληκέναι αὐτὸν ἐπιγνῶναι ἔχομεν. εἰσὶ δὲ οἱ λόγοι οὗτοι· Καὶ εἶπεν ὁ θεός· Ἰδοὺ Ἀδὰμ γέγονεν ὡς εἷς ἐξ ἡμων τοῦ γινώσκειν καλὸν καὶ πονηρόν. οὐκοῦν εἰπὼν Ὡς εἷς ἐξ ἡμῶν, καὶ ἀριθμὸν τῶν ἀλλήλοις συνόντων καὶ τὸ ἐλάχιστον δύο μεμήνυκεν. οὐ γάρ, ὅπερ ἡ παρ' ὑμῖν λεγομένη αἵρεσις δογματίζει, φαίην ἂν ἐγὼ ἀληθὲς εἶναι ἢ οἱ ἐκείνης διδάσκαλοι ἀποδεῖξαι δύνανται, ὅτι ἀγγέλοις ἔλεγεν ἢ ὅτι ἀγγέλων ποίημα ἦν τὸ σῶμα τὸ ἀνθρώπειον· ἀλλὰ τοῦτο τὸ τῷ ὄντι ἀπὸ τοῦ πατρὸς προβληθὲν γέννημα πρὸ πάντων τῶν ποιημάτων συνῆν τῷ πατρὶ καὶ τούτῳ ὁ πατὴρ προσομιλεῖ [referring again to Prov. 8, and quoting Josh. 5. 13-6. 2, concerning the ἀρχιστράτηγος κυρίου]. IRENAEUS, *haer.* i. 18, says that Menander and Saturninus said that the angels said "Let us make man" to one another: *ibid.* i. 28. 3, that the Ophites said that Ialdabaoth said it to the six powers. His own exegesis agrees with Justin: *ibid.* iv. *praef.*, *homo est autem temperatio animae et carnis qui secundum similitudinem dei formatus est et per manus eius plasmatus est, hoc est per filium et spiritum sanctum quibus et dixit Faciamus hominem: ibid.* v. 1. 3, *non enim effugit Adam manus dei ad quas pater loquens dicit Faciamus hominem ad imaginem et similitudinem nostram: ibid.* v. 15. 4, *idem ipse qui ab initio plasmavit Adam, cum quo et loquebatur pater, Faciamus hominem secundum imaginem et similitudinem nostram,* in the latter days formed clay from the earth and restored the eyes of the blind. TATIAN, *fragm.* 6. 7 (Otto, quoted from Clement of Alexandria and Origen), said that γενηθήτω φῶς was εὐκτικόν, a prayer of the demiurge to the supreme god.

ORIGEN, *comm. in Ioa.* ii. 14, p. 67 (of course independently of Tertullian and perhaps of Justin), quotes Ps. 148. 5, Αὐτὸς γὰρ εἶπε καὶ ἐγεννήθησαν, αὐτὸς ἐνετείλατο καὶ ἐκτίσθησαν, and comments, ἐνετείλατο γὰρ ὁ ἀγέννητος θεὸς τῷ πρωτοτόκῳ πάσης κτίσεως καὶ ἐκτίσθησαν, οὐ μόνον ὁ κόσμος καὶ τὰ ἐν αὐτῷ ἀλλὰ καὶ τὰ λοιπὰ πάντα, εἴτε θρόνοι εἴτε κυριότητες εἴτε ἀρχαὶ εἴτε ἐξουσίαι· πάντα γὰρ δι' αὐτοῦ καὶ εἰς αὐτὸν ἔκτισται καὶ αὐτός ἐστι πρὸ πάντων (Col. 1. 16). The letter of the ANTIOCHENE SYNOD to Paul of Samosata (Routh, *R.S.*, vol. iii. p. 292) shows acquaintance with both Tertullian and Origen: quoting Ps. 148. 5, they say, ὁ δὲ ἐντελλόμενος ἑτέρῳ ἐντέλλεται τινί· ὃν οὐκ ἄλλον πεπείσμεθα ἢ τὸν μονογενῆ υἱὸν τοῦ θεοῦ θεὸν, ᾧ καὶ εἶπε Ποιήσωμεν ἄνθρωπον κατ' εἰκόνα καὶ καθ' ὁμοίωσιν ἡμετέραν: then follow the usual references to John 1. 3: Col. 1. 16: Prov. 8. 30: Gen. 18. 1 (one of the three who appeared to Abraham): Gen. 19. 24 (fire and brimstone from the Lord): with the remark that God who appeared to the patriarchs is called sometimes angel, sometimes Lord, sometimes God, and τὸν μὲν γὰρ θεὸν τῶν ὅλων ἀσεβὲς ἄγγελον νομίσαι καλεῖσθαι. HILARY OF POITIERS, *de trin.* iv. 16 sqq. and *tract. in psalm.* cxlviii. 4, repeats the same texts with similar comments.

What may be the real significance of the plural *Faciamus* it is not easy to say. Those who describe it, and the plural *Elohim*, as a relic of primitive polytheism have not explained how such a relic occurs in the last and most uncompromisingly monotheistic stratum of the Old Testament, the exilic or post-exilic priestly document.

Aut numquid angelis loquebatur?

JUSTIN (*loc. cit.*) mentions, only to reject, this suggestion: the present parallel should be added to Otto's note rejecting Thirlbey's emendation παρ' ἡμῖν. Maranus (in the note quoted by Otto) gives no actual instance of Jewish teachers offering this explanation. Cf. NOVATIAN, *de trin.* 17, *aut numquid angelum cum angelis dicit descendentem et dicentem, Venite et mox descendamus, etc.?*: *ibid.* 22, *sed nec in angelis formam dei legimus.*

Spiritus in sermone.

Tertullian perhaps means the same as ORIGEN, *comm. in Ioa.* ii. 10, καὶ τάχα αὕτη ἐστὶν ἡ αἰτία τοῦ μὴ καὶ αὐτὸ (sc. τὸ ἅγιον πνεῦμα) υἱὸν χρηματίζειν τοῦ θεοῦ, μόνου τοῦ μονογενοῦς φύσει υἱοῦ ἀρχῆθεν τυγχάνοντος. οὗ χρῄζειν ἔοικε τὸ ἅγιον πνεῦμα διακονοῦντος αὐτοῦ τῇ ὑποστάσει, οὐ μόνον εἰς τὸ εἶναι ἀλλὰ καὶ σοφὸν εἶναι καὶ λογικὸν καὶ δίκαιον καὶ πᾶν ὁτιποτοῦν χρὴ αὐτὸ νοεῖν τυγχάνειν κατὰ μετοχὴν τῶν προειρημένων ἡμῖν Χριστοῦ ἐπινοιῶν.

Quasi cum ministris et arbitris,

"as with confidential agents". Cf. below, *Christo assistente et ministrante.*

Deus hominem, etc.

Pamelius restored the scriptural text, ⟨*Et fecit*⟩ *deus hominem, ad imaginem dei fecit illum*: there is no pressing need for the restoration in this case, but (as is shown by the necessity of supplying *virga directionis* in the next chapter) the manuscripts are not faultless in this respect, and the missing words are best restored.

Erat autem ad cuius imaginem, etc.

"But there was one in whose image he was making him, the Son in fact, who because he was to be the truer and more veritable Man, caused to be described as his image the man who at the creation had to be formed of clay, and was the image and similitude of the true." *Excidit sibi Septimius.* In what follows he says that God who spake is the Father, and God who made is the Son: in that case God who made man will be the Son and *ad imaginem dei* should mean not the Son's image but the Father's. *Imago veri et similitudo* is a recollection of Heb. 1. 3 and 9. 24 in view of Gen. 1. 26: according to Tertullian, *de bapt.* 5, *imago in effigie, similitudo in aeternitate censetur.*

Ipse statim sermo, etc.

There is no question here of the Word coming into existence when God said, "Let there be light". Tertullian only says that the Word was not yet made manifest, *nondum apparente*: but the Word himself is *statim*, without preamble or without intermediary, the true Light, and consequently when God says "Let there be light", the *mundialis lux* comes into existence through him. Kroymann has rashly altered the text, against all the MS. evidence, and against the requirements of sound theology. Tertullian, contrary to frequent custom, reads *venientem*, i.e. makes ἐρχόμενον in John 1. 9 agree with ἄνθρωπον.

Ceterum <etsi> ubique teneo.

Teneo and *teneam* have equal MS. authority. *etsi* was added by Rigaltius. Oehler, reading *ceterum ubique teneam*, remarks that it it not unknown for Tertullian to omit the concessive conjunction and put the verb in the subjunctive: but he gives no examples.

Nam nec iuberet, etc.

It is difficult to make sense of these two sentences as Oehler prints them, and Kroymann's alteration hardly helps. The difficulty lies in *dum iuberet fieri per eum* and in *aut sine iussu*, where *sed* is required to balance *haud.* I should suggest reading, *nam nec iuberet si ipse faceret dum iuberet fieri: per eum tamen iubebat, aut sibi iussurus si unus esset, aut sine iussu facturus, quia non expectasset ut sibi iuberet.* "For neither would he be commanding if himself were the maker when he commanded things to be made: yet he did command ⟨them to be made⟩ by him, though if he had been alone he would either have commanded himself or would have made them without a command, since he would not have waited to command himself." The objection to this is that the second *aut* should have been *vel potius*. Most of the difficulty would vanish if we could omit *dum iuberet fieri per eum.*

XIII. *These and other texts where the titles God and Lord are in the same context applied to two Persons are not by us taken to mean that there are two Gods or two Lords. They cannot however be disregarded, but must be taken as meaning what they say. Those who deny that the titles are rightly applied to our Lord should recollect that in two places the designation "gods" is applied to men who by faith have become sons of God:* a fortiori *it can be applied to the only Son of God. The plural expressions are a safeguard against the idea that it was the Father who was born and who died. The Old Testament used the titles God and Lord of two Persons, with the intention that when Christ came they should not be denied to him, and that it should not be supposed that it was the Father himself who came down from heaven. When Christ did come, the meaning of those indications of the Trinity was made clear, and the Father himself was made more fully manifest. Christians however, with the purpose of discountenancing the polytheism of the gentiles, do not use the titles in the plural: else they would put out their candle and would weaken their courage against persecution. Consequently, if the Father and the Son are mentioned together the Father is called God and Jesus Christ is called the Lord; though, by the apostle's authority, Christ by himself can be called God, even as the sun's ray is called sun (though the sun is not called the ray). For the sun and the ray are two aspects of one undivided substance, as also God and his Word are two, yet of one substance.*

Once more Tertullian is largely, though not entirely, quoting texts already collected by Justin and Irenaeus. JUSTIN, *dial.* 42, cites Is. 53. 1, not like Tertullian (§ 11) as spoken by the Holy Spirit, but ὡς ἀπὸ προσώπου τῶν ἀποστόλων λεγόντων τῷ χριστῷ ὅτι οὐχὶ τῇ ἀκοῇ αὐτῶν πιστεύουσιν ἀλλὰ τῇ αὐτοῦ τοῦ πέμψαντος αὐτοὺς δυνάμει: *ibid.* 56, maintaining that he who appeared to the patriarchs ἕτερός ἐστι τοῦ τὰ πάντα ποιήσαντος θεοῦ, he takes the rain of fire and brimstone as his main argument, and adds, as further proof that παρὰ τὸν νοούμενον ποιητὴν τῶν ὅλων ἄλλος τις κυριολογεῖται ὑπὸ τοῦ ἁγίου πνεύματος, Ps. 110. 1 and Ps. 45. 6, 7. IRENAEUS, *haer.* iii. 6. 1, has (with one exception) all the texts quoted by Tertullian: *neque igitur dominus neque spiritus sanctus neque apostoli eum qui non esset deus definitive et absolute deum nominassent aliquando nisi esset vere deus: neque dominum appellassent aliquem ex sua persona nisi qui dominatur omnium deum patrem et filium eius qui dominium accepit a patre suo omnis conditionis, quemadmodum habet illud, Dixit dominus, etc.: patrem enim filio collocutum ostendit qui dedit ei haereditatem gentium et subiecit ei omnes inimicos. vere igitur cum pater sit dominus et filius vere sit dominus merito spiritus sanctus domini appellatione signavit eos. et iterum in eversione sodomitarum scriptura ait, Et pluit dominus, etc.: filium enim his significat, qui et Abrahae collocutus sit, a patre accepisse potestatem iudicandi sodomitas propter iniquitatem eorum. similiter habet illud, Sedes tua deus, etc.: utrosque enim dei appellatione signavit spiritus, et eum qui ungitur filium et eum qui ungit, id est patrem. et iterum, Deus stetit, etc., de patre et filio et de his qui adoptionem perceperunt dicit: hi autem sunt ecclesia. haec enim est synagoga dei, quam deus, hoc est filius ipse, per semetipsum collegit. de quo iterum dicit, Deus deorum, etc. quis deus? de quo dixit, Deus manifeste veniet, deus noster, et non silebit: hoc est filius, qui secundum manifestationem hominibus advenit, qui dicit, Palam apparui his qui me non quaerunt. quorum autem deorum? quibus dicit, Ego dixi, etc., his scilicet qui adoptionis gratiam adepti sunt per quam clamamus Abba pater.* Tertullian's own contribution to the discussion is confined to the texts Is. 45. 14 and 53. 1.

There is at first a certain irony in the suggestion that he will help his adversaries by producing further texts in support of their objection that he is a dualist: but Tertullian proceeds to be carried away by his own phantasy, so as to suggest that the Old Testament is deliberately dualist, and that it is only at the coming of Christ that strict monotheism makes its appearance. The statement that in Christian practice the Father is addressed as God and Jesus Christ as Lord is supported in general by the ancient liturgies.

Puta interim,

i.e. (1) until I am able to explain that the Old Testament of set purpose has these dualistic expressions, so that there may be scriptural support for the Christian statement that Christ is God, yet is not identical with the Father, and (2) until I am able to point out that, the purpose of these dualistic expressions being fulfilled, the New Testament uses strictly monotheistic language.

Thronus tuus, deus, etc.

The primary authority for the application of this text to our Lord is Heb. 1. 8, 9. Westcott (*ad loc.*) claims that the best rendering is "God is thy throne": to which one can only reply that in that case it is strange that none of the ancient fathers, who presumably were fairly expert in the Greek language, had even a suspicion that *ὁ θεός* is anything but a vocative. In classical Greek the article with the nominative, when used for the vocative, is somewhat peremptory or somewhat contemptuous: in Coptic the article is regularly used with the vocative, and the Alexandrian translators were possibly influenced by the vernacular usage. Also "God is thy throne" goes too far: if God is the Son's throne, then the Son is greater than God, which is rather more than the apostolic writer means to prove. *Virga directionis* has to be restored, as Kroymann remarks.

Si ad deum loquitur, etc.

The text as printed seems the simplest restoration, involving only a slight variation from the MS. authorities, i.e. *affirmat et* for *affirmat sed* (Kroymann). *Pro virga regni tui* presents more difficulty: it is not easy to make sense of it, and possibly the four words are the misplaced relic of a marginal note bearing on the need to insert *virga directionis* above.

Esaias ad personam Christi.

Persona once more is used in almost a dramatic sense: Christ is, so to speak, one of the interlocutors in a dialogue, in this instance the person addressed. The quotation, from Is. 45, 14, consists of selected phrases: the complete Greek text is, [*Οὕτως λέγει κύριος σαβαώθ, Ἐκοπίασεν Αἴγυπτος καὶ ἐμπορία Αἰθιόπων, καὶ*] *οἱ Σαβαεὶμ, ἄνδρες ὑψηλοὶ, ἐπί σε διαβήσονται* [*καὶ σοὶ ἔσονται δοῦλοι*] *καὶ ὀπίσω σου ἀκολουθήσουσιν δεδεμένοι χειροπέδαις* [*καὶ διαβήσονται πρός σε*] *καὶ προσκυνήσουσί σοι* [*καὶ ἐν σοὶ προσεύξονται*] *ὅτι ἐν σοὶ ὁ θεός ἐστιν* [*καὶ οὐκ ἔστιν θεὸς πλὴν σοῦ*]· *σὺ γὰρ εἶ θεὸς καὶ οὐκ ᾔδειμεν, ὁ θεὸς τοῦ Ἰσραήλ*. Tertullian alone seems to apply this text *ad personam Christi*: the words are evidently addressed to Jerusalem (see verse 13), and *οὐκ ἔστιν θεὸς πλὴν σοῦ*, discreetly omitted by Tertullian, probably means "there is no god except the God who is in thee": *σὺ γὰρ εἶ θεὸς καὶ οὐκ ᾔδειμεν* is evidently the prayer addressed to God in Jerusalem by the Sabaeans. *Erat* for *erant* and *Christum* for *spiritum*, Turner's corrections, are beyond question right.

Alius penes quem.

A mutilated note among the fragments of SUETONIUS (Roth,

p. 314), from the lost work *pratum*, reads *inter apud et penes, apud personam significat*: probably the note continued *penes (significat) locum*. Tertullian treats the two prepositions as interchangeable: *adv. Marc.* v. 6, *sapientia enim huius mundi stultitia est penes deum: penes quem deum?*

Domine, quis credidit, etc.

The text, Is. 53. 1, is often quoted, but not before Tertullian with this deduction from the repeated *domine . . . domini*: the commentators were probably well aware of the Hebrew practice of repeating the substantive instead of using the pronominal termination, especially in stock phrases like "arm of the Lord".

Et pluit dominus, etc.

Gen. 19. 24, quoted by Justin and Irenaeus with the same interpretation. The true explanation is probably, as in the previous instance, that *dominus* is the only possible subject of *pluit* and that emphasis was intended to be laid on the fact that retribution came *de caelo a domino*: there would be no particular point in *de caelo a se*, even if such a turn of phrase were possible in Hebrew.

Ego dixi, etc.

This argument is drawn from John 10. 34, where the same quotation from Ps. 82. 6 receives a similar comment, εἰ ἐκείνους εἶπε θεοὺς πρὸς οὓς ὁ λόγος τοῦ θεοῦ ἐγένετο, κτἑ. APHRAATES, whose thought is hardly advanced even to the second-century standard, makes it the basis of his argument in the tractate xviii, *Of Christ the Son of God*. Kirkpatrick remarks that *elohim* in this psalm are the judges of Israel, appointed by God to their office, and called into council by God to have judgement passed upon them: he also approves of Westcott's observation that the citation in John is more than an *argumentum ad hominem*, in that the Old Testament contains within it a foreshadowing of the Incarnation. This is rather like special pleading: it is not impossible that *elohim* was used as equivalent to *shophetim* without any specific divine implication.

Et tempora et causas scripturarum.

Tertullian here enunciates the principle that divine revelation is progressive: elsewhere, e.g. in the treatise against Marcion, he maintains the concurrent principle that it is a self-consistent whole.

As a disciple of the Paraclete he claims to have good understanding of the way in which successive stages of revelation fit their *tempora*, occasions, and serve their ultimate purposes (*causae*). He probably means by this that the Montanist prophets received revelations explanatory of such matters; but, apart from this idiosyncrasy, he is following the principle enunciated by St Paul, "comparing spiritual things with spiritual", or "investigating spiritual things for spiritual men". Elsewhere, e.g. *de praescr. haer.* 19, *scorp.* 12, he maintains that the true sense of Scripture is only understood by the apostles and in the Churches which have learned from them: which is probably what he means here by *quod non licet credi quoniam non ita traditum est.*

Sed quoniam retro, etc.,

"but because previously two were proclaimed as God and two as Lord, so that when Christ came he might be acknowledged as God and addressed as Lord, as being the Son of him who is God and Lord". There is no need to strain Tertullian's paradox into the statement that the Old Testament preaches two gods and two lords.

Praeter unus deus.

Oehler's Index has references for *praeter=praeterquam* (or *nisi*): e.g. *scorp.* 8, *Danielem nullius praeter dei supplicem. Descendisse* refers to the theophanies, not to the descent into hell.

Ut quia nationes.

Ut . . . et (Ursinus for *et . . . ut*) seems a necessary change. *Quia* must apparently be understood to mean *eo consilio ut.*

Ex conscientia qua scimus.

Conscientia means rather more than *scientia*: it occurs several times in *de carne Christi*, 3, for Christ's knowledge of himself or of his own nature, which (on certain suppositions with which Tertullian does not agree) might differ from the impression made upon those who saw him: here it means that private knowledge which we have of the doctrine of the holy Trinity which we might (though we ought not to) use to excuse us if we were to make a public profession of polytheism and so escape persecution.

Sed apostolum sequar.

Tertullian correctly states the New Testament practice, by

which θεός means God (the Father) and κύριος means our Lord. The exceptions to this practice are rare: notably John 20. 28: Rom. 9. 5.: 1 Tim. 1. 1 and perhaps 3. 16, and the Old Testament quotations in Heb. 1, where θεός is used of our Lord: κύριος seems always to mean our Lord except in quotations from the Old Testament (in 2 Cor. 3. 17 sqq. it is interpreted by St Paul as meaning the Holy Spirit).

Etsi soles duos faciam.

Non was inserted by Ursinus, who (strangely for him) missed the point, which is that by calling both the orb and the beam the sun I give the superficial impression of making out that there are two suns, which in fact I do, though only in the same sense in which I speak of the Father and the Son as two, reserving the safeguard that they are of one indivisible substance.

XIV. *Our contention that there are two ⟨who are designated God and Lord⟩ is supported by the fact that though God says "No man can see my face and live", the Scriptures also say that on certain occasions God was seen. Therefore he who was seen must be understood to have been Another, and we must suppose that the Father is invisible and the Son visible, even as no one dare look at the sun though our eyes can bear the sight of its ray. Someone may object that the Son also, as being Word and spirit, is invisible, equating the attributes of the Father and the Son with the intention of maintaining their identity (though we have pointed out that the Scripture differentiates them by the attributes of invisibility and visibility). Such objectors add that if it was the Son who spoke to Moses, it was the Son who said that his face could not be seen, being himself the invisible Father under the name of Son. So, they say, the same one is both visible and invisible, both Father and Son: and they quote texts which they think prove this. But our interpretation of the Scriptures is appropriate to the Son. For we say that the Son also, being in his own nature invisible, before his Incarnation became visible to certain people as it were in visions or dreams. The statement that God spoke to Moses face to face is therefore proleptic, and became true only at the Transfiguration, since all the Son's appearances before the Incarnation were "as in a glass, darkly". If God had already spoken to Moses face to face, why did Moses afterwards ask to see God's face? Moreover, Jacob says, "I have seen God face to face and my life is preserved": so there must be another "face of God" which no man can see and live. It was then the Son whom Jacob saw, and "my face", which Moses cannot see, means the invisible Father, the breath of whose person is Christ the Lord: for since the Father is Christ's head,* a fortiori *he is his face.*

It is tempting to see, in the change of ground which Tertullian is driven to make in the course of this chapter, a trace of the oral discussions which may have preceded the writing of the treatise. The distinction between the Father essentially invisible and the Son capable of becoming visible (or assuming visibility) cannot be maintained, and has to be relinquished. It has moreover a gnostic flavour (though, as is shown below, Tertullian by no means derived it from gnostic sources): for it seems to remove the Father into the region of the unknown and unknowable, but with the difference that while the gnostics made the unbegotten Father absolutely unknowable, Tertullian asserts the scriptural truth that the Father is known to and revealed by the Son. Also the distinction has in it at least the germs of Arianism: for if the Father is essentially incapable of being visible, while the Son can make himself visible (or, alternately, if the glory of the Father is such that the sight of it causes death, while the lesser glory of the Son can be seen with impunity) there would appear to be a difference of nature between the two divine Persons such as the Arians imagined. Tertullian therefore in the present passage, while retaining the traditional theory that the theophanies were appearances of the Son, denies their substantive reality and suggests that they were no more than visions and dreams, "as in a glass, darkly", and will have it that in his own Person the Son was not seen until the Incarnation. That this was not his previous view of the matter is shown by the following passages from other works, in two of which he says that what the patriarchs saw was a real body created expressly as a vehicle for each theophany: though even so he would still be able to maintain (as he does here) that the Son was not seen in his divine nature but as it were *in speculo et in aenigmate.*

Adv. Marc. ii. 27, *nam et profitemur Christum semper egisse in dei patris nomine, ipsum ab initio conversatum ipsum congressum cum patriarchis et prophetis, filium creatoris, sermonem eius quem ex semetipso proferendo filium fecit et exinde omni dispositioni suae voluntatis praefecit, diminuens illum modico citra angelos . . . qua diminutione in haec quoque dispositus est a patre quae ut humana reprehenditis, ediscens iam inde a primordio, iam inde hominem*[1] *quod erat futurus in fine. ille est qui descendit, ille qui interrogat, ille qui postulat, ille qui iurat. . . . igitur quaecunque exigitis deo digna, habebuntur in patre invisibili incongressibilique et placido et ut ita dixerim philosophorum deo: quaecunque autem ut indigna reprehenditis deputabuntur in filio et viso et audito et congresso, arbitro patris et ministro miscente in semetipso hominem et deum, in virtutibus deum in pusillitatibus hominem, ut tantum homini conferat quantum deo detrahit.*

Ibid. iii. 9. The two angels who visited Lot had real, not putative, bodies. *Ideo et ipse* (sc. *Christus*) *cum angelis tunc apud Abraham in veritate quidem carnis apparuit, sed nondum natae quia nondum moriturae, sed et discentis iam inter homines conversari.* Cf. *ibid.* 6, *persona spiritus nostri Christus dominus, qui ab initio vicarius patris in dei nomine et auditus sit et visus.*

De carne Christi, 6: [to the same effect, in almost identical language].

Adv. Iud. 9. *nam qui ad Moysen loquebatur ipse erat dei filius, qui et semper videbatur. deum enim patrem nemo vidit unquam et vixit. et ideo constat ipsum dei filium Moysi esse locutum, etc.* When he says to the people "Behold I send my angel before thy face", the angel is Joshua, even as in Malachi the angel is John the Baptist.

The patristic view of the theophanies is discussed by Bull, *Def. Fid. Nicaenae*, lib. I cap. I, from which most of the following references are taken: almost without exception, from Justin onwards, they are regarded as manifestations of the Son.

Justin, *apol.* i. 63. The Jews even now teach that it was the unnameable God who spoke with Moses. For this lack of insight they are rebuked by the prophetic Spirit (Is. I. 3) and by our Lord (Matt. II. 27). The Λόγος is also called "angel" and "apostle", because he is the *messenger* of the Father who *sent* him. Hence the Angel who spoke to Moses at the Bush, ἐγώ εἰμι ὁ ὤν, is the Son of God, καὶ ἐν ἰδέᾳ πυρὸς ποτὲ φανείς, ποτὲ δὲ καὶ ἐν εἰκόνι ἀσωμάτων (*quaero an legendum* ἐνσωμάτων).

[1] Perhaps read *iam inde a primordio hominem <indutus id esse> quod, etc.*, or possibly, regarding *iam inde hominem* as a marginal note, read *iam inde a primordio id esse quod, etc.*

Dial. 56 sqq. A long section of the *Dialogue* is an argument to prove from the theophanies the existence of "another who is called God" besides the invisible Father. As it was apparently Justin who worked out this theory and made it common form for his successors, his method of approach is of interest. Justin says that God who appeared to Abraham at Mamre in company with two angels was sent by another, and therefore cannot be identified with that other. One of the Jews objects: Not so, but the episode is in two stages: first God appeared, and after his departure came the three men (i.e. three angels), one of whom was sent to Sara, the other two to Sodom. Justin replies that this explanation cannot stand, for the one who spoke to Sara promised to return, which he did when Isaac was grown [an evident misunderstanding of the text of Genesis]. Trypho having expressed the view that all three were angels, Justin undertakes to prove that God who appeared to Abraham, to Isaac, and to Moses, *ἕτερός ἐστι τοῦ τὰ πάντα ποιήσαντος θεοῦ, ἀριθμῷ λέγω ἀλλ' οὐ γνώμῃ.* He quotes the texts, "The Lord rained down fire and brimstone from the Lord", "The Lord said unto my Lord", "Thy throne, O God, is for ever and ever . . . God, even thy God, hath anointed thee", remarking that in each case there are two called "the Lord". Returning to the Mamre-Sodom narrative he suggests that its whole tenor shows that the Lord is in converse with Abraham and Sara until the end of Abraham's prayer; that then the two angels go alone into Sodom, and only when Lot comes out of Sodom does the Lord again appear, and sends down fire and brimstone from the Lord. Trypho acknowledges the point as proved, but has doubts whether the Lord ate the food which Abraham prepared. Justin replies that eating must be understood in a figurative sense, as we say that fire eats. Trypho agrees, and asks for an explanation *πῶς οὗτος ὁ τῷ Ἀβραὰμ ὀφθεὶς, θεὸς καὶ ὑπηρέτης ὢν τοῦ ποιητοῦ τῶν ὅλων θεοῦ, διὰ τῆς παρθένου γεννηθεὶς ἄνθρωπος ὁμοιοπαθὴς πᾶσιν ὡς προέφης γέγονεν.* Justin prefers to give the rest of his proofs first: God, he says, gave Jacob advice about the sheep-breeding, wrestled with him, blessed him after the death of Deborah, appeared to him in the dream at Bethel: he also appeared to Moses at the Bush. Here Trypho suggests that it was an angel who was in the flame of fire, but God himself who spoke to Moses: to which Justin replies that you cannot suppose that the Maker of all things himself left the heavens and appeared in a small part of the earth. There are subsequent references to the Captain of the Lord's host who appeared to Joshua, and to God's appearance to Moses in the cleft of the rock at Sinai. In § 127 the argument is summed up in these terms:—*ὁ γὰρ ἄρρητος πατὴρ καὶ κύριος τῶν πάντων οὔτε ποι ἀφῖκται οὔτε περιπατεῖ οὔτε καθεύδει οὔτε ἀνίσταται, ἀλλ' ἐν τῇ αὐτοῦ χώρᾳ ὅπου ποτὲ μένει, ὀξὺ ὁρῶν καὶ ὀξὺ ἀκούων, οὐκ ὀφθαλμοῖς οὐδὲ ὠσὶν ἀλλὰ δυνάμει ἀλέκτῳ . . . οὔτε οὖν Ἀβραὰμ οὔτε Ἰσαὰκ οὔτε Ἰακὼβ οὔτε ἄλλος ἀνθρώπων εἶδε τὸν πατέρα καὶ ἄρρητον κύριον τῶν πάντων ἁπλῶς καὶ αὐτοῦ τοῦ χριστοῦ, ἀλλ' ἐκεῖνον τὸν κατὰ βουλὴν τὴν ἐκείνου καὶ θεὸν ὄντα υἱὸν αὐτοῦ, καὶ ἄγγελον ἐκ τοῦ ὑπηρετεῖν τῇ γνώμῃ αὐτοῦ.*

Tertullian was undoubtedly acquainted with Justin's work: his use of the same series of texts can hardly be accidental. But the purpose of the two discussions is different, Justin's being to prove the existence of Another, Tertullian's to prove that that other (whose existence his adversaries admit) is not a mere phase of the one. Consequently Justin stresses the transcendence of the Father, so that he may claim that the visible God of the theophanies is the Son. Tertullian could hardly repudiate Justin; yet (since his adversaries accepted Justin's argument and used it in their own interests) he finds the distinction a liability rather than an asset, and is driven back to acknowledge the transcendence of the Son, even at the cost of surrendering the objective reality of the theophanies.

To Theophilus, expounding to a Greek the divine transcendence, it is the theophanies which present the difficulty, and the doctrine of a not always transcendent Λόγος is a means of easing the situation. *Ad Autol.* ii. 22, in answer to an anticipated question, how the infinite God can be supposed to have walked in the Garden, he says: *ὁ μὲν θεὸς καὶ πατὴρ τῶν ὅλων ἀχώρητός ἐστι καὶ ἐν τόπῳ οὐχ εὑρίσκεται· οὐ γάρ ἐστιν τόπος τῆς καταπαύσεως αὐτοῦ. ὁ δὲ λόγος αὐτοῦ, δι' οὗ τὰ πάντα πεποίηκεν, δύναμις ὢν καὶ σοφία αὐτοῦ, ἀναλαμβάνων τὸ πρόσωπον τοῦ πατρὸς καὶ κυρίου τῶν ὅλων, οὗτος παρεγίνετο εἰς τὸν παράδεισον ἐν προσώπῳ τοῦ θεοῦ καὶ ὡμίλει τῷ Ἀδάμ*: consequently it says, "Adam heard the Voice of the Lord God"—*φωνὴ δὲ τί ἄλλο ἐστὶν ἀλλ' ἢ ὁ λόγος ὁ τοῦ θεοῦ, ὅς ἐστιν καὶ υἱὸς αὐτοῦ;* This is language which would have pleased the monarchians: but a little later (having introduced the idea that the λόγος ἐνδιάθετος became προφορικός for the purpose of creating the world) he uses expressions of which Tertullian would have approved: θεὸς οὖν ὢν ὁ λόγος καὶ ἐκ θεοῦ πεφυκώς, ὁπόταν βούληται ὁ πατὴρ τῶν ὅλων πέμπει [*leg.* πέμπειν] αὐτὸν εἴς τινα τόπον, ὃς [*del.* ὃς] παραγενόμενος καὶ ἀκούεται καὶ ὁρᾶται πεμπόμενος ὑπ' αὐτοῦ, καὶ ἐν τόπῳ εὑρίσκεται.

IRENAEUS is in controversy with gnostics who have removed the ineffable Father to such remote transcendence that there is need for angels of inferior rank to act as mediators in creation and in the work of the world. The Jews, he says (*haer.* iv. 14), have revolted from God in refusing to accept his Word: they think they can know the Father in himself, without the aid of the Son. But it was the Son who from the beginning ordered all divine revelation, *non indigente patre angelis ut faceret conditionem et formaret hominem propter quem et conditio fiebat . . . sed habente copiosum et inenarrabile ministerium. ministrat enim ei ad omnia sua progenies et figuratio sua, id est filius et spiritus sanctus, verbum et sapientia, quibus serviunt et subiecti sunt omnes angeli.* From which it is evident that, to Irenaeus, the Word and the Holy Spirit are not, like the angels, inferior powers, for all that they are mediators in the revelation of the Father to men. With the theophanies in mind, Irenaeus says (*ibid.* iv. 34. 7), *verbum dispensator paternae gloriae factus est . . . hominibus quidem ostendens deum, deo autem exhibens hominem, et invisibilitatem quidem patris custodiens ne quando homo fieret contemptor dei et ut semper haberet ad quod proficeret: visibilem autem rursus hominibus per multas dispositiones ostendens deum, ne in toto deficiens a deo homo cessaret esse: gloria enim dei vivens homo, vita hominis visio dei.* Already (*ibid.* 6) he has said, quoting *Nemo videbit deum et vivet*, that the reason for this is man's disability and not God's lack of power; for God, when he will, is seen by men, *a quibus vult et quando vult et quemadmodum vult.* The theophanies therefore are real events, for only on a real present experience could the patriarchs and prophets have based a prophecy of the future: *ibid.* 8, *necessario oportebat eos per quos futura praedicabantur, videre deum quem ipsi hominibus videndum [=visum iri] intimabant, uti non solum dicatur prophetice deus et dei filius, et filius et pater, sed et ut videatur . . . secundum hanc igitur rationem et filium dei hominem videbant conver-*

satum cum hominibus, id quod futurum erat prophetantes, eum qui nondum aderat adesse dicentes et impassibilem passibilem annuntiantes, etc. Tertullian accepts this view of the prophetic character of the theophanies, adding to it, apparently of his own, the idea that the Word was habituating himself to the assumption of human attributes: but since he has been driven to admit the transcendence, as of the Father, so of the Son before the Incarnation, he has to regard the theophanies as no more than visions and dreams. But the passage *adv. Marc.* ii. 27 (quoted above), with its ironic reference to the placid philosopher's God, suggests that Tertullian was at times too wise to push transcendence to the point of abstraction: and consequently what his present argument amounts to is that, on scriptural testimony, God cannot be seen with impunity, and God has been seen with impunity, and therefore the authority of Scripture is with us when we say that there are two who are named God and Lord, and when we maintain that the Son is not the same Person as the Father. When, as in § 16, he presses to the utmost the transcendence of God, he insists that the Son in his divine nature is transcendent as well as the Father, and that it is only because the Scriptures compel us that we consent to believe the theophanies at all.

Cum enim Moyses . . . qui viderit.

This sentence should be treated as parenthetic, adducing the scriptural authority for the rule or principle *deum invisibilem esse.* The next sentence, *Invenimus enim, etc.*, states how this rule *nobis adsistit*: the apparent exceptions to it require explanation, which is what our doctrine provides. *In Aegypto* is incorrect: Exod. 33. 13, 18, 20 takes place *in eremo*: possibly the correction should be made (but see note on § 23).

Secundum hominum capacitates.

IRENAEUS, *haer.* iv. 34. 5 (quoted in part above), had already used similar language wherein he made it clear that the impossibility of seeing God is due to man's incapacity to see, not to God's incapacity to be seen: Tertullian means the latter, and it is the mainspring of his argument. Irenaeus wrote: *praesignificabant igitur prophetae quoniam videbitur deus ab hominibus, quemadmodum et dominus ait: Beati mundo corde quoniam ipsi deum videbunt. sed secundum magnitudinem quidem eius et mirabilem gloriam nemo videbit deum et vivet: incapabilis enim pater: secundum autem dilectionem et humanitatem, et quod omnia possit, etiam hoc concedit iis qui se diligunt, id est videre deum, quod et prophetabant prophetae: quoniam quae impossibilia apud homines possibilia apud deum. homo etenim a se non videt deum. ille autem volens videtur ab hominibus, a quibus vult et quando vult et quemadmodum vult. potens est enim in omnibus deus: visus quidem tunc per spiritum prophetice, visus autem et per filium adoptive, videbitur et in regno caelorum paternaliter, spiritu quidem praeparante hominem in filium dei, filio autem adducente ad patrem, patre autem incorruptelam donante in aeternam vitam, quae unicuique evenit ex eo quod videat deum.*

Cum invisum aut cum visum.

The MSS. readings are unintelligible. Probably the easiest way out is to delete *cum invisum aut* as already contained in the previous clause. We are then left with a triple dilemma. Either (1) they ought to have died, or (2) the Scripture is false in saying that God said he could not be seen, or (3) it is not true that they saw God: since (1) they did not die, and (2), (3) the Scripture cannot lie, *iam ergo alius erit qui videbatur.*

Pro modulo derivationis

is illustrated by *pro temperatura portionis*, where *temperatura* means "lower temperature" (not "mixture"), and *portio* is "apportionment" rather than "part" (see note on § 9). IRENAEUS, *haer.* iv. 6, *omnia enim mensura et ordine deus facit, et nihil non mensum* (οὐδὲν ἄμετρον) *apud eum quoniam nec incompositum* (μηδὲν ἀναρίθμητον): *et bene qui dixit ipsum immensum patrem in filio mensuratum: mensura enim patris filius, quoniam et capit eum* (*capit*=χωρεῖ).

Ex diverso . . . aliquis,

"some one of the opposite party": as in § 15, *quis ex diverso non argumentabitur.*

Sed diximus, etc.

Tertullian is going to be forced to shift his ground, but on one point he remains immovable, namely that the Scripture does make a distinction between God visible and God invisible, and this distinction implies difference of persons, *differentiae patrocinari.* With that safeguard he admits that the Son, as Word or Spirit, is invisible: he goes further, and instead of saying (as do Justin and Theophilus) that the Son, by nature invisible, becomes visible as occasion requires, he allows that the Son until the Incarnation was always invisible and that the theophanies were no more than visions and dreams. But still, the Scripture makes a distinction, and if the Son is in his divine nature invisible, *a fortiori* the Father is.

Nam et illud adiciunt.

An obvious point for the monarchians to score: if the Son was the subject of the theophanies, then it was the Son who said (*tunc* at Exod. 33. 20) that his face could not be seen, and consequently the Son *may* be identified with the Father. It takes Tertullian all his skill to surmount this difficulty, which he does (with more ingenuity than conviction) at the end of this chapter. Kroymann wishes to read *pronuntiarit*, perhaps wrongly: Tertullian reports the monarchians' arguments in the imperfect subjunctive, his own statement in the indicative (*loquebatur*).

Ac per hoc, etc.

A further step in the monarchian argument: immediately before Moses' request to see God's face, the request that was denied, it is written (Exod. 33. 11) that the Lord spake to Moses face to face, and it is written that Jacob (Gen. 32. 30) said he had seen the Lord face to face: therefore God is both visible and invisible. *Et quia idem utrumque*, and because the same Person has both attributes, it *must* be that the Father himself, though invisible, is, as Son, visible.

Quasi non . . . filio competat.

But our interpretation is equally suitable: for the moment Tertullian will say no more than that. This use of *competere* is almost unparalleled in Tertullian: but cf. *ad nat.* ii. 13, *sed neque hoc potest competere numini.* He would perhaps have written *expositioni . . . filius competat* except for the consideration that ideas must conform to the Son rather than the Son conform to ideas. The MSS. read *visibilitate*, which is possible if *patre seposito* is parenthetic, the last three words going closely with *filio*: so Engelbrecht, and Kroymann's alterations are unnecessary.

Dicimus enim, etc.

Tertullian admits one part of the monarchian argument: he takes it even further, *iam nunc*, since the Incarnation. *Et qua*

***deus . . . spiritus dei*;** this clause perhaps began as a marginal gloss, *et qua deus*, amplifying *qua sermo* in the previous line, the other words being added (still in the margin) to indicate its place in the text.

Etsi fuerit, etc.

Num. 12. 6 sqq. LXX has *ἐὰν γένηται προφήτης ὑμῶν κυρίῳ, ἐν ὁράματι αὐτῷ γνωσθήσομαι καὶ ἐν ὕπνῳ λαλήσω αὐτῷ. οὐχ οὕτως ὁ θεράπων μου Μωυσῆς . . . στόμα κατὰ στόμα λαλήσω αὐτῷ, ἐν εἴδει καὶ οὐ δι' αἰνιγμάτων.* The additional words are Tertullian's explanations: the quotation 1 Cor. 13. 12 is introduced to justify the equation *aenigma=imago.* This promise regarding Moses, Tertullian says, was only fulfilled at the Transfiguration: and consequently in past time (*retro*) all the theophanies, including those to Moses, must be understood to have been visions and dreams. IRENAEUS held the same view: *haer.* iv. 34. 8, as regards Moses: *et dictum est ei, Sta in loco alto petrae . . . non enim videt homo faciem meam et vivet: utraque significans, quoniam et impossibilis est homo videre deum, et quoniam per sapientiam dei in novissimis temporibus videbit eum homo, in altitudine petrae, hoc est in eo qui est secundum hominem eius adventu. et propter hoc facie ad faciem confabulatus est cum eo in altitudine montis, adsistente etiam Helia, quemadmodum evangelium retulit, restituens in fine pristinam repromissionem*: and as regards the other prophets, a little lower down, quoting Ezek. 1. 1 sqq. he comments, *ne quis putaret forte eum in his proprie vidisse deum intulit, Haec visio similitudinis gloriae domini . . . quae autem ab his videbantur erant similitudines claritatis domini et prophetiae futurorum.*

Et ipse quidem dominus, etc.

Tertullian will go even further than his adversaries wish to press him: "And though it is true that the Lord himself *spoke* face to face, yet a man would not *see* his face as he is (1 John 3. 2), but at the most in a mirror, darkly". Even during his earthly life, our Lord was not really *seen.* ***Si forte**, nisi forte*, generally have lost the sense of "perhaps" and have taken on the function of admitting a suggestion with which the writer does not disagree, e.g. *adv. Val.* 2, *si forte praestat minus sapere quam peius, errare quam fallere*: see Oehler's index.

Denique si sic Moysi, etc.

A final contrast of texts to be considered: at Exod. 33. 11 it is said that the Lord spake to Moses face to face, and yet ***statim atque ibidem*** (Exod. 33. 13, 18) Moses is still asking to see God's face and having his request refused. Moreover Jacob had long ago seen God's face and lived (Gen. 32. 30) at Peniel.

Aut quae est facies, etc.

In these sentences, which clinch the question and state Tertullian's answer, Kroymann's punctuation is preferable: Turner suggests *alia debet esse facies quae* ⟨*visa est, alia quae*⟩ *si videatur occidit*, which Kroymann's punctuation would make unnecessary. ***Etsi facie :*** the MSS. have *facies*.

Quis enim pater ?

The sentences to the end of the chapter are meant to justify the equation *facies filii=invisibilis pater*. Common idiom gives the equation *facies=auctoritas*: it is the greater who gives authority to the lesser: the Father is greater than the Son, and gives the Son authority: therefore the Father is the Son's face: and this conclusion is in conformity with Scripture (Lam. 4. 20). Tertullian has taken the idiom *faciem mihi praestat* and (no doubt illicitly) equated it with *facies mea est*, so as to lead to the conclusion *facies filii erit pater*: which is more resourceful than convincing. A mark of interrogation is needed after *praestat*.

Nam et scriptura, etc.

There seems no precedent for Tertullian's reading ***personae eius :*** LXX has πνεῦμα προσώπου ἡμῶν: the Hebrew is fairly represented by LXX. Justin, *apol.* i. 35, has πνεῦμα πρὸ προσώπου ἡμῶν: IRENAEUS, *haer.* iv. 11. 22, *spiritus faciei nostrae*.

Ergo si Christus, etc.

The editors have made heavy weather of this sentence: Kroymann has altered the text almost beyond recognition. Much of its difficulty vanishes with the moving of a few commas (as in the present text) and on observing that ***suam***, though not a common substitute for *eius*, is not unknown. So we translate: "If then Christ is the spirit of the Father's person, rightly did the Spirit (as the author of the Old Testament) declare that he whose the person was—namely, the Father—is his (i.e. the Son's) face, *ex unitate scilicet*, because *persona* and *facies* are synonymous terms". The unexpressed antecedent of *cuius* is the object of *pronuntiavit*. CLEMENT OF ALEXANDRIA, *strom*. vii. 58, makes a similar deduction from a different text, Ps. 24. 6, ζητούντων τὸ πρόσωπον τοῦ θεοῦ Ἰακώβ: συντόμως οἶμαι τὸν γνωστικὸν ἐμήνυσεν ὁ προφήτης· κατὰ παραδρομὴν ὡς ἔοικεν ἡμῖν θεὸν εἶναι τὸν σωτῆρα ἀπέδειξεν ὁ Δαβὶδ πρόσωπον αὐτὸν εἰπὼν τοῦ θεοῦ Ἰακώβ, τὸν εὐαγγελισάμενον καὶ διδάξαντα περὶ τοῦ πατρός.

XV. *Our interpretation of these Old Testament texts is confirmed by the New Testament, in which the apostles and evangelists on the one hand declare that God is invisible, and on the other hand testify that Christ has been seen. Our adversaries reply that that is their position: that the Father, invisible before the Incarnation, is the same person as the Son, visible in the Incarnation. In that case what do they make of the appearances before the Incarnation, and what of the statements, made after the Incarnation, that God is still invisible? Who was it the apostles said they had seen? It was, according to John, the Word of life, the only-begotten Son, whom he declares to be God: and yet he immediately adds (to confound our opponents) that no man hath seen God. What God has not been seen? Not God the Word: for concerning him he says, "We have seen and heard and handled". Him Paul also saw—not the Father—and him he calls "God over all, blessed for ever": him he "openly sets forth", namely Jesus Christ the visible Son of God, the Word of God (for "Christ" is an appellation of the Word made flesh). The Father, he says, is invisible, alone has immortality, dwells in light unapproachable: to the end that, again on his testimony, we might affirm the opposites of these of the Son, visibility, mortality, approachable light—though even this approachable light was scarcely tolerable to Paul, or to Peter and James and John, who, hardly bearing the glory of the Son, would at once have died if they had seen the Father. Thus the Scripture is consistent with itself: in both the Old and the New Testaments it is the Son who is seen, converses, works—of course by the Father's authority and will, since the Son can do nothing of himself; but what he sees the Father doing in thought, that he accomplishes in act, and so "all things were made" by the Son, and "without him was not anything made".*

Si hunc articulum, etc.

Articulus means "text" or "passage of scripture": see Oehler's index, e.g. *adv. Marc.* ii. 24, *nam et apud Graecos interdum malitiae pro vexationibus et laesuris, non pro malignitatibus ponuntur, sicut et in isto articulo*, i.e. "the passage under discussion", viz. Jonah 3. 10, *paenituit dominum de malitia quam dixerat facturum se illis. Quaestiones scripturae veteris* seems to mean "enquiries made of the Old Testament": Oehler's index gives no help here. *Reputare* is used by Tertullian for *deputare*: see Oehler's note *de carne Christi*, 3: and *defendere* is used for *vindicare*: *adv. Marc.* i. 26, *cur enim prohibet admitti quod non defendit admissum?*

Condicionis utriusque.

Condicio seems to mean something more than "attribute". Cf. *adv. Marc.* i. 7, *non nomini sed statui, nec appellationi sed condicioni eius, summum magnum et adscribo et vindico*, where *condicio* is coextensive with *status* which (cf. § 2) is one and the same in the case of all three divine Persons. In the present passage Tertullian seems to go back somewhat from that position, maintaining a distinction which almost amounts to a difference of quality, the difference between absolute invisibility and potential visibility—"with an evident personal distinction between the two qualities". See a note on § 3.

Exclamat quodammodo.

Tertullian seems to mean that the text *Deum nemo vidit unquam* at John 1. 18 comes almost (*quodammodo*) as a surprise, not being led up to by what precedes. Later in this chapter he quotes the same text from 1 John 4. 12 (as is clear from the next sentence, *praedictum est*, referring to 1 John 1. 1): there, he observes, the statement is *ex abundanti*, "there being no special need for the remark"—which is true in the sense that the connexion of thought would have been clear without it.

Sed nec videri potest.

Pamelius, perhaps rightly, read *videre* as below in this chapter, when the text is quoted again.

Porro si ipse est Christus, etc.

"Further, if Christ himself is both Father and Son".

Qui ex diverso nobis,

"our opponent": Turner's improvement on *quis ex diverso non.* Cf. *de res. carn.* 19, *diversa pars*, "my opponents"; and *supr.* § 14, *ex diverso dicet aliquis.*

Aeque si idem, etc.

"Likewise, if the same one is visible after the Incarnation, how is he even now pronounced invisible by the apostles? Unless it is that there is one who even of old was seen darkly, and whom now the Incarnation has made more fully visible—namely, the Word who was also made flesh—and another whom no man hath ever seen—namely the Father, whose the Word is." *Nisi* before *pater* is rightly omitted by Kroymann, and the comma must be removed from after *pater.*

Glorificati a patre invisibili.

Evidently a reference to John 12. 28, καὶ ἐδόξασα καὶ πάλιν δοξάσω.

Ne adiuvaret adversariorum praesumptionem.

Praesumptio apparently means no more than "assumption", as at *apol.* 25, *illa praesumptio dicentium Romanos pro merito religiositatis diligentissimae in tantum sublimitatis elatos ut orbem occuparint* : *de pud.* 7, *diversae partis praesumptionem.* At *apol.* 21, *quasi sub umbraculo insignissimae religionis certe licitae aliquid propriae praesumptionis abscondat*, the sense perhaps is "something it has assumed and made its own", though Souter translates "some of its own arrogance", and at *ibid.* 25 "prejudiced assertion": both of which seem too strong.

Apud quem deus erat sermo, etc.

This is the MS. reading: there was no need to alter *deus* to *deum* (Ursinus, followed by Oehler). "In whose presence (i.e. "with whom," John 1. 1) the Word, the only-begotten Son, who himself hath declared the bosom of the Father, was God." *Qui sinum patris, etc.* This, the reading of *MF*, is evidently correct: cf. John 1. 18 and the note on § 8. *P* reads *est in sinu*, which has caused more trouble than it need have done: see Oehler's footnote.

Phantasma . . . contrectatus

refers to Luke 24. 39, ψηλαφήσατέ με καὶ ἴδετε, ὅτι πνεῦμα

σάρκα καὶ ὀστέα οὐκ ἔχει, as well as to 1 John 1. 1, αἱ χεῖρες ἡμῶν ἐψηλάφησαν.

Quorum patres, etc.

See the note of Sanday and Headlam, *Romans*, pp. 233 sqq., who observe that the fathers almost without exception take the whole of this text as referring to Christ: and indeed, as Bull remarks, there is no sense in taking it otherwise.

Ostendit et ipse, etc.

Perhaps bears a reference to Gal. 3. 1, προεγράφη.

A se novissime visum.

1 Cor. 15. 8, ἔσχατον δε πάντων . . . ὤφθη κἀμοί.

Sine rationis et amentia.

Kroymann would omit *et amentia qui*: needlessly, for (as Rigaltius remarked) the phrase means *sine periculo rationis et sine amentia*, with reference to ἔκφοβοι γὰρ ἐγένοντο and μὴ εἰδὼς ὃ λέγει in the accounts of the Transfiguration.

Qui si non passuri filii gloriam.

Oehler appears to take *passuri* for a nominative plural: there is no doubt that it is a genitive singular: delete the commas after *si* and after *gloriam*, and insert *essent* before *credo* (Engelbrecht), "who, if they had seen the Father, and not ⟨just⟩ the glory of the Son who was due to suffer, would, I believe, have died on the spot".

Pater enim sensu agit.

Sensus means "mind" or "thought" as in § 6, *immo et facta iam quantum in dei sensu*: also § 24, *pater in filio non visu sed sensu videbatur*. The conjecture *quod* for *qui* (Ursinus) improves the sense. There is a reference to John 5. 19. "For the Father acts by thought; but the Son, while he sees what is in the Father's thought, makes it an actuality", or (retaining *qui*) "but the Son, who is in the mind of the Father, sees and makes actual". These last sentences lead to the next step in the argument, that at the beginning, and since the beginning, all things done by God in the world have been carried out by the Son as agent.

XVI. *Not only the creation of the world but also all divine acts in the world since the beginning have been wrought by the agency of the Son. The texts which state that the Father has delivered to the Son all power, all judgement, and so forth, imply that the Son at all times holds and has held these prerogatives: for "all" includes all time. The theophanies of the Old Testament had the Son for their subject. He was by them preparing for the Incarnation—preparing himself and preparing our faith. He who at length assumed human substance, flesh and soul, prepared for that by assuming human affections. Hence all those Old Testament episodes which heretics lay hold upon as unworthy of God. What these reject as unworthy even of the Son, our present opponents ascribe to the Father. But how could the invisible God, whose attributes are so transcendent, have appeared among men in human form and in human activities? It would not have been proper to believe such things of the Son unless they had been written: perhaps we should have been wrong to believe them of the Father though they had been written. Yet our opponents bring the Father down into Mary's womb, to Pilate's judgement seat, to Joseph's sepulchre. Forgetting that, since the beginning, all divine acts in the world have been administered by the Son, they fall into the error of attributing to the Father the human affections which the Son assumed.*

In sinu eius.

The same text is quoted at § 21 with *in manu*, which may be the true reading here.

Ex quo a primordio . . . a primordio tamen.

Kroymann tries to remove the awkwardness of the sentence by omitting the first *a primordio*. But both appear necessary: the real difficulty is *tamen* where one would have expected *utique*.

Linguasque disperdens.

Ursinus suggested *dispertiens*, which however receives no support from LXX, συγχέωμεν . . . συνέχεεν: but LXX also have καὶ διέσπειρεν αὐτοὺς κύριος, and in view of that Tertullian may have written *dispergens*.

Quem erat persecuturus.

Quem is due to Ursinus: the MSS. read *quae*: possibly *qui* would be right.

Ediscebat.

Cf. *adv. Marc.* iii. 9, *ideoque et ipse cum angelis in veritate quidem carnis apparuit, sed nondum natae quia nondum moriturae, sed et discentis iam inter homines conversari*, where if *discentis* is right (the MS. reads *discentes*) Tertullian has made a curious slip involving a contradiction with the whole argument of *de carne Christi* (perhaps we should read *discens etiam*): *de carne Christi* 6, *Christum . . . qui iam tunc et liberare et iudicare humanum genus ediscebat in carnis habitu.* Possibly there is a reminiscence of Heb. 5. 8, ἔμαθεν ἀφ' ὧν ἔπαθεν.

Si qua haeretici adprehendunt.

The Marcionites are here meant: cf. *adv. Marc.* ii. 27, a chapter which has some verbal similarities with the present. Marcion objected to such expressions as "it repented God", "the evil which God said he would do", to his apparent ignorance of facts, as in the questions, "Where art thou?" "Where is thy brother?" and in "I will go down now and see . . . and if not I will know", and to statements that the Lord sware by himself: to all of which Tertullian gives something rather better than the obvious common-sense answers (§§ 24-26) and proceeds (§ 27) to solve *cetera . . . quaecunque adhuc ut pusilla et infirma et indigna colligitis ad destructionem creatoris.* (1) God could not have entered into human relationships except by assuming human thoughts and passions (*humanos et sensus et affectus*), so as to mitigate the force of his majesty by a humility unworthy indeed of God but necessary for man, and so also worthy of God, since nothing is so worthy of God as man's salvation. Marcion himself admits that God humbled himself to the death of the cross: and the humilities of the Old Testament create a presumption that Christ, who was made the sport of human passions (*humanis passionibus obiectum*), belongs to that God of the Old Testament whose humilities Marcion thinks so objectionable. *Nam et profitemur Christum semper egisse in dei patris nomine, ipsum ab initio conversatum, ipsum congressum cum patriarchis et prophetis . . . quem . . . exinde omni dispositioni suae voluntatique praefecit, diminuens illum modico citra angelos . . . qua diminutione in haec quoque dispositus est a patre quae ut humana reprehenditis, ediscens iam inde a primordio †iam inde hominem† quod erat futurus in fine. . . .* (2) All these acts are *sacramentum humanae salutis*: God conversed with man on man's terms so that man might learn to converse with God on God's terms.

Minoratus a patre, etc.

Ps. 8. 5: Heb. 2. 9: *adv. Marc.* ii. 27: and below, § 23, *minoravit filium modico citra angelos ad terram dimittendo, gloria tamen et honore coronaturus illum in caelos resumendo.*

Quae tu ipsi patri inducis,

"with which you becloud the Father himself".

Quanquam filius hominis, etc.

Kroymann makes a period at *apparuerit*, and thereafter punctuates as follows: *quanquam filius hominis est dictus et in imagine et speculo et aenigmate scilicet et haec, nec de filio dei credenda fuissent, si scripta non essent, fortasse non credenda de patre, licet scripta, quem isti in vulvam, etc.* What he snpposes this to mean is not very evident, and he is clearly in error in separating *quanquam filius hominis est dictus* from *quartus apparuerit*: the most that can be said is that he departs from the MSS. only in writing *fuissent* for *fuisse.* Oehler's text, which follows the old editors, is not much more intelligible: *ni haec in imagine, etc.*, can hardly be right, for what Tertullian means is that under no circumstances could the Father be thought to have made these appearances, and a conditional clause is therefore out of place. The easiest way out, possibly too rash, would be to omit *et in imagine et speculo et aenigmate* as having crept in from elsewhere or as being the intelligent criticism of some reader who thinks he is answering Tertullian out of his own previous language; and to read: . . . *dictus? scilicet et haec nec de filio dei credenda fuissent si scripta non essent, fortasse non credenda de patre licet scripta, etc.* This at least makes sense. Dan. 3. 25 actually says, "the form of the fourth is like a son of the gods": LXX, ὁμοίωμα ἀγγέλου θεοῦ: Theodotion, ὁμοία υἱῷ θεοῦ. It is just possible that *quanquam filius hominis est dictus* is a mistaken marginal objection to Tertullian's inclusion of this episode (the objector thinking of Dan. 7. 13: 10. 16), and that *et in imagine* is a further comment based on ὁμοίωμα, to which *et speculo et aenigmate* could have been added through recollection of § 14. If everything from *quanquam* to *aenigmate* were omitted all trouble would disappear.

Omnem ordinem divinae dispositionis per filium decucurrisse.

So Tertullian summarises his contention that all the theophanies of the Old Testament were theophanies of God the Son, and, more than that, that from the creation onwards the whole course of the world and the progressive revelation of God has been administered by the Son. That this was already established doctrine is evident from the passages cited in the notes to § 14: that it has at least some scriptural basis would appear from such places as John 8. 56-58 and 1 Cor. 10. 4, where the very allusiveness of the language is an indication of how deep the doctrine already was in the Christian mind. This is not the place to trace in detail the influence of Eusebius of Caesarea in causing to sink into the background of Christian thought, and eventually almost to vanish from it, a theory which previous generations had accepted as an evident truth.

XVII. *They have been more ready to think that the Father has acted in the Son's name than that the Son has acted in the Father's name, although the latter is what our Lord says of himself and what the Scripture testifies of him. The Name of the Father involves the titles God Almighty, the Most High, the Lord of Hosts, the King of Israel, I am. On scriptural authority we say that these titles belong to the Son also: for he says "all things that the Father hath are mine", and "all things" must include the names. The titles belong to the Son because he fulfils the functions indicated by each of them. I shall reply elsewhere to their suggestion that the name of Christ belongs to the Father: meanwhile, since they doubt the propriety of giving the Son the title "Almighty", I remark that the Son of the Almighty is almighty for precisely the same reason as the Son of God is God.*

The argument here is in three stages:

(1) The monarchian contention, if admitted, would require that in the theophanies, as in the Incarnation, it was the Father who was acting, albeit in the name of (i.e. under pretence of being) the Son. The scriptural statements are however to the opposite effect, that the Son is acting in the name (i.e. with the authority) of the Father. At this point Tertullian takes a step which is by

no means essential to the argument, though it makes an easier transition to what follows. The idiomatic phrase "in my Father's name" probably means only a little more than "as my Father's representative", "with my Father's authority": Tertullian gives the word "name" its full sense in all the texts quoted, John 5. 43: Matt. 21. 9: John 17. 6. In this last, "I have manifested thy name", that interpretation seems natural and necessary: its transference to the other texts is in accordance with the common tendency to try to make the same word have the same meaning wherever it occurs—a tendency sufficiently common in interpreters both ancient and modern to need no illustration. The connexion recurs § 23: *glorifica nomen tuum—in quo erat filius.* At *de orat.* 3 Tertullian goes even further and almost personifies the name, suggesting that the Name of the Father is the Son himself: *nomen dei patris nemini proditum fuit. etiam qui de ipso interrogaverat Moyses aliud quidem nomen audierat. nobis revelatum est in filio. iam enim filius novum patris nomen est. Ego veni, inquit, in nomine patris: et rursus, Pater, glorifica nomen tuum: et apertius, Nomen tuum manifestavi hominibus.* See the discussion of φωνὴ βοῶντος, Origen, *comm. in Ioa.* vi. 17 sqq., where there is first a personification of φωνὴ as being the Baptist himself, but finally the common-sense suggestion that the phrase means Ἐγώ εἰμι περὶ οὗ γέγραπται φωνὴ βοῶντος, ὥς βοῶντα εἶναι τὸν Ἰωάννην, καὶ τούτου τὴν φωνὴν ἐν τῇ ἐρήμῳ βοᾷν, Εὐθύνατε τὴν ὁδὸν κυρίου.

(2) The divine name involves the divine attributes. The name is not a fortuitous appendage, but is the peculiar property of the person, essentially descriptive of the person: and consequently it summarises all those descriptive titles which indicate the essential attributes of the person. Since the Son is come in the Father's name, these titles and the attributes they imply are his also.

(3) Actually each of these titles can be shown, on scriptural authority, to be applicable to the Son: from which it follows that the God of the Old Testament is not, as the monarchians and others alleged, God the Father only, but is God, namely the Son revealing the Father. See below, § 21, *subiungens autem, Neque vocem eius audistis unquam neque formam eius vidistis, confirmat retro non patrem sed filium fuisse qui videbatur et audiebatur. denique dicit, Ego veni in patris mei nomine et non me recepistis:*

adeo semper filius erat in dei et regis et domini omnipotentis et altissimi nomine.

Condicente etiam scriptura.

Condicere in Tertullian means not "promise" but "agree": *adv. Hermog.* 11, *cum pecora condixerint bestiis*, "when lambs dwell with wolves": *adv. Marc.* ii. 2, *cui et apostolus condicet*, "the apostle will be found to agree with Isaiah". See Oehler's note, *scorp.* 14, *condixerat Petrus*. The Scripture here referred to is Ps. 118. 26, not Matt. 21. 9 and its parallels, which are not Scripture but the shout of a fickle multitude.

Deus omnipotens: אל שדי, Gen. 17. 1, etc., Exod. 6. 3. *Altissimus:* עליון, Gen. 14. 18, etc. *Dominus virtutum:* יהוה צבאות, 1 Sam. 17. 45, etc. *Rex Israelis*, 1 Sam. 12. 12: Deut. 33. 5, but only by implication, not as an express title. *Qui est:* אהיה, ὁ ὤν, Exod. 3. 14.

Filius suo iure deus omnipotens.

Omnipotens is inserted by the editors: it appears to be required by the general tenor of the sentence. *Suo iure* cannot mean "without reference to or derivation from the Father"—which would involve ditheism: it apparently means "in his own proper person". The sentence *Cum ergo legis . . . et non sunt* means that when these titles are read in the Old Testament it is the Son who is meant, and that they are to be taken as strong evidence for his existence *suo iure*, as a Person distinct from the Father.

Omnium accepit potestatem: Matt. 28. 18: the Son is God Almighty on two grounds, by nature as *sermo omnipotentis* (see below) and because all authority has been given to him. *Dextera dei exaltatus:* Acts 2. 33. *Omnia subiecta sunt illi:* 1 Cor. 15. 27, quoted from Ps. 8. 6. *Sors gentis istius*, Deut. 32. 9. *Filii dicuntur et non sunt*, Rom. 9. 8 sqq.

Si autem volunt, etc.

Some of the monarchians seem, like the adoptionists, to have distinguished a divine Christ from a human Jesus, and to have identified (as the adoptionists did not) the former with the Father: see below, § 28.

Ego dominus qui est, etc.

The monarchians' argument seems to have been that this sentence of the Apocalypse is spoken by Christ: that the title "Almighty" is not appropriate in the mouth of any except the Father: and that therefore Christ must be regarded as identical with the Father. Tertullian replies that omnipotence, like deity, belongs to Christ by virtue of his sonship, there being as good reason for the one as for the other. *Quasi qui venturus, etc.* The meaning of the sentence seems clear enough, though the text is in some disorder: the MSS. read *quasi qui venturus sit omnipotens*, which will not construe: Oehler inserts *non* after *sit*, which is hardly better: Kroymann reads *quasi qui venturus sit omnipotentis filius non sit omnipotens*, which makes sense: the simplest alteration would be to read, *quasi qui venturus sit ⟨non sit⟩ omnipotens*, and to translate, "as though he who is to come were not almighty, the fact being that the Son of the Almighty is almighty precisely as the Son of God is God".

XVIII. *They hesitate to acknowledge that the Son shares the Father's titles, on the ground that the Scripture pronounces that there is one only God. When we reply, as we have done, that the same Scripture sets forth two ⟨who are⟩ God and Lord, they reply that those two are therefore one and the same. But the Scripture does not need human subtlety to help it not to contradict itself: it has its reasons in both cases and is competent to explain itself. God does not cease to be the only God by having a Son: for he is named alone, without the Son, when reference is to the Father as the primary Person. So "there is one God, the Father" and "beside him there is none else". When God said that, he said it not to deny the Son, but to exclude another god: and the Son is not another god. If statements of this kind are carefully examined they are seen to be directed against idolatry: and the Son is to be understood as included in the unity, inseparable from the Father, the more so as he is not mentioned. The mere mention of him in such circumstances would have implied separation, or would have been otiose, since the Son is in the Father. The insistence upon one God is therefore directed against idolaters and against heretics, who fabricate other gods, the former with their hands, the latter with words: it is intended to preclude the idea that Christ came from any other god except him who declared his own unity, a unity which includes the Son.*

Ideo ambo unus, etc.

This seems the best way to punctuate: Oehler and Kroymann place the comma after *idem*, making a very awkward sentence.

De tua argumentatione succurras,

"come to its assistance with your subtleties". Oehler (index s.v.) remarks that *argumentari* is equivalent to *argutiis agere*. Of the references given, the following seem to bear that sense: *adv. Prax.* 26, *volent quidem et hic argumentari, sed veritas praevalebit: de carne Christi,* 16, *argumentandi libidine ex forma ingenii haeretici: de res. carn.* 37, *peccatores . . . quos monumenta* (i.e. John 5. 28) *intellegendos argumentantur haeretici: ibid.* 53, *corpus animale animam quidam argumentantur: ibid.* 60, *de officiis quoque membrorum argumentantur: adv. Hermog.* 3, *argumentari tibi videor? de anima,* 37, *ego ad deum potius argumentabor hunc modum temporis, ut decem menses decalogo magis inaugurent hominem, ut tanto temporis numero nascamur quanto disciplinae numero renascimur.* Possibly also *de carne Christi,* 6, *his vero quae insuper argumentantur nos resistemus:* and, *adv. Prax.* 15, *quis non ex diverso argumentabitur?*, probably has the same meaning. In the present passage the substantive seems to mean "subtle reasoning": so *ad nat.* ii. 2, *in incertum abiit etiam quod invenerant, et facta est argumentationum inundatio de stillicidio uno atque alio veritatis: ibid.* 4, *sed quid ego cum argumentationibus physiologicis.* But, *de anima,* 3, where he opposes *argumentationes originales id est philosophicas* to *definitiones caelestes id est dominicas* the word seems to mean "inductions": cf. *adv. Marc.* ii. 5, *haec sunt argumentationum ossa quae obroditis,* where it appears from what follows that the word means "arguments", or perhaps "cavils". Tertullian seems never to use *argumentari, argumentatio,* for reasoning of which he approves.

Habet rationem.

Rationem habere apparently means "has reasonable cause", cf. CICERO, *in Verrem,* II. ii. 115, *quid tandem habuit argumenti aut rationis res quam ob rem in eo potissimum . . . praemium poneretur?*

Non enim desinit esse, etc.

Delete the comma after *filium*, and translate, "For he who has a son does not cease to be himself singular, I mean when considered in himself, as often as he is mentioned without his son". The reference here and in the following sentence is to fathers and sons in general: the particular reference to God is resumed at *igitur unus deus.*

Unus deus pater: 1 Cor. 8. 6. ***Absque eo alius non est,*** Is. 44. 6: 45. 5, 18. ***Ipse inferens,*** God himself who introduces this statement, being himself the speaker in Is. 45.

Ceterum alius a patre, etc.

Supply *deus* from the previous sentence: otherwise Tertullian's case is given away.

Habens tamen filium.

A construction according to sense: the participle depends on *unio divinitatis*, which is equivalent to *unus deus.*

Individuum,

"undivided", synonymous with *inseparatum*: cf. § 6, *habentem in se individuas suas rationem et sophiam.* ***In patre reputandum,*** "must be supposed to be included in ⟨the mention of⟩ the Father, although not specifically named".

Si nominasset.

Such a mention would either (*a*) stultify the pronouncement by suggesting the existence of another even while denying it, or (*b*) would be otiose, as in the illustration which follows.

Propter haereticos.

Both Marcionites and gnostics deduced their Christ from another god who was not the God of the Old Testament, and so fabricated a second god and a second so-called christ.

Caelum solus extendit.

Is. 45. 18, *οὕτως λέγει κύριος ὁ ποιήσας τὸν οὐρανόν . . . Ἐγώ εἰμι καὶ οὐκ ἔστιν ἔτι*, suggests Is. 44. 24, *ἐξέτεινα τὸν οὐρανὸν μόνος*, and so provides the transition to the next chapter: cf. Job 9. 8, *ὁ τανύσας τὸν οὐρανὸν μόνος*. The Hebrew in both cases reads נֹטֶה, "stretcheth out".

XIX. "*I alone have spread out the heavens*" (*Is.* 44. 24), *which our adversaries use to support their case, was intended to guard against gnosticism. It will only suit the monarchians if they are prepared to forget that at the creation Wisdom was also present* (*Prov.* 8. 30).

When the prophet says "Who hath known the mind of the Lord or been his counsellor?" he evidently means, "Who besides Wisdom", that is "besides the Son", Christ who alone knows the mind of the Father. Therefore at the creation God was not alone, for he had a companion within himself: he was alone, in that there were no other gods present. The evangelist (John 1. 1) and the psalmist (Ps. 33. 6) testify that the Word, i.e. the Son, was present at the creation: so again proving that God was not alone except in the sense that no other gods were there. The verses which follow "I alone have spread out the heavens", mention the Son—"establishing the words of his Son", which God did when he said "Hear him" (Matt. 17. 5): by adding this reference to the Son he shows in what sense we must understand the word "alone". Moreover it is the Son who says, "I alone have spread out the heavens", as is proved by the text of Proverbs and by what is said in this same discourse, "I am the first" (Is. 41. 4): the first must be the Son, since the Father is outside the order of numeration. If then they are anxious to safeguard the divine unity, it is safeguarded by the statement that God, being one, has also a Son, as the Scripture testifies: we have already drawn attention to this testimony, and have explained how the fact that there are two who are called God and Lord does not mean that there are two gods or two lords: for the Son must be called God because of his unity with the Father.

Qui et ipsum creatorem, etc.

The MS. reading, Oehler's text, seems to mean: "They make out that the creator is either an angel, or else a being contrived for other external purposes such as the fabrication of the world—ignorant ⟨of the true God⟩ in either case". The Valentinians distinguished between the creation of the suprasensible ideal world and the subsequent creation of the actual visible world: Tertullian here seems to be hinting at that distinction. There is however nothing in the Valentinian system which suggests that the supramundane creator was an angel or that the maker of the visible world was a being specially fabricated or suborned for the purpose: though gnostic speculations were so elastic that it is impossible to say that such a theory was not held by someone or other. Kroymann's suggestion, *aut ab aliqua extrinsecus virtute volunt ad opera mundi*, is therefore unnecessary, though his reference to Achamoth is to the point: Engelbrecht's *ad alia quae extrinsecus sunt opera mundi* preserves the necessary distinction, and may be correct: but it has nothing to balance the previous *aut.*

Isti . . . haeretici.

Tertullian here for the first time calls the monarchians heretics: but their doctrine is called heresy in § 1.

Et si dixit.

Oehler, following Ursinus, adds *apostolus*, referring to Rom. 11. 34: Engelbrecht suggests *Esaias*, referring to Is. 40. 13. Possibly both are wrong: Tertullian may have forgotten that the speaker in Is. 40. 13 is the prophet in his own person. If God were the speaker, as in the previous quotations, *praeter sophiam non fuit*, the reading of one MS., would stand. *Praeter sophiam fuit* (*PM*) would also stand: the question is whether *praeter* means "without" or "besides". *Consilio fuit* (for LXX σύμβουλος) occurs only here: *adv. Marc.* v. 14. 18, *adv. Hermog.* 17, *scorp.* 7, *consiliarius.*

In ipso tamen et cum illo, etc.

The sentences are somewhat interlaced: *in ipso tamen* is the apodosis of *et si dixit*, as though *utique praeter sophiam, etc.*, had not intervened: *praeter sophiam autem, etc.*, develops *utique praeter sophiam*, as though *in ipso tamen, etc.*, had not been there. The natural subject of *compingebat* is *sophia*: "yet in him and in company with him ⟨Wisdom⟩ established all things, seeing he was not ignorant of what he was doing". But there may conceivably be a *constructio ad sensum*, *ipso* and *illo* being masculine by anticipation of the equation *sophia=filius*: "Yet in the Son and with the Son for associate he established all things, and the Son was not ⟨like the supposed demiurge of the gnostic⟩ ignorant of what he was doing". But the sequence would be easier if we could read *in ipso etenim*. *Dicit* cannot mean "he means" since *praeter sophiam* is not a quotation but a supposition: translate "'without Wisdom' means 'without the Son'".

Spiritus qui in ipso est.

Here, as elsewhere, "the Spirit" is interpreted as meaning "the Son".

Atque adeo statim,

i.e. in the verses immediately following *Extendi caelum solus,* Is. 44. 25, 26, τίς ἕτερος διασκεδάσει σημεῖα ἐγγαστριμύθων καὶ μαντείας ἀπὸ καρδίας, ἀποστρέφων φρονίμους εἰς τὰ ὀπίσω καὶ τὴν βουλὴν αὐτῶν μωρεύων, καὶ ἱστῶν ῥήματα παιδὸς αὐτοῦ; where παῖς, as the Hebrew shows, means not Son but Servant. The same collocation of Is. 44. 26 with Luke 9. 35 occurs *adv. Marc.* iv. 22, *Sistens enim, inquit, verba filii sui, dicendo scilicet, Hic est filius meus dilectus, hunc audite.*

Proinde et filii erit vox.

The divine discourse Is. 41. 1-50. 3 is, like the other theophanies, a theophany of the Son. Since the Father is *cum filio unum* (not *unus*), and since the Son alone ministered the Father's activity, the Son *also* can say, *Extendi caelum solus.* *In sermone . . . paratum est caelum* comes from Ps. 33. 6: *sophia . . . adsistente* from Prov. 8. 30, συμπαρήμην. But Tertullian will carry his case further: unless the Son is the speaker in this discourse the language is unsuitable to the Father, for it contains the sentence *Ego primus, etc.* (Is. 41. 4), and the Father cannot be the first, seeing that he is outside all order of numeration. *Ceterum pater . . . non potest videri: primus non potest videri* is evidently what is meant, and probably *primus* should be restored to the text (so Kroymann).

Duos deos . . . duos dominos.

The sequence shows that, as in several similar passages, the numerals are to be taken as the direct object and the substantives as predicative. Tertullian can, if he wishes, choose his phraseology carefully, as in *cum filio solus, cum filio unum* earlier in this chapter, and as in *dei non duo nec domini* later in this sentence: and it is difficult to resist the impression that by such a collocation as *duos deos* he is making a deliberately provocative phrase with the intention of shocking his opponents into attention to his explanation. The end of this sentence repeats the substance of §§ 2 and 9.

Vocari habeat.

Habere with the infinitive may mean either "may" or "must": in many of the instances quoted by Oehler, *de fuga,* 12 note, possibly "must" is the meaning, though "may" is all one could insist on: but *de cult. fem,* i. 1, *propter tuum meritum, id est mortem, etiam filius dei mori habuit*, the meaning is certainly "had to die". So probably here, not "may be called God" but "has to be called God"—his unity with the Father necessarily, not permissively, involves his being called by the divine name. But below, § 21, *quid retro fuerit qui caro fieri habebat*, perhaps no necessity is implied, but only contingent futurity, "who was to be made flesh". *Ex unitate patris*, probably "because of his unity with the Father": or else, the very fact that the Father's unity is so categorically stated makes the deity of the Son a necessary deduction: the former seems preferable.

XX. *But ⟨for all we have given this explanation⟩ we still need to rebut their subtleties: we have to attend to whatever they will extract from the New Testament to suit their purpose, while they overlook all those other texts which observe the rule while yet the divine unity is safeguarded. Just as in the Old Testament they reject all else in favour of, "I am God and beside me there is none else", so in the Gospel they cling to three sentences in our Lord's reply to Philip, and expect the whole of both Testaments to yield to these—though the few instances ought to be understood in the light of the many. But all heretics do that: they advocate a few texts against the many, and take up the cause of later instances in disregard of precedents—whereas in every sphere the rule as originally established in precedents prescribes also for later instances, as of course for the fewer in number.*

Si quid de scripturis.

Probably read *novis scripturis*. We leave here the discussion of Old Testament texts and pass on to consider the three New Testament texts put forward by the monarchians, and to give them an interpretation in accordance with the general sense of the Gospel. *Regulam servant:* either the Rule of the Faith, rehearsed in § 2, which states the fact of the Trinity, or perhaps the rule enuntiated at the end of this chapter that earlier instances prescribe for later ones and the larger number for the smaller. The former interpretation gives a better connexion with what follows: the gospel texts observe the trinitarian rule of the faith while yet not denying the divine unity and the impressive sound of monarchy. So read *salva* and *sonitu* with *P*. *Sonitus*, which refers back to *monarchiam sonare* in § 3, means not a mere sound but a loud or impressive sound: cf. Cicero, *ad Att.* i. 14. 4, *nosti iam in hac materia sonitus nostros*. Kroymann, reading *salvo* and substituting *statu* for *sonitu*, produces a text which can only mean "preserving also the fact of the case by the unity of divinity and monarchy", which is probably not what he intended it to mean. For *unione* one would at first sight have expected *unitate*: but cf. *de res. carn.* 2, *sic multos inretitos videmus, dum ante de resurrectione carnis eliduntur quam de unione divinitatis elidunt: de monog.* 4, *perseveravit unio coniugii in auctoribus generis ad finem usque*, i.e. Adam never had any wife except Eve: from which it appears that *unio* means "singularity" and is somewhat stronger than *unitas*—certainly it has not its original sense, "act of uniting".

Ego et pater unum sumus.

John 10. 30, not from the reply to Philip but from a controversy with the Jews: the other two texts, John 14. 9, 10, were spoken to Philip.

Proprium omnium haereticorum.

Cf. *adv. Marc.* iv. 19, *ipse, inquiunt, contestatur se non esse natum dicendo, Quae mihi mater et qui mihi fratres? ita semper haeretici aut nudas et simplices voces coniecturis quo volunt rapiunt, aut rursus condicionales et rationales simplicitatis condicione dissolvunt, ut hoc in loco: adv. Hermog.* 19, *itaque occasiones sibi sumpsit quorundam verborum, ut haereticis fere mos est simplicia quaeque torquere: nam et ipsum principium in quo deus fecit et caelum et terram aliquid volunt fuisse quasi substantivum et corpulentum quod in materiam interpretari possit: ibid.* 27, *hae sunt argutiae et subtilitates haereticorum simplicitatem communium verborum torquentes in quaestionem.*

Utique et in paucioribus.

So the MSS.: editors, following Ursinus, have read *pauciora*, which still leaves the sentence one-sided. Engelbrecht would omit the four words. They will however make sense as they stand, if they are taken not grammatically but as a summary statement of the "greater and lesser number" parallel to *regula . . . constituta in prioribus et in posteriora praescribit*: this, written out in full, would have been *uti et quae in pluribus constituta et in pauciora praescribit*, which would have made a very awkward sentence and is briefly, perhaps somewhat impatiently, summarised "and likewise in the case of the fewer".

XXI. *A multitude of texts in the Gospel before Philip's question establish the precedent. The Evangelist's preface indicates two Persons: the Word who was from the beginning, and God with whom he was. It was the Word, not he whose Word he is, who was made flesh, whose glory was seen, who hath declared the bosom of the Father: for God, it says, no man hath seen. The Lamb of God means the Son of God, not God whose Son he is. Nathanael's confession, which our Lord approved, as he did Peter's elsewhere, was "Thou art the Son of God". The Temple is "my Father's house". In conversation with Nicodemus our Lord says that God gave his only-begotten Son, and that God sent his Son into the world. John the Baptist again says "The Father loveth the Son and hath delivered all things into his hand", and what follows. To the Samaritan woman our Lord declared himself the Messiah, which means Christ the Son, not the Father. To his disciples he says that his work is to do the will of his Father, and to the Jews he says, "My Father worketh hitherto, and I work": indeed in the whole of that discourse concerning the paralytic he distinguishes between the Father and the Son, as he does also in the discourse concerning the Bread of Life: and at the end of both these discourses he affirms that no man has seen the Father, thus distinguishing the Father from himself whom they then saw. And again Peter acknowledges him to be the Christ, which means the Son, not the Father.*

In this collection of the texts of St John's Gospel which indicate the distinction of the Father and the Son, Tertullian's principle of interpretation is the sound one, *Haec non aliter accipi licet quam quomodo scripta sunt*. In the one place where his deduction seems a little fanciful (i.e. in his explanation of *Deus glorificatus est in illo*, § 23 *ad fin.*) he errs through too much, not too little, adherence to his rule, giving the preposition more weight than it was perhaps intended to bear. The same principle can be seen working, on a broader field, in his anti-Marcionite comments on the Marcionite New Testament (*adv. Marc.* iv. v.). What scriptural interpretation could become in the hands of gnostics whose imagination was stronger than their understanding is apparent in the specimens of their work which Irenaeus quotes as their own sufficient refutation: the Valentinian exposition of John 1. 1-3 (*haer.* i. 1. 18) is a fair sample. How suggestive, though often unpersuasive, it could become in the hands of a reverent Christian seeker, is evident from the almost contemporary work of Origen. If by the side of this Tertullian seems dull and pedestrian, he has at least the merit of having made an exhaustive collection of texts bearing on his thesis, and of insisting on their being understood in their natural and literal sense.

The Johannine evidence is taken first, and exhaustively (§§ 21-25) because the three stock monarchian texts came from this gospel. In accordance with the rule that the less usual must be interpreted in terms of the more usual, it was necessary first to discover what the general Johannine usage is, and to apply it to the three debated texts. In subsequent chapters the concurrence of the other gospels and of St Paul is summarily exemplified.

Fieri habebat.

See note on § 19.

Alium sermonem dei, etc.

The accusatives in this sentence have no government, a fact which does not seem to have troubled the editors—except Kroymann, who has changed them all to nominatives.

Quo alium dicamus, etc.

Quo can only here mean "where". The second *non eundem* is Oehler's addition: *alium* would have done just as well.

Hic unicus sinum patris, etc.

Reading *unicus* with Engelbrecht (representing *μονογενής* in John I. 18). As already remarked, Tertullian takes *κόλπον* as the object of *ἐξηγήσατο*.

Inde et si agnus dei, etc.

"Next also, if by John he is called Lamb of God, he is not called God whose beloved he is." The Baptist's language is of course sacrificial, as Tertullian himself observes, *adv. Iud.* 9, *lucerna ardens et lucens qui non tantum vias eius parabat in eremo, sed et agnum dei demonstrando illuminabat mentes hominum praeconio suo, ut eum esse intellegerent agnum quem Moyses passurum nuntiabat.* How he arrives at the equation *agnus=dilectus* it would be difficult to say, unless there is an implied reference to Nathan's parable. In Irenaeus, *haer.* iii. 11. 9, *Ecce filius meus dilectissimus* is quoted in close connexion with Nathaniel's *Tu es filius dei* and a reference to Peter's confession. Possibly Tertullian had this passage in mind.

Quod et patrem senserat

seems meaningless, and perhaps should be ejected, if one could explain how the interpolation arose. Kroymann brackets for removal *et patrem*, thus making sense. Engelbrecht makes the four words a parenthesis, "To whom flesh and blood had not revealed it—because he had perceived the Father—but the Father".

Qui Petro revelaverat, etc.,

"who had revealed to Peter what Peter acknowledged, that Christ is the Son of God". *Quod* is a relative pronoun, not a conjunction, and the accusatives are of indirect speech.

Quid de Iesu cum tingeret.

Cum tingeret is Engelbrecht's conjecture for the MSS. *contingeret*. Kroymann, taking this a step further, reads *cum interrogaret qui de Iesu cur tingeret*: this is hardly in accordance with John 3. 26, for no one asked the Baptist why Jesus was baptizing. He was hardly asked a question at all, but presented with a piece of information involving an implied question, which is sufficiently indicated by *interrogaretur quid*.

Si Messiam . . . filium utique.

The equation *Christus=filius* comes from Matt. 16. 17 as Tertullian here says: see again at the end of this chapter, and § 22, *nunquam Christus pater scriptus est venturus*.

Pater et ego, filius dicit.

The sense is quite general—"My father and I" is what a son says.

Pater enim diligit filium.

The second *demonstravit* should be *demonstrabit*: John 5. 20, δείξει. After *quomodo enim* insert *pater*. *Transit* stands for *transiit*, μεταβέβηκεν. *Vitam aeternam:* the adjective, both times, is Tertullian's addition to the text. *Et iudicium dedit, etc.*, a paraphrase for (or a quotation from memory of) καὶ ἐξουσίαν ἔδωκεν αὐτῷ κρίσιν ποιεῖν. *Sicut et filius dei per spiritum eius.* See a note on § 2.

Subiungens autem, etc.

This sentence and the next claim the authority of the Gospel for the theses maintained in §§ 16, 17: (*a*) that the Son was the subject of the theophanies, and (*b*) that he there appeared not only with the Father's authority but with the Father's dignity and titles. ***Retro . . . semper*** "always in the past": cf. § 22, *at cum subiungit, Abraham diem meum vidit et laetatus est, nempe demonstrat filium Abrahae retro visum, non patrem.*

Offert si velint, etc.,
a pregnant expression for "suggests that they also may like to go away", *offert et ipsis ut discedere liceat si velint*, which goes a little beyond the strict meaning of *μὴ καὶ ὑμεῖς θέλετε ὑπάγειν;* ***Patrem illum esse, etc.***, depends on *respondit*, the intervening quotation being parenthetic.

XXII. *In the conversations which took place at the Feast of Tabernacles, namely with the Jews who marvelled at his doctrine, with the servants of the high priests and Pharisees sent to take him, and with the Jews who believed on him: again in the matter of the man blind from birth, and in the parable of the Door of the sheep: and again at the Encaenia: our Lord preserves the distinction between himself and his Father. When we reach the text, "I and my Father are one", our opponents wish to make a stand: though this text also is in our favour, since "I and my Father" and "are" are plural expressions, and "one" in the neuter gender signifies not singularity but unity, community, equality. Moreover, in the same conversation in which this text occurs, our Lord stresses the duality; and it appears that the Father and the Son are one* (unum) *by community of work* (per opera) *being two in one exercise of power* (in una virtute).

Cuius autem doctrinam, etc.,
"Whose does he say that doctrine was that they marvelled at?", John 7. 15-17 (a reference omitted by Oehler).

Utique non pater, etc.,
"evidently not the Father, but the Son". Any Jew (and it was Jews who were discussing him) knew that Christ is not the Father: therefore they must (without being aware of it) have meant the Son: so below: *nam usque in hodiernum diem Iudaei Christum dei, non ipsum patrem sperant, quia nunquam Christus pater scriptus est venturus.* *Neque nescitis* (Oehler) is rather far-fetched, though

it gives the sense of the Greek κἀμὲ οἴδατε: the MSS. read *neque me scitis*, for which Kroymann substitutes *meque scitis*: perhaps read *Meque scitis, inquit, et scitis unde sim*, κἀμὲ οἴδατε καὶ οἴδατε πόθεν εἰμί. ***Apud illum***, as though the Greek were παρ' αὐτῷ instead of παρ' αὐτοῦ.

Ad invadendum eum.

John 7. 32, ἵνα πιάσωσιν αὐτόν, which Tertullian apparently misread as ἐπίωσιν αὐτῷ.

Duos dixit ignotos, quod si.

Kroymann punctuates . . . *duos dixit ignotos, quod, si ipsum nossent*, etc., "he said there were two whom they did not know, because, if they had known him they would have known the Father". A period after *sine altero potest*. ***Per individuitatem***, "because of their inseparability": so below, *individuorum duorum*, "two who are inseparable".

Interpretante extrinsecus scriptura,

i.e. the evangelist's words as distinguished from our Lord's, ***extrinsecus***, "from outside", "as an interpolation". ***Ecce dedi, etc.***, Jer. 1. 9, is evidently not a Messianic text: ***Dominus dat, etc.***, Is. 50. 4, may be so regarded.

Sed sicut me docuit.

Perhaps add *pater* (Kroymann).

Ut quidam arripiunt huius dicti occasionem.

John 8. 42, ἐγὼ γὰρ ἐκ τοῦ θεοῦ ἐξῆλθον καὶ ἥκω. These are apparently the same people as those referred to by ORIGEN, *comm. in Ioa.* xx. 18, p. 331, ἄλλοι δὲ τό, Ἐξῆλθον ἀπὸ τοῦ θεοῦ, διηγήσαντο ἀντὶ τοῦ, Γεγέννημαι ἀπὸ τοῦ θεοῦ· οἷς ἀκολουθεῖ ἐκ τῆς οὐσίας φάσκειν τοῦ πατρὸς γεγεννῆσθαι τὸν υἱόν, οἱονεὶ μειουμένου καὶ λείποντος τῇ οὐσίᾳ ᾗ πρότερον εἶχε τοῦ υἱοῦ [so Brooke: perhaps read πατρὸς] ἐπὰν γεννήσῃ τὸν υἱόν, ὡσεὶ νοῆσαι τις τοῦτο καὶ ἐπὶ τῶν ἐγκυμόνων. ἀκολουθεῖ δὲ αὐτοῖς καὶ σῶμα λέγειν τὸν πατέρα καὶ τὸν υἱόν, καὶ διῃρῆσθαι τὸν πατέρα, ἅπερ ἐστὶ δόγματα ἀνθρώπων μηδ' ὄναρ φύσιν ἀόρατον καὶ ἀσώματον πεφαντασμένων, οὖσαν κυρίως οὐσίαν. οὗτοι δὲ δῆλον ὅτι ἐν σωματικῷ τόπῳ δώσουσι τὸν πατέρα, *καὶ τὸν υἱὸν τόπον ἐκ τόπου ἀμείψαντα σωματικῶς ἐπιδεδημηκέναι τῷ βίῳ, καὶ οὐχὶ κατάστασιν ἐκ καταστάσεως ὥσπερ ἡμεῖς ἐξειλήφαμεν.* Origen takes the whole text to refer to the Incarnation: AUGUSTINE (quoted by Westcott, *ad loc.*—no reference given) takes *processi* to refer to the eternal generation, and *veni* to the Incarnation. [Westcott's note on the subtle difference between *ἐκ*, *παρὰ*, and *ἀπό* must be reviewed in the light of the fact that Origen uses the three prepositions indiscriminately without a suggestion of any difference between them (*comm. in Ioa.* xx. pp. 330, 331).] Tertullian, as the three similes show, refers the text to the eternal generation. The variation ***ex semine*** for the more usual *ex radice* is probably no more than accidental.

Pater enim quod mihi dedit, etc.

So *PM*, agreeing with *cod. Vat.*, *ὁ πατήρ μου ὃ δέδωκέν μοι πάντων μεῖζόν ἐστιν*: the reading of *F* almost corresponds with *cod. Alex.* and the received text, *ὁ πατήρ μου ὃς δέδωκέν μοι μείζων πάντων ἐστιν.* The reading of *F* would better suit the reference to the sheep: if the better attested reading is adopted this reference is only obtained by making *omnibus* apply to the sheep, "than they all".

Tum quod Unum sumus, non Unus sumus.

Kroymann adds ⟨*dicit*⟩: possibly the missing word is *sit*, and the meaning, "lastly that *Unum sumus* is not the same as *Unus sumus*". In the next sentence a period is required after *videtur* and only a comma after *generis*: "and so, since there are two of the masculine gender, he says *unum* in the neuter, which pertains not to singularity, but to unity, to likeness, to conjointness, etc.". Cf. *de res. carn.* 55: at the resurrection, by the change that takes place, the man . . . *non ita alius efficitur ut cesset idem esse, immo nec alius efficitur sed aliud*, i.e. he will differ in quality, not in personality. The phraseology used here and a little later (*per opera . . . in una virtute*) does not necessarily imply much more than a moral unity: but Tertullian's position as regards unity of substance is sufficiently expressed elsewhere.

Unum esse patrem.

Add *et filium* (Ursinus).

Adeo totum hoc, etc.

"And so his consistent purpose was to reach this result and this alone (*totum hoc*), that they might believe in two, yet two in one operative act, because it was impossible for them to believe in the Son unless it were the case that there were two to believe in." For ***perseverare*** see § 25, *quae in finem evangelii perseverant in eodem genere sermonis*: and *de pall.* 4, *si post incentivum* ⟨*Achilles*⟩ *puellam perseverasset*. On ***in una virtute*** see John 5. 19, where it is said not that the Son's works are similar to the Father's, but that they are identical: and 14. 10 (quoted below, § 24), *pater autem manens in me facit opera.*

XXIII. *Not only was Martha not in error when she confessed Jesus to be Christ the Son of God, but our Lord also on the same occasion addressed himself as Son to the Father. Further, when his soul was troubled* ⟨*when the Greeks came desiring to see him*⟩, *he both spoke to the Father and was answered by the Father from heaven. Of course the Father is everywhere, and the Son is with him everywhere: yet in the Dispensation it was the Father's will for the Son to be on earth, the Father being in heaven. Heaven is God's throne: the Son he made a little lower than the angels by sending him down on earth, but with the purpose of glorifying him—as it says here, "Glorify thy name", and "I have both glorified it and will glorify it again", for the Son is in the Father's Name. Any suggestion that the Father in heaven is identical with the Son on earth accuses both of mendacity: and besides, why should the Son pray to himself or the Father make promises to himself? Even if, as our opponents say, we are making two separate gods, better two separate gods than one chameleon god. It was for their sake, as our Lord here says, that that Voice came—so that they might believe in the Father and the Son, each in his own name and person and location. Again, in what follows, our Lord distinguishes himself, as sent, from the Father who sent him, explaining that belief in the Son is the way to belief in the Father, since the Son conveys the Father's message. The evangelist—a better authority than Praxeas—explains this when he says that Jesus knew that the Father had given all things into his hand, and that he was come from God and was going to God. If Praxeas were right Judas would have been the betrayer of the Father, whereas in fact it was the Son who was betrayed and the Son who was glorified: for "God is glorified in the*

Son of Man", i.e. God the Word is glorified in the flesh: and moreover "God shall glorify him", i.e. the Father shall glorify the Son (whom he has "in himself" even while on earth) by the conquest of death through the Resurrection.

Martha

was substituted for *Maria* by Pamelius, in view of John 11. 27. The mistake may be Tertullian's: that he was capable of such a slip of memory is shown by his wrong attribution of John 10. 30 (§ 20) and by *in Aegypto* (§ 14), where *in eremo* would have been correct. *Statim didicisset* means not "she would have been told she was mistaken", but that if she had been mistaken and had not called our Lord the Son of God, she would have learned to call him so from his address to the Father in verse 41.

In conturbatione animae.

John 12. 27, νῦν ἡ ψυχή μου τετάρακται.

In quo erat filius.

Tertullian slightly personifies the Name, by taking literally the idiomatic expression "in the name": cf. § 17. A similar literalism is often found in interpretations of ἐν ἀρχῇ, Gen. 1. 1 and John 1. 1 (see a note on § 5).

Inde scilicet suffecerat, etc.

The note of Junius, quoted by Oehler, is beside the point, which is: that the Son's address to the Father (Glorify thy name) would have been sufficient to establish our argument; but, *ex abundantia*, for more abundant proof, the Father, who had already (at the Baptism and the Transfiguration) testified from heaven to the Son, here again refers to that testimony (*glorificavi*), and promises further glorifying, by which he meant "at the Resurrection" (see at the end of this chapter): the Son's address to the Father would have been sufficient, and so the Father's answer to the Son is more than sufficient. *Contestaturus* is Oehler's correction of the MSS. reading *contestatur*: *contestatus* would be better, since the Baptism and the Transfiguration had preceded the present episode. For the identification, the Son *is* the Father's name, see note on § 17.

Sed vi et potestate.

Tertullian is no pantheist, and therefore thus qualifies his statement of God's ubiquity—a ubiquity in which the Son, as *individuus*, shares. By the Father's will, in the Incarnation (*in ipsa οἰκονομίᾳ*) the Son is on earth, and the Father in heaven: (*haberi* meaning both "to be" and "to be seen to be"): yet this is not a separation of the Son from the Father, but a divine dispensation: even such appearance of separation as is involved in the distinction "on earth", "in heaven", will be brought to an end at the Ascension. Meanwhile the possibility of the distinction "on earth", "in heaven", is proof that Father and Son are two Persons.

Hanc sedem suam voluit pater . . . minoravit, etc.

This is the reading of the two eleventh-century MSS. *PM*: the fifteenth-century MS. *F*, which occasionally preserves traces of an older text, reads . . . *voluit pater mihi turmis minoravit, etc.*, on the ground of which Kroymann brilliantly conjectures . . . *voluit pater: 〈In caelo, inquit, mihi thronus. hinc et〉 minoravit, etc.*

Itaque ad istos, etc.

Isti are those who stood by and said that it thundered, or that an angel spoke to him: *hi*, in the next sentence, are the monarchians.

Auctoritas credendi filio pater est,

i.e. by the command *Audite illum.*

Dominus enim . . . sermonem.

Kroymann takes the quotation from Is. 50. 4 as a parenthesis explanatory of *mandatum dedit*, and, reading *quae* for the MSS. *quem*, understands it as beginning a new quotation from John 12. 50. But the MS. text will construe if the quotation from Isaiah is made parenthetic and *sermonem quem, etc.*, is regarded as a comment on it.

De suo sensu,

"of his own mind": i.e. John 13. 1-3 are not words of our Lord, but the evangelist's comment. *Et se ex deo esse:* Ursinus (followed by Kroymann) perhaps needlessly reads *exisse* (Greek ἐξῆλθεν).

Deus glorificatus est in illo.

Tertullian's explanation of this text seems to be his own idea: the expression *filius dei qui erat in filio hominis* is one which would have pleased Nestorius. ORIGEN's explanation is no doubt the correct one, *comm. in Ioa.* xxxii. p. 446, εἶτ' ἐπεὶ οὐκ ἔνεστι δοξασθῆναι τὸν χριστὸν μὴ ἐνδοξαζομένου ἐν αὐτῷ τοῦ πατρὸς, διὰ τοῦτο πρόσκειται τῷ Νῦν ἐδοξάσθη ὁ υἱὸς τοῦ ἀνθρώπου τό Καὶ ὁ θεὸς ἐδοξάσθη ἐν αὐτῷ: the whole comment, §§ 25-29, is worth consultation. But Tertullian was concerned to preclude a possible monarchian suggestion that God being glorified in the Son of Man implies that the Son of Man is the Father, himself incarnate: and the expression to which we have taken exception is safeguarded by the paraphrase *sermo patris, qui erat in filio hominis, id est in carne*, which is almost scriptural.

In qua et glorificatus, etc.

The MSS. read *et ante Iesum*: the nominative is evidently required: Jesus had already, even before this, been glorified, that is to say, by his miracles (*virtute*) and by the voice from heaven (*sermone*). Tertullian misses the point, which Origen sees, that the exit of Judas was a glorification of the Son of Man because it was to occasion that uplifting by which he would draw all men to himself: he makes ἐδοξάσθη refer entirely to the past, reserving δοξάσει for the future as indicating the Resurrection.

XXIV. *Our Lord, in his answer to Thomas, "I am the way, etc.", says that he is the way to the Father, whom from henceforth the disciples have known and seen: which brings us to Philip's request, "Shew us the Father", and our Lord's reply. The disciples ought by that time to have known Jesus; but is there any reason for thinking that they ought to have known him to be the Father? The prophecies of the Old Testament pointed to him as the Christ of God: our Lord's own pronouncement and the Father's testimony declared him to be the Son of God. It was as Christ the Son that the disciples believed in him and the Jews disbelieved: as such he had represented himself to them, giving the Father preference and honour: and his expostulation, "Have I been so long time with you, etc.", implies that they had not yet fully apprehended the meaning of his sonship. "He that hath seen me hath seen the Father" must be understood in the same sense as "I and my Father are one"—namely that Jesus came from the Father, and is the way to the Father, and is the Father's deputy both in act and in word, the Father himself being invisible. That is why Philip is rebuked for asking to see the Father, because the Father is to be seen in the Son—in mighty works, but not in person. Moreover the sentence which follows, "I am in my Father and my Father in me", quite overthrows the monarchian contention: for it would have been quite easy, if it had been true, to say "I am my Father": while this that he does say he proceeds to interpret, showing how the Father, abiding in the Son, seen through the Son's works of power and words of doctrine, is seen in the Son, not with the eyes but with the mind.*

Nec intellegens quomodo visum patrem audisset,

"not understanding in what sense he had just heard Jesus say 'Ye have seen him'".

Quem dicit cognosci ab illis debuisse, etc.

With Oehler's (the MS.) reading, *quem* is a relative pronoun: "Him whom he says they ought to have known—this alone is at issue between us—does he say they ought to have known as Father or as Son?" Engelbrecht suggests *debuisse se*, making *quem* an interrogative pronoun. "As whom does he say they ought to have known him . . . as Father or as Son?" ***Non dico intellegi:*** understanding is concerned with the truth, and is too good a word for such an error as Praxeas would here make: ***aestimari*** (the Platonic δόξα) is good enough.

Nobis omnes scripturae, etc.

This distinction here drawn, between the Old Testament as prophesying concerning the Christ of God and the pronouncements recorded in the New Testament that Jesus is the Son of God, will be admitted to be for the most part true; though there are in the Old Testament a few passages commonly regarded as Messianic where "Son" is the term used, e.g. Ps. 2. 7: 2 Sam. 7. 14: 1 Chron. 22. 10: 28. 6: Ps. 89. 26, 27 (cf. Heb. 1. 5). The New Testament pronouncements quoted are from the narrative of the Transfiguration (Matt. 17. 5) and the reference to it and confirmation of it at John 12. 28 (referred to already, § 23). But Tertullian's point here is not the distinction between the two Testaments, but their concurrence in using the genitive phrase "Christ of God", "Son of God".

Et apparere iam potest, etc.

Here Tertullian comes to the point, the true explanation of the saying, "He that seeth me seeth the Father". (*a*) It must be taken as parallel to "I and my Father are one" and receive a similar interpretation. (*b*) This interpretation will be on the lines of the texts, "I came forth from God" and the others quoted: which indicate that the Son came from the Father, is the way which leads to the Father, receives to himself those whom the Father draws to him, has received all authority from the Father, and gives life even as the Father does: so that the knowledge of the Son carries with it the knowledge of the Father. (*c*) The text last quoted, "If ye know me, ye know my Father also", is the climax of a series which shows the Son as *vicarius patris*, in whose works the Father is seen, in whose words he is heard, and in whom he is known; not that the Son displays the Father's Person, but that the Father is manifested in his own acts which the Son does. Consequently, if the Son is *repraesentator patris*, that is because the Father, abiding in the Son, doeth the works, as our Lord says, "I am in my Father, and my Father in me".

Denique si patrem eundem filium, etc.

Tertullian regularly writes *eundem et*, as § 25, *ad fin.*, *demonstrationem eiusdem patris et filii*: but he is capable of omitting the conjunction altogether, as § 26, *hic spiritus dei idem erit sermo.* "If he wished the Father to be understood to be the same as the Son . . . why does he add . . .?" *Quomodo* apparently means *quare*, as does *quo* in *quo exaggeravit*.

Aut quo exaggeravit, etc.

"Or why did he repeat himself, except that he made clear what he wished to be understood, namely, that he is the Son." The "exaggeration", or piling up of sentences, is the repetition, John 14. 11, of "I am in the Father and the Father in me", from verse 10: this, says Tertullian, is explained by the fact that our Lord is anxious that a wrong meaning should not be put upon "He that hath seen me hath seen the Father".

Filius repraesentator patris.

The *duarum personarum coniunctio* makes it otiose for Philip to ask "Show us the Father": the Son makes the Father present.

But this also needs to be safeguarded by the interpretation which our Lord gave when he showed in what sense the Father is in the Son and the Son in the Father, namely by means of the words and the works. *Filius repraesentator patris* is in (apparently) designed contradiction with *non ex personae repraesentatione* above: the latter represents the theological accuracy of the matter, while the present phrase is a paradoxical exaggeration introduced because it demands and gives occasion for the explanation that follows. *Repraesentator* means more than "representative"—which is *vicarius*: it means one who *patrem repraesentat*, "makes the Father present" or one in whom the Father is present: cf. *de anima*, 57, *atquin in resurrectionis exemplis, cum dei virtus sive per prophetas sive per Christum sive per apostolos in corpora animas repraesentat, solida et contrectabili et satiata veritate praeiudicatum est hanc esse formam veritatis, ut omnem mortuorum exhibitionem incorporalem praestigias iudices: de res. carn.* 14, *plenitudinem perfectionemque iudicii non nisi de totius hominis repraesentatione constare, totum porro hominem ex utriusque substantiae concretione parere* (where *repraesentatio* almost means production in court: *parere*, to appear in court): *ibid.* 17, *carnem repraesentandam: ibid.* 22, *<resurrectio> etsi in agnitione sacramenti fruticat, sed in domini repraesentatione florescit atque frugescit* (where *repraesentatio* means the παρουσία): *ibid.* 23, *adeo contemplatio est spei in hoc spatio per fidem, non repraesentatio nec possessio, sed expectatio* ("real presence"). Tertullian is a realist, and in such a phrase as (*de poen.* 3) *animus sibi repraesentat*, he means (in terms of Stoic psychology) that in the act of memory or imagination the mind does in some sort of quasi-physical way make present to itself the things it remembers or imagines: so that *adv. Marc.* i. 14, *panem quo ipsum corpus suum repraesentat*, means "the bread in which he makes his body present" in a physical or quasi-physical sense which need not necessarily differ from what we should mean by a mental sense, though possibly in this case that is not the whole meaning: see pages 215 and 321.

Hoc quoque interpretatus est.

The interpretation or explanation of "I am in my Father and my Father in me" (the text which makes the Son *repraesentator patris*) is that "the words that I speak unto you I speak not of myself: the Father abiding in me doeth the works" (a text in which appears the *proprietas utriusque personae*): which gives the conclusion, as against the monarchians, that the Father is seen in the Son by identity of operation but not in identity of person, and that he is so seen ***non visu sed sensu***, not with the eyes but with the mind. For the meaning of *sensus* see a note on § 6.

XXV. *To the end of this gospel the distinction is maintained between the Father and the Son, with the added distinction of "another" Paraclete, whom the Son promises to send from the Father. We have already explained what is meant by "another". The Paraclete, he says, will receive from the Son, as the Son receives from the Father: so there is a series of three, and the three are* unum, *one substance, not* unus, *one person. The distinction recurs in the parable of the vine and the husbandman, as also when the Son on earth lifts up his eyes to the Father in heaven when commending the disciples to him. The words from the cross addressed to the Father are not recorded in this gospel; but after the Resurrection, when the time of his humility was past and our Lord, if he had been the Father, could have openly professed to be he, he speaks once and again of ascending to the Father. Finally, the evangelist's concluding words expressly describe Jesus as Christ the Son of God, and consequently those who identify the Son with the Father are striving against the clear sense of the Gospel.*

Post Philippum, etc.

Substantia seems here to mean "occasion" or "attendant circumstances". Kroymann, following Latinius, reads *perseverat*; but the sentence as it stands makes a perfectly good sense, if it is understood that ***perseverant*** does double service, as the predicate both of the relative clause and of the principal sentence.

Ita connexus, etc.

Cf. §§ 2, 7.

Percurre adhuc, etc.

Kroymann's correction, ***vitem*** for *vice*, is so evidently right that one can only wonder that it did not occur to earlier editors. ***Uti*** is equivalent to *sicut et*.

Exposita necessitate, etc.

Exponere is frequently used by Tertullian for *deponere, exuere*; e.g. *de res. carn.* 45, *Expone enim, inquit, secundum pristinam con-*

versationem veterem hominem—non secundum alicuius substantiae senium, neque enim carnem praecipit deponamus. The Resurrection marks the term of Christ's voluntary humiliation (Phil. 2. 8), and if that humiliation had been such as the monarchians supposed, a humiliation of Father into Son, then would have been the time for him again to call himself the Father—which, on the evidence of the two texts quoted, he did not do.

Clausula evangelii.

Westcott, *Commentary*, vol. ii. p. 359, says "there is no evidence to show that the Gospel was published before the appendix [i.e. chapter 21] was added to it": *Introduction to the Study of the Gospels*, p. 258, he refers to differences of language which by no means amount to a proof of difference of authorship, but only of a difference of date, and affirms the "universal concurrence of all outward evidence". It is good enough reason for Tertullian's omission to refer here to chapter 21, that there is nothing in it which bears on the present subject: that the chapter was known to him is evident from *de anima*, 50, *obiit et Ioannes quem in adventum domini remansurum frustra fuerat spes.* The index to CLEM. ALEX. does not refer to the chapter: though it was known to ORIGEN (see Brooke's index). But the expression *clausula evangelii* still needs explaining: is it possible that in Tertullian's copy John 20. 31 had been transferred to the end of 21?

Ad demonstrationem eiusdem patris et filii,

i.e. *ad demonstrandum eundem esse patrem atque filium*: the substitution of substantive for gerund throws the dependent substantives into the genitive, and *et* is for *atque* in Tertullian's usual manner.

XXVI. *On account of Philip's question and our Lord's answer we have made a tour of St John's Gospel. I need add no more from the other gospels, except the angelic annunciation that, because of the action of the Spirit of the Lord and the power of the Most High, the virgin's Son would be called the Son of God. Our adversaries will quibble even here: they say that the Spirit of God is God, the power of the Most High is the Most High. But in that case why did not the angel say openly "God shall come upon thee and the Most High shall overshadow thee"? By "Spirit" in this text is meant what*

John means by "Word", since spirit is the substance of the Word and word is an operation of the Spirit: so that when John says "Word" we understand "spirit", and when the angel says "the Spirit" we understand "the Word". But the Word and the Spirit are not identical with God whose Spirit and Word they are: for nothing which is "of" anything is the same thing as that of which or whose it is. Certainly, when something is "from God" and is his because it is "from him", it is of the same quality as he from whom it is and whose it is. So the Spirit is God and the Word is God, as being "from God", yet is not he from whom he is. Since the Spirit of God, which is substance, while being God, is not God himself, even less will the power of the Most High, which is not substance but attribute, be identical with the Most High. Because the Spirit, the Word, the power, came upon the virgin, that which is born of her is the Son of God. He himself testifies to this as a boy in the Temple: Satan acknowledges it at the temptation: the devils confess it: he prays to the Father: he accepts Peter's profession: and so on through the Gospel, which ends with the command to baptize in the name of three Persons, not one only.

Secundum omnia, etc.

Cf. § 20 *ad fin.* and *de res. carn.* 19, *et haec itaque dispectio tituli et praeconii ipsius, fidem utique defendens vocabulorum, illuc proficere debebit ut si quid pars diversa turbat obtentu figurarum et aenigmatum, manifestiora quaeque praevaleant et de incertis certiora praescribant: ibid.* 21, *et utique aequum est, quod et supra demandavimus, incerta de certis et obscura de manifestis praeiudicari, vel ne inter discordiam certorum et incertorum, manifestorum et obscurorum, fides dissipatur, veritas periclitetur, ipsa divinitas ut inconstans denotetur.* ***Etiam adversus suos sensus*** could, but evidently should not, be construed closely with *interpretandus*, "even though our interpretation should contradict the plain sense of the passage".

Ceterum ut alia, etc.

On the subject of this chapter see the Introduction, pp. 63-70. For ***annuntiari*** Kroymann plausibly suggests *annuntiali*: but if *annuntiaris* is a possible side-form of *annuntiarius*, the MS. reading should be retained as having an active sense, which is here required, not the passive sense ("announced" or "object of announcement"), which is the natural meaning of the *-alis* termination.

Inicere.

Perhaps here it has its natural sense "foist in". But cf. *apol.* 23, *quid autem inici potest adversus id quod ostenditur nuda sinceritate?* where it means "suggest", or "allege": *de anima*, 34, *iniecerat angelos condere*, "suggested to himself", "decided": *de praesc. haer.* 22, *Christum reprehensioni inicientes* (=*Christo reprehensionem inicientes*), "casting blame upon". Below, § 27, *haec iniectio eorum*, "this suggestion (theory) of theirs".

Dicens autem, etc.

The MSS. reading *etsi spiritus dei* is evidently wrong, and Pamelius writing *spiritum* does not improve matters: Ursinus reads *etsi spiritus dei deus*, which makes sense, but I have preferred to read *etsi spiritus deus*, which is equally near the MSS. and is a deduction by simple conversion from the frequently quoted text John 4. 24, *deus spiritus est*. *Directo*, a grammatical term meaning "in the upright case", i.e. the nominative or accusative, as opposed to the *casus obliqui*, the genitive, dative, and ablative: the expression *spiritus dei* uses the word *deus* not *directo*, but in genitive dependence, and so indicates *portionem totius*. On *portio* see note on § 9. *In filii nomen*, a term of accountancy: "was to pass to the Son's account". This cannot mean that a portion of the whole deity was going to be separated off and designated "son": the Son already existed before the Incarnation, as Tertullian maintains throughout. It must be admitted that the language here used is dangerously liable to misunderstanding: similar language, equally dangerous, is used in § 9 of the eternal generation of the Word: but in both cases the danger is less if *portio* means not "part" but "assignment" and *totius* is a descriptive, not a partitive, genitive—a testamentary sense which is included in the verb *cessura erat*.

Hic spiritus dei idem erit sermo.

Hic is probably here the demonstrative pronoun, not the adverb, and *atque* must be understood before *sermo*. Tertullian's failure to understand that the function of the Holy Spirit at the incarnation of the Word is the miracle of the virginal conception, causes him to need at all costs to reconcile Luke 1. 35 with John 1.

14, and so to identify "Spirit" and "Word". This is not to say that he identifies the Word with the Holy Spirit, but only that he claims that when St Luke says "the Spirit of the Lord" he means the same as St John means by "the Word", for since the Word is God and God is spirit, spirit is the substance of the Word and word (discourse or reason) is an operation of Spirit, which is the kind of substance God is: i.e. "Spirit" is a common term which can refer to any one or all of the three Persons, and in this text of St Luke, if he is to agree with St John, it must be taken as referring to the Second Person. But his treatment of the two texts is subsidiary to his main argument here, that whether you say "Spirit of God" or "Word of God" the genitive relationship precludes the personal identification of the Word or the Spirit with God himself of whom they are. *Nulla res alicuius, etc.*, states the general rule, that nothing in genitive dependence can be that on which it is dependent: *plane cum quid, etc.*, qualifies this by allowing that though the two are not identical, yet when the possessor is not only possessor but is also the source or origin of the being of the other, there is a likeness of character (*tale quid quale*) between them: *et ideo, etc.*, draws from *plane cum quid, etc.*, the conclusion that the Spirit and the Word, being *ex deo*, are God, and from *nulla res alicuius, etc.*, the reservation that yet they are not personally identical with him who is their source or origin.

Quodsi spiritus dei, etc.

The MSS. reading is meaningless: *quodsi* is due to Ursinus: *spiritus* seems to me so obvious that I have presumed to substitute it for *deus*. The Stoic logic recognised four categories (πρῶτα γένη), namely ὑποκείμενον (=*substantia*), ποιόν, πως ἔχον, and πρός τί πως ἔχον, the last three being συμβαίνοντα τῷ ὑποκειμένῳ (*accidentia uniuscuiusque substantiae*): see Ritter and Preller (8th ed.), pp. 404-5. There is however some reason to think that Tertullian was not unacquainted with Aristotelian logic, with which his language here is equally consistent. *Quod est spiritus: quod* is a relative pronoun, not a conjunction: it is in the neuter, in spite of the fact that its antecedent is feminine, for the same reason as *hoc* (two sentences further on) is neuter though its reference is to *filius*, namely, to generalise the sense: *substantiva res quae est spiritus* would have meant "that particular substantive thing which is spirit", but what Tertullian wants to say is "it is not a substantive thing, as spirit is", and that is what *quod* enables him to say.

Hic quoque,

i.e. in the same context as the preceding quotation: but *affirmat* supplies a verb for a series of oblique quotations from the rest of the Gospel. *A patre defensi,* "avenged": cf. *adv. Marc.* i. 26, *cur enim prohibet admitti quod non defendit admissum*, and frequently, of the punishment of crime; but Oehler's index gives no parallel to the present use, of the avenging of an injured person.

Nec semel sed ter . . . tinguimur.

Apparently in the African Churches baptism was administered by threefold immersion accompanying the recipient's confession of faith: cf. *de cor.* 3, *dehinc ter mergitamur, amplius aliquid respondentes quam dominus in evangeliis determinavit*, i.e. something more than the bare trinitarian formula. This, if the Egyptian Church Order is the work of Hippolytus, was the practice of the Roman Church in the third century: in the second century, according to Justin, the minister pronounced the formula (ἐπιλέγοντος)—in this case also a somewhat expanded one (*apol.* i. 61).

XXVII. *They introduce further darkness into things manifest by attempting a distinction between the Flesh, which they say is the Son, namely Jesus, and the Spirit, which they say is God or Christ. Here they are dividing things inseparable, whereas hitherto they have been attempting to identify Persons distinct. Moreover, the idea of a distinction between Jesus and Christ is gnostic in conception. We have already shown that they are wrong in identifying the Word, Wisdom, and power of God with the Father: they make it necessary to say more. "That thing which shall be born shall be called the Son of God": see, they say, that which is born is the flesh, and therefore the Flesh is the Son. But, we reply, the Virgin conceived of the Holy Spirit, and what she conceived is what was born, namely Emmanuel. The flesh is not God, but he who was born in the flesh is God, and he is no other than the Word or Spirit. The Word was not changed into flesh, but was clothed with the flesh: for the Word, being God, cannot change. Nor can there be any question of such a mixture of deity and humanity as would result in neither the one nor the other, but something between. For Jesus is both God and Man, as the psalmist says, "God as man was born in her", and as the apostle confirms (Rom.* I. 3, 4). *In the apostle's two sentences we observe a double status, not by confusion but by conjunction, God and Man in one Person, conserving the attributes and activities of both substances, the miracles showing the godhead, the sufferings the manhood. Otherwise, if there had been confusion or mutation, the characteristics of one nature or the other, or of both, would have disappeared. Flesh cannot become spirit, nor spirit flesh, though the facts show that both can coexist in one Person. Therefore the angel calls him, according to the Spirit, the Son of God, reserving for the flesh the designation Son of Man: and the apostle, calling him mediator, agrees. Finally, if you say that "Son of God" means the Flesh, what will you say "Son of Man" means?—evidently not the Spirit, for you have already said that the Spirit is the Father.*

The attempt of a section of the monarchians to distinguish between a divine Christ (whom they identify with the Father) and a human Jesus, is a conflation (not apparently elsewhere mentioned) of the doctrines of Noetus with those of Theodotus the adoptionist. Tertullian reserves for the next chapter his exposition of the evident fact that the office of Messiah is by the nature of the case a human office and that to attempt to distinguish between a divine Christ and a human Jesus is culpable ignorance. Here he remarks (1) that there is some inconsistency in those who, having made a point of combining three divine Persons into one, now attempt to divide one Person into two: and (2) that the idea is akin to gnosticism. HIPPOLYTUS, after his custom of suggesting in such cases direct and conscious borrowing, expressly states that Theodotus of Byzantium stole his opinion from the school of the gnostics and Cerinthus and Ebion, describing it in these terms: *καὶ τὸν μὲν Ἰησοῦν εἶναι ἄνθρωπον ἐκ παρθένου γεγενημένον κατὰ βουλὴν τοῦ πατρός, βιώσαντα δὲ κοινῶς πᾶσιν ἀνθρώποις καὶ εὐσεβέστατον γεγονότα ὕστερον ἐπὶ τοῦ βαπτίσματος ἐπὶ τῷ Ἰορδάνῃ κεχωρηκέναι τὸν Χριστὸν ἄνωθεν κατεληλυθότα ἐν εἴδει περιστερᾶς* (*philos.* vii. 35). Neither this nor the similar but rather more fanciful opinion of Theodotus the tanner (*ibid.* 36) is precisely what

Tertullian here describes: these placed the union between the divine Christ and the human Jesus at the occasion of the baptism by John, whereas Tertullian's opponents placed it at the Annunciation. (3) Tertullian has already confuted the opinion which identifies Christ with the Father: he now deals with it in another way (*aliter*) by explaining what did happen at the Incarnation.

This exposition, which anticipates the language of Cyril of Alexandria and the Council of Chalcedon, rejecting in passing opinions afterwards proposed by Apollinarius and by Eutyches, and expressing itself in terms similar to those of Leo's Epistle to Flavian, is notable in that it answers in advance questions which a later age needed to settle by controversy. It is somewhat surprising that it was not quoted as authority by the orthodox theologians of the fifth century, as for example among the *testimonia* cited by Leo at the end of his 134th epistle, *ad Leonem Augustum*: though probably the Pope thought it good policy to quote only doctors of undoubted orthodoxy. The attitude of posterity to Tertullian generally coincided with that of HILARY OF POITIERS, a much broader-minded man than Leo: *comm. in Matth.* v. 1, *de orationis autem sacramento necessitate nos commentandi Cyprianus vir sanctae memoriae liberavit. quamquam et Tertullianus hinc volumen aptissimum scripserit: sed consequens error hominis detraxit scriptis probabilibus auctoritatem.*

Tertullian's contemporaries express their positive teaching in similar though not identical terms, and without his remarkable anticipation of later errors. If Tertullian suggests the language of Leo, HIPPOLYTUS writes in terms which might have appealed to Cyril: *c. Noet.* 17, 18, καινὸς ἄνθρωπος γενόμενος, τὸ μὲν οὐράνιον ἔχων τὸ πατρῷον ὡς λόγος, τὸ δὲ ἐπίγειον ὡς ἐκ παλαιοῦ Ἀδὰμ διὰ παρθένου σαρκούμενος. οὗτος προελθὼν εἰς κόσμον θεὸς ἐν σώματι ἐφανερώθη, ἄνθρωπος τέλειος προελθών· οὐ γὰρ κατὰ φαντασίαν ἢ τροπὴν, ἀλλ' ἀληθῶς γενόμενος ἄνθρωπος. οὕτως οὖν καὶ τὰ ἀνθρώπινα ἑαυτοῦ οὐκ ἀπαναίνεται ἐνδεικνύμενος θεὸς ὤν, ὅτε πεινᾷ καὶ κοπιᾷ, κτἑ. But whereas Tertullian, as afterwards Leo, describes the *virtutes* and the *passiones* as *distincta documenta utriusque substantiae*, Hippolytus describes both the one and the other as acts of one and the same Person, οὗτος ὁ θεὸς, ὁ ἄνθρωπος δι' ἡμᾶς γεγονὼς, ᾧ πάντα ὑπέταξεν πατήρ.

That NOVATIAN was acquainted with Tertullian's work can

hardly be denied, though he approaches the subject at a different angle. He is in controversy not with monarchians of a Noetian type, but with humanitarians who were apparently not even adoptionists. His purpose is not to prove the distinctness of three divine Persons, but to establish the deity of Christ. He says (*de trin.* 11): *si probatio haec ex infirmitatibus Christi illuc proficit ut homo ex infirmitatibus comprobetur, probatio divinitatis in illo collecta ex virtutibus illuc proficiet ut etiam deus ex operibus asseratur.* But he makes his case not, like Tertullian and Hippolytus, by reference to the Gospel narrative, but by reference to the Old Testament prophecies and to the theological statements of the New Testament: *tam enim scriptura etiam deum annuntiat Christum, quam etiam hominem ipsum annuntiat deum . . . nam quomodo est qua homo ex Abraham, sic est etiam qua deus ante ipsum Abraham . . . et quomodo ad patrem qua homo vadit, sic oboediens patri qua filius inde descensurus est. ita si mediocritates in illo approbant humanam fragilitatem, maiestates in illo affirmant divinam potestatem.*

Novatian's opponents having maintained that the Son of Man is *as such* Son of God, and having cited the angel's annunciation to prove their case, he expounds that text as follows: (1) The Scripture does not say *propterea quod ex te nascetur sanctum*: if it did, we could still disprove their suggestion: it says, *propterea et quod, etc.*, and the addition of the conjunction signifies *non principaliter hoc sanctum quod ex illa nascitur, id est istam carnis corporisque substantiam, filium dei esse, sed consequenter et in secundo loco: principaliter autem filium dei esse verbum dei incarnatum per illum spiritum de quo angelus refert, Spiritus veniet in te, etc.* (2) Novatian, *ibid.* 24 (as it were in passing, and without discussion), takes the same view as Tertullian of the meaning of *Spiritus dei veniet in te: Legitimus filius dei . . . dum sanctum istud assumit et sibi filium hominis annectit et illum ad se rapit atque transducit, conexione sua et permixtione sociata praestat,*[1] *et filium illum dei facit, quod ille naturaliter non fuit: ut principalitas nominis istius filius dei in spiritu sit domini qui descendit et venit . . . ut dum filius hominis adhaeret in nativitate filio dei, ipsa permixtione faeneratum et mutuatum teneret quod ex natura propria possidere non*

[1] Fausset, *ad loc.*, suggests that *praestat*=κυροῖ, or else that *et filium illum dei facit* should be moved to the end of the sentence so that *praestat* may govern *quod ille naturaliter non fuit.* I suspect rather that *praestat* means " has the preeminence," sc. over the human nature.

posset. This language is evidently not Nestorian, even superficially: *filius hominis* means no more than fifth-century doctors meant by *homo illius*, or what Cyril (following St John) preferred to call ὁ ναὸς αὐτοῦ. Neither is *permixtio* intended to have a Eutychian sense: Novatian is feeling for the best language, and wisely balances the possible danger of this word by adding *faeneratum et mutuatum*, which by themselves might have suggested the opposite error. (3) Tertullian's argument makes it advisable for him to insist on the reality and permanence of the *substantiae* of both godhead and manhood: Novatian is more concerned to maintain the unity of Christ's Person. *Ac sic facta est angeli voce . . . inter filium dei hominisque cum sua tamen sociatione distinctio, urgendo illos uti Christum, hominis filium hominem, intellegant quoque dei filium, et hominem dei filium (id est dei verbum . . . deum) accipiant, atque ideo Christum Iesum dominum ut ita dixerim ex utroque contextum atque concretum, et in eadem utriusque substantiae concordia mutui ad invicem foederis confibulatione sociatum, hominem et deum . . . cognoscant.*

Undique enim obducti, etc.

Obducere, "confute", "convince": see Oehler's note to *apol.* 46, where examples are given, including *de res. carn.* 2, *obducti dehinc de deo carnis auctore et Christo carnis redemptore iam et de resurrectione carnis revincentur.* ***Distinctione:*** Oehler's insertion of *de* is only necessary if *obducti* means "convinced" and if the distinction referred to is the objective distinction between the divine Persons; but ***obducti*** here means "confuted", as at *de ieiunio*, 11, *altercatio diversae partis obducitur* (for there is no reason to suppose that his opponents were convinced), and the *distinctio* is the scriptural practice of referring to the divine Persons as not identical, "by" which (not "concerning" which) the monarchian position is shown to be false.

Unare

occurs only here. It was apparently invented by Tertullian to avoid the objectivity of *unire*, which would mean unite in fact, whereas all that is needed here is the allegation of a non-existent unity.

Non enim ipse, etc.

This point has already been made, *ex praetractatis*, i.e. in the preceding chapter. *In isto capitulo,* "in the present chapter": *iste=hic* is sufficiently common, e.g. § 1, *in isto commeatu. Revincentur:* observe the close juxtaposition of *obducti* and *revincentur* at *de res. carn.* 2 (quoted above).

Propterea quod nascetur, etc.

That *sanctum* should be construed with *vocabitur*, not with *quod nascetur*, appears from the citation below, *vocabitur sanctum filius dei.* Tertullian omits, or allows his opponents to omit, the καὶ of which Novatian makes much. *Caro itaque nata est, etc.*, is the monarchians' explanation of the text: Tertullian's follows, *immo de spiritu, etc.* Twice more in this chapter *immo* introduces a statement which Tertullian regards as evidently true.

Quoniam deus homo, etc.

Ps. 87. 5. Where Tertullian found the text in this form does not appear: no previous writer quotes it in any form, and neither *deus homo* nor *voluntate patris* seems to occur except in this chapter. The Latin vulgate has: *Numquid Sion dicet, Homo et homo natus est in ea et ipse fundavit eam Altissimus?*, which (except for *numquid*) well enough represents the Hebrew. LXX has Μήτηρ Σειών, ἐρεῖ ἄνθρωπος, καὶ Ἄνθρωπος ἐγενήθη ἐν αὐτῇ, καὶ Αὐτὸς ἐθεμελίωσεν αὐτὴν ὁ ὕψιστος. Tertullian takes *in ea* to mean *in carne*: *de patris voluntate natus est* would naturally refer to the Incarnation, by which the Word or Spirit was born in the flesh; but *sermo et spiritus qui cum sermone . . . natus est* would better apply to the eternal generation of the Word and the procession of the Spirit: if *cum sermone* were removed all would be well.

Igitur sermo in carne, etc.

Dum et seems to mean *ut interea. Indutus carnem* is the correct answer to the question: if that is rejected, the alternative is *transfiguratus in carne,* which would give two possible theories: (1) such a change of godhead into flesh as would involve the destruction (*interemptio*) of godhead, or (2) such a mixture of godhead and manhood as would produce *tertium quid*, neither the one nor the other. The former seems, in a modified form, to have been the theory of the later Apollinarians, to exclude which σαρκωθέντα ἐκ πνεύματος ἁγίου καὶ Μαρίας τῆς παρθένου was inserted in the Constantinopolitan form of the Nicene Creed:

the latter was the theory of Eutyches rejected at Chalcedon and tacitly dropped by the monophysites. Both theories, says Tertullian, are untenable in view of the immutability of the divine nature: the second also because in that case Jesus will be neither God nor man. He adds that by the former alternative also Jesus will not be man, since "Word" converted into flesh will not be true flesh. He has not with his usual precision disentangled the two theories: they are dealt with in alternate sentences. ***Transfiguratus, transfiguratio***, involve more than a mere change of appearance: ***figura*** in Tertullian means "shape", including the essential reality of a thing: cf. *adv. Marc.* iv. 40, *acceptum panem et distributum discipulis corpus suum illum fecit, Hoc est corpus meum dicendo, id est figura corporis mei: figura autem non fuisset nisi veritatis esset corpus: ceterum vacua res, quod est phantasma, figuram capere non posset*: where the whole point of the argument is lost if *figura* means no more than "type", for it is Tertullian's intention to show that the Old Testament types of the Passion had to be realities so that they could be types of a reality. Hence *figura* is allied to *forma*: see the notes on § 2, where *forma* appertains to each divine Person distinctively, while *substantia* appertains to God as God: and so here, *Sermo* . . . *manet in aevum* (Is. 40. 8), *perseverando scilicet in sua forma*. Consequently *transfiguratio*, either as conversion of something into something else or as mixture with something else, would be *interemptio pristini*, not a mere change of appearance, but utter destruction. ***Informabilis*** (*deum inmutabilem et informabilem*) must, by the context, mean *intransformabilis*, just as ***configurari*** (*si non capit configurari*) would imply change of shape, as at *de anima*, 9, *in Adam concreta et configurata corpori anima*: so that it is unnecessary (with Ursinus and Kroymann) to alter the word.

Quia et cetera, etc.,

"because the other texts also demand this interpretation", i.e. the rest of the Gospel, not merely the words of the Annunciation.

Neque homo caro.

Kroymann's omission of *caro* is unnecessary: intelligent punctuation is all the alteration needed: there is a balanced antithesis between "for neither will Jesus be God" and "nor will his manhood be flesh", and the reason given in each case.

Sed enim invenimus, etc.

Directo "in the accusative or nominative case", i.e. not in genitive dependence: cf. note on § 26. *Secundum utramque substantiam, etc.:* The proof of the permanence of both the divine and the human substance in the Word incarnate consists of (1) the proof texts Ps. 87. 5, *deus homo, etc.*, and Rom. 1. 3, *ex semine David* (i.e. *homo et filius hominis*), combined with 1. 4, *definitus filius dei secundum spiritum* (i.e. *deus et sermo, dei filius*): and (2) the general tenor of the Gospel narrative which shows the operation of one who is both God and Man. Rom. 1. 3, 4 is quoted by IRENAEUS, *haer.* iii. 31. 1, to prove the reality of Christ's human nature taken from Mary, as against gnostic docetism. *Distantem* must be construed with *substantiam* (not with *illum* or with *deum et hominem*).

Videmus duplicem statum, etc.,

"we observe a double quality, not by confusion but by conjunction, Jesus in one person God and Man". This anticipation of fifth-century language collects the sense of the two texts just quoted. *Status* appertains to deity as deity (§ 2) and to manhood as manhood: it also (§ 2) is consequent upon *substantia*, and carries with it in each case its distinctive *potestas*. Hence, *salva est, etc.*, "that which each substance specifically is (including its attributes and activities) is preserved", as is clear from the Gospel narrative which exhibits *distincta documenta utriusque substantiae*. The question of the meaning of the title "Christ" is deferred to the next chapter. On *non confusum* cf. *de anima*, 12, where it is said that *animus* and *anima* are one: *et quaeretur quomodo unum utrumque, ex duarum substantiarum confusione an ex unius dispositione: nos autem animum ita dicimus animae concretum, non ut substantia alium sed ut substantiae officium* (where *concretus* means condensation or congelation: i.e. *animus* is *anima* in the same way as ice is water).

Ex translatione.

Tertullian is still discussing at the same time the two possible theories (1) of conversion of the godhead into flesh, and (2) of confusion of substance, though the latter is chiefly in his mind: in such a case either (1) the two substances would exchange properties and activities or (2) an intermediate substance would be formed with the properties and activities of neither. Tertullian's exposition, like Leo's, fails (except verbally) to do complete justice to the unity of Christ's Person: there is a sense, *ex translatione*, in which it is possible to say "The Son of Man ascended up where he was before", and "The Son of God laid down his life for us", because of the *communicatio idiomatum*, the fact that the *proprietas utriusque substantiae* is communicated or held in common by one Person. Tertullian's exposition therefore, like Leo's, answers no questions, but serves to safeguard the important fact of the truth of both the divine and the human substances and the permanence of their attributes and activities, each *in statu suo*. There can, of the nature of things, be no change of flesh into spirit or of spirit into flesh: but both can exist in one person, evidently, *plane*, because the Gospel narrative shows the coexistence of their *operae et exitus*. ***Exitus*** (pl.), as appears from § 29, means the departure of the spirit and the death of the flesh.

Dei et hominum sequestrem.

1 Tim. 2. 5, μεσίτης θεοῦ καὶ ἀνθρώπων, can only by implication bear on the present subject. It is quoted *de carne Christi*, 15, to controvert the Valentinian notion that the flesh of Christ was of spiritual origin: and again, *de res. carn.* 51, to prove that human flesh has a place in heaven, *hic sequester dei atque hominum appellatus ex utriusque partis deposito commisso sibi carnis quoque depositum servat in semetipso, arrabonem summae totius: quemadmodum enim nobis arrabonem spiritus reliquit, ita et a nobis arrabonem carnis accepit, et vexit in caelum pignus totius summae illuc quandoque redigendae.* ***Sequester***, meaning "partaker of both", is not a satisfactory equivalent for μεσίτης: *de carne Christi*, 15, has *mediator*. Irenaeus, *haer.* v. 17. 1, uses the text in the sense in which the apostle intended it: *propitians quidem pro nobis patrem in quem peccaveramus, et nostram inobedientiam per suam obedientiam consolatus: nobis autem donans eam quae est ad factorem nostrum conversationem et subiectionem.*

Novissime, etc.

A final argument, a *reductio ad absurdum*.

XXVIII. *In equating "Christ" with the Father, you show your ignorance of the meaning of this name, or rather this appellation: for "anointed" is a participle like other participles, not a personal name. Further, how could the Father be anointed, and by whom? The scriptural testimony is to the effect that the Son of God is "anointed" by the Father—"thy holy Son whom thou hast anointed"—"God hath made this Jesus both Lord and Christ". John stresses the importance of believing that Jesus is the Christ: and Paul invariably speaks of God the Father and the Lord Jesus Christ as two Persons, and of Jesus as the Christ, one Person. The name Jesus is a proper name: the appellation Christ is descriptive of the effect of anointing and can only be appropriate to the Son, not the Father. Also, if Christ were the Father, the text "I ascend to my Father" would point to another god superior to the Father, as would other texts of Scripture: and "God who raised up Christ from the dead" would mean that the Father died and was raised again by some other god superior to him.*

Tertullian's language, of the general correctness of which there can be no doubt, needs strengthening in one respect. The appellation "Christ" is not a mere participle, but has become a title of office: yet "the office of Christ is the office of a man", or, as he says in § 29, *Christus humanae naturae vocabulum.* The subject is discussed *adv. Marc.* iii. 15, on the same principles but with a different purpose: The name of God is a kind of natural noun, which can be applied to everything for which divinity is claimed, even to idols—so 1 Cor. 8. 5, "gods many . . . either in heaven or on earth"; but the name of Christ belongs to the Old Testament revelation, and could not be used with propriety by one who (as Marcion alleged) was unconnected with the God of the Old Testament: *Christi vero nomen, non ex natura veniens sed ex dispositione, proprium eius efficitur a quo dispositum invenitur.* The deficiencies of human language sometimes lead us to use terms in an improper sense, by κατάχρησις: but God does not suffer from deficiencies, and would have used a new term for a new thing, if it had been new. Moreover, *si Christus unctus est, ungui utique corporis passio est*: which is another argument against Marcion, who denies the reality of our Lord's body. Cf. *de bapt.* 7, *Christus dicitur a chrismate, quod est unctio, quae domino nomen accommodavit, facta spiritalis quia spiritu unctus est a deo patre,* quoting Acts 4. 27 (as here).

Et habes <per> totum instrumentum eius, etc.

This (Kroymann's) reading is nearer to the MSS. than the traditional *tota instrumenta.* "And throughout the Pauline collection you have statements couched in this form, setting forth two, God the Father and our Lord Jesus Christ." For *instrumentum* see *de res. carn.* 39, *resurrectionem apostolica quoque instrumenta testantur: ibid.* 38, *instrumentum Ioannis* (the Apocalypse): *de carne Christi,* 2, *his opinor consiliis tot originalia instrumenta Christi delere, Marcion, ausus es* (all the narratives of the Nativity). The MSS. read *deum patrem: et* was added by the early editors, who no doubt had in mind τὸν θεὸν καὶ πατέρα τοῦ κυρίου ἡμῶν Ἰησοῦ Χριστοῦ.

Qui solidat tonitruum, etc.

Amos 4. 13 LXX, διότι στερεῶν βροντὴν καὶ κτίζων πνεῦμα καὶ ἀπαγγέλλων εἰς ἀνθρώπους τὸν χριστὸν αὐτοῦ, through a misreading of משיחו for מה־שחו "what is his thought", lat. vg. *eloquium suum.*

Haec dicit dominus, etc.

Is. 45. 1, quoted already, § 11, to prove the distinction between two who are called *dominus.* We must read *Christum* with Kroymann: the whole passage is couched in monarchian terms, so as to reduce to absurdity by applying it in all cases their contention that Jesus *qua* Christ is the Father.

Qui suscitavit Christum, etc.

Kroymann by omitting *est* (after *suscitaturus*)—which could easily have slipped in through the copyist's recollection of Rom. 8. 11—gives a meaning to the MS. reading *tanquam,* for which previous editors had substituted *iamque.*

XXIX. *Which is blasphemy. Let it be sufficient that it was Christ the Son of God that died: and that only because the Scripture says so. Even the apostle, when he says that Christ died, has to add "according to the Scriptures". In Christ are two substances, an immortal and a mortal: it was the mortal, the human, that died: and therefore when the apostle says that Christ died he indicates that the appellation "Christ" applies to the human nature. That, say our adversaries, is what we mean when we say that the human nature is the Son: how then do we blaspheme? But they do, for they transfer to the Father the curse which attaches to one crucified: whereas we, when we say that Christ was crucified, are quoting the curse of the Law (as the apostle did) and are not blaspheming: there is no blasphemy in speaking the truth. An alternative suggestion is that the Father "suffered with" the Son: this is blasphemy by implication, and moreover it admits the distinction of Father and Son which our adversaries have hitherto denied. To "suffer with" is to suffer: and if the Father is impassible he can do neither. The Father, as also the Son, is impassible in his godhead: and when the Son suffered the Father was no more affected by suffering than the fountain is defiled when the stream becomes turbid. Moreover the Spirit suffered not in itself: for we also cannot suffer for God's sake unless the Spirit of God be in us, yet the Spirit does not suffer in us, but gives us the strength to suffer.*

Non sine onere.

Onerare occurs as a quasi-legal term meaning "accuse", *de spect.* 26, *cum oneraretur immundus spiritus*: *de pat.* 10, *si levius defendaris insanies, si uberius oneraberis: de pud.* 5, *oneravit moechiam.* Hence perhaps, "not without risk of objection", against which he guards himself by claiming scriptural authority. *Duritiam pronuntiationis* is a reminiscence of John 6. 60, σκληρός ἐστιν οὗτος ὁ λόγος, "hard to bear" (not "hard to understand").

Quanquam cum duae substantiae, etc.

Tertullian's language is carefully chosen: Christ died *qua caro et homo et filius hominis*, not *qua spiritus et sermo et dei filius.* There is some risk of a Nestorian dualism in all these attempts to distinguish, but against this Tertullian guards himself by insisting that, though in his godhead Christ did not die, he did as one Person bear the curse of the cross.

Censeantur.

See note on § 5.

Maledictione enim, etc.

Oehler's text will translate, if *maledictione* is treated as equivalent to *propter maledictionem* or as instrumental to *blasphematis*. Kroymann reads *maledictionem enim*, and omits

Christum, which gives a clear sense and is perhaps preferable The MSS. read *maledictio*: Engelbrecht would read *in Christum patrem*.

Ergo nec compassus.

Modern discussion of the impassibility of God has got into difficulties through failure to distinguish impassibility from impassivity. No living religion can have any use for an impassive god. But when it is said that God is impassible and that Christ in his divine nature is impassible, it is not meant that God is incapable of feeling but that he is incapable of being injured from without: which is what Tertullian has in mind here. Hence *compassus* does not mean "have compassion" but "be injured in company with". Clearly the divine nature of Christ is not injured along with the human nature: yet it is against Christ as one Person that the injury is directed, albeit it is only the human nature which is affected by the injury. *Compati* is quoted in Oehler's index only from *de res. carn.* 40, and *scorp.* 13, both of them quotations of Rom. 8. 17.

Separatur a filio, non a deo.

It is not easy to find a satisfactory meaning for this sentence. Possibly the argument is: But, you object, how could the Son suffer, if the Father could not suffer with him? I answer that the distinction begins from (*separatur a*) the Son's Person, not from the Deity itself. . . . The divine nature in the Son is impassible, the human nature is passible.

Ita et spiritus dei, etc.

The MSS. read: *ita et spiritus dei qui pati possit in filio quia non in patre pateretur sed in filio pater passus non videretur sed sufficit nihil spiritum dei passum suo nomine quia si quid passus est in filio quidem erat ut pater cum filio pateretur in carne quia hoc retractatus* (*retractatum*, *PF*). I would suggest the following punctuation: *ita et spiritus dei qui pati possit in filio? quia non in patre pateretur sed in filio, pater passus non videretur? sed sufficit nihil spiritum dei passum suo nomine; quia si quid passus est in filio* ⟨*possibile*⟩ *quidem erat ut pater cum filio pateretur in carne. quin hoc retractatum, nec quisquam negabit.* "So also how could the Spirit of God (i.e. the divine Word) suffer in the Son? Because he was not suffering in the Father but in the Son, would it appear that the Father had not suffered? Perhaps: but it is enough that the Spirit of God suffered nothing as Spirit of God: since if he did suffer aught in the Son, it was feasible for the Father to have suffered along with the Son, in the flesh. But we have dealt with this question, and no one will gainsay us." This involves the insertion of only one word, *possibile*, and the alteration of one letter, *quin* for *quia*: and it gives a sense which seems to hang together with what precedes and what follows. If *quidem* had not required some significant word preceding it, *possibile* would not have been necessary: *esse* in the sense of "be possible" is sufficiently common, e.g. *de res. carn.* 3, *est quidem et de communibus sensibus sapere in dei rebus: ibid.* 49, *de antecedentibus discere est.*

XXX. *Our opponents will have difficulty in interpreting the cry, "Why hast thou forsaken me?" If it was the Son suffering, forsaken by the Father, evidently it was not the Father suffering. If it was the Father suffering, to what god did he cry? The cry is the cry of flesh and soul, i.e. of manhood, not of godhead, and shows the impassibility of the godhead which forsook the manhood in delivering it to death. So the apostle says, "God spared not his own son" and Isaiah agrees, "He delivered him for our offences". However, the Father did not forsake the Son; for the Son commended to him his own spirit: and so to be forsaken by the Father meant that the Son died. Consequently, according to the Scriptures, the Son's death as well as his resurrection was the Father's act. Having descended into the lower parts of the earth, the Son ascended into the highest heaven and sits at the Father's right hand—not the Father at his own right hand. Stephen saw him still standing at God's right hand: thereafter he sat, and will sit, until the Father puts all enemies under his feet: also he will come again in like manner as he ascended. Meanwhile he has received from the Father, and has poured forth, the Holy Spirit, the third divine Person, preacher of one God, interpreter of the economy, and leader into all the truth.*

Committere,

"bring into conflict with"—a classical use of the word.

Uti dicam quid de isto quaeris?

I can make no satisfactory sense of this. *Dicam* can perhaps mean *rogem*, though one would have preferred *uti quaeram* . . .

dicas. But ***de isto*** can hardly refer to *pronuntiatione*, which would require *ista*: and *iste* is not a word which even Tertullian would use for *ille=Christus*.

Ut quid me dereliquisti?

The monarchians' interpretation of this text, as signifying the dereliction of the human Jesus by the divine Christ-Father, has a gnostic flavour, though something like it was to some extent current in orthodox circles as late as the fourth century: see a discussion by the Benedictine editors of Hilary of Poitiers, *praef. gen.* § 4 (Migne, p. 78). IRENAEUS, *haer.* i. 1. 16, gives this from the Valentinians: καὶ τὰ πάθη δὲ αὐτῆς (sc. Achamoth), ἃ ἔπαθεν ἐπισεσημειῶσθαι τὸν κύριον φάσκουσιν ἐν τῷ σταυρῷ· καὶ ἐν μὲν τῷ εἰπεῖν, Ὁ θεός μου, εἰς τί ἐγκατέλιπές με; μεμηνυκέναι αὐτὸν ὅτι ἀπελείφθη ἀπὸ τοῦ φωτὸς ἡ Σοφία καὶ ἐκωλύθη ὑπὸ τοῦ Ὅρου τῆς εἰς τοὔμπροσθεν ὁρμῆς: which is so far-fetched as not to require an answer. A view widely held among orthodox writers is thus expressed by HILARY OF POITIERS, *in Matth. comm.* 33: *clamor vero ad deum corporis vox est recedentis a se verbi dei contestata dissidium*. Elsewhere, however, Hilary writes (*comm. in psalm.* 141), *quanquam enim potestatem haberet ponendi animam suam et resumendi, tamen semper per reverentiam filii honorem paternae maiestati reservavit, cum orat, Pater, clarifica me; cum proclamat, Deus meus, quare me dereliquisti? in his enim non est infirmitatis suae confessio sed paternae virtutis praedicatio*. TERTULLIAN seems to reject this interpretation and, by his citation of Rom. 8. 32 (see below), to suggest that the dereliction of the Son by the Father was in some sense a moral one: and with this CHRYSOSTOM (*hom. in Matth.* 88) is, somewhat briefly, in agreement, remarking also that Jesus afterwards (Matt. 27. 50) cried again with a loud voice, showing that he was still alive, and that he was laying down his life κατ' ἐξουσίαν, "of himself" (quoting John 10. 18). ORIGEN, *in Matth. comm.* 35, comes nearer to the root of the matter, saying that the dereliction of the Son by the Father began when he caused him to take the form of a servant, and was continued in the crucifixion, the reviling, the indignity of being numbered with malefactors, and that its climax is indicated by the darkening of the sun. He concludes: *forsitan autem et videns peccata hominum pro quibus patiebatur dicebat,*

Quare me dereliquisti ut fierem quasi qui colligit stipulam in messe et sicut qui colligit racemos in vindemia, cum non sit botrio ad manducandum primitiva? et haec dico, Quia periit timoratus a terra, et qui corrigat inter homines non est (Micah 7. 1, 2). *unde non existimes humano more salvatorem ista dixisse propter calamitatem quae comprehenderat eum in cruce: si enim ita acceperis non eris audiens magnam vocem in qua ista locutus est, nec digna voce divina requires.* This still leaves room for something *dignum voce divina.* As it is the case that Christ bare our sins in his own body on the tree, he bore also the consequences of sin, one of which is separation from God, which to him would be utter desolation: hence the cry represents no mere periphrasis for dying, nor is it a mere quotation from a psalm, but the expression of a real moral experience—which in this context is perhaps more important than metaphysics.

Hominem eius,

"his humanity". The phrase is commonly used by Latin writers in this sense. Strictly speaking it involves Nestorianism, "his man", but it is continually used without any such intention by writers of unimpeachable orthodoxy, and even in controversy with Nestorius was used without any sense of danger: so, *Tu ad liberandum suscepturus hominem non horruisti virginis uterum,* which probably was intended to mean "when thou tookest upon thee manhood to deliver it, etc.": cf. AUGUSTINE, *de fide et symbolo* 8: *ut totum hominem credat a verbo dei esse susceptum, id est corpus, animam, spiritum.* The Latin writers had in fact no other word they could use: *humanitas* can only mean, not the physical or metaphysical constitution of man, but the social virtues of civilised men.

Si pater filio non pepercit.

This mistranslation of Rom. 8. 32, ὅς γε τοῦ ἰδίου υἱοῦ οὐκ ἐφείσατο, has through the Latin vulgate suggested, or been used in support of, that theory of the Atonement which regards it as involving vicarious punishment or retribution. A better translation would be *proprii filii parcus non fuit*: for οὐκ ἐφείσατο does not mean "was ruthless with" but "was generous of": cf. Aristophanes, *Acharn.* 319, τί φειδόμεσθα τῶν λίθων; and Euripides, *Herc. Fur.*, 1146, τί δῆτα φείδομαι ψυχῆς ἐμῆς; In this sense it is understood by CHRYSOSTOM, *ad Rom. hom.* 16, ὃ δὲ λέγει τοιοῦτόν ἐστιν· εἰ τὸν υἱὸν αὐτοῦ ἐχαρίσατο, καὶ οὐχ ἁπλῶς ἐχαρίσατο ἀλλὰ καὶ σφαγῇ παρέδωκε, τί λοιπὸν περὶ τῶν ἄλλων ἀμφιβάλλεις, τὸν δεσπότην λαβών;

Adhuc stantem . . . exinde sessurum.

Tertullian apparently thinks that our Lord had remained standing until Stephen saw him, and shortly afterwards sat down. I know of no parallel to this view, but cf. Hebrews 10. 11, 12.

Tertium nomen, etc.

See previous notes, §§ 2, 8. *Sacramentum* apparently means the Creed, or the *regula fidei*: cf. *de praescr. haer.* 20, *eiusdem sacramenti una traditio.*

XXXI. *To believe in one God while refusing to believe in the Son and the Spirit is Judaism. Apart from that, what difference is there between the Jews and us? To what purpose is the Gospel, unless from thenceforth we believe one God in three Persons? God renewed the covenant in order that his unity might be understood in a new way by the mediation of the Son and the Spirit, so that he who aforetime was preached by the Son and the Spirit and not understood might now be known face to face in his own names and Persons. Let then these antichrists see to it, for they deny the Father and the Son: they deny the Father by identifying him with the Son, and the Son by identifying him with the Father. We, confessing Christ the Son of God, have God abiding in us: we believe the witness of God, which he testified concerning his Son, "He that hath not the Son hath not life": and no one has the Son who regards him as other than Son.*

Substantia novi testamenti.

Substantia here goes back almost to one of the primary senses of ὑπόστασις, firm ground beneath the mire, Ps. 69. 2, ἐνεπάγην εἰς ἰλὺν βυθοῦ καὶ οὐκ ἔστιν ὑπόστασις: hence Heb. 11. 1, ἐλπιζομένων ὑπόστασις "certainty concerning things hoped for": and here "raison d'être".

Novare sacramentum,

"make a new covenant".

INDEX OF SCRIPTURE TEXTS

INDEX SCRIPTORUM ANTIQUORUM

INDEX LOCORUM IPSIUS TERTULLIANI

INDEX VERBORUM LATINORUM ATQUE GRAECORUM

www.ingramcontent.com/pod-product-compliance
Lightning Source LLC
LaVergne TN
LVHW021115300926
849160LV00010B/748
9780444504838